A SHORT HISTORY
OF WRITING INSTRUCTION

From Ancient Greece to Modern America

Second Edition

Edited by

JAMES J. MURPHY

HERMAGORAS PRESS
An Imprint of Lawrence Erlbaum Associates, Publishers

Lawrence Erlbaum Associates, Inc., Publishers
10 Industrial Avenue
Mahwah, NJ 07430

Cover design by Kathryn Houghtaling Lacey

Library of Congress Cataloging-in-Publication Data

A short history of writing instruction from ancient Greece to modern
America / edited by James J. Murphy.—2nd ed.
          p. cm.
Rev. ed. of: A short history of writing instruction from ancient Greece to
twentieth-century America. 1990.
     Includes bibliographical references and index.
ISBN 1-880393-30-1 (alk. paper)
1. Authorship—Study and teaching—History. 2. Rhetoric—Study and
teaching—History. I. Murphy, James Jerome. II. Short history or writing instruction from ancient Greece to twentieth-century America.
PN181 .S54   2001
808′.007′1 —dc?1   00-057684
                                                                CIP

Books published by Lawrence Erlbaum Associates are printed on acid-free
paper, and their bindings are chosen for strength and durability.

Printed in the United States of America
10 9 8 7 6 5 4 3 2

DEDICATED TO THE MEMORY OF

JAMES A. BERLIN

(1942–1994)

Teacher, Historian, Friend

Contents

Introduction

James J. Murphy

The prevalence of writing systems in the world argues that writing must be one of the most powerful human instincts. While we in the West rely largely on a Roman alphabet, countless other cultures have developed sophisticated systems using everything from knotted cords to notched sticks and pictographs. Even the genus "alphabet" has many species: Ogham, Runic, Coptic, Etruscan, Slavonic, and Phrygian, to name a few. The point is that the urge to record, to pass on information, seems so universal that humans everywhere have struggled for thousands of years to find ways to do so. While many "oral" cultures—that is, those without a writing system—have used oral memory as a recording device for their histories and literatures, it is also true that many such cultures eventually developed a writing system that supplanted the oral.

This book, as its title indicates, is concerned with the European-American segment of this worldwide historical phenomenon. It is our belief here that we cannot understand the present state of affairs unless we also understand how that state of affairs came to be. Moreover, as the linguist Louis G. Kelly is quoted as saying at the end of chapter 2, we can learn useful things for present use by examining what has been done before in language instruction. It is possible, for example, that a modern teacher can use in his or her classroom some specific methods employed in Roman, medieval, or American colonial schools.

The primary thesis of this book is that because writing is something that needs to be taught, we owe it to ourselves to discover how people have been and are teaching this powerful human tool.

1

Our intent, then, is to trace the developments in writing instruction in Europe from ancient Greece and Rome through the Middle Ages and Renaissance, and then to follow those pedagogical patterns as they were transplanted to America. Over time, these European patterns were reexamined in America, and new forms appeared in the nineteenth and twentieth centuries. The book concludes with some observations about possible futures in writing instruction.

It is important to note at once that the term *instruction* is a key element in this history. The basic principle of the European-American tradition is that writing must be taught. For example, one of the major influences in the European phase of this history, the Roman educator Marcus Fabius Quintilianus, writing about AD 95, observes that writing, unlike speech, has to be acquired through education by someone other than the learner. A small child, he says, can acquire oral language simply listening to and imitating those around him. But the child cannot acquire writing ability in this way. The tremendous investment of time and resources in writing instruction over many centuries would seem to reinforce Western belief in this principle.

A second major principle in the tradition is that such instruction should take place in "schools." We are so accustomed to schools today that we may overlook the fact that this principle was accepted only after a major debate about whether individual tutors should teach writing in the home, as opposed to gathering students in groups for instruction by a teaching master. The debate was still going on during the first century of the Christian era, but the Roman Empire quickly moved to support schools with public money and, in fact, used the schools as a means of Latinizing their conquered lands. The acceptance of standardized teaching methods made it possible for Roman schools scattered around the world to have substantially the same classroom regimes—not because of any mandated curriculum ordered from above, but simply because the methods worked. The school tradition itself has proved so strong that even dissident or excluded groups have organized writing schools for their own purposes, from illegal "hedge schools" in occupied Ireland to mechanics institutes in nineteenth-century England and female academies in America of the same period. The school thus serves both the established and the non-established, simply because it works.

This is not to say that every school in every place and time has done the same thing. Yet the key point is that school as mechanism has served the Western world quite well over the years, regardless of variations in detail. What is important is the continuity of writing instruction itself as a desired goal.

This book also aims to describe the various changes in writing instruction that have occurred over time. Certainly, for example, the social and cultural objectives of a Roman classroom teacher were vastly different from those of a classroom teacher in eighteenth-century Wales or an American high school teacher in the 1950s. One of the objectives of this book, therefore, is to discover whether the instructional methods differed as much as their environments did. That is why each chapter seeks to outline the dominant cultural milieu in which instruction occurred in order to measure the extent to which such forces affected the instruction. It is for this reason that the chapters are arranged chronologically—not to argue a presumptive continuity, but rather to allow readers to determine for themselves how each generation decides either to follow a traditional path or to move in some new directions.

It would not be fair, even if it were feasible, to attempt to summarize here the eight chapters that follow. Each chapter covers a unique period in human history, each with its own complexities. In the same sense that it is said that every translation is a lie, so any short summary of such intricate subhistories would undoubtedly result in a kind of unconscious misrepresentation.

Instead, it might be worth calling attention to two themes that cut across chronological lines: power and the physical task of writing.

WRITING AND POWER

In all the periods covered in these studies, the ability to communicate well was a source of public power. In many societies, including the ancient Greek, the cultural memory of the group was reserved originally to an elite. When writing became accessible to the non-elite in Greece, as Richard Leo Enos demonstrates in chapter 1, a powerful force of democratization was unleashed. While we see in chapter 2 that the paired faculties of speaking and writing were important to the Romans, each supporting the other, writing in late antiquity and the early Middle Ages became the primary transmission mode. The revolutionary decision of Benedictine monks in the sixth century to begin copying antique manuscripts preserved a vast treasury of ancient thought for later use; in turn, the need to train scribes for this purpose made writing instruction an integral part of monastic life for the next millenium. Carol Dana Lanham, in chapter 3, describes the rise of the new *ars dictaminis*, or art of letter-writing, introducing the practical application of writing skills for the specific needs of chancery offices and other official bodies; the practitioners of this art wielded great power for centuries, acting as transmitters of messages sent out by Popes, kings, and all sorts of governing bodies, especially since they dealt with the language not available to the common people—that is, Latin. In the later Middle Ages, as Marjorie Curry Woods points out in

chapter 4, the close study of written texts became a means of encouraging
the composition of poetry in both Latin and the emerging vernaculars.

With the Renaissance and its revival of Roman educational practices,
the systematic pairing of the oral and the written returned as a means of
upward mobility; both the English "grammar school" and the Jesuit educational program stressed careful writing, as Don Paul Abbott indicates in
chapter 5. In this same period, writing in the vernacular became increasingly popular, vastly expanding the range of readership beyond the
Latinate few and thus empowering larger and larger segments of popula-
tions across Europe. The English grammar school was exported intact to
colonial America. While the European model prevailed in America well
into the nineteenth century, the last three chapters of this book deal with a
multitude of specifically American responses to the challenges of providing writing instruction for the citizens of a democracy; these responses are
predicated on the deeply ingrained presumption that writing leads to
power.

One measure of writing as power is that it is independent of time and
place. An oral statement is time-and-place bound and evaporates with the
last sound uttered. An oral protest, for example, can be quashed by batons
and tear gas, but in written form, it can be anywhere, anytime. One of the
most famous examples of this power is that of Martin Luther. When he
posted his famous 95 Theses on the church door in Wittenburg on Octo-
ber 31, 1517, calling for a public debate about indulgences, nothing much
happened. But two weeks later, when the theses were printed in pamphlet
form, a wave of support sprang up. Both Latin and German vernacular
versions were circulated. Scores of pamphlet writers on both sides of the
issue soon entered the fray. While it is true that books were later to become
the main tools of the ensuing Reformation debates throughout Europe, it
was the vernacular pamphlet that informed the initial struggle for power.
Often badly written and poorly printed, the pamphlet nevertheless engaged, and hence empowered, masses of lay people in an unprecedented
shift of power from the clerical establishment. Suddenly, it was no longer
necessary to ask ecclesiastical permission to write about religion. Both
Protestant and Catholic leaders saw the urgent necessity of capturing this
source of power, and it was not long before systematic educational programs emerged to serve their respective causes—Melanchthon and Sturm
on the Protestant side, the Jesuits on the Catholic. It was a classic case in
which recognition of power created a demand for the pedagogical means
to achieve that power. Chapter 5 outlines some of the instructional consequences of that recognition.

Writing as democratizing has many other examples in the chapters that
follow. They need not be detailed here, but it seems important to alert the

reader to keep an eye out for the many instances that occur throughout the book.

THE PHYSICAL DIFFICULTY OF WRITING

Another factor that underlies most of this history is the speed of thought compared to the slowness of the writing which records that thought. The mind is fast, the hand is slow. While not every chapter cites complaints about this problem (possibly because the matter is so obvious to each generation that it hardly needs saying) the complaints that emerge from time to time indicate that it is not far from writers' minds. Consequently, it might be useful to look briefly at the technology of writing over the centuries.

Surprisingly little has been written about the sheer physical difficulty of inscribing alphabetic characters on some sort of surface. Nevertheless, until very recent times, this difficulty has been a factor in the writing process and therefore in the instructional process. This matter deserves more attention.

The earliest widely used writing surface was woven from the papyrus plant and manufactured on long sheets, which were then rolled up for storage after the writing was inscribed on one side. The *codex*, or "book" as we know it, was not developed until late antiquity; in this form, written pages were stitched together at one edge. Since it was not necessary to roll the sheets, writing could be placed on both sides.

Another surface was the scraped hide of an animal, known as *parchment* from the supposed place of its invention in Pergamum. The finest form of parchment was also known as *vellum*. A complete book could require the hides of a herd of sheep and was therefore extremely expensive. It has been estimated, for example, that the cost of a medieval parchment book of 200 pages would be the equivalent of a modern Porsche or BMW luxury automobile. The cost of parchment was important for two reasons: first, it restricted parchment writing to rich foundations, universities, or patrons, making such writing a product of elite groups; but second, it militated against classroom use for exercises or practice.

Wax tablets, thin pieces of wood with a thin layer of wax, were in use from ancient times until at least the Renaissance period. A stylus was used to scratch letters in the wax. They were commonly used in the classroom for drafts and notes. The wax could be erased by heating it with the palm of a hand and then smoothing it over. One problem with the wax was that it did not work well with cursive writing (i.e., writing using connected letters) because of wax buildup in front of the stylus after a few letters.

Paper, though extremely expensive in the beginning, was a revolutionary advance in the democratization of writing and the broadening of classroom uses. Apparently it was invented in China in the year AD 105, but did not reach Europe until the twelfth century. The first American paper factory was set up in 1690 at Germantown near Philadelphia. Printing created a high demand for paper, which in turn encouraged the increase in the number of paper mills and a subsequent reduction in prices. By the late nineteenth century, paper was so common that it ceased to be mentioned as a factor in writing.

The instruments for inscribing on a page, however, remained a problem until very recently. Early tools were the stylus, a simple scratching rod, or the pen, a tool for laying ink on a surface. Pens were made from metal or wood, then later with quills of birds like the goose; any nonmetal pen required constant sharpening, so that a knife became a constant companion of the writer. (This is the origin of the term *pen knife*.) Note in chapter 5 that English grammar school students are enjoined to keep sharpened pens and to learn how to make their own ink. The fountain pen, a pen containing a reservoir of ink that is fed automatically to the nib, appeared only in the 1880s. It was prone to leakage, however, with disastrous consequences for clothing as well as the papers of students and their teachers, and many schools preferred to use regular steel pens; even after World War II, it was common to see school desks with recesses to hold ink bottles.

While wooden pencils using carbon fillers are mentioned as early as 1565 in Switzerland, the practical pencil, as we know it today, was perfected only in 1898. Very little has been written about the use of pencils in writing instruction.

The now-ubiquitous ball-point pen, using a rotating ball to draw on an interior ink supply, came into common use only as recently as 1946. It solved both the leakage problem and the inkwell problem, and its cheapness made it available at all economic levels. It has become the most democratic of writing tools.

In terms of machine writing, Mark Twain was the first major American writer to use a typewriter. (Ironically, the much-berated "qwertyuiop" sequence of keyboard letters was introduced initially as a way to slow down the fingers of typists who might have gone so fast that they would jam the machine.)

These technological factors are important to note because, until recently, they were limiting factors for both the would-be writer and the writing instructor. Today, when a whole class's compositions can be posted on a web site for all to see, it may be difficult for a modern generation to understand the difficulties faced by their writing forebears.

The history of punctuation is another neglected aspect of the writing process. Modern punctuation is essentially a product of the print age, when habits of rapid reading created by the flood of printed material made readers reluctant to use traditional methods of interpreting texts. Ancient Greek and Roman texts did not usually have word separations, since the reader sensitive to oral patterns could easily work out the sounds intended by the written words. In addition, it must be remembered that "reading" in ancient times (and medieval times as well) was vocalized, that is, sounded out. Note in chapter 2 that Quintilian advises his students about the methods of reading their texts in this way. Concepts like a visual "paragraph" appeared in the Middle Ages, though first-line indentation did not, but complexities like colon/semi-colon were standardized only with printing. The quotation mark, for example, was a post-printing device, but even in sixteenth-century texts, quotation marks can be found opposite every quoted line, unlike the present practice of using them only at the beginning and the end of the quotation.

For the historian of writing instruction, then, it is critical to understand, for each period, the writing technologies and the linguistic presuppositions (e.g., like punctuation) which have a bearing on teaching methods and their intended results.

Everyone who has ever lived has lived in what was to him or her "modern times." The following chapters, then, are not mere antiquarian curiosities looking at quaint old teaching practices, but descriptions of each age's effort to solve the problems of what to teach and how to teach it, for every person discussed in these pages considered writing to be an important human activity and therefore one worth doing well.

Chapter 1

Ancient Greek Writing Instruction

Richard Leo Enos

Key Concepts. *Oral culture* • *Memory versus writing* • *Alphabet* • *Writing as public activity* • *Writing and thinking* • *Literacy* • *Writing as labor craft* • *Women and writing* • *Family education* • Progymnasmata *as graded composition exercises* • Paideia • *Homeric rhapsodes* • *Syllabaries* • *Sophists* • *Logography* • Melete • *Rhetoric* • *Writing in education* • *Plato's objections to writing* • *Aristotle's use of writing* • *Writing as intellectual process* • *Isocrates's curriculum based on talent, education, practice* • *Letteraturizzazione*

INTRODUCTION

The history of writing instruction in ancient Greece is a record of the discoveries of the powers of literacy and how those powers could be taught systematically. At first glance, the study of writing instruction does not appear to seem complex. If we consider literacy to be nothing more than learning the skill of how to read and write, then writing instruction would be nothing more than learning the rudiments of a technique that would serve as an aid to memorizing speech. Before writing, Greece was exclusively an oral culture. Thoughts and sentiments were preserved by long-term memory and transmitting those thoughts from mentor to apprentice. While being facile in long-term memory was valuable in Greek culture, it was hardly a widespread trait. Skill in memorizing massive amounts of language for preservation and transmission became viewed as a specialized craft that required years of training. That is, controlling Greek "literature" was the job of the expert and not a broad-based public skill. The ties between writing, reading, and speech were particularly strong in ancient Greece. In fact, there is very good reason to believe that most ancient Greeks never learned to read silently. From this perspective, writing instruction would be a tremendous skill if it were nothing more than simply a recording device. It is also important to note that the alphabet made this recording device very easy to learn and to use. Mastery in writing and reading allowed not only a broad dissemination of literature but also a skill that could be acquired by children. Writing provided the conditions under which not just an expert but a community, such as Athens, could become literate. In short, writing had demonstrable benefits over techniques to stimulate long-term memory, the procedure used by early Greeks to capture the fleeting, momentary utterances of oral discourse.

There is little doubt that writing instruction aids oral discourse by "freezing" speech so that it is stable. Yet, stabilizing oral discourse through writing offers many more benefits than merely holding the language still and in place. Ancient Greeks realized that extraordinary abilities in memory were the gift of a few, and that skill was subject to the fragility of personal recall. As this chapter shows, however, ancient Greeks realized that writing offered benefits that extended far beyond the value of recording oral discourse for preservation. Writing also facilitated the production and quality of discourse. By its very nature, the act of writing required authors to slow down their thinking much more than was necessary in oral discourse. Moreover, once written, that discourse was readily available for pondering, recall, and self-reflection. From this perspective, writing was thought to help stimulate abstract thought, creativity, and long-term problem-solving. Although these concepts sound contemporary, and even progressive, they were features of writing that ancient Greeks recognized and, accordingly, assimilated into their writing instruction. The history of writing instruction in ancient Greece is much more than mastery of lock-step prescriptive methods; it is the evolution of a mentality that came to understand that writing was itself a heuristic for both preserving and creating new modes of thought and expression.

Ancient Greeks also recognized that writing had another, social dimension. One of the most important features in the development of writing instruction in ancient Greece was that it evolved into a public activity. That is, by comparison with other contemporary cultures, more members of Greek societies, such as Athens, participated in reading and writing. This social dimension to writing had an enormous impact not only on shaping writing instruction but also in sharing the advantages of literacy beyond the individual expert. Not the least of these advantages was that writing served as a recording device and as an activity that facilitied widespread complex thinking. That is, a community of writers and readers could benefit from the interaction of comment and response, much like a collection of individuals could benefit from the interchange inherent in the oral dynamics of discussion. One of the earliest and most important features to understand about writing instruction in ancient Greece is that it became a public activity. Writing instruction was done in Greek not just to train the scribe but to enrich education by facilitating higher-level modes of thought and expression than had been available through oral discourse alone. Yet, awareness of the cognitive benefits of writing was not immediately recognized and was the subject of considerable debate among thinkers such as Plato. To understand the evolution of writing instruction in Greece, the issues inherent in determining the place of writing instruction in Greek education, and its eventual impact on higher education, some modern presumptions about writing and its relationship to thinking must first be reassessed.

In one respect, writing is a technology and, in ancient Greece, the alphabet was the essence of that technology. By modification and adaptation of earlier Semitic scripts, ancient Greeks were able to construct a writing system that evolved to only twenty-four letters, each of which was intended to capture a discrete but essential sound of the utterances of their language. When arranged together, these discrete sounds could be echoed to reconstruct the vocal patterns of everyday speech. The alphabet was ingenious in its simplicity and monumental in its impact. Earlier writing systems were, by comparison, slow, cumbersome, complex, and imprecise. The alphabet, however, could be easily learned, written, and readily remembered, even by children. The Greek alphabet facilitated public writing instruction and became a feature of widespread education. In his volume, *A Study of Writing*, I. J. Gelb asserts that the Greek development of the alphabet was "the last important step in the history of writing."[1] For those of us who wish to better understand the history of writing instruction in ancient Greece, the opposite view would seem to be true. That is, the devising of the alphabet signaled the beginning of writing instruction in ancient Greece. The simple, yet ingenious, manufacturing of letters that captured each discrete sound into a group of twenty-four symbols would appear to be the first—not the last—of achievements. If we take Gelb's remark to mean that the structure of writing was so ingeniously simplified that any child could learn to write and, therefore, any advancement would only be limited to adding or modifying letters, then we would agree with Gelb's view. Writing instruction in ancient Greece, however, was much

---

[1]I. J. Gelb, *A Study of Writing* (Chicago: U of Chicago P, 1974) 184.

more than imparting directions about the arrangement of individual letters of the alphabet. It soon became apparent to Hellenic practitioners, educators, and politicians that the alphabet was the medium for unleashing thoughts and sentiments that were otherwise constrained when limited to oral expression. Ancient Greeks realized that writing could do much more than label and serve as an aid to memory; writing could also function as a heuristic, an aid to creating discourse and refining patterns of thinking.

CAUTIONS AND CONDITIONS

Reconstructing the history of writing instruction in ancient Greece is difficult because, from a retrospective view, modern writers' perspectives and capacities toward writing are assumed to be similar to those of Hellenic writers and, correspondingly, it is assumed that instruction would be based on such shared traits. Starting with the presumption that writing and its instruction are synonymous with current practices presupposes many unwarranted inferences. For example, writing is such a powerful intellectual force that it is used as a marker for the educational and intellectual achievements of societies. By modern standards, writing is both a skill and a sign of higher education. We go so far as to judge not only individuals but also entire societies by labeling them as "literate" or "non-literate." Societies that demonstrate any evidence of literacy, widespread or otherwise, are lauded for their sophistication and erudition. Such present-day stereotyping and generalizations distort our understanding of the development of writing instruction and its evolution toward importance in ancient Greek culture. Generalizations about writing and its instruction are based on the belief that *literacy* is univocal in meaning. Correspondingly, we associate literacy with the privileged; that is, if any members of a society were literate, it would be the rich, the powerful, and the intellectual luminaries. We tend to think that those who have learned how to read and write possess some kind of cultural superiority or, what may be even more inaccurate, that these individuals are representatives of their cultures. One of the most fundamental current assumptions about writing instruction centers on the association of literacy with intellectual capability. Writing today is viewed as a heuristic, a conceptual tool, for problem-solving and as a mark of creative artistry. By current standards, those who are eloquent are judged so through literacy. The command of language, by the standards of present society, is evaluated by control over written language.

As we learn more about the history of writing instruction, especially with respect to ancient Greece, we realize that many of our current assumptions, such as those just outlined, are inaccurate. This chapter shows that *literacy* has a range of meanings, that facility in writing was not always the possession of the intellectual elite, and that writing underwent a transformation from a pragmatic labor-craft to an intellectual heuristic or skill for rational analysis and expression that eventually found its place in the higher education of Hellenistic Greece. By the standards of archaic Athens, writing was initially learned for functional purposes. The standards for eloquence were not written but oral expression. The impact of literacy was, in part, a change from the view of writing as a mundane recording device to the standard for artistic prose expression. The transformation of writing during this period was both caused by and reflected in the writing instruction of Athenian society. The best way to view the nature and evolution of writing instruction, from a labor skill to its intellectual flowering with the school of Isocrates, is to understand the forces in operation that brought about this change.

As mentioned earlier, another condition concerning writing instruction in ancient Greece needs to be underscored: its emergence from an oral society. Many groups of people, entire civilizations in fact, have come and gone without any known writing system. Walter J. Ong has argued that thousands of languages are known to have existed—doubtless many more have faded from memory—but only a few more than one hundred writing systems are known to have existed. Yet, the impact of those writing systems has been astounding in their facilitation of virtually every dimension of those literate societies: law, education, politics, and the ways histories are recorded. The relationships between these disciplines and orality and literacy were also important in the development of writing instruction in ancient Greece.

Writing instruction is a dynamic research topic, in part because its place and importance are only now beginning to be understood. This dynamism is particularly apparent in understanding the place of women in ancient Greek writing instruction. It must be stated at the outset that the role of women in the history of rhetoric in general, and Greek writing instruction in particular, is under-researched and woefully incomplete. There is, however, current scholarship that provides evidence indicating that women were far more involved in Greece's literate revolution than previously suspected. Recent scholarship by Andrea Lunsford, Susan C. Jarratt, C. Jan Swearingen, and Cheryl Glenn has made an important contribution toward understanding the place of women in Greek rhetoric (e.g., *Reclaiming Rhetorica* and *Rhetoric Retold*). There is evidence pointing toward the possibility of women participating in schools of rhetoric in Athens, teaching rhetoric, and even establishing their own educational centers. The constraint inherent in such research, however, is that the sources and social status in Athens, and many other Greek city-states, were so heavily oriented toward male control that the quest for primary evidence remains the foremost concern before a full and detailed accounting can be made. Such scholars as those mentioned above, however, have demonstrated that the activity and place of women in writing instruction were far greater than suspected. Further, epigraphical evidence reveals the possibility that education for women in Athens may not be representative of all of Greece. All this is to say that the role of women in writing instruction in ancient Greece is a current and very exciting topic of inquiry.

The impact of writing instruction reveals much more than the nature of writing within a culture: it tells us about the culture itself. Few societies better illustrate the impact of literacy than ancient Athens. Given these preliminary cautions, what then should be said about Gelb's assertion about the alphabet as the last great achievement of writing? Gelb's assertion should be viewed as accurate and, at the same time, incomplete. It is true that the alphabet was a monumental achievement, but it is also true that this achievement set into motion a series of events that led to system-ized writing instruction which, in turn, led to the emergence, perhaps for the first time, of a literate community: Athens.

THE HOMERIC TRADITION OF ORAL EDUCATION AND THE EMERGENCE OF WRITING INSTRUCTION

Ancient Greeks relied on oral discourse to express thoughts and senti-ments; their culture was oral, including their educational practices. If three adjectives were used to characterize what is known about the earliest forms of Greek education, they would be oral, musical, and athletic. The earliest known educational practices in Greece were direct and personal, often associated with family relationships. Elders of the family, both male and female, participated in educating their children personally and di-rectly. Although the earliest Greeks did not have an education that could be described as communal or systematic, the "curriculum" was fairly com-mon, at least among the higher classes of citizens. The one clear exception was Sparta, whose citizens had their own mode of communal education and chose to de-emphasize literacy to the point that some Spartans even bragged about their inability to read and write. In most other settings, however, the responsibility of education centered on the family. In addi-tion to the skills necessary for managing the economy of property and (in many cases) animal husbandry, youthful citizens were "educated" by learning Homer, engaging in athletic contests oriented toward military and agonistic skills, and acquiring (to some degree) proficiency in music.

Such knowledge, especially at this earliest, preliterate phase of instruc-tion, was oral, aural, and physical. At the heart of this education was the *sumposium*. That is, wisdom was imparted to youth from family elders; in the case of young boys, education passed through elder males and was seen as a means for not only imparting wisdom but also strengthening kinship bonds. Females had parallel forms of instruction, primarily directed toward learning domestic skills. In both instances, and before writing was introduced, the family-bound education was cemented through orality. Home-based, family-centered education was strongly associated with kinship. Eventually, education was de-centered away from the family and home in two respects. First, centers, such as the gymnasium, evolved from sites of military and athletic training to include other forms of education. One of the most important aspects of this education was elementary rhetorical exercises called *progymnasmata*. Although these early exercises are most closely associated with the more formalized educational practices of the later Hellenistic and Roman periods of writing instruction, scholars such as D. A. Russell strongly argue that they were evident early in Greek education.[2] Second, instruction from the home was extended, and correspondingly diminished, by foreign educators (*metics*), who were attracted to Athens. In fact, many of the most famous Sophists were non-Athenian but saw in Athens a site that offered both the freedom and reward for their pedagogical skills. The novelty and diversity of these educators attracted students to their schools and away from family teachers and what amounted to home schooling.

Understandably, the mode of expression that dominated these earlier forms of education was oral. Orality is apparent even in the transmission of what is known today as *literature*. For centuries, the transmission of this literature had been oral. Tales woven out of the *Iliad* and *Odyssey* were composed for oral performance, lauding virtue and condemning vice. Homeric bards, or *aoidoi*, and later rhapsodes emerged as experts skilled in the telling and preservation of Homeric literature. The cultural values and social standards of Homeric literature became the foundation for what ancient Greeks termed *paideia* or the virtue of intellectual excellence. Over the centuries, this Homeric heritage, which served as the basis for education, was challenged, and writing was a central issue in the transformation of the concept of *paideia* or what it meant to be educated. Greek writing instruction is a study of the evolution of *paideia*, for as writing became part of the education of ancient Greeks, their notion of *paideia* changed dramatically, influencing the very fabric of their society. Writing became a part of the *paideia* of Greek education when it was considered to be a pedagogical value and not merely an instrument; that is, writing became a means for attaining intellectual excellence. Yet, writing was not initially seen as an intellectual source of power but rather as a functional skill that served, at best, as a facilitator of the oral tradition of education.

---

[2]D. A. Russell, *Greek Declamation* (London: Cambridge UP, 1983) 3.

The history of writing instruction in ancient Greece is a history of this transition from oral-only to oral-and-literate educational practices. Writing instruction was closely tied with, to the point of being inextricably bound to, orality. This relationship was fostered, in part, because of the bond that existed among reading, writing, and orality. Today, the language arts are treated in terms of either orality or literacy. In the most literal sense, writing instruction in ancient Greece was oral and literate, one and the same. Ancient Greeks, with rare exceptions, never learned to read and write silently. Compositions were written to be recited aloud and were meant not only to be seen but also to be heard. At its highest and most polished levels, writing instruction pointed toward compositions that were intended to be performed aloud. Writing instruction in ancient Greece, then, was more closely tied with the oral/aural than it is today. To discuss writing instruction is implicitly to discuss reading instruction. Whereas the association between writing and reading is viewed as a natural connection today, the emphasis and expertise between writers and readers in ancient Greece diverged as writing was introduced and as writing/reading instruction evolved. Some groups, principally of Athenian social classes, received writing instruction for varying purposes: some became composers as a trade; others were principally readers who learned only rudimentary skills of writing that would carry them through their daily business.

THE (R)EVOLUTION OF WRITING INSTRUCTION
DURING THE ARCHAIC PERIOD

The impact of writing instruction was so dramatic that some scholars have characterized it as a "literate revolution." The introduction of writing and its instruction is considered, by some scholars, a startling and immediate "event," something akin to a society being invaded and taken over by an alien force. A more accurate representation, however, is that writing instruction was an evolution and that the impact of literacy, which flowered in the late fifth and early fourth centuries BC, began centuries earlier. To understand the nature and impact of this literate revolution, we must first understand the "(r)evolution" of writing instruction.

As with some other groups, early (pre-alphabetic) Greeks both developed and borrowed symbols to transcribe and therefore "freeze" ideas. These symbols were both descriptive and representational in that the earliest Greek scripts (written well before the alphabet was invented) captured meaning through pictures (presentational symbols) and phonetic symbols to represent sounds. Influenced by contact with other groups of people, particularly the seafaring Phoenicians, early Greeks evolved their pre-alphabetic writing systems into syllabaries, pronunciation systems based on sound clusters. For example, a syllabic writing system would have three

FIG. 1.1. Abortive abecedarium (courtesy of The American School of Classical Studies: Agora Excavations).

signs approximating the vocalization for each cluster of sounds in the word *in-struc-tion*. The two most famous of these early Greek writing systems emerged during the Bronze Age and are known as Linear A and Linear B. At this early level, however, any sort of writing instruction was idiosyncratic and learned because of the pragmatic utility of the symbols, principally for commercial and economic reasons. These forms of writing were used for counting, recording, and remembering. These early, crude systems were not writing systems as we think of them today. They were not used to record long prose narratives or to help in the explication of complex modes of reasoning; rather, they were shorthand methods for recording that served as aids-to-memory (e.g., in recording jars of oil or number of oxen).

Although these early Greek writing systems had pragmatic functions, they were nonetheless difficult to learn, making instruction all the more selective. Early Greek syllabaries normally comprised scores of characters, requiring no small degree of commitment to learn. There is, moreover, no direct evidence of how this earliest Greek writing instruction was actually taught. The prevailing belief, however, is that writing instruction paralleled the normal patterns of early Greek instruction, particularly the habits for acquiring oral compositional techniques. Most likely, these complex systems were taught by mentor to apprentice and sustained by individuals who saw the benefits of recording economic data and possessions and had the resources to utilize it. These early Greek writing systems, the forerunners to the alphabet, helped to stabilize a system of expression that would be refined into the alphabetic script.

FIG. 1.2. Bone styli used for writing (courtesy of The American School of Classical Studies: Agora Excavations).

As mentioned earlier, what Gelb means by the last great invention—the development of the alphabet—is the finalization of a system that could be learned simply and used widely. The alphabet could be learned by children without great difficulty and, as ancient Greeks discovered, was useful in ways that extended far beyond counting and chronicling. The elegant simplicity of the alphabet made instruction much easier as well. That is, the "expert" did not need to know the scores of characters that are required by Greece's earlier syllabaries but a comparatively few number of characters with distinct phonetic equivalents. This explains why earlier, pre-alphabetic writing instruction was a craft-tool used for the employment of economic concerns and not artistic production or educational development. The possibilities of the alphabet, however, were enormous, extending the benefits across society and making the system of writing so simple that it could be learned only a few years after birth.

Not the least of the alphabet's public consequences was that the need for a scribe became less essential. This type of "craft" literacy, such as the scribe necessary for mastering the intricacies of Egyptian hieroglyphics, diminished to largely civic and administrative functions. Yet, the increased dissemination of writing brought into existence another kind of craft literacy, the need for artisans who could inscribe and engrave this new writing for widespread public dissemination. In this respect, Gelb's last phase of writing—the emergence of the alphabet—is the solidification of a system that would begin an evolution toward public literacy. The progress of that evolution is the progress and refinement of writing instruction. It is for these reasons that, while earlier Greek writing systems existed, the attention to the development of writing instruction started—not ended as Gelb implies—with the emergence of the alphabet in Greece around 800 BC. The technological ease of the alphabet meant that writing skill could be acquired publicly. The potential of the Greek alphabet meant that not only was communal literacy possible but also that writing instruction could be systematized.

EARLY WRITING AND SPECIALIZED INSTRUCTION: ARTISTS AND ARTISANS

The evolution of literacy in ancient Greece took several hundred years. As already indicated, the emergence of alphabetic writing is known for certain around 800 BC and was probably in existence quite some time prior to that date. Knowledge of alphabetic writing and its widespread instruction, however, are two different matters. During this early period, the ninth and eighth centuries BC, Greece was in a transitional phase known as *preliteracy*. Alphabetic writing had some use and its familiarity was spreading (doubtless due to its utility in trade and commerce) but was not widely employed. In brief, writing was known throughout Greece, but there is little evidence that most people knew how to read and write to the extent that widespread, public literacy could be claimed. In this respect, writing instruction was in a transitional period, evolving from a specialized craft into what would later become a public skill. By the Archaic period (late seventh century to early fifth century BC), this early manifestation of writing instruction as a craft appeared in two dominant groups: the Homeric rhapsodes and the artisans of the Archaic period.

The Homeric rhapsodes were bards who orally transmitted the tales of Homer and other forms of poetry. As the etymology of their Greek name implies, they were "stitchers of odes" who wove their compositions into tales. Rhapsodes evolved into a specialized guild out of the early Homeric *aoidoi*, the earliest balladeers that appear within the works of Homer (e.g., *Odyssey*, IX). As the singers of Homeric tales, rhapsodes took pride in being the linguistic guardians for the "proper" pronunciation of Homeric Greek, acquiring their reputations from their ability to orally chant recitations of Homeric literature and to do so in a tongue that was becoming increasingly distant from the numerous, evolving dialects of Greece.

Homeric rhapsodes began a system of writing instruction which was designed to preserve the words and the oral quality of the Homeric tongue. In an effort to record, and thereby preserve Homer, as well as capture the correct orthography of the Homeric tongue, many rhapsodes began to use writing as an aid-to-memory and soon saw writing instruction as a part of their craft. Rhapsodes transmitted their thesaurus of Homeric literature from mentor to apprentice, and it is doubtless that through this process, writing was taught. Such a form of writing instruction, however, is far from public. Rhapsodic composition was more akin to the specialized craft skill mentioned earlier, a system used to preserve the oral features of epic poetry. Accounts indicate that the texts of the *Iliad* and the *Odyssey* that we have today came about because a group of rhapsodes gathered to codify and transcribe the spoken tales of Homer, thus stabilizing and establishing the inscribed text. Unlike the function of earlier, pre-alphabetic syllabaries, however, rhapsodes used this craft literacy in a way that would become a part of their art. Instruction in the writing of Homeric discourse was pragmatic but, as evidenced by Plato's *Ion*, this instruction was learned for the purposes of preserving semidivine (oral) literature. Hellenic rhapsodes were among the first Greeks to show expert ability in writing and its instruction as a group. Their educational practices, however, were not directed to the public but rather to other apprentice-rhapsodes, who learned reading and writing as a technology to help sustain Homeric oral features.

The second major group of individuals to demonstrate any sort of expertise in writing that required specialized instruction was the artisans of the Archaic period. A few inscriptions, possibly dating back to the Homeric period, have been discovered on objects that have words and phrases scratched on the surface. As we move through the Archaic period, however, this form of writing becomes much more stylized and even a part of the art itself. In one example, an urn portrays a Homeric rhapsode and words from Homer are "spoken" from the figure's mouth. As Greek plastic art evolved, writing became a common trait and was associated with physical features of artistic expression; in short, the sort of prestige of stylized writing associated with earlier Egyptian hieroglyphics or later medieval calligraphy became (to a limited degree) part of the art of ancient Greece. Names of gods and heroes were included on pottery and artisans dedicated objects of art (probably at the request of their patrons) to beneficiaries of these precious gifts.

The association of writing with fine art also applies to architecture. Existing monuments and public structures reveal that artisans inscribed buildings; lists of individuals and chronicles of events label important structures throughout Greece. The ever-increasing occurrence and popularity of this form of public writing makes it apparent that artisans, coming from the *thetes* or labor class, learned to write first as a part of their build-

ing trade and later as a trade in its own right. Thus, in two specialized occupations that seem somewhat distant from each other—the Homeric
rhapsode and the *thetes* artisan—writing was learned as a craft literacy.

The writings of Homeric artists and common artisans provided material that nurtured public literacy and more popular forms of writing instruction. The proliferation of writing was directed more and more toward
public readers; while writing was done by craft experts for defined tasks,
the reading was directed toward larger audiences. There should be little
question about the connection between these early forms of writing instruction and the spread of literacy. Yet, generalizations about instruction
should be made with caution. Although the presence of writing is a sign of

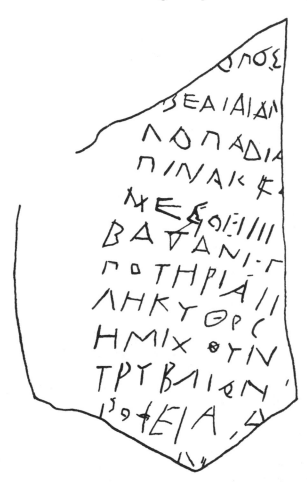

FIG. 1.3.   A fourth-century BC shopping list (courtesy of The American
School of Classical Studies: Agora Excavations).

some sort of instruction, it is not a basis for inferring that that instruction was widespread or systematic, nor can we infer widespread literacy from evidence of writing at various sites throughout archaic Greece. These two forms of specialized literacy, however, should evoke questions about the increasing spread of literacy, for while these two forms of writing comprise the bulk of the available evidence, it is clear that there was some sort of ever-increasing literate public who were the beneficiaries. That is, the rhapsodes and artisans were the "composers," but they were composing for listeners and readers.

What writing exists from "non-expert" writers during the Archaic period is little more than childlike scratch marks. There is some evidence of *abecedaria* (fragments of the alphabet written out for practice) that has been excavated this century from the Athenian Agora, which shows that the learning of "letters" had a place in the *sumposium* education of Athenian citizens. It is likely, however, that this education could better be classified as reading rather than writing instruction, for, with the exception of short, pithy phrases of dedication and brief messages, the literacy instruction of most Athenians was undertaken to benefit from what was written by the two groups of experts: the artists and the artisans of the Archaic period. By degree of emphasis, writing was being composed and produced as a craft of a select group with reading being the emphasis for the remaining citizenry.

THE CLASSICAL PERIOD: WRITING INSTRUCTION IN THE SERVICE OF ORALITY

As Athens moved from the Archaic period into the Classical period of the fifth and fourth centuries BC, the nature of writing instruction, and even its purposes and benefits, altered dramatically. We have seen that writing during the Archaic period was little more than a recording device learned as a trade in the service of the upper classes. The wealthier and more aristocratic classes of Athens did, indeed, learn to write. During this early period, however, these classes learned writing as an aid in carrying out the routine and mundane tasks of the day. The emphasis in literacy for these upper-class Athenians was more in reading, and there is some evidence to support the belief that reading knowledge was fairly widespread during the Classical period.

The Classical period, however, ushered in significant changes in writing and, accordingly, altered its instruction dramatically. While it is accurate to state that writing-in-order-to-read was still (by degree) the orientation of the upper classes, that emphasis was shifting during the Classical period. During the Archaic period, writing was done to stabilize texts for their permanence. Hence the works of Homer, the chronicling of histori-

cal events, and the finalization of laws dominated the more formal
craft–skills of artisan writers. The Classical period continued to utilize artisan writers, but newer, more specialized writing tasks developed and with
them more specialized writers. The distinguishing feature of this emerging form of writing instruction is that it was done in the service of orality.
The *progymnasmata* provided elementary drills and exercises. In these sessions, students typically developed skills in composing narratives, fables,
rudimentary issues and points of law, and argumentation. What is persistent in the exercises of *progymnasmata* is the close ties between oral and
written composition. Later this chapter discusses how this close association
between oral and written composition was extended into the more sophisticated and advanced educational exercises which Greeks called *melete* and
Romans called *declamatio*.

Athens offers the most explicit example of writing in the service of
orality. As democracy stabilized political procedures in Athens, the need
for writers to record specific events of oral and civic functions increased.
Writing was also helpful in recording the oral deliberations necessary in
the operations of the *polis*; it was used to record events that had immediate
and pragmatic impact. For example, during this period the *hupogrammateus* emerged as a secretary charged with the responsibility of recording
oral transactions of civic deliberation. Such recordings were, on occasion,
subject to time constraints since orators were limited by the *klepsydra* (or
water-clock) and, correspondingly, so were those who had to transcribe
their speeches.

The new conditions of writing in the service of orality modified the nature of writing instruction, at least writing instruction done for these specialized tasks. The momentary and fleeting discourse that is the nature of
speech prompted the *hupogrammateus* to develop shorthand systems of
writing called *tachygraphy*. Diogenes Laertius claimed that Xenophon was
the first Athenian to use shorthand symbols.[3] Unfortunately, there is no
extant evidence of Xenophon's work or any direct examples of systematic
tachygraphy until the early Christian centuries.[4] Even these artifacts, unfortunately, come from Egypt, not Athens. If the account of Diogenes
Laertius is accurate, however, it constitutes a very important piece of evidence about the (r)evolutionary emphasis of writing moving into the upper classes. Xenophon was from an old and established aristocratic family.
The fact that he would "create" a writing heuristic to aid orality provides
an instance of the diminishing stereotype of writing as a lower-class craft
while, at the same time, demonstrating its use by a member of the upper
classes of Athenian society.

---

[3]Diogenes Laertius, *Xenophon* 2.48.
[4]Eunapius, *Vitae sophistarum* 489.

FIG. 1.4. Ostraka used in fifth-century BC voting (courtesy of The American School of Classical Studies: Agora Excavations).

There is, however, other, more abundant evidence of writing developing in the service of orality and its ever-increasing emphasis among the upper classes of Athens during the Classical period. Much of the credit for integrating higher-level writing functions goes to the Sophists. One of the most important aspects of this advanced, foreign education is that many of these Sophists readily assimilated writing into the course of advanced studies, thereby encouraging the view that writing was a part of advanced instruction. Practice in compositions for the law courts, public and ceremonial occasions, and the writing of history all revealed more sophisticated dimensions (and benefits) of the writing process. These educators, concentrating on advanced studies, encouraged extending education into young adulthood.

Logography is one illustration of how a long-established pragmatic skill evolved into a higher-level study of writing in the service of orality. The concept of *logography* existed during the Archaic period as a specialized skill to record accounts of important events. In this respect, early chroniclers and even Herodotus, the father of historians, would be considered logographers. Here too, however, this form of specialized writing altered during the Classical period because it was applied to the immediate constraints of orality. During the Classical period, logography evolved to become a profession in which individuals composed speeches for others, normally during legal proceedings where each male citizen was compelled to speak for himself. Logographers wrote these speeches for a price and instructed clients in their "readings," that is, in the preparation for their oral performance before courts. Evidence shows that the most successful of logographers, such as Lysias and quite possibly Isocrates, were popular because they composed oral arguments well for others. At least some of these logographers, including Lysias and Isocrates, came from the upper classes but, due to their own financial misfortunes, had to use these writing skills to earn a living. The success of logographers began to alter the perception of writing, which came to be viewed more and more as part of an intellectual process. Eric A. Havelock's research has revealed the importance of writing in the service of orality. One of Havelock's most important (but debated) claims is that such writing served to facilitate abstract thought. That is, writing speeches helped to stabilize oral arguments by shaping and molding words that would otherwise be thought of as "winged" if left to the fleeting notions of oral discourse and memory alone.

There are other arenas that illustrate the impact of writing in the service of orality during the Classical period of Athens. One such kind of writing might best be considered "composing for the gods." Most scholarly attention to writing instruction has been oriented toward the more civic functions typical of Athenian rhetoric, that is, the writing used in the orally based activities of the *Ekklesia*, or public assembly, and the courts. The current view of writing instruction for epideictic discourse (i.e., rhetoric that is often ceremonial and occasional) has been limited and narrow, with the exception of Donovan J. Ochs's recently published *Consolatory Rhetoric* (1993). If, however, the notion of epideictic rhetoric is extended to other ceremonial functions, the pervasive influence of writing in the service of orality can be illuminated.

The best and most substantial examples of writing instruction being assimilated into the arts of expression are in the literary festivals actively attended by Athenians. The Olympic Games are, of course, the most famous of all Greek festivals. There were, however, other religiously rooted festivals, such as the Isthmian Games of Corinth and the games held at Delphi. These games included athletic contests, but often literary and oratorical contests as well. Although many of these major games were held every four years, many other smaller games were held annually. In sum, literary and oratorical contests for Athenian citizens were widely available and, based on epigraphical evidence, regularly attended by Athenians both as spectators and participants.[5]

Contest winners from these literary games were recorded on marble and other durable material, often listing not only events but also the names and origins of victors. The evidence from games held at the Amphiareion at Oropos, a site approximately thirty miles from Athens, show

---

[5]Richard Leo Enos, *Roman Rhetoric: Revolution and the Greek Influence* (Prospect Heights: Waveland, 1995) 87–96.

that Athenians regularly participated in these contests, which included such events as satire, comedy, rhapsodic odes, and tragedy. It is reasonable to infer that these Athenians, as well as contestants from throughout Greece, would have used writing to aid in the preparation and recording of their literary performances. This sort of composing, done to honor the gods at various religious festivals, reveals that the processes of writing were becoming a part of the creative process. Although these festivals never lost their oral emphasis, it is also reasonable to assume that part of instruction in poetry and the fine arts would have increasingly incorporated writing into its training. Other types of physical evidence lend support to the claim that writing was becoming integrated into artistic expression and education in general. Vase paintings, for example, depict youths practicing their musical instruments, reciting aloud, and learning their letters— all within the same scene. Writing instruction was becoming a part of the arts of expression.

WRITING INSTRUCTION IN ANCIENT ATHENS
AFTER 450 BC AND THE *RATIO ISOCRATEA*

More and more, writing was becoming a part of daily life at all class levels. Recent archaeological evidence, excavated this century at Athens's Agora, demonstrates the pervasiveness of everyday writing throughout the Ar-

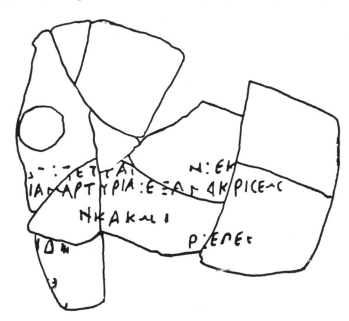

FIG. 1.5.   Lid of a pot used to hold copies of written evidence, fourth century BC (courtesy of The American School of Classical Studies: Agora Excavations).

chaic and into the Classical period. Personal notes of affection appear on pottery. Such personal possessions as spear-butts are labeled for ownership. Shopping lists for parties have been scratched on pottery fragments. As mentioned above, several *abecedaria*, lists of the alphabet–writing for practice, have also been unearthed. The majority of this writing is not sophisticated and certainly does not match some of the elegant inscriptions of the artisans mentioned earlier. What it does demonstrate, however, is that writing, while still used for functional purposes, was becoming more widely used by Athenian citizens.

The most complete sources of this functional writing come from Athens, but it is clear, primarily through the efforts of such epigraphists as L. H. Jeffery, that such writing also is in evidence throughout Greece. This evidence proves that writing was increasingly studied for its everyday use and that literacy was widespread. During the fifth century BC, however, Athenian education underwent significant changes. As advanced levels of education assimilated writing, its importance shifted from a functional tool to a heuristic for advanced thought. The upper levels of Athenian society began to complement their ever-increasing emphasis on reading with writing to clarify and record advanced intellectual problems.

The Classical period of Greece (the fifth and fourth centuries BC) is famous for the flowering of Athenian democracy, the emergence of intellectual luminaries, and the stabilization of higher education. Many historians of rhetoric believe that writing played a part in these achievements of the Classical period. As mentioned earlier, operations of government and the systematization of legal procedure, both of which remained predominantly oral, included writing as a way of recording and disseminating deliberative and forensic activities. Prominent thinkers and artists, moving away from a strictly oral tradition, included writing as a feature of work ranging from philosophy to history to theatrical composition. In short, by widespread practice, writing was manifested throughout Athenian society. For the purposes of this inquiry, it is important to see how this popularity relates to instruction.

By the Classical period, the traditional, Homeric form of education was being replaced. Music lost emphasis and writing gained increasing status. This influence of writing instruction, which flowered during the subsequent Hellenistic period, grew into the *paideia* of Greek education, eventually reaching all levels. The small child (*paidion*) learned letters necessary for reading and writing from the grammatist (*grammatistes*) at the primary level. The older child (*pais*) was taught more advanced levels in reading and writing by the grammarian (*grammatikos*). This secondary emphasis, for children ranging from 7 to 14 years of age, covered the more sophisticated levels of exposition, interpretation, and criticism. The culmination of the grammarian's curriculum was instruction in *krisis*, or arguing for an evaluative judgment. From the ages of 15 to 20, males underwent military education as *epheboi*. In Athens, this form of education was formalized in an Ephebic College. Finally, and normally after required military service, an adolescent male (*meirakion*) could elect to study rhetoric with a Sophist. It should be understood that this latter phase altered and upset the traditional form of education and faced resistance.

As mentioned earlier, the traditional oral features of education were being complemented by writing instruction at all levels. Preliminary exercises in rhetoric, *progymnasmata*, were introduced that extended the earlier training of grammarians by integrating oral and written assignments that ranged from the analysis of fables to composing arguments for legal and popular debate. The advanced form of these exercises, *melete*, had a very important impact not only on writing instruction but also on the perception of rhetoric itself. Russell argues that instruction in this type of composition played "a large part in the development of literature."[6] Proficiency in complex declamatory exercises became a feature of higher education in the Greco-Roman world. Writing, brought into existence to aid in the pragmatic needs of functional speech, became in effect an art. That is, the mastery of technique became increasingly valued not only for its functional effect but also for its aesthetic merits. *Melete*, and later Roman *declamatio*, represented, for Russell, a shift of rhetoric "from discourse to literature."[7]

The changes in writing instruction that would be stabilized and fully integrated in Hellenistic and Roman education were not assimilated without resistance. Conservative citizens, those who wished to preserve the long-standing modes of education, saw writing instruction by Sophists as disrupting the strong family-oriented bonds of education associated with the *sumposium*. Others doubtless continued to see writing as a form of manual labor associated with the trades of the lower *thetes* class. If we understand these underlying tensions about writing and the uneasiness that some established families had over having their sons taught by non-Athenians, we can gain a much more sensitive understanding of Plato's objections to writing instruction and sophistic rhetoric in general, as well as Aristotle's cryptic but critical views of *technographers* in the opening passages of his *Rhetoric*.

Plato expressed great concern about writing because he felt that it destroyed the dynamic and interactive exchange that took place in the (necessarily) oral deliberations of dialectic. The assimilation of writing into the highest forms of education can be credited, in large part, to the Sophists. Most Sophists were not Athenian citizens but *metics*, non-Athenian Greeks

---

[6]Russell 3.
[7]Russell 15.

who came to Athens to teach for a price. Some of these Sophists were famous orators and others were logographers. Many Sophists recognized
the benefits of writing in higher levels of education and actively promoted
the use of writing among their aristocratic Athenian students. As mentioned earlier, the *sumposium* methods of Athenian education were both
oral and family centered. Sophists ruptured this traditional *paideia* both as
foreigners and as non-family teachers of writing. Socrates's views against
writing instruction are well expressed through the dialogues of his student
Plato, particularly in the *Gorgias* and the *Phaedrus*. Plato viewed writing as
a constraint because it mediated the essential function of primary, direct,
oral interaction between thinkers. Plato valued memory and believed that
writing would limit and devalue the important role that memory has in internalizing knowledge. Plato further believed that writing instruction by
Sophists was not an instrument for knowledge but rather a technical skill
and should be seen as such.[8]

Plato's criticism of writing instruction as taught by the Sophists was
echoed by his student Aristotle, who clearly believed that these technographers emphasized "supplements" and missed the heuristic potential
for rhetoric. In the opening passages of his *Rhetoric*, Aristotle criticizes
technographers who taught and practiced only the surface techniques of
their craft and did not understand rhetoric as an "art," that is, a *techne* for
creating rational proofs.[9] An understanding of the emergence of writing
instruction in higher education through the Sophists helps clarify Aristotle's views. At the time that Aristotle wrote his *Rhetoric*, writing was shifting in emphasis from an aid to oratory to an art unto itself. The revolution
of literacy, however, was not so much that more and more people could
read and write, although that appears to be the case, but rather that writing instruction could be a system for enhancing more complex patterns of
thought and expression. It is important to recognize that in the *Rhetoric*,
Aristotle clearly sees writing as an important feature and treats it as a part
of the process of thought and expression. In a rarely cited passage of the
Rhetoric, Aristotle explicitly comments on how the exactness of writing
composition (*akribestate*) aids in stylistic precision.[10] Moreover, Aristotle
later comments on how epideictic rhetoric is especially suited to writing,
since it is intended to be read.[11] Aristotle's observation complements Russell's belief that *progrymnasmata* and *melete* were forms of writing instruction that aided in the development of literature. It is also significant to
note why Aristotle claims he wrote the *Rhetoric*. Aristotle asserts in the be-

---

[8]Plato, *Protagoras* 236 C,D.
[9]Aristotle, *Rhetoric* 1354a–55.
[10]Aristotle 1413b.
[11]Aristotle 1414a.

ginning of his *Rhetoric* that he wishes his work to be a corrective for the then current Sophistic practices. Given the views of Aristotle discussed above, it is clear that he believed that the Sophists did not fully realize the potential (*dunamis*) for writing as a heuristic for complex discourse. There is strong reason to believe, in addition and more specifically, that Aristotle was contesting the views of Isocrates, whose instruction he associated with the Sophists.

The advancement of writing instruction in ancient Greece came with Isocrates and his important school of rhetoric. Enormous changes took place in writing instruction from the Archaic into the Classical periods. Writing instruction moved from a labor skill to an intellectual process. This ultimate phase of its development, however, only became apparent with Isocrates and his school, which Friedrich Solmsen called the *Ratio Isocratea*.[12] Isocrates's views on writing are best understood by contrasting his mode of instruction with the practices of his contemporaries. During the Classical period, writing was used increasingly in higher education for the more aristocratic citizens. Sophists, in fact, saw writing as a feature of higher education, often incorporating writing instruction into the educational practices of their oldest and most distinguished students. By all accounts, however, Sophists did not fully recognize the heuristic potential of writing. Yet, where the Sophists valued the functional features of writing, Plato viewed writing and its instruction as a necessary evil at best, while Aristotle saw writing's potential as unrealized by the educators of his day. Plato had strong reservations about writing because it was a poor alternative to the dynamics of primary, direct oral interaction. Aristotle saw the Sophists (a group in which he unfairly included Isocrates) as embracing the technical features of transcription and recording. Aristotle clearly acknowledged advantages to writing and says so in his *Rhetoric*, but his recognition of writing as a dynamic heuristic process is nowhere as apparent as it is within the writings of Isocrates.

Isocrates's distinguished career as an educator is well chronicled by both his contemporaries and by current scholars. Yet, it is only recently that scholars have come to understand how important his view of writing instruction is in education and how it modified the concept of *paideia*. For Isocrates, writing instruction was an integral part of intellectual growth. Two of Isocrates's treatises are especially valuable in revealing his views on writing instruction. *Against the Sophists* was composed fairly early in his career. Isocrates wished to distance himself from the Sophists, to illustrate that his mode of instruction was based on his own version of philosophy. Attacking the pretentiousness of the Sophists, Isocrates sought to demon-

---

[12]Friedrich Solmsen, "The Aristotelian Tradition in Ancient Rhetoric," *American Journal of Philology* 62 (1941): 190.

strate his genuine concern for the worth of the individual. At the same time, however, Isocrates also distanced himself from Plato. Isocrates's notions of *philosophy* and *truth* were not based on, or even derived from, Plato's belief that knowledge was predicated on universals nor the idea that the apparatus for securing such knowledge was through dialectic. Isocrates had his own philosophy and in *Against the Sophists*, he reveals how this knowledge is derived from a study of people and cultures, how social knowledge and normative values are a type of knowledge which, when applied, can help to promote justice and wise choices about human affairs, social conduct, and ethics. For scholars such as Werner Jaeger, Isocrates is the father of the humanities, principally because Isocrates's theory of knowledge and the grounding for action centers on, and is derived from, social and communal standards.

In many respects, the ideas that Isocrates presents in *Against the Sophists* are elaborated on in his later work, *Antidosis*. Written at the age of 82, and thus several decades after *Against the Sophists*, Isocrates's *Antidosis* is the statement of an educator whose reputation was secure. The *Antidosis* provides a much more detailed explanation of his views on education and the place of writing. For Isocrates, writing was a way of coming to understand. Yet, as he pointed out, his writings were not the writings of the sycophants of legal logographers but rather speeches composed with the intent of resolving social issues. His ideas about education were a synthesis of all that we associate with classical education: the conditioning of the body with the development of the mind; the orchestration of talent, practice and experience; the harmony that comes from self-knowledge and self-restraint. All of these ideas were, for Isocrates, "composed" through writing, for it was through writing, Isocrates believed, that wisdom and eloquence could be united in the pursuit of virtue (*arete*) and justice (*dike*). If we fail to be impressed by Isocrates's motives, we should be impressed by the seriousness of his beliefs. So complex was Isocrates's curriculum that, as pointed out in the *Antidosis*, some of his students studied three to four years. In short, writing was not, for Isocrates, a skill mastered as a technical craft nor something one learns only as a child. For Isocrates, writing was a central part of a process of social knowledge and language interaction that could only be mastered (when it is mastered) at the pinnacle of one's education and only with the most rigorous training of the best minds. A reading of these two treatises of Isocrates will not only make apparent why the *Ratio Isocratea* was a mainstay of classical education, but also why writing had emerged as one of its central features.

While Isocrates provides us with the particulars of his writing instruction in his *Antidosis*, we also can thank ancient authorities such as Plutarch, and modern scholars such as R. C. Jebb, H. I. Marrou, and R. Johnson, for synthesizing and expanding on Isocrates's comments. As already mentioned, Isocrates stressed relationships in his educational philosophy. He believed that mind and body should complement each other and that education was based on talent, practice, and experience.[13] Marrou calls Isocrates's education the development of "mental culture."[14] Isocrates believed in a broadly based education that included such subjects as history, political science, poetry, ethics, geography, literary studies, mathematics, and oral and written rhetoric. In fact, rhetoric was at the core of all of these subjects and composition was at the heart of his literary rhetoric. As Johnson points out, Isocrates's curriculum "is centered on rhetorical composition."[15] Isocrates's writing instruction prepared students by developing writing as a source of civic power. As Jebb argues, writing was "recognized as a mode of influencing public opinion on the affairs of the day."[16] In fact, if we were to condense Isocrates's educational philosophy, it would be that he considered writing instruction to be the art of expressing good judgments to others about civic matters.

Athens is well known for moving from an oral culture to an oral and literate culture. Some contemporary scholars, such as Havelock, consider this shift as nothing less than a "revolution." Isocrates's methods of writing instruction reveal his revolutionary mode of literary rhetoric. Although Isocrates taught many students over his own distinguished career, he instructed small numbers of students at a time, probably no more than eight. Study by imitation was important, but Isocrates also sharpened critical thinking by debate exercises, pitting students against one another in agnostic verbal warfare. There is also evidence that Isocrates encouraged his students to discuss and evaluate in groups, so that they would have comments coming not only from him but from peers as well. He taught excellence in writing through exercises that bonded oral with literary composition. Isocrates's students declaimed from written speeches and doubtless his own experiences as a logographer grounded his writing instruction.

In terms of writing instruction, Isocrates was the educator behind Athens's literate revolution, the educator who established the importance of writing in the classical curriculum. Of all the educators of the Classical period, Isocrates is credited as the first to realize the full potential for writing instruction, that is, as a method for facilitating thought and expression in higher education. Marrou has called Isocrates the first literate rhetorician. Isocrates, himself an excellent and prolific writer, encouraged writing

---

[13]Isocrates, *Antidosis* 187.

[14]H. I. Marrou, *A History of Education in Antiquity*, trans. George Lamb (Madison: U of Wisconsin P, 1982) 83.

[15]R. Johnson, "Isocrates' Method of Teaching," *American Journal of Philology* 80 (1959): 31.

[16]R. C. Jebb, *The Attic Orators from Antiphon to Isaeos*, vol. 2 (1875; New York: Russell, 1962) 47.

among his students, many of whom ranked among the most respected of Athenian citizens. In his writings, Isocrates makes it clear that education directed toward human concerns and immediate social issues is noble and a philosophical orientation in its own right, albeit a more pragmatic and directed one than that of Plato or Aristotle. If we judge educators by the merits of their students, we begin to see the merits of Isocrates's mode of instruction. His school produced not only leading politicians but also historians and educators. Isocrates established writing as endemic to the highest, most complex, and most serviceable of all levels of education. It is not too much to say, and significant to note, that no great thinker or statesman emerged in Athens after Isocrates who is not also known for his literate ability. Marrou has called Isocrates and Plato the two pillars upon which classical education was built. Although there are profound differences between Isocrates and Plato, especially in their views on writing instruction, there is no doubt that both were highly literate and that it is through their respective accomplishments in writing, and the writings of their students, that their importance and impact are measured.

CONCLUSION

How can we best understand how the "(r)evolution" of writing came about so quickly? How can we explain how thinkers such as Plato, Isocrates, and Aristotle, who exhibited such control over writing that they became the standards of literacy for their culture, seemed to spring into existence so quickly? What we witness with such individuals as Plato, Isocrates, and Aristotle is a phenomenon of rhetoric that is normally discussed only with reference to macroscopic views of cultures and societies: the phenomenon of *letteraturizzazione*. George Kennedy's treatment of *letteraturizzazione*— first introduced to readers of English in his 1980 edition of *Classical Rhetoric and Its Christian and Secular Tradition from Ancient to Modern Times*—is as a concept that is meant to explain what happens when literacy is introduced into oral cultures. *Letteraturizzazione* is the process by which features of oral rhetoric are appropriated and applied to writing. The analogy would be akin to the principles of typing being transferred and applied to word processing on the computer. Early versions of personal computers borrowed heavily from the systems invented for manual typewriters. Over time, however, certain techniques that were helpful remained, whereas those techniques of typing that were not useful were removed or replaced with a more "user-friendly" approach. Personal computing evolved into its own system, but the residue of the principles of mechanical typing can still be found. Likewise, written rhetoric appropriated some of the techniques of oral rhetoric, discarded others, and created new heuristics that were

unique to writing. As with personal computing, written rhetoric still has
the residue of some of its primary oral antecedents, such as a writer's
"tone" and "voice."

This overview of writing instruction in ancient Greece reveals the evidence of the dynamic power of writing which, when realized, facilitates
stunning intellectual advancements. What we see with individuals such as
Plato, Isocrates, and Aristotle is the phenomenon of *letteraturizzazione*
manifested on a personal level. That is, all three of these individuals were
so proficient with writing that they were able to apply that system to
higher-level problems. Each manifested his power of advanced proficiency in writing in very different but dynamic ways. For Plato, writing was
an aid to abstract concepts of ontology that refined his philosophy. For
Isocrates, writing in terms of political issues and history helped to explain,
account for, and interpret social activity and human conduct. For Aristotle, writing was an essential heuristic in his quest to provide taxonomical
systems that enabled him to analyze and synthesize in order to organize
phenomena for better understanding. Studying in the respective schools
of these three thinkers meant not only studying their orientations but also
studying how writing facilitated thought and expression in their respective
domains of inquiry. The evolution of writing, much like a plane taxiing on
a runway, builds speed until the moment that it is airborne. For these
three thinkers, writing moved beyond a recording device to become an instrument that freed them and their students into the higher levels of abstract thought and expression.

The luxury of history is that we can retrospectively see that those educators who integrated writing instruction into the highest levels of education
prospered. Isocrates, considered the first of the literate rhetoricians, established educational practices that became the cornerstone of Hellenistic
education. In this respect, the school of Isocrates is a pivot between the
culmination of classical education and the entry into the zenith of Greek
education, the Hellenistic period. The evolutionary role of writing into
and throughout the *paideia* of Greek education is the marker for such
change. Perhaps Marrou's analogy of Plato and Isocrates as the classical
pillars on which Hellenistic and Roman education was built should be
modified, reconfiguring Marrou's imagery into a tripod, to include Aristotle's role in bringing writing instruction into the foundation of the classical curriculum.

Chapter 2

The Key Role of Habit
in Roman Writing Instruction

James J. Murphy

Key Concepts. Habit (hexis) • *Roman education as a system* • Public schools • *Concept of curriculum* • *Writing and oral language* • *Quintilian* • *Facility* (facilitas) • *Tutorial teaching* • *Isocrates's influence* • *Male-centered education* • *Five parts of Latin rhetoric* • *Cicero as model* • *Theory and practice* • *Triad of precept, imitation, practice* • *Inheritance from Greek pedagogy* • Grammaticus • Rhetor • *Grammar and rhetoric as precept* • *Seven steps of imitation* • *Form preceding free expression* • *Graded composition exercises* (Progymnasmata) • *Hermogenes and Apthonius* • *Declamation* • *Sequencing* • *Modern criticisms of the system*

The remarkable thing about Roman education is that it took the comparatively loose ideas of Greek educators and molded them into a coherent system, which instilled in its students a Habit (*hexis*) of effective expression. Moreover, the Romans embedded the system in a network of "public" schools (i.e., classrooms of numerous students, each under one master), which used a common curriculum throughout the Roman world.

Virtually every individual element found in the Roman education pattern was inherited from the Greeks. What was not inherited, however, was the deftly designed correlation of these elements into a learning system that could be replicated worldwide as a tool of Roman public policy equal in geopolitical value to the legions of soldiers and the tax collectors in making the world Roman.

The basic principle of this system is that students can be habituated into both skill and virtue. Skill of language comes from the adroit use of precept, imitation, and practice in the classoom, while moral and political virtues are absorbed through the contents of the texts and orations studied there.

To understand the unique qualities of this Roman educational program, then, it will be useful to examine not only the role of writing but the manner in which the full system came to supplant the old private, tutorial method, which had been the practice in the early days of the Republic.

It is clear that writing and oral language go hand in hand in the Roman educational program. If oral eloquence was the desired product of the schools, writing was a major means to that end.

"In writing are the roots, in writing are the foundations of eloquence." This judgment, written in AD 95 by Marcus Fabius Quintilianus in his *Institutio oratoria*,[1] was not unique to him. It was an idea already pervasive in Roman culture. Quintilian quotes Marcus Tullius Cicero as saying a century and a half earlier that the pen is "the best modeler and teacher of eloquence." Three centuries after Quintilian, the young Aurelius Augustinus, a teacher of rhetoric later to be Christian bishop and one of the four Latin Fathers of the Church, describes in his *Confessions* his own efforts to teach oral and written composition to the unruly young in North Africa. The Christian encyclopedists of the sixth and seventh centuries still insist on the same point.

The Roman educational system—and indeed it was truly a "system"— had rhetorical efficiency as its primary goal. Quintilian's term for this objective is Facility (*facilitas*), or the habitual capacity to produce appropriate and effective language in any situation. This result was to be achieved by a carefully coordinated program of reading, writing, speaking, and listening. The process carried boys from beginning alphabet exercises at age six or seven through a dozen years of interactive classroom activities designed to produce an adult capable of public improvisation under any circumstances.

Writing was an integral part of this process, inseparable from the other elements. As Quintilian notes:

> I know that it is often asked whether more is contributed by writing, by reading, or by speaking. This question we should have to examine with careful

---

[1] *Institutio oratoria* X.3.1. Quotations from books 1, 2, and 10 are from *Quintilian on the Teaching of Speaking and Writing: Translations from Books One, Two, and Ten of the Institutio oratoria*, ed. James J. Murphy (Carbondale: Southern Illinois UP, 1987). Quotations from other books will be from *The Institutio oratoria of Quintilian*, trans. H. E. Butler, 4 vols (Cambridge: Harvard UP, 1921–22).

attention if in fact we could confine ourselves to any one of these activities; but in truth they are all so connected, so inseparably linked with one another, that if any one of them is neglected, we labor in vain in the other two—for our speech will never become forcible and energetic unless it acquires strength from great practice in writing; and the labor of writing, if left destitute of models from reading, passes away without effect, as having no director; while he who knows how everything ought to be said, will, if he has not his eloquence in readiness and prepared for all emergencies, merely brood, as it were, over locked-up treasure. (*Institutio* X.1.1)

Since Roman writing instruction was so firmly embedded in such a complex process, then, the modern reader needs to understand all the elements of the system itself in order to appreciate the role played by writing. Consequently, the following section describes the manner in which rhetorical education supplanted the "Old Education" in Rome during the first century before Christ. The next sections discuss that educational process as described in Quintilian's *Institutio oratoria*, followed by a brief analysis of the advantages and disadvantages of the Roman educational pattern.

THE ROMAN TRANSITION TO SYSTEMATIC RHETORICAL EDUCATION

The first century before Christ was the turning point in the Roman transition from the Old Education of the conservative Republic to the more systematic rhetorical program, which dominated European practice for the next two millennia.

The change was from a native Latin, tutorial process to a Greek-originated "school" system. In a real sense it was a triumph of Isocratean educational principles over a familial approach that had emphasized private tutors and apprenticeship. The historian Cornelius Tacitus, writing later in the middle of the first Christian century, looks back fondly on "the good old days" before there were "professors of Rhetoric":

Well then, in the good old days the young man who was destined for the oratory of the bar, after receiving the rudiments of a sound training at home, and storing his mind with liberal culture, was taken by his father, or his relations, and placed under the care of some orator who held a leading position at Rome. The youth had to get the habit of following his patron about, of escorting him in public, of supporting him at all his appearances as a speaker, whether in the law courts or on the platform, hearing also his word-combats at first hand, standing by him in his duellings, and learning, as it were, to fight in the fighting-line. It was a method that secured at once for the young students a considerable amount of experience, great self-possession, and a

goodly store of sound judgment: for they carried on their studies in the light
of open day, and amid the very shock of battle, under conditions in which
any stupid or ill-advised statement brings prompt retribution in the shape of
the judge's disapproval, taunting criticism from your opponent—yes, and
from your own supporters' expressions of dissatisfaction. So it was a genuine
and unadulterated eloquence that they were initiated in from the very first;
and though they attached themselves to a single speaker, yet they got to
know all the contemporary members of the bar in a great variety of both civil
and criminal cases. Moreover a public meeting gave them the opportunity of
noting marked divergences of taste, so that they could easily detect what
commended itself in the case of each individual speaker, and what on the
other hand failed to please.[2]

Thus in this older, conservative program, there were three levels of education: home training, military service, then apprenticeship to some
prominent orator to learn the practical ways of the world. Cicero's father,
for instance, placed him with Q. Mucius Scaevola Augur; however, the
young boy's advisers had earlier warned him away from the new-fangled
Latin rhetorician L. Plotius Gallus, and Cicero went off instead to Rhodes
to study Greek rhetoric there before taking up his apprenticeship with the
orator.

If Roman education was male centered, it was because the society was
male centered. Women had little status under the law, and children—even
adult sons with their own careers—were regarded as subjects of their fathers in many circumstances. This was not so much a conscious social decision as it was a continuation of assumptions common to many ancient societies, including the Greek and the Judaic. It is important therefore for a
modern reader, even while deploring this situation, to look beyond that
feeling to assess the teaching methods actually employed. Plutarch tells us
how the elder Cato (234–149 BC) taught his own son two centuries before
Christ:

When his son was born, no duty (save perhaps some public function) was so
pressing as to prevent him from being present when his wife bathed the
child and wrapped it in its swaddling clothes. His wife suckled the child with
her own milk, and would often give her breast to the children of her slaves,
so as to gain their affection for her son by treating them as his brothers. As
soon as the boy was able to learn, Cato took him personally in charge and
taught him his letters, although he owned an accomplished slave, named
Chilon, who was a schoolmaster and gave lessons to many boys. But Cato, to
use his own words, would not have a slave abuse his son nor perhaps pull his

---

[2]*Cornelius Tacitus, A Dialogue on Oratory*, trans. Sir William Peterson (Cambridge: Harvard
UP, 1946) 105–06.

ears for being slow at his lessons; nor would he have his boy owe a slave so precious a gift as learning. So he made himself the boy's schoolmaster, just as he taught him the laws of Rome and bodily exercises; not merely to throw the javelin, to fight in armour or to ride, but also to use his fists in boxing, to bear heat and cold, and to swim against the currents and eddies of a river. And he tells us himself that he wrote books of history with his own hand, and in large characters, so that his son might be able even at home to become acquainted with his country's past; that he was as careful to avoid all indecent conversation in his son's presence as he would have been in presence of the Vestal virgins; and that he never bathed with him. This last point seems to have been a Roman custom, for even fathers-in-law were careful not to bathe with their sons-in-law to avoid the necessity of stripping naked before them.[3]

Significantly, the resident schoolmaster Chilon was both Greek and a slave. The militant Romans had conquered Greece, so that many educated Greeks were brought back to Rome as slaves. During the republican period, then, most teachers had a very low social status since they were enslaved members of a conquered class.

Matters Greek were thus to be despised in that period. Despite a popular visit to Rome in 168 BC by the grammarian and literary scholar, Crates of Malos, there was general resentment against Greek philosophy and against certain Greek practices like nudity in athletics. In 161 BC, the Roman Senate passed a decree enabling the Praetor to expel all Greek teachers of philosophy and rhetoric.

The first clear evidence of a Latin, as opposed to Greek, teacher of rhetoric comes from 93 BC. In that year, L. Plotius Gallus began teaching in Latin, but was stopped almost at once. In 92 the two Censors, Cn. Domitius Aenobarbus and L. Licinius Crassus, issued the following edict, which was aimed not only at Plotius Gallus but at other unnamed teachers:

A report has been made to us that certain men have begun a new kind of teaching, and that young men are going regularly to their school; that they have taken the name of teachers of Latin rhetoric (*Latini rhetores*): and that our young men are wasting their whole days with them. Our ancestors ordained what lessons their children were to learn, and what schools they were to frequent. These new schools are contrary to our customs and ancestral traditions (*mos maiorum*), and we consider them undesirable and improper. Wherefore we have decided to publish, both to those who keep these schools and to those who are accustomed to go there, our judgement that we consider them undesirable.[4]

[3]Quoted in Aubrey Gwynn S.J., *Roman Education from Cicero to Quintilian* (1926; New York: Columbia Teachers Coll., n.d.) 19.
[4]Quoted in Gwynn, *Roman Education* 61.

The tone of this decree would make it appear that the phenomenon of Latinized rhetoric was a recent and even sporadic or unusual occurrence. Yet two almost simultaneous publications, both issued shortly after the decree, show instead that there already existed a well-organized and comprehensive system of Latin rhetoric which included provisions not only for theory but for teaching.

Since the study of that rhetoric was such an integral part of the Roman educational system, it may be useful to describe that subject briefly before turning to the role of writing in the whole pedagogical process.

It is not known exactly how a rather generalized rhetoric from the time of Aristotle (died 322 BC) became a specifically organized and standardized five-part system by about 100 BC. The names of some Greek teachers, especially those on the island of Rhodes, are known, as well as some lost treatises like that of Hermagoras of Temnos, mentioned by both Cicero and Quintilian. Of the precise transition to the five-part theory of rhetoric, however, comparatively little is known.

One thing known is that a young Roman, Marcus Tullius Cicero, wrote a rhetorical treatise circa 89 BC titled *On Invention* (*De inventione*).[5] In it, Cicero declares that rhetoric is divided into the five "parts": Invention, Arrangement, Style, Memory, and Delivery. Cicero discusses only the first of these five, promising to write later about the other four; he never carried out the promise, however.

What is also known is that an anonymous author (Cornificius?) published a book circa 86 BC which treated all five parts named by Cicero. Since the book is addressed to one Gaius Herennius, it has traditionally been titled the *Rhetorica ad Herennium* (*The Book of Rhetoric Addressed to Herennius*).[6] Its full treatment of the five parts makes the *Rhetorica ad Herennium* the first complete Latin rhetoric. It is a rigorously practical manual. The author says he will treat only what is pertinent to speaking: "That is why I have omitted to treat those topics which, for the sake of futile self-assertion, Greek writers have adopted." Moreover, he uses only his own Latin examples throughout the book (as he explains in IV.6.9–10).

The remarkable correspondence between these two books suggests the prior existence of a standardized theory of rhetorical education, dating perhaps to 100 BC or even earlier. The adolescent Cicero is clearly reporting only what he had been taught some time earlier, while the older author of the *Ad Herennium* not only admits the influence of "my teacher"

[5]Cicero, *De inventione. De optimo genere oratorem. Topica*, trans. H. M. Hubbell (Loeb Classical Library: Harvard UP, 1968). Cicero was only nineteen when he wrote the *De inventione*.

[6]Cicero, *Ad C. Herennium De ratione dicendi* (*Rhetorica ad Herennium*), trans. Harry Caplan (Loeb Classical Library: Harvard UP, 1954). Caplan's Introduction (especially xxi–xxxii) has interesting notes on the possible author of the book and its possible relation to the *De inventione* of Cicero.

and refers to students studying in schools (*utuntur igitur studiosi*), but specifically declares that rhetorical skill is to be attained through the three means of Precept, Imitation, and Exercise (I.2.3).

Rhetoric, then was the "Precept" portion of the Roman educational triad. As such, it was embedded in a consciously organized program designed to translate the "rules" into activities that would transform the students into rhetorical men. In fact the author of the *Ad Herennium* says that the five parts of rhetoric are what should be "in the orator" (*in oratore*), a phrase Harry Caplan translates as "faculties." In other words, the whole apparatus aimed at practical ability rather than mere knowledge. This ability was to be "in" the person, not in his books.

The striking homogeneity of Roman rhetorical theory at this early period may be seen clearly in the similar definitions of the five parts as given by Cicero and the author of the *Ad Herennium:*

Cicero	*Rhetorica ad Herennium*
Invention is the discovery of valid or seemingly valid arguments to render one's cause plausible	Invention is the devising of matter, true or plausible, that would make the case convincing.
Arrangement is the distribution of arguments thus discovered in the proper order.	Arrangement is the ordering and distribution of the matter, making clear the place to which each thing is to be assigned.
Expression is the fitting of the proper language to the invented matter.	Style is the adaptation of suitable words and sentences to the matter devised.
Memory is the firm mental grasp of matter and words	Memory is the firm retention in the mind of the matter, words, and arrangement.
Delivery is the control of the voice and body in a manner suitable to the dignity of the subject matter and the style.	Delivery is the graceful regulation of voice, countenance, and gesture.

Both books accept Aristotle's view that speeches are of three kinds: Forensic, dealing with legal accusation and defense; Deliberative or Political, dealing with public policy; and Epideictic, dealing with praise or blame.

The similarity of the two books is so great that, during the Middle Ages and early Renaissance, it was commonly assumed that Cicero was the author of both. Medieval writers called the *De inventione* Cicero's "First Rhetoric" (*Rhetorica prima*) or "Old Rhetoric" (*Rhetorica vetus*), relying on Cicero's statement that he planned to write on all five parts of rhetoric; these same writers believed that the *Rhetorica ad Herennium* was Cicero's carrying out of this promise, terming it his "Second Rhetoric" (*Rhetorica secunda*) or, more frequently, his "New Rhetoric" (*Rhetorica nova*). It was only in the late fifteenth century that humanists like Raffaele Regio began to question Cicero's authorship of the *Ad Herennium*.[7]

Though there are some differences between the books (e.g., the *Ad Herennium* offers two methods of Arrangement whereas Cicero proposes only one), the basic doctrines are substantially similar. These rhetorical precepts remained standard for antiquity, the Middle Ages, and the Renaissance, and had currency well into the eighteenth century. It is fair to say that there is such an entity as "Roman Rhetoric," characterized by the five-part division of the subject and by standard treatments of each of the parts.

This standardization was achieved by a resolute rejection of eclecticism after about 100 BC. The *Ad Herennium* draws on a number of Greek sources ranging from pre-Aristotelian to contemporary Rhodean ideas. But this "synthesis of various teachings" (to use translator Caplan's term) petrifies the chosen ideas into a lasting framework. Cicero simply assumes that the five-part plan is standard, "as most authorities have stated" (I.6.9).

The basic theoretical proposal of this Roman rhetoric is that the speaking process involves four chronologically arranged interior steps, followed by one exterior step. The speaker finds ("invents") ideas, then arranges them in an order, then puts words to them, then remembers all of this; finally, the exterior expression ("delivery") occurs through vocal sound, facial expression, and bodily gesture. By analogy the writing process is almost the same, with the physical handwriting (*orthographia*) replacing oral delivery as the final step.

Invention was accomplished through two major processes. One was the use of "status" or "issue" questions, which could be asked in any controversy. "Every subject which contains in itself a controversy to be resolved by speech and debate," Cicero says, "involves a question about a fact, or about a definition, or about the nature of an act, or about legal process" (I.8.10). The other method was to discover ideas through the use of "topics" or commonplaces" such as Division, Consequence, Cause, Effect, or Definition; each of these was considered a "region of an argument," a mental pathway that could lead the mind to find a useful line of argument. So important was this method that Cicero wrote a separate book (*Topica*) on the subject.

---

[7]For an account of the medieval reception of the book see Murphy, *Rhetoric in the Middle Ages: A History of Rhetorical Theory from Saint Augustine to the Renaissance* (U of California P, 1974) 106–114. Interestingly, the book was virtually unknown until late antiquity. For an account of Regio's argument against Cicero's authorship, see James J. Murphy and Michael Winterbottom, "Raffaele Regio's 1492 *Quaestio* doubting Cicero's authorship of the *Rhetorica ad Herennium*: Introduction and Text," *Rhetorica* 17 (1999): 77–87.

Arrangement specified six parts of an oration: Exordium or introduction, Narration or statement of facts, Division or the outline to be followed, Confirmation or proof, Refutation or attack on the opposition's arguments, and Peroration or conclusion.

Style included both general discussion of desirable wording and a very specific treatment of "figures" like Synecdoche, Metaphor, Antithesis, and Isocolon. The fourth book of the *Rhetorica ad Herennium*, in fact, presents the first systematic treatment of Style in Latin, with the first discussion of 64 figures (*exornationes*) which give "distinction" (*dignitas*) to language. Declaring that there are three levels of style (Plain, Middle, and Grand), the author says that good style should have the three qualities of Taste, Artistic Composition, and Distinction. This Distinction is achieved by two kinds of figures:

> To confer distinction upon style is to render it ornate, embellishing it by variety. The divisions under Distinction are Figures of Diction and the Figures of Thought. It is a figure of diction if the adornment is comprised in the fine polish of the language itself. A figure of thought derives a certain distinction from the idea, not from the words. (IV.13.18)

Then follow definitions and examples for 45 figures of speech (diction) and 19 figures of thought; the treatment of the figures occupies more than a fourth of the total length of the book, primarily because of the extensive examples the author feels necessary to make his definitions clear. It is interesting to note that this particular set of figures, not particularly well organized and not always mutually exclusive, became a sort of canon for writers as late as the sixteenth century. The figures became an accepted part of Style for Roman rhetoricians from Cicero onwards, and Quintilian regards them as so important that he devotes two entire books (eight and nine) of his *Institutio oratoria* to their analysis.

Memory, "the storehouse of invention," was described as being either natural or artificial. The natural memory could be improved by exercise, just like a bodily muscle. The artificial or artistic memory employed a mnemonic system of "Images" and "Backgrounds," in which the mind could store symbols (Images) set in a visualized neutral space (Background). Here too the *Rhetorica ad Herennium* is the first to describe the image-background system, though the theory may well have been commonly known.

Delivery, the final exteriorization, involved detailed consideration of vocal tones, facial expressions, and body movements, including the management of posture, arms, and fingers.

This five-part division of rhetoric had the virtue of being analytic, permitting further study of the individual parts without neglecting their relation to the whole. Cicero, as it has already been demonstrated, could write an entire book dealing only with Invention, and, within that area another treating only the Topics. Quite naturally there were technical debates about subpoints, for instance, the question whether there were really four issues in Invention or as few as three or as many as five. Nevertheless, the main framework held steady for centuries. Perhaps it was the logicality of the process description, the theory that idea-collection precedes arrangement which precedes style and memory. As a working hypothesis for speech preparation, it seems to have had a recognized value for a very long time.

At the same time, the written treatises had the defect of being schematic at best and mechanical at worst. The technical could, and did, become hypertechnical at times. When Cicero grew older, he began to react against what he saw as an over-technical approach he had favored in his youthful *De inventione*. His dialogue, *De oratore*,[8] written in 55 BC, argues that a liberal education is more important for the orator than "rules"; while Cicero's spokesman Crassus accepts the familiar doctrines of Roman rhetoric, he also declares that "the prize must go to the orator who possesses learning" (III.35.14). The character Crassus in *De oratore* is the same historical personage, Crassus, who was one of the censors prohibiting the Latin teachers of rhetoric from operating their schools in 92 BC, and Cicero has him explain his motives for the act; Crassus replies that they had no sense of the humanities and "so far as I could see these new masters had no capacity to teach anything except audacity" (III.24.94). In a sense, Cicero's *De oratore*, with its plea for a broad general education, is the last major objection against a well-organized, discourse-centered teaching program which was clearly already well rooted in Roman society.

Yet the treatises of *praecepta* were only a part of the picture. The *Rhetorica ad Herennium* concludes with an insistence on *exercitatio*: "All these faculties we shall attain if we supplement the rules of theory with diligent practice (*diligentia . . . exercitationis*)" (IV.56.69).

What, then, does *exercitatio* mean in this context? What is the nature of the system in which rhetoric is embedded? The evidence indicates that the system was as standardized as its rhetorical precepts.

THE ROMAN EDUCATIONAL SYSTEM
AS DESCRIBED BY QUINTILIAN

The most complete description of the Roman educational system appears in a work published in AD 95, almost a century and a half after the death

---

[8]Cicero, *De oratore*, trans. E. W. Sutton and H. Rackham, 2 vols (Cambridge: Harvard UP, 1967.)

of Cicero but reflecting a process already under way during Cicero's lifetime; it was destined to continue in substantially unchanged form throughout antiquity, to survive the barbarian invasions of late antiquity, and to become a major force in medieval and Renaissance education.

What makes Quintilian's *Institutio oratoria* so valuable as a source of our understanding is that it was written by Rome's acknowledged master teacher, based both on twenty years of classroom experience and on years of courtroom practice.[9] Moreover, because it is Quintilian's method not only to discuss his own methods but to compare other approaches and to analyze the advantages and disadvantages of each, the book offers a wide-ranging treatment of educational issues in addition to its specific descriptions of the Roman process.

Quintilian was born about AD 35 in Callaguris (modern Calahorra) in Spain.[10] When he was about sixteen he went to Rome, attaching himself, as was the custom, to a famous orator, Domitius Afer. At sixteen he would already have finished his formal education in Spain and taken on the toga of an adult. When Domitius Afer died in 59, Quintilian returned to Spain. He must have taken up a career as pleader and orator with some success, for he was among those who went to Rome in 68 with the governor of Spain, Galba, who became emperor in January 69.

Quintilian was both teacher and pleader in Rome. He mentions (IV.1.19) that he once pleaded a case before Queen Berenice, sister of the King Agrippa who questioned Saint Paul in Caesarea before the apostle was sent to Rome for trial. He also says (IV.2.86) that in many trials "the duty of setting forth the case was generally entrusted to me"—certainly a mark of his peers' respect for his oratorical abilities. He says (VII.2.24) that he published one of his courtroom speeches; however, the text has been lost.

His reputation as a teacher, however, was even greater. He was among the rhetoricians provided an annual subsidy from the public treasury in 72 by the Emperor Vespasian. A famous epigram by Martial a few years later, in 84, is evidence of his continuing reputation:

Quintiliane, vagae moderator summe iuventae,
Gloria Romanae, Quintiliane, togae.

---

[9]"The Empire's greatest professor of rhetoric," according to Brother E. Patrick Parks F.S.C. in *The Roman Rhetorical Schools as a Preparation for the Courts Under the Early Empire* (Baltimore: Johns Hopkins UP, 1945) 98.

[10]For biography, see George A. Kennedy, *Quintilian* (New York: Twayne, 1969). There is, of course, a considerable bibliography. For a select bibliography see Murphy, *Quintilian On the Teaching of Speaking and Writing* xiv–li. Keith V. Erickson has published a listing of about one thousand items in "Quintilian's *Institutio oratoria* and Pseudo-*Declamationes*," *Rhetoric Society Quarterly* 11 (1981): 78–90. See also Kennedy, *The Art of Rhetoric in the Roman World* (Princeton UP, 1972) 45–62.

O Quintilian, supreme guide of unsettled youth,
Glory of the Roman toga, O Quintilian.
                                    —*Epigrams* 2.90.1–2

Even the satirist Juvenal remarked on Quintilian's good influence on the
young, while his pupils included such famous figures as Pliny the Younger
and perhaps the historians Tacitus and Suetonius. The Emperor Domitian
entrusted the education of his two grandnephews to Quintilian even after
he had retired from teaching. His career was financially successful, as he
himself notes (VI. Preface 4); on the other hand, as he laments in the same
section, he suffered the loss of a beloved son, then his young wife, and finally a second son. Upon his retirement about the year 90, the Emperor
Domitian granted him consular rank, a remarkable honor at that time for
a rhetorician. There is no record of Quintilian after the murder of
Domitian in 96, and Kennedy suggests that he may have died within a year
or two of the publication of his *Institutio oratoria* in 95.

Quintilian says that he spent two years of his retirement preparing to
write the *Institutio*, after refusing for a while the requests of his friends that
he write a book on the "art of speaking." In his Preface, addressed to
Marcellus Victorius, he charges that other books on the subject have failed
to recognize that such an art depends on the educational foundation of
the orator; he says that a visible eloquence depends on an invisible preparation, "as the pinnacles of buildings are seen, while the foundations are
hid." Hence his program is a comprehensive one:

> For myself, I consider that nothing is unnecessary to the art of oratory, with-
> out which it must be confessed that an orator cannot be formed, and that
> there is no possibility of arriving at the summit in any subject without previ-
> ous initiatory efforts: therefore, I shall not shrink from stooping to those
> lesser matters, the neglect of which leaves no room for the greater, and shall
> proceed to regulate the studies of the orator from infancy, just as if he were
> entrusted to me to be brought up. (Preface 5)

The result is a work, divided into twelve books, which proposes an educational process beginning in the cradle and lasting into retirement from
public life. It starts with what we would call language acquisition and ends
with a discussion of honorable leisure in old age. Quintilian includes a detailed description of elementary and secondary education, with a book
(ten) on adult self-education, and a lengthy treatment of the five parts of
rhetoric. The final book, twelve, discusses the ideal orator as "a good man
speaking well."

Charles E. Little describes the *Institutio* as four books blended into one:
a treatise on education, a manual of rhetoric, a reader's guide to the best

authors, and a handbook on the moral duties of the orator.[11] Quintilian's own description includes the moral flavor permeating the work:

> The first book, therefore, will contain those particulars which are antecedent to the duties of the teacher of rhetoric. In the second book we shall consider the first elements of instruction under the hands of the professor of rhetoric and the questions which are asked concerning the subject of rhetoric itself. The next five will be devoted to invention (for under this head will also be included arrangement); and the four following, to elocution, within the scope of which fall memory and pronunciation. One will be added, in which the orator himself will be completely formed by us, since we shall consider, as far as our weakness shall be able, what his morals ought to be, what should be his practice in undertaking, studying, and pleading causes, what should be his style of eloquence, what termination there should be to his pleading, and what may be his employments after its termination. (I. Preface 21–22)

What then of the subject of rhetoric itself? Quintilian follows this passage with the statement that rhetoric will be taught throughout the whole program, where suitable:

> Among all these discussions shall be introduced, as occasion shall require, the art of speaking, which will not only instruct students in the knowledge of those things to which alone some have given the name of art, and interpret (so to express myself) the law of rhetoric, but may serve (also) to nourish the faculty of speech, and strengthen the power of eloquence; for in general, these bare treatises on art, through too much affectation of subtlety, break and cut down whatever is noble in eloquence, drink up, as it were, all the blood of thought, and lay bare the bones, which while they ought to exist and be united by their ligaments, ought still to be covered with flesh. (I. Preface 23–24)

In other words, Quintilian provides an integrated approach in which a major subject, rhetoric, is shown in its proper setting. The author of the *Rhetorica ad Herennium* specifies that the three elements of Precept, Imitation, and Exercise are necessary to the art, but leaves unspecified what he means by Imitation and Exercise. It is quite possible that he felt it unnecessary to do so for his contemporary readers, who would know, from their own experience, what went on in the schools. (As a matter of fact he does remind his readers [II.24.38] of the way "students in rhetorical schools" are taught to use Dilemma in argument.) As already shown, Quintilian complains that previous books on rhetoric ignored the fact that the subject

---

[11]Charles E. Little, *Quintilian the Schoolmaster*, vol 2 (Nashville: George Peabody Coll. for Teachers, 1951) 41.

is embedded in a total learning process; this great book fastens on the person learning, not merely on the subject itself. The subject of rhetoric, important though it may be, is but one of the tools in that learning process. Quintilian's title is "The Education of the Orator" (*Institutio oratoria*), not "A Book of Rhetoric" (*De rhetorica*).

As Aldo Scaglione has observed, what we today call "composition" had no equivalent in ancient and medieval literary theory.[12] Instead, the movement from silent voice or empty page to fully fashioned appropriate language was the province of rhetoric as assisted by its ancillary, grammar. The oralness or writtenness of the language was regarded as less important than its wholeness in fitting the situation at hand; that is why there is no separate "art of letter-writing" in Roman antiquity (as there is in the Middle Ages), no separate "art of historiography" or separate "art of poetry-writing."[13] The movement toward future language is the concern of an entire educational program built around rhetoric in its broadest sense but including much more than rhetoric itself.

The objective of the program is the shaping of an adaptive man of discretion, with an ingrained "habit" of adjusting his language to suit any subject or occasion. This sort of schooling does not attempt to lay down "rules":

> But let no man require from me such a system of precepts as is laid down by most authors of books of rules, a system in which I should have to make certain laws, fixed by immutable necessity, for all students of eloquence . . . for rhetoric would be a very easy and small matter, if it could be included in a short body of rules; but rules must generally be altered to suit the nature of each individual case, the time, the occasion, and necessity itself. Consequently, one great quality in an orator is discretion, because he must turn his thoughts in various directions, according to the various bearings of his subject. (II.13.1–2)

Nevertheless, even if Quintilian disdains reliance on "rules," he describes a systematic, programmatic educational program. However, it is possible that a modern reader, untrained in the technical processes of Roman education, may well overlook the architectonic framework lying behind Quintilian's readable style and sensible advice.

---

[12] Aldo Scaglione, *The Classical Theory of Composition from Its Origins to the Present: A Historical Survey*, U of North Carolina Studies in Comparative Literature 53 (U of North Carolina P, 1972) 3

[13] For the close correspondence between Horace's *Ars poetica* and the standard rhetorical lore of the day, see George Converse Fiske and Mary A. Grant, *Cicero's De oratore and Horace's Ars poetica*, U of Wisconsin Studies in Language and Literature 27 (U of Wisconsin P, 1929). There was, of course, a separate art of verse-writing in the Middle Ages; see Marjorie Curry Woods in chapter 4 of this volume and Murphy, *Rhetoric in the Middle Ages* 135–193.

It has been noted that if there is an art that conceals art, Quintilian has an art which conceals method. His Latin style makes extensive use of periodic sentences, with frequent parallel structures, sometimes quite complex by modern standards. (A good example may be found in the passage just quoted or in the preceding quotation on the role of rhetoric in the teaching program.) Also, since he usually presents various viewpoints before declaring his own judgment on each point, only the most careful reader will be able to track his main threads of thought through such discussions. His highly personalized accounts of his own teaching methods may also mislead an unwary reader into believing falsely that the *Institutio* is more of an autobiography than an exposition. All of this makes Quintilian extremely difficult to summarize.

ROMAN TEACHING METHODS

Virtually every individual element found in the program described by Quintilian was inherited from the Greeks. What was not inherited, however, was the deftly designed correlation of these elements into a "system."[14] As a system the process could be—and was—replicated over time and space. As a system it could be promoted worldwide as a tool of public policy equal in geopolitical value to the legions and the tax collectors in making the world Roman. As the television commentator Alastair Cooke once remarked, "Language is a dialect with an army and a navy," and history does in fact tell us that for more than half a millennium, the Latin language and its schools served as a kind of social cement throughout the Western world.[15]

Quintilian is not the inventor of this system; he is merely describing a process already familiar to Romans for almost two centuries. However, he is one of our best sources for both its philosophy and its details. Donald A. Russell suggested that Quintilian could even be used as a guide to understanding earlier Greek developments:

> The conservatism of rhetorical teaching over such a long period makes it possible to give an account of it as a system, based on the late textbooks

---

[14]For a schematic overview of the five elements of the Roman teaching methods, see the Appendix at the end of this chapter.

[15]Robert Pattison offers a useful analysis of the power of the Latin language "in the service of authority" in his book, *On Literacy: The Politics of the Word from Homer to the Age of Rock* (Oxford UP, 1982): "As it began its expansion, Rome also began to develop formal, written Latin for the business of the Empire. The soldier and the grammarian proceeded in lockstep to spread the Roman way, one by conquering the world, the other by providing it with correct Latin as a medium of organization" (67).

which survive, without feeling that one's conclusions are likely to be fundamentally wrong for the earlier period. Quintilian is undoubtedly the best
guide.[16]

Some modern critics have argued that Quintilian is presenting an ideal-
ized or even wistfully utopian view of education. They point to his insistence on morality as a reaction to the decadence he saw around him, noting that many of his examples hearken back to the presumably more
virtuous days of the pre-Imperial Republic. Yet he says that he bases the
Institutio oratoria on his own teaching experience in a career that won the
approbation of at least two Emperors, Vespasian and Domitian, and attracted the plaudits of writers like Juvenal and Martial.

What is more important, though, is that what Quintilian describes is
consistent with other evidence about Roman education from the time of
Cicero up to the fall of Rome to the barbarians in the fifth Christian century. It is also generally consistent with the evidence about the early Middle Ages, up to the late twelfth century at least. Obviously not every student went all the way through the course, just as today there are many
"dropouts" in even the best of schools. The poor sent their children for
only the most elementary education with the *ludi magister* for grammar or
the *calculator* for basic numbers.[17] No doubt many students had to content
themselves with the instruction in grammar without ever proceeding to
more advanced studies with a rhetorician. Nor did every teacher have the
mastery of a Quintilian; Seneca tells the story of the Spanish schoolmaster
Porcius Latro who could declaim brilliantly before his pupils but was para-
lyzed with fright when called upon to speak in public.[18]

If nothing else, the homogeneous longevity of the system proves its efficiency. Pierre Riché remarks that even in the sixth century teachers of
grammar, rhetoric, and law were still listed in the public budget under
"barbarians" like Theodoric and his successor Athalaric. "When we look
inside the schools of the grammarian and the rhetor," Riché adds, "we can
observe that the program and methods of instruction also had not
changed."[19] The ever-practical Romans surely did not continue the system

---

[16]Donald A. Russell, *Criticism in Antiquity* (U of California P, 1981) 25. S. F. Bonner also
stresses the systematic, devoting 162 pages of his *Education in Ancient Rome from the Elder Cato
to the Younger Pliny* (U of California P, 1977) to a section titled "The Standard Teaching
Programme."

[17]The most comprehensive account of ancient education is that of Henri I. Marrou, *A History of Education in Antiquity*, trans. George Lamb (New York: Sheed, 1956). He discusses Roman education in chapters 4 through 7 (265–313). For a discussion of terms like *calculator*,
see E. W. Bower, "Some Technical Terms in Roman Education," *Hermes* 89 (1961): 462–77.

[18]Cited in Gwynn, *Roman Education* 67.

[19]Pierre Riché, *Education and Culture in the Barbarian West Sixth through Eighth Centuries*,
trans. John J. Contreni (U of South Carolina P, 1976) 40.

out of any philosophical regard for "liberal arts"—Cicero's *De oratore* in 44 BC was apparently the last major Roman stand on that issue—but rather for the quite pragmatic reason that it worked. It provided literacy for many, competence for some, excellence for a few. The dividing line separating these three levels of accomplishment was based simply on the length of time the student could spend in the program.

What Quintilian demonstrates, then, is the complete system. Whether this or that student benefited fully from it depended more on socioeconomic factors than on the integrity of the system itself.

Consequently, it would seem useful to examine in a bit more detail the actual methods designed to produce what Quintilian calls *facilitas*, the ability to produce appropriate language on any subject in any situation. This examination covers Precept (Rhetoric and Grammar), Imitation, the two exercise programs of Progymnasmata and Declamation, and Sequencing.

Precept

Both grammar and rhetoric are included here. The *Rhetorica ad Herennium*, as has been shown, defines *praecepta* as "a set of rules that provide a definite method and system of speaking." Cicero's *De inventione* defines Eloquence as speaking based on "rules of art." Quintilian, as seen from his Preface, cautions that such "rules" should be not followed slavishly, and he adds in another place that "these rules have not the formal authority of laws or decrees of the plebs, but are, with all they contain, the children of expediency (*utilitas*)" (II.13.6). For him they serve as guides rather than commandments. No doubt this attitude was that of the best rhetors, though we can imagine the worse masters, just as today, driven to a helpless reliance on the rules because they do not know their subject well enough to be flexible.

The exact Roman method of teaching rhetoric as precept is not clear. Quintilian suggests that the precepts operate throughout the program; this could mean either that the master introduced precepts at each stage or that separate times were set aside for them. The *Institutio oratoria* does not describe any separate segment for teaching precepts, though it would seem logical that the older students preparing for Declamation would have to know the principles of at least deliberative and forensic rhetoric, the major fields covered in the imaginary cases students were asked to plead.

The Roman boy's educational progress was divided into three main steps: the acquisition of the most basic language skills, especially reading and writing; then a period of exercises with the *grammaticus*; then, when he was ready, training under the teacher of rhetoric (the *rhetor*). Book 2 of the *Institutio* covers the teaching done by the rhetorician. One might expect a discussion of *praecepta* at this point. Yet what Quintilian describes is not a systematic instruction in rhetorical precepts, but instead a more advanced version of the same types of classroom exercises already handled under the *grammaticus*. In fact, Quintilian declares that the exercises are more important than the precepts: "I will venture to say that this sort of diligent exercise will contribute more to the improvement of students than all the precepts of all the rhetoricians that ever wrote" (II.5.14). When he does come to a treatment of rhetoric in book 2, he adds another caution about the relation of precept to exercise:

> For the present I will only say that I do not want young men to think their education complete when they have mastered one of the small text-books of which so many are in circulation, or to ascribe a talismanic value to the arbitrary decrees of theorists. The art of speaking can only be attained by hard work and assiduity of study, by a variety of exercises and repeated trial, the highest prudence and unfailing quickness of judgment. (II. 13.15)

Since his discussion of rhetoric occupies eight of the twelve books of the *Institutio*, however, it is clear that he regards the subject as important. Yet Quintilian's whole approach is to teach students, not subjects. The most likely explanation is that rhetorical precept was not taught in a block, all at once or even on assigned days; rather, individual concepts must have been introduced whenever they suited the exercise at hand. When Quintilian discusses Narration of histories under the teacher of rhetoric (II.4.3–19), for example, he outlines the qualities of good narration and then refers to his later treatment of the subject under Judicial Oratory in his rhetoric section. Quintilian's recurrent principle for the assignment of individual exercises to the student is "When he is ready." He criticizes grammarians (II.1.2) for taking upon themselves some aspects of rhetorical instruction for which the boys will not yet be ready.

One thing is certain. The rhetoric treatise was not a student "textbook" in the modern sense of the word, with each student having a copy to study. The 'textbook' in our sense of the word is a product of the printing age, when books became cheap enough to distribute in a classroom. In any case, Roman rhetoric was so homogeneous that any reasonably well-educated teacher could master and transmit the principles orally without much difficulty. There were rhetoric texts available for study (they apparently sold well), even if public libraries were comparatively rare.

No doubt students were asked to memorize some materials. For example, the "commonplaces" (topics) would be useful for students to have ready to hand. Certainly it is known that they were obliged to memorize poetry and prose for the process of Imitation, and in fact Quintilian prefers this over having them memorize their own writing, even if doting parents preferred to hear their sons recite their own compositions from memory for public presentations. His argument is that they might as well memorize the best authors rather than perpetuating their own errors. But he makes no mention of memorizing precepts.

Grammar was another matter. Although Quintilian refers to "those rules which are published in the little manuals of professors" (I.5.7), the subject of grammar was not nearly as well developed in his day as rhetoric had already been for more than two centuries. There was no standard treatise on the subject. As a consequence, he feels obliged to devote a significant portion of book 1 (chapters 4–7) to such matters as "word," analogy, usage, spellings, barbarisms, solecisms, vocal tones, and the differences between Greek and Latin. Chapter 7 deals with Orthography, the art of writing words correctly on the page. He justifies this attention to apparently minor matters by arguing that correct language is the basis for every good use of language. "These studies," he says, "are injurious, not to those who pass through them, but only to those who dwell immoderately on them" (I.7.35).

Grammar is regarded as so foundational that students must be taught its precepts directly, especially in the earliest stages. And in the exercise of Imitation, the fine points of grammar are noted carefully in meticulous critiques of the models being studied. These two types of instruction are pointed out in his definition of the subject. Quintilian defines grammar in what was already a traditional way: "the art of speaking correctly, and the interpretation of the poets" (I.4.2). Thus it includes what we would today call the "rules" of correctness, and also the study of what we would call "literature."

(Later Roman teachers had access to a standard textbook on grammar. By the fourth Christian century, a widely accepted manual of basic Latin grammar, the brief *Ars minor* of Aelius Donatus [fl. AD 350][20] was available. This book petrified for later centuries the concept of "eight parts of speech"; another work, his larger *Ars grammatica* (*Ars maior*), not only treats the eight parts of speech in greater detail but includes a section dealing with *schemes* [figures of speech] and *tropes*, which would ordinarily have been treated by the rhetor rather than the grammarian. It was another two centuries before the appearance of what was to become the standard advanced Latin grammar text for more than a thousand years, that is, the *Ars grammatica* of Priscian [fl. AD 500], who was a teacher of Latin grammar in the Greek-speaking city of Constantinople. This work contains eighteen

---

[20]It has been translated by W. J. Chase in *The Ars Minor of Donatus*, U of Wisconsin Studies in the Social Sciences and History 36 (U of Wisconsin P, 1926). The Latin text is in Henry Keil (ed.) in *Grammatici Latini* 7 vols (Leipzig, 1864) 4, 355–66.

books, the last two dealing with "construction" [syntax], or the elements of composition.[21])

Even without such books in the earlier periods of Roman history, however, all the evidence indicates a consistency of grammatical instruction in the schools. The *grammaticus*, after all, received a young boy who had only the rudiments of reading and writing skills; the exigencies of standard-setting through all the complex classroom exercises provided ample opportunity for the grammarian not only to teach the rules themselves but to insist on their proper application in both writing and speaking.

What is to be remembered, above all, about the role of Precept in the Roman schools is that it was only a part of an integrated system designed to produce not merely knowledge but ability. Quintilian reminds his readers of this fact in book 10: "But these precepts of being eloquent, though necessary to be known, are not sufficient to produce the full power of eloquence unless there be united to them a certain Facility, which among the Greeks is called *hexis*, 'habit'" (X.1.1). This facility is resident in the psyche of the person, not merely in his knowledge.

To comprehend how the Romans produced this habit in young men, it is necessary to understand the precise role played in the schools by Imitation and by the graded composition exercises known as Progymnasmata.

Imitation

The concept of *Imitatio* (*Mimesis*) is much misunderstood today. On one hand, it could mean the artistic re-creation of reality by a poet or artist; on the other, it could mean the deliberate modeling of an existing artifact or text.[22] Actually it was for the Romans the second of these, a carefully plotted sequence of interpretive and re-creational activities using preexisting texts to teach students how to create their own original texts. Each phase in the sequence has its own purpose, but takes its value from its place in the sequence. It would be a mistake, therefore, for a modern reader to assume that each of the parts is independent of the others or to think that the set of compositional activities is a kind of smorgasbord to be picked up and used at random. It is not mere eclecticism.

The concept is certainly an ancient one. Plato has Protagoras say that when schoolboys memorize the great poets they imbibe not only the poetry but the moral qualities of the great men described in the poems (*Protagoras* 325–326). Isocrates makes it a key teaching tool (*Antidosis* 276–277). Aristotle begins his discussion of drama with a statement of

---

[21]Text in Keil, *Grammatica Latini* 4 367–402. Priscian was the first Latin grammarian to discuss syntax.

[22]There is a good brief survey of ancient views in Russell, *Criticism in Antiquity* 99–113.

principle: "Imitation is natural to man" (*Poetics* 1148b). The *Rhetorica ad Herennium*, as we have seen, begins and ends with the injunction to use Imitation as well as Exercise to learn the art of speaking. Cicero, the object of fervid imitation during the Renaissance,[23] opens the second book of his *De inventione* with the statement that he has taken the best from many sources, just as the painter Zeuxis of Heraclea chose the five most beautiful girls from Croton as models for a painting of Helen the city had commissioned for its Temple of Juno. The continuity of Imitation was so strong throughout the Roman period that the first Christian rhetorician, Saint Augustine, writing in AD 426, declares in his *De doctrina Christiana* (IV.3) that Imitation is more important than Precept for the newcomer to rhetoric.

The Roman school system perfected a seven-step process of Imitation, with writing or the analysis of written texts being coupled to oral performance by the students before master and peers in the classroom. What today would be called peer criticism is an integral part of the scheme; in the Roman interactive classroom the student-critic shapes his own critical judgment by assessing publicly what he hears and reads. The teacher is not merely to tell the students what to think, Quintilian says, "but frequently to ask questions upon them, and try the judgment of his pupils" (II.5.13).

A brief explanation of these seven steps may show how Imitation works in the Roman classroom.[24]

A. Reading Aloud (lectio).   Either the master or one of the students could read a text aloud. Models are to be carefully chosen for their linguistic virtues, though occasional faulty ones may be used to illustrate how defects may occur. In the later stages when speeches become the texts for study, the master may declaim a speech or even declaim one of his own (though Quintilian prefers that the master use an acknowledged orator like Cicero rather than his own work). Quintilian introduces implicitly a major educational principle at this point, namely, that no exercise should be conducted for a single purpose only. The students hear not only the form of a text, including its rhythmical or other sonic patterns, but also take in unconsciously its subject matter and moral tone. Hence the insistence on histories as well as poems, as offering salutary models of conduct.

---

[23]See Izora Scott, *Controversies Over the Imitation of Cicero as a Model for Style and Some Phases of Their Influence on the Schools of the Renaissance* (Davis: Hermagoras, 1991). It is important to note, however, that some Renaissance discussions of Imitation deal with adults deciding which authors to imitate in their own literary works, while others do deal with Imitation in educating the young.

[24]A useful account of Imitation may be found in Donald Lemen Clark, *Rhetoric in Greco-Roman Education* (Columbia UP, 1957) 144–176. Clark's account may be particularly interesting to readers concerned with teaching method, since he consistently analyzes the rationale for the exercises more clearly than other historians like Marrou or Bonner.

B. *Analysis of the Text (praelectio).* This is the beginning of the application of judgment. The master literally dissects the text. The immediate intent is to show the students how the author made good or bad choices in wording, in organization, in the use of figures, and the like; the long-range objective is to accustom the student to what today we could call a "close reading" of texts. Since it is a written text done orally, the exercise also trains the "ear" of the student for later exercises in analyzing the oral arguments used in orations. Both good models and bad models are to be presented. Quintilian's brief summary in book 2 of the *Institutio* seems straightforward enough; in the following passage he is explaining the method in respect to analyzing an oration, though the method is exactly the same for a poem or a history (as he points out in I.8.13–21):

> The master, after calling for silence, should appoint some one pupil to read (and it will be best that this duty should be imposed on them by turns), so that they may thus accustom themselves to clear pronunciation. Then, after explaining the cause for which the oration was composed (so that what is said will be better understood), he should leave nothing unnoticed which is important to be remarked, either in the thought or the language: he should observe what method is adopted in the Exordium for conciliating the judge; what clearness, brevity, and apparent sincerity is displayed in the statement of facts; what design there is in certain passages, and what well-concealed artifice (for that is the only true art in pleading which cannot be perceived except by a skilful pleader); what judgment appears in the division of the matter; how subtle and urgent is the argumentation; with what force the speaker excites, with what amenity he soothes; what severity is shown in his invectives, what urbanity in his jests; how he commands the feelings, forces a way into the understanding, and makes the opinions of the judges coincide with what he asserts. In regard to the style, too, he should notice any expression that is peculiarly appropriate, elegant, or sublime; when the amplification deserves praise, what quality is opposed to it; what phrases are happily metaphorical, what figures of speech are used; what part of the composition is smooth and polished, and yet manly and vigorous. Nor is it without advantage, indeed, that inelegant and faulty speeches—yet such as many, from depravity of taste, would admire—should be read before boys, and that it should be shown how many expressions in them are inappropriate, obscure, timid, low, mean, affected, or effeminate. (II.5.6–10)

When Quintilian and his colleagues say that they will "leave nothing unnoticed," they mean exactly that. The dissection of the text is intended to be microscopic. While a reader may cover whole sections with a sweep of the eye, the composing writer/speaker must commit himself to one word or even one syllable at a time as he creates a text. Hence the truly analytic

2. HABIT IN ROMAN WRITING INSTRUCTION

reader needs to reach back through the wholeness of paragraph or argument to identify the microcosmic decisions made by the composer.

An excellent example of this Roman micro-analysis may be found in a
later work written by the grammarian Priscian about AD 500. Priscian's
Analyses of the First Lines of the Twelve Books of Virgil's Aeneid is an extremely
meticulous work, occupying 54 pages in the standard edition of Henry
Keil. The beginning section provides a good example of the method:

Scan the line *Arma virumque cano Troiae qui primus ab oris.*

How many caesurae are there?

Two.

What are they?

The penthemimera and the hephthemimera [*semiquinaria, semiseptenaria,*
Priscian says in his barbarous Latin]. Which is which?

The penthemimera is *Arma   virumque cano,* and the hephthemimera *Arma
virumque cano Troiae.*

How many "figures" has it?

Ten.

Why has it got ten?

Because it is made up of three dactyls and two spondees.

[Priscianus takes no notice of the final spondee.]

How many words ["parts of speech"] are there?

Nine.

How many nouns?

Six—*Arma, virum, Troiae, qui* [sic], *primus, oris.*

How many verbs?

One—*cano.*

How many prepositions?

One—ab.

How many conjunctions?

One—*que.*

Study each word in turn. Let us begin with *Arma.* What part of speech is it?

A noun.

What is its quality?

Appellative.

What kind is it?

General.

What gender?

Neuter.

How do you know?

All nouns ending in -*a* in the plural are neuter.

Why is *Arma* not used in the singular?

Because it means many different things.[25]

This kind of methodical treatment, carried on over all kinds of texts for ten or a dozen years, must surely have promoted a high degree of linguistic sensitivity in the students. It must be remembered, too, that the same treatment was given to the students' own compositions.

On the other hand, the mere analysis of others' texts could produce a sort of compositional paralysis, with the writer fearing his inability to do as well as the models. Quintilian is quite aware of what we would call "writer's block." He tells the story of a young man named Secundus, whose uncle, Julius Florus, found him in a dejected state one day; Secundus told his uncle that he had been trying for three days to write an introduction to a subject he had to write upon for school. Florus responded smilingly, "Do you wish to write better than you can?" (X.3.14). For improvement, Quintilian adds, there is need of application, but not of vexation with ourselves.

The close analysis of texts was of course not the only method used. It took its value from its place in the system. The next steps called upon the student to apply his own energies.

C. *Memorization of Models.* Quintilian is convinced that memorization of models not only strengthens the memory in the way that physical exercise strengthens a muscle but also provides the student with "an abundance of the best words, phrases, and figures" for possible use later on (II.7.4). Memorization is especially useful for the very young, who do not yet have the capacity for intellectual analysis of their texts. "The chief symptom of ability in children," he says, "is memory" (II.3.1). (He says the same thing about teaching a foreign language to the very young.) He is quite adamant about the virtue of memorizing good models rather than one's own writing, and in fact says that such memorization will equip the student better to recall his own compositions when necessary. As usual, though, he has a keen eye for the pedagogical opportunity: a student may be allowed to recite his own work from memory only as a reward, when he has produced "something more polished than ordinary" (II.7.5). The problem he sees is that otherwise the student may end up perpetuating his faults if he memorizes his own work.[26]

---

[25]Quoted in Marrou, *History of Education in Antiquity* 279–280.

[26]There is a brief analysis of Quintilian's view of memory in Frances A. Yates, *The Art of Memory* (Chicago, Chicago UP, 1966), pp. 21–26.

D. *Paraphrase of Models.* The re-telling of something in the students' own words begins at the earliest stages of the program—for example, with first an oral and then a written paraphrase of a fable of Aesop (I.9.2)—but continues throughout the instruction of both the *grammaticus* and the *rhetor*. The more advanced students deal with more complex types of narrations such as plots of comedies or the accounts found in histories (II.4.2); here Quintilian refers to the concepts of narration to be found in rhetorical doctrine, though he expressly reminds the reader that the exercise is a continuation of that begun earlier under the *grammaticus*. (Here too is another example of the way in which formal rhetorical precepts are fed into the system as the need arises.)

The ultimate purposes of paraphrase are two: to accustom students to fastening on the structure of the model rather than its words, and to begin the development of a personal style in narration. "It is a service to boys at an early age," he says, "when their speech is but just commenced, to repeat what they have heard in order to improve their faculty of speaking. Let them accordingly be made, and with good reason, to go over their stories again, and to pursue them from the middle, either backward or forward" (II.4.15).

It is in this section, dealing with the first efforts of the students to compose in their own terms, that Quintilian lays down his principles of classroom correction. The students should be shown the faults in their writing and speaking, but should also be praised for whatever they have accomplished. If the performance is so bad that the student is asked to write again on the same subject, he should be told that he can indeed do better, "since study is cheered by nothing more than hope" (II.4.13). Quintilian applauds exuberance in compositions by the young, if it is made clear that later on a more sophisticated standard will be demanded. He comments that "the remedy for exuberance is easy, but barrenness is incurable by any labor" (II.4.6). Elsewhere he refers to an ancient aphorism that "it is easier to prune a tree than to grow one" (II.8.9). Accordingly he urges the master to promote freedom of invention in the early stages of the student's development, tolerating (though noting) some stylistic faults which can be corrected as the student becomes more adept in language.

E. *Transliteration of Models.* There is no precise English term for the Roman exercises in text re-casting. The process could take several forms: direct translation of the text from Greek to Latin or Latin to Greek; recasting of Latin prose to Latin verse; re-casting of Latin prose to Greek verse, or vice versa; making the model shorter, or longer, whether in verse or prose; altering the style from plain to grand or vice versa. Transliteration could be an extremely sophisticated assignment, demanding precise knowledge of verse forms and prose rhythms as well as an extensive vocabulary. Indeed, Quintilian notes, the difficulty of the exercise makes it valuable for teaching a keen awareness of language. A sure knowledge of the model is a prerequisite. As for critics of this method, he points out agreement on the principle: "About the utility of turning poetry into prose, I suppose no one has any doubt" (X.5.4). Once the principle of usefulness for re-casting is established, he implies, there is no reason to shy away from other modes of accomplishing the same end.

A monolingual culture like the American, in which knowledge of foreign languages is severely limited, might be hard put to use some translative forms of the method, but other forms (e.g., verse-prose or prose-verse, or plain style-grand style) might well be considered as classroom tools.

F. *Recitation of Paraphrase or Transliteration.* The oral-written relationship is so strong in Roman educational practice that even Quintilian does not always make explicit what he clearly expects everyone to take for granted. This relationship is spelled out at the very beginning of his discussion of teaching methods: "Not only is the art of writing combined with that of speaking, but correct reading also precedes illustration" (I.4.3). The student, having "read" his text analytically, writes his own paraphrase or transliteration of it, and then brings his own work into the public classroom for oral presentation. Sometimes it will be recited from memory, sometimes read aloud.

G. *Correction of Paraphrase or Transliteration.* The admonitions of the master concerning this performance are shared with all who hear, thus raising the standards of everyone. Quintilian argues that this is the prime advantage of public over private tutorial education:

> At home he can learn only what is taught himself; at school, even what is taught others. He will daily hear many things commended, many things corrected; the idleness of a fellow student, when reproved, will be a warning to him; the industry of anyone, when commended, will be a stimulus; emulation will be excited by praise; and he will think it a disgrace to yield to his equals in age, and an honor to surpass his seniors. All these matters excite the mind; and though ambition itself be a vice, yet it is often the parent of virtues. (II.2.21–22)

This "exercise of judgment," as Quintilian calls it, could also enroll the students themselves as critics. Not only was the Roman schoolroom interactive between master and students, but between students and students as well. Quintilian is quite explicit about this for the older boys doing formal declamations or practice orations: "Shall a pupil, if he commits faults in declaiming, be corrected before the rest, and will it not be more serviceable to him to correct the speech of another? Indubitably" (II.5.16). Even though he does not make the same kind of statement about the earlier stages of the program, the whole tone of the book, especially chapter 2 of book 1 on the virtues of the public classroom, argues for what he continually refers to as "activity of the mind" among the students. There is no reason to believe that this would exclude what we call "peer criticism." Perhaps Quintilian intends only the older boys to comment on each others' work, but everything else he says throughout the book is at least consistent with the possibility that he encourages student criticisms at every stage.

Two principles govern his use of correction. The first is that oral correction should be tailored to the capacities of the student involved; however, since correction is public, the master must keep in mind the other hearers in the classroom, "who will think that whatever the master has not amended is right" (II.6.4). The second is that some early faults can be tolerated, as part of the student's natural development of a particular skill.

For the adult practitioner he discusses in book 10, there is another kind of self-correction involved in the practice of writing. This involves personal decisions about what to add, to take away, or to alter (X.5.1), rather than the public pronouncements in a classroom about something just recited. Even so, it is logical to assume that Quintilian would ask the adult writer to analyze his own written text with the same methods used earlier in the classroom process of Imitation. He proposes lifetime use of methods learned in school.[27]

The process of Imitation, then, is for Quintilian and other Romans a specific sequence of learning activities for students from the youngest to the oldest. The method remains the same over time, the only change being in the models imitated. The young lad who begins with a simple fable of Aesop ends up years later as a young adult doing the same thing with a complex speech of Demosthenes or Cicero. The student learns political science, history, morals, and literature by a kind of intelligent osmosis. His attention is focused on the style and structure of the particular text, but he cannot escape an awareness of historical circumstances or ethical problems as he moves through the various steps.

The objective, of course, is to enable the student eventually to compose his own texts: "For what object have we in teaching them, but that they may not always require to be taught?" (II.5.13). Free composition must be based on knowledge of the options available to the writer, and this knowledge comes only from Imitation. Imitation is thus a life-long pursuit.

---

[27]Accordingly, Quintilian includes in book 10 a lengthy section (X.1.37–2.26) analyzing a wide range of authors and orators worthy of imitation by the adult learner. He concludes the section by saying that "we should do well to keep a number of different excellences before our eyes."

Quintilian remarks early in the *Institutio* that a child learns spoken language easily through natural imitation, so that even a two-year-old can speak and understand what is said to him. Writing, however, must be taught to him. The boy follows the forms of the letters of the alphabet before he is allowed to write them for himself, tracing indented patterns with his stylus to accustom his hand kinesthetically to the form of a letter before he writes it freely. "By following these sure traces rapidly and frequently, he will form his hand, and not require the assistance of a person to guide his hand with his own hand placed over it" (I.1.27). This kind of tactile Imitation is based on exactly the same principles as the school exercises and the self-learning activity recommended in book 10 for adults to continue even into retirement. To put it into abstract terms, form precedes freedom. The writer who knows only one mode of writing is not free, but is bound to that one mode.

As valuable as Imitation is, however, it too is but one part of the total educational system. The Roman student also underwent a parallel program of specific writing/speaking exercises (*Progymnasmata*).

Progymnasmata (Graded Composition Exercises)

This is one area of methodology in which Quintilian is less than thorough, perhaps because of what he calls "this haste of mine" (II.1.12). In the opening chapter of book 2 he discusses the proper spheres of *grammaticus* and *rhetor,* arguing that the teacher of rhetoric (as well as the teacher of grammar) "should not shrink from the earliest duties of his profession" (II.1.8). What he means is that both should teach the "little exercises" that ultimately prepare the boy to be an adept user of language. Then he rapidly lists nine exercises: narration, praise, blame, thesis, commonplaces, statement of facts, eulogy, invective, and refutation; then in chapter 4, he discusses some of these exercises and adds three more: comparison, cause and effect (which he calls a *chreia*), and praise or censure of laws. Earlier (I.8.3), he had named *prosopopoeiae* in connection with proper oral reading. This makes thirteen altogether. He concludes chapter 4, with this observation: "On such subjects did the ancients, for the most part, exercise the faculty of eloquence" (II.4.41). In other words, he is simply listing rapidly a number of exercises long known and undoubtedly familiar to his readers—hence his brevity.[28]

What he writes about here is a set of graded composition exercises which had long since come to be called *progymnasmata* (though he himself does not use that term). The name comes from the function of the exercises: if the highest forms of school training are the Declamations or ficti-

---

[28]Hock and O'Neill 10–22.

tious speeches (*gymnasmata* in Greek), then that which prepares for them is Pre-Declamation (*progymnasmata*). Even though the term itself is Greek, and the major ancient writers of textbooks on the subject were Greek, it is clear from Quintilian's account that the use of the exercises is already solidly entrenched in Latin schools.

The earliest surviving textbook defining and illustrating the exercises is that by Aelius Theon of Alexandria, writing probably in the latter half of the first Christian century—a contemporary of Quintilian though probably unknown to him. Two of the most popular Greek textbooks come long after Quintilian, written by Hermogenes of Tarsus[29] (second century) and Aphthonius of Antioch[30] (fourth century). Both these books had impact well beyond antiquity. Hermogenes's treatise was translated into Latin as *Praeexercitamenta* by the Latin grammarian Priscian around AD 500, and had use during the Middle Ages and Renaissance. Aphthonius, however, eclipsed Hermogenes in antiquity by far, mainly because he included useful examples, and his work became a standard Byzantine textbook as well; when introduced to the Latin West during the fifteenth century, it achieved a new popularity extending even to colonial America.

Quintilian's concern with the proper role of the grammarian proved to be a prophetic one. It was not a question of whether the *progymnasmata* should be taught, but rather a question of who should teach them. Quintilian urges the rhetorician to keep some control, even if it means taking up "the earliest duties of his profession" by working with very young students just beginning narrations of fables. History tells us that the grammarians eventually won out in Roman schools, taking over these exercises for themselves. As a practical matter, this development may have meant little to the boys who came through the system, since they received the instruction in any case.

We see in Quintilian, then, a comparatively early stage in which these exercises still fall under the purview of both masters. It is true, nevertheless, that his brief account can show us their relation to the schools' objectives. Specifically, he argues that the exercises train students in the exact functions needed in the real world:

> But what is there among those exercises, of which I have just now spoken, that does not relate both to other matters peculiar to rhetoricians, and, indisputably, to the sort of causes pleaded in courts of justice? Have we not to make statements of facts in the forum? I know not whether that department of rhetoric is not most of all in demand there. Are not eulogy and invective often introduced in those disputations? Do not commonplaces, both those

---

[29]Translated by Charles S. Baldwin, *Medieval Rhetoric and Poetic* (New York: Macmillan, 1928) 23–38.

[30]Translated by Ray Nadeau, *Speech Monographs* 19 (1952): 264–285.

which are leveled against vice (such as were composed, we read, by Cicero), and those in which questions are discussed generally (such as were published by Quintus Hortensius, as, "Ought we to trust to light proofs?" and "For witnesses and against witnesses"), mix themselves with the inmost substance of causes? These weapons are in some degree to be prepared, so that we may use them whenever circumstances require. He who shall suppose that these matters do not concern the orator, will think that a statue is not begun when its limbs are cast. (II.1.10–12)

This argument is coupled with the proposal that the *grammaticus* continue to teach the students part of the time even after they join the *rhetor*. This, he says, will show the students the continuity of their instruction while providing them with variety in their masters. "Nor need there be any fear," he adds, "that the boy will be overburdened with the lessons of two masters. His labor will not be increased, but that which was mixed together under one master will be divided. Each tutor will thus be more efficient in his own province" (II.1.13). Perhaps the futility of his argument lay in the fact that both masters used the same methods anyway, with the exception of Declamation belonging clearly to the *rhetor*.

In any case, Quintilian does not define or illustrate most of the terms he uses for the exercises, so we must look elsewhere. The *Progymnasmata* of Hermogenes of Tarsus is as good a source as any, since it transmitted the well-accepted definitions which even the more popular Aphthonius used later as the basis for his own book. Even though Hermogenes is writing in the second Christian century, he reflects a tradition going well back before the time of Cicero.

Donald Lemen Clark has an incisive statement about the educational value of the *progymnasmata* as found in Hermogenes and his successors:

> They all give patterns for the boys to follow. They present a graded series of exercises in writing and speaking themes which proceed from the easy to the more difficult; they build each exercise on what the boys have learned from previous exercises . . . yet each exercise adds something new.[31]

The key term here is "graded." Like other elements of the Roman system, the *progymnasmata* are taught not for themselves but for habit-building in the mind of the student. With each accomplishment of the student, there comes a new and more difficult challenge, just as Imitation moves by steps from the oral reading through model-based writing to the final free composition of the student. The "how" is carefully spelled out at each stage.

---

[31]Clark, *Rhetoric* 181. For a modern adaptation of this idea, see John Hagaman, "Modern Use of the Progymnasmata in Teaching Rhetorical Invention," *Rhetoric Review* 5 (1986): 22–29.

Hermogenes presents twelve *progymnasmata*: fable, tale, *chreia,* proverb, refutation and confirmation, commonplace, encomium, comparison, impersonation (*prosopopoeia*), description, thesis, and laws. (Aphthonius makes these into fourteen by separating refutation and confirmation, and by making censure the opposite of encomium; Quintilian, as we have seen, adds cause and effect.)

> The twelve can be divided according to the three types of rhetoric:
>
> Deliberative rhetoric: fable, tale, *chreia,* proverb, thesis, laws.
>
> Judicial rhetoric: confirmation and refutation, commonplace.
>
> Epideictic rhetoric: encomium, impersonation, comparison, description.

However apt this kind of division might be in terms of future usefulness to the student, though, it does not represent the order in which the *progymnasmata* were taught. (Indeed the concept of "three genera of speeches," introduced by Aristotle and followed by the Romans, was always more theoretical than practical in terms of speeches made in the real world; any one oration might require elements of all three genera, as Cicero's performances have shown.) The exercises were taught in a certain order, for the good reason that they naturally succeeded each other.

The following abstract of the twelve *progymnasmata* of Hermogenes is necessarily brief, since the inclusion of overnumerous examples would produce an account as long as the book itself; examples are provided only in those cases (e.g., the *chreia*) which might otherwise be difficult for a modern reader to understand.[32]

1. Fable. The first exercise is the retelling of fables from Aesop. The retelling may be either more concise than the original, or expanded beyond it with invented dialogue or additional actions to enhance the tale.

2. Tales. This is the recounting of something that happened (a history) or of something as if it had happened (an epic, a tragedy, a comedy, a poem). Hermogenes names five modes: direct declarative, indirect declarative, interrogative, enumerative, comparative.

3. Chreia. This is an exercise in amplification, dealing with what a person said or did. Hermogenes says there are three types of *chreia* to be used in this way:

> Of words only: "Isocrates said that education's root is bitter, its fruit is sweet" (*Chreia* 43).

---

[32]The following account is based largely on Clark.

Of actions only: "Crates, having met with an ignorant boy, beat the boy's tutor" (Quintilian I.9.5).

Mixed, with both words and actions: "Diogenes, on seeing a youth misbehaving, beat his tutor and said, 'Why are you teaching such things?'" (*Chreia* 26).

Hermogenes notes that a *chreia* differs from a maxim in three ways: a maxim has no character speaking, does not involve actions, and does not have an implicit question and answer.

The main point, of course, is the amplification asked of the student. Hermogenes suggests a sequence of eight methods to write about a *chreia:* praise of the speaker quoted, an expanded restatement of the *chreia,* its rationale, a statement of the opposite view, a statement from analogy, a statement from example, a statement from authority, and an exhortation to follow the advice of the speaker.

Ronald F. Hock and Edward N. O'Neill have recently published translations of the *chreia* of seven ancient authors including Quintilian; an appendix listing 68 *chreia* shows a remarkable similarity among the various collections, whether the "speaker" named is Demosthenes, Diogenes, or Plato.[33] This is not surprising, since the books are written for teachers rather than students; and utility not variety is the standard.

4. *Proverb.* This is an exercise in amplification of an aphorism (*sententia*). It is not radically different from the preceding exercise, but is intended as incremental repetition. Hermogenes suggests methods similar to those for the *chreia,* though of course without praise for a speaker or an action. The *Rhetorica ad Herennium* (IV.43.56-58) cites the Proverb as an element of a figure of speech called Dwelling On One Point (*expolitio*); seven means of amplification are offered for the proverb "Often one who does not wish to perish for the republic must perish with the republic."

5. *Refutation and Confirmation.* This involves disproving or proving a narrative. Quintilian (II.4.18-19) makes credibility the main heading to be considered. Hermogenes, however, says that the elements of Destructive Analysis are obscurity, incredibility, impossibility, inconsistency, unfittingness, inexpediency, or obscurity. Constructive analysis takes the opposite of these.

6. *Commonplace.* This exercise asks the student to "color," that is, to cast a favorable or unfavorable light upon an established fact, a thing admitted. Aphthonius says the Commonplace is practice in arousing the

---

[33]See footnote 26.

emotions of an audience in the face of an established fact—for example, the discovery of a temple robber:

> Begin with the contrary, analyzing it, not to inform, for the facts are assumed, but to incite and exasperate the auditors. Then introduce a comparison to heighten as much as possible the point you are making. After that introduce a proverb, upbraiding and calumniating the doer of the deed. Then a digression, introducing a defamatory conjecture as to the past life of the accused; then a repudiation of pity. Conclude the exercise with the final considerations of legality, justice, expediency, possibility, decency, and the consequences of the action.[34]

This treatment is called a Commonplace, he says, because it can be applied commonly to any temple robber or other miscreant.

7. *Encomium*. This is an exercise in praise of virtue and dispraise of vice, either in a thing or in a person. (Aphthonius makes the positive [Encomium] and negative sides [Vituperation] of this exercise into two separate items, but most others keep them as one.) Since praise and blame are the function of Epideictic oratory, the exercise of Encomium could draw upon all the lore of that section of rhetorical theory. Theon is reported to have developed the topics of Encomium in 36 divisions and subdivisions. Hermogenes contents himself with ten ways to praise a person: marvelous events at his birth, his nurture, his education, the nature of his soul, the nature of his body, his deeds, his external resources, how long he lived, the manner of his end, and the events after his death. Quintilian praises this exercise both because "the mind is thus employed about a multiplicity and variety of matters" (II.4.20), and because it furnishes the students with many examples for later use.

8. *Comparison*. This exercise builds on the preceding one of Encomium by doubling the subjects to be treated in one composition. The same methods are to be used.

9. *Impersonation*. Here the student is asked to compose an imaginary monologue that would fit an assigned person in certain circumstances. The task is to make the language appropriate not only to the person (age, background, and emotional state) but to the circumstances in which he speaks. For example, what might Achilles say to the dead Patroclus, or what might Niobe say over the bodies of her dead children? There were three standard divisions: *Ethopoeia* is the imaginary statement of a known person; *Prosopopoeia* is the imaginary statement of an imaginary person;

---

[34]Quoted in Clark, *Rhetoric* 194.

and *Eidolopoeia* are lines written for the dead to speak. Despite these theoretical divisions of the textbooks, the term *Prosopopoeia* (as in Quintilian) is often used to denote the whole range of impersonative exercises.

10. Description.   The exercise in vivid description (*ecphrasis*) asks the student to write and speak so that he is "bringing before the eyes what is to be shown"—a phrase used by Theon, Hermogenes, and Aphthonius as well as Quintilian. Quintilian discusses this kind of imaging in Book Eight under Ornateness; the figure *enargeia* (Vivid Illustration), he says, portrays persons, things, and actions in lively colors, so that they seem to be seen as well as heard (VIII.3.61). Clark (203) uses the term "Epideictic word-painting" for *ecphrasis,* and quotes Hermogenes as saying that "The virtues of the ecphrasis are clearness and visibility." It requires a careful attention to detail, and here the *ecphrasis* builds on the earlier exercises of Commonplace and Encomium. The student does not simply say a wall is large, but describes its stones, its height, its thickness, its circumference, its battlements—dilation of detail until the reader/hearer can "see" it in his mind.

11. Thesis.   This advanced exercise asks the student to write an answer to a "general question" (*quaestio infinita*)—that is, a question not involving individuals. Cicero states in his *De inventione* (I.6.8) that rhetoric does not deal with such General Questions, but only with those involving individuals. Quintilian too notes that a general question can be made into a persuasive subject if names are added (II.4.25). That is, a Thesis would pose a general question such as "Should a man marry?" or "Should one fortify a city?" (A Special Question on the other hand would be "Should Marcus marry Livia?" or "Should Athens spend money to build a defensive wall?") Hermogenes distinguishes the Thesis from the Commonplace by declaring that the Commonplace amplifies a subject already admitted, while the Thesis is an inquiry into a matter still in doubt. Since both negative and positive answers may be supported, the exercise calls on the student to marshal arguments, using his rhetorical skills on the chosen side; as a consequence both Hermogenes and Aphthonius recommend the same structure that is used in orations.

12. Laws (Legislation).   This final exercise asks the pupil to compose arguments for or against a law. Quintilian regards this as the most advanced of the set of exercises: "The praise or censure of laws requires more mature powers, such as may almost suffice for the very highest efforts" (II.4.33). That is, it requires almost as much skill as the most advanced student activity, the Declamation. He says that the chief topics to be considered are whether the law is proper or expedient; under "proper" he includes consistency with justice, piety, religion or similar virtues; the "expedient" is determined by the nature of the law, by its circumstances, or by its enforceability. Quintilian also complains that some teachers make too many divisions of the two topics he discusses; as a matter of fact Hermogenes lists the six topics of evident, just, legal, possible, expedient, and proper.

The *progymnasmata,* then, offered Roman teachers a systematic yet flexible tool for incremental development of student abilities. The young writer/speaker is led step-by-step into increasingly complex compositional tasks, his freedom of expression depending, almost paradoxically, on his ability to follow the form or pattern set by his master. At the same time he absorbs ideas of morality and virtuous public service from the subjects discussed, and from their recommended amplifications on themes of justice, expediency, and the like. By the time he reaches the exercise of Laws he has long since learned to see both sides of a question. He has also amassed a store of examples, aphorisms, narratives, and historical incidents which he can use later outside the school.

The student is, in short, ready to take on the most complex of all the Roman school's learning experiences—the Declamation (*declamatio*), or fictitious speech. Declamation is the cap, the culmination of the whole process.

Declamation

The Declamation is a rhetorical exercise designed to develop skill in deliberative (political) and forensic (judicial) oratory.[35] The two main types, in fact, are the *suasoria* in which the speaker urges an assembly or person either to act or not to act, and the *controversia,* in which the speaker prosecutes or defends a person in a given legal case. Here again the Romans adapt for the schools a Greek practice apparently in use well before the time of Aristotle. The earliest Latin rhetorical treatises take it for granted. The author of the *Rhetorica ad Herennium* describes several deliberative exercises he finds useful; for example, one finds Hannibal debating with himself whether to return to Carthage or stay in Italy (III.2.2). Cicero says in his *De oratore* that every day he made up fictitious cases and made practice orations on them.

Besides the school practice sessions there was a public form of declamation, first among friends for mutual edification and entertainment (as in the time of Cicero), then under the Empire as a regular type of public display or even competition—the Emperor Nero himself "won" such a competition on one occasion. Later, under the period of oratorical virtuosity

---

[35]S. F. Bonner, *Roman Declamation in the Late Republic and the Early Empire* (UP of Liverpool, 1949). For pre-Roman declamation see D. A. Russell, *Greek Declamation* (Oxford UP, 1983). Clark has an account in *Rhetoric* 213–261. There are shorter descriptions in Gwynn, Marrou, Parks, and Kennedy.

known as "The Second Sophistic," the public declaimers attracted crowds and wealth which today only a rock star could command.[36]

Declamation thus has a curious history. Obviously any would-be orator would want to practice, and there is the famous story of Demosthenes delivering a practice oration on shore against the sound of the breakers to improve his speaking voice. No doubt speakers since the very earliest days have practiced their skills in made-up controversies, and it would not be surprising to find Greek teachers like Gorgias or Isocrates putting their students through such drills.

The great virtue of Declamation for the Roman schoolmaster, though, was that the whole technical apparatus of rhetorical theory was available as resource for the classroom activity of the oration. All that was needed was a set of subjects on which to deliver speeches. It is significant that Quintilian, after devoting most of the first two books of the *Institutio* to the early education of the student, turns briefly to Declamation (II.10.1–15) and then begins the detailed exposition of rhetoric which occupies eight of the ten remaining books. Once Declamation is reached, in other words, rhetoric becomes the master's concern. The complete oration, even in the classroom, demands a full appreciation of the five parts of rhetoric: Invention, Arrangement, Style, Memory, and Delivery. Heretofore, rhetoric has been used piecemeal in the preliminary exercises, the precepts being introduced wherever useful. Now every skill of the student has to be harnessed toward one goal.

The student facing an audience of colleagues and master, and often facing a student opponent as well, had rhetorical problems similar to those in the outside world. Quintilian has high expectations for Declamation, rather sarcastically answering critics who see no value in it:

> For, if it is no preparation for the forum, it is merely like theatrical ostentation, or insane raving. To what purpose is it to instruct a judge who has no existence? To state a case that all know to be fictitious? To bring proofs on a point on which no man will pronounce sentence? This is nothing more than trifling; but how ridiculous is it to excite our feelings, and to work upon an audience with eagerness and sorrow, unless we are indeed preparing our-

---

[36]See, for instance, Eunapius's account of the declamation which Prohaeresius delivered in Athens in the third century as part of his candidacy for the highly-paid position of *rhetor* in that city; the crowds were so great that soldiers had to be used to control the situation. Prohaeresius started his extempore speech on one side of a difficult theme, then switched to the opposite side—then challenged the shorthand reporters to check his accuracy as he repeated both impromptu speeches word for word! The story is in Eunapius, *Lives of the Philosophers*, in Philostratuus and Eunapius, *Lives of the Sophists*, trans. Wilmer C. Wright (Cambridge: Harvard UP, 1922) 495–97.

selves, by imitations of battle, for serious contests and a regular field? (II.10.8)

These "imitations of battle" take a standard format in the Roman schools. The master assigns a problem ("theme") to one or more students; they prepare and deliver an oration before the class in reply to the problem posed in the theme; the master delivers an oral comment on the orations, perhaps adding to it a declamation of his own to show how it might be done better. Quintilian in fact proposes that the master ask the students to evaluate his own declamation as a means of sharpening their critical skills (II.2.13). An easy variation involves matching two students against each other, especially in the forensic declamations (*controversiae*).

Typically the declamation is divided into the four parts of proem, narration, proofs, and peroration (i.e., conclusion). A division after the narration could lay out the overall plan the speaker intends to follow; for example he might divide his remarks into Letter of the Law (*ius*) versus Spirit of the Law (*aequitas*). Classroom practice encouraged amplification as a means of testing the students' powers, particularly in the use of weighty statements (*sententiae*) or in the devising of novel approaches (*colores*). To go into greater detail here about the methodology of the Declamation would be to rehearse the entirety of rhetorical theory. This is of course not our main concern.

What part did writing play in the exercise of Declamation? The answer is not clear. Quintilian does not specifically mention writing, though he does say of Declamation that "it comprehends within itself all those exercises of which I have been treating, and presents us with a very close resemblance to reality" (II. 10.2). Certainly writing plays a major part in Imitation and in the *progymnasmata* which go before. Quintilian mentions the practice of providing written outlines for students to follow in their declamations (II.6.2). Given Quintilian's whole orientation toward the relation of speaking and writing, it would not be surprising to find various written forms behind the oral performance. For one thing his constant admonitions about storing examples for future use imply written record as well as strong memory. And what he says in book 10 about the writing orator (e.g. X.3.10) seems to imply that at least some of the oral was first the written. The Declamation itself was of course purely oral, but we are not yet sure how much writing lies behind it.

However, Quintilian's advice to adults about writing may well indicate his attitude toward writing for the young. Certainly Quintilian urges the adult speaker to use writing both as a general preparation and as a tool for shaping certain parts of a speech in advance of its delivery: "By writing we speak with greater accuracy and by speaking we write with greater ease"

(X.7.29). He makes this remark, one of his most famous aphorisms, in discussing the value of meditation as compared to the value of writing:

> As to writing, we must certainly never write more than when we have to speak much extempore; for by the use of the pen a weightiness will be preserved in our matter, and that light facility of language, which swims as it were on the surface, will be compressed into a body as husbandmen cut off the upper roots of the vine (which elevate it to the surface of the soil) in order that the lower roots may be strengthened by striking deeper. And I know not whether both exercises, when we perform them with care and assiduity, are not reciprocally beneficial, as it appears that by writing we speak with greater accuracy, and by speaking we write with greater ease. We must write, therefore, as often as we have opportunity; if opportunity is not allowed us, we must meditate; if we are precluded from both, we must nevertheless endeavor that the orator may not seem to be caught at fault, nor the client left destitute of aid. But it is the general practice among pleaders who have much occupation, to write only the most essential parts, and especially the commencements, of their speeches; to fix the other portions that they bring from home in their memory by meditation: and to meet any unforeseen attacks with extemporaneous replies. (X.7.28–30)

Quintilian adds (X.7.30–31) that Cicero and many other orators used written memoranda as aids in preparing their speeches.[37] His personal recommendation is to use short notes and small memorandum-books which may be held in the hand while speaking. In his discussion of Memory in book 11 there are constant references to written texts of orations for which the memory must be used (esp. XI.2.25–49). If the adult speaker is urged to use writing, it certainly seems likely that the young student preparing to be an orator would be given the same instructions.

There have been many critics of the Declamation, both ancient and modern. Tacitus complains in his *Dialogue on Oratory* (AD 85) about "the training merely of tongue and voice in imaginary debates which have no point of contact with real life.[38] Quintilian himself says that "The practice however has so degenerated through the fault of the teachers, that the license and ignorance of the declaimers have been among the chief causes that have corrupted eloquence" (II.10.3). To this, however, he immediately has a positive reply: "But of that which is good by nature we may surely make a good use."

---

[37]For a discussion of the role played by writing in Cicero's oratory, see Richard Leo Enos, *The Literate Mode of Cicero's Legal Rhetoric* (Southern Illinois UP, 1988) Orthography—the physical task of writing—is important to Quintilian, he urges writers to use wax tablets for drafts to speed up composition without breaking the pattern by having to dip a pen in ink (X.3.31–33). For a brief history of the wax tablet, see Richard and Mary Rouse, "Wax Tablets," *Language and Communication* 9 (1989): 175–191. See also Albertine Gaur, *A History of Writing* (London: The British Library, 1984); the illustration of pens and a stylus on p. 52 may help illuminate Quintilian's remarks noted above.

[38]Tacitus, *Dialogue,* 31 95.

Many of the criticisms concern the subjects chosen for classroom use.[39] Manifestly such subjects must be difficult enough to challenge the capacities of the students, yet generalizable enough to permit the students to work on them without vast research. As a consequence a large array of fantastic or even incredible topics came to be associated with Declamation, and especially with the forensic type. They feature pirates, seducers, wronged heirs, poison cups, cruel husbands, contradictory laws, cures for the blind, shipwrecks, and a host of other calamities and dilemmas calculated to present the student orator with difficulty. The deliberative type was generally more staid ("Cato deliberates whether to take a wife"), but the Romans always considered the forensic the more difficult and therefore exercised more ingenuity in posing its problems. One example from the collection of Seneca the Elder may suffice to show the level of complexity which was employed:

The Daughter of the Pirate Chief

"A young man captured by pirates writes his father for ransom. He is not ransomed. The daughter of the pirate chief urges him to swear that he will marry her if he escapes. He swears. Leaving her father, she follows the young man, who, upon his return to his home, takes her to wife. A well-to-do orphan appears on the scene. The father orders his son to divorce the daughter of the pirate chief and marry the orphan. When the son refuses to obey, the father disowns him." (*Controversiae* I.6.6)[40]

S. E Bonner, one of the most perceptive modern students of the Declamation, defends such classroom subjects on the very grounds that critics use to attack them. The subjects are deliberately more complex than real life, he says, as a test of the student's powers: "they were deliberately designed to provide an almost, but not quite, impossible hurdle."[41]

The publication of declamatory texts also shows a public interest in the topics and their treatment. While the published *Progymnasmata* of Hermogenes and Aphthonius were for the use of teachers, the sets of declamations published by the elder Seneca and by the Pseudo-Quintilian[42] were intended for a general reader. Such works were successful enough

---

[39]"The world of the declamation was a fantastic and melodramatic one," writes Martin Lowther Clarke, "and for that reason perhaps popular in a humdrum age." He makes the remark in *Rhetoric at Rome. A Historical Survey* (London: Cohen, 1953) 91.

[40]Quoted in Clark, *Rhetoric* 231.

[41]Bonner, *Roman Declamation*, 83.

[42]See Seneca the Elder, *Controversiae. Suasoriae*, ed. and trans. Michael Winterbottom, 2 vols (Cambridge: Harvard UP, 1974). Seneca says he wrote the declamations for his sons, but the work had a more general circulation anyway. Michael Winterbottom has edited the *Minor Declamations Attributed to Quintilian* (New York: Walter de Gruyter, 1984), with a commentary which includes treatment of the subject of possible authorship of the collection.

that someone wrote two collections to which Quintilian's name became attached. The reason, of course, is that there were popular public declamations put on by adult orators to demonstrate their rhetorical virtuosity; the
throngs attending such displays of extempore eloquence might well treasure a written form of what they had heard, just as sports fans today read
eagerly the newspaper account of a game seen the day before.

In any case history shows that the Declamation served the Roman
schools for many centuries—again, a case in which the very longevity of
the practice demonstrates its perceived value. The Declamation is the remote ancestor of the *disputatio* of the medieval university, and of scholastic
debate beginning in colonial American colleges and lasting into the present time. Like the *Progymnasmata* and Imitation, Declamation may well
have had far-reaching influences in Western culture not yet completely
recognized by modern scholars.

Sequencing

The systematic ordering of classroom activities in Roman schools was to
accomplish two goals: Movement, from the simple to the more complex;
and Reinforcement, by reiterating each element of preceding exercises as
each new one appears. To these can be added another principle: no exercise should be done for just a single purpose.

It is these principles which lead to the constant interrelating of writing,
speaking, reading, and listening. Writing is a solitary activity, Quintilian
notes, but recitation of the written is a public one. What is written by one
student is heard by another when recited. What is read—and we must remember that even private reading in ancient times is generally vocalized,
and therefore "heard" by the reader—becomes the model for the written.
Writing makes speaking precise, Quintilian says, just as speaking makes
writing easy. Listening prepares the student for analysis of the oral arguments he will later hear his opponent raise against him in forum or courtroom. Everything fits: there are no random activities in the Roman schoolroom.

CONCLUSION

Habituation is the key to success in the Roman school. For example a
dozen years of re-telling stories, from simple Aesop to complex Demosthenes, make narrative skill second nature by adulthood. Likewise the analytic phases of Imitation make critical reading the norm. The step-by-
step progression through the *Progymnasmata* equips the student with powerful tools of amplification, just as the Declamation prepares him to see in-

stinctively the two sides to any controversy. Quintilian declares Habit (*hexis*) to be the ultimate goal of the program. What he means is something a bit different from the modern idea of habit as something fixed and somewhat out of our control. His "habit" means a deep-rooted capacity (his word is *facilitas*) to employ language wherever needed, on whatever subject, in whatever circumstances. His meaning is close to Aristotle's, who defines rhetoric as a "faculty" of observing the available means of persuasion in a given case; this 'faculty' for Aristotle is seen as virtually a part of the personality (*ethos*) of the rhetor. In a sense, for both men, the person *becomes* rhetorical.

It is for this reason that Quintilian and other Roman masters are willing to set up this grueling sequence of sometimes petty and dull exercises. The goal is no less than the perfect orator, whose molding is worth every effort. Quintilian would probably say that the way to train an architect is to start him as a boy on building bricks; the child need not know what a wall is, when he begins to make bricks, but later he can be taught how to make small brick piles, then walls, then houses, then palaces, and then even cities. This is just the way Roman schools approach language use. The master envisages word-cities even from the time the child begins to trace letters with his stylus, and then leads him incrementally through a nicely coordinated sequence of learning experiences which make efficient language use virtually a part of his personality. The letter of the alphabet becomes years later a stirring oration in the Roman Senate.

Many of the individual exercises can be used profitably today, of course, since each is largely self-explanatory. Nevertheless a modern reader should understand that the full power of their use resides in their interrelation to each other, and in their place in a proven sequence.[43]

It was an efficient system, producing a habit of language use designed to last a lifetime. As the next three chapters demonstrate, the core concepts of the Roman educational program lasted in a recognizable fashion through late antiquity, the Middle Ages, and the Renaissance. And later chapters show the massive social and cultural changes in Western society which eroded the coherence of the system even while fragments of its teaching methods continue in use, often unrecognized, to this day.

It is a story of system and continuity. It seems inconceivable that any human activity of such longevity could be valueless.

This is not to say that the enterprise was perfect or without fault. Its very longevity has provided ample opportunity for criticism, from Cicero and Tacitus to modern detractors like Martin Lowther Clarke who notes that

---

[43]For a comment on modern use of the system see Murphy, "The Modern Value of Roman Methods of Teaching Writing, with Answers to Twelve Current Fallacies," *Writing On the Edge* 1 (1989): 28–37.

"The Romans had administrative capacity in their bones, and it could survive even the follies of the lesser rhetoricians."[44] He complains that the
schools fostered a cult of ornateness; that the system of Imitation and Invention by Topics prevented students from thinking for themselves; that
truth was made less important than imagination; that directness in speech
was discouraged; and that the same educational labor could well have
been spent on something better. He concludes with the observation that
Pliny is narrower than Cicero, and Fronto is narrower than Pliny. Others
complain that the education was purely literary (word-centered) thus
training declaimers rather than orators. Still others maintain that the student was given no real sense of history, no training in philosophy except
for a scattering of ethical commonplaces, no unifying picture of society or
government; another criticism is that as an elitist mechanism the schools
merely perpetuated the order of a ruling class.[45]

At the same time its pedagogical values surely seem worth studying. It
might be well to conclude this chapter with an observation from a modern
historian of language, Louis G. Kelly:

> Nobody really knows what is new or old in present-day language teaching
> procedures. There has been a vague feeling that modern experts have spent
> their time in discovering what other men have forgotten; but as most of the
> key documents are in Latin, moderns find it difficult to go to original
> sources. In any case, much that is being claimed as revolutionary in this cen-
> tury is merely a rethinking and renaming of earlier ideas and procedures.[46]

APPENDIX

OVERVIEW OF ROMAN TEACHING METHODS
DESCRIBED IN THE *INSTITUTIO ORATORIA*

They fall into five categories: (1) Precept, (2) Imitation, (3) Composition
exercises (*Progymnasmata*), (4) Declamation, and (5) Sequencing.

   1. Precept: "a set of rules that provide a definite method and system of
      speaking." Grammar as precept deals with "the art of speaking cor-

---

[44]Clark, *Rhetoric* 162.

[45]For a succinct array of charges against the system, see Robert A. Kaster, *Guardians of Language: The Grammarian and Society in Late Antiquity* (U of California P, 1988) 12–13. Kaster also provides (231–440) demographic records of hundreds of teachers for the period AD 250–440.

[46]Louis G. Kelly, *25 Centuries of Language Teaching. An Inquiry into the Science, Art, and Development of Language Teaching Methodology 500 B.C.–1969* (Rowley: Newbury, 1969) ix.

rectly, and the interpretation of the poets." Rhetoric as precept occupies eight of the twelve books of the *Institutio oratoria*:

   a. Invention
   b. Arrangement
   c. Style
   d. Memory
   e. Delivery

2. Imitation: the use of models to learn how others have used language. Specific exercises include:

   a. Reading aloud (*lectio*)
   b. Master's detailed analysis of a text (*praelectio*)
   c. Memorization of models
   d. Paraphrase of models
   e. Transliteration (prose/verse and/or Latin/Greek)
   f. Recitation of paraphrase or transliteration
   g. Correction of paraphrase or transliteration

3. Composition exercises (*Progymnasmata* or *praeexercitamenta*): a graded series of exercises in writing and speaking themes. Each succeeding exercise is more difficult and incorporates what has been learned in preceding ones. The following twelve were common by Cicero's time:

   a. Retelling a fable
   b. Retelling an episode from a poet or a historian
   c. *Chreia*, or amplification of a moral theme
   d. Amplification of an aphorism (*sententia*) or proverb
   e. Refutation or confirmation of an allegation
   f. Commonplace, or confirmation of a thing admitted
   g. Encomium, or eulogy (or dispraise) of a person or thing
   h. Comparison of things or persons
   i. Impersonation (*prosopopeia*), or speaking or writing in the character of a given person
   j. Description (*ecphrasis*), or vivid presentation of details
   k. Thesis, or argument for/against an answer to a general question (*quaestio infinita*) not involving individuals
   l. Laws, or arguments for or against a law

4. Declamation (*declamatio*), or fictitious speeches, in two types:

   a. *Suasoria*, or deliberative (political) speech arguing that an action be taken or not taken

      b. *Controversia,* or forensic (legal) speech prosecuting or defending a fictitious or historical person in a law case

  5. Sequencing, or the systematic ordering of classroom activities to accomplish two goals:

      a. Movement, from the simple to the more complex

      b. Reinforcement, by reiterating each element of preceding exercises as each new one appears

Perhaps the most important aspect of these methods is their coordination into a single instructional program. Each is important for itself, but takes greater importance from its place within the whole.

Chapter 3

Writing Instruction from Late Antiquity to the Twelfth Century

Carol Dana Lanham

Key Concepts. *Latin as dominant language* • *Continuity of content and method* • *Role of Christianity* • *Types of sources* • *School reading texts* • *Grammar* • *Rhetoric* • Progymnasmata • *Glossaries,* differentiae, scholia • Sententiae • *Exempla* • *Colloquies* • *Formula and letter collections* • *Teaching anthologies and manuals* • *Narrative sources* • *Writing instruction* • Lectio divina • *Influence of poetry on prose* • *Style and diction* • *Rhythm* • Progymnasmata *and prose composition* • *Imitation, paraphrase, variation* • Compilatio • Dispositio • Ars dictaminis, *the art of letter-writing* • Progymnasmata *and epistolography*

THE SOCIAL, CULTURAL, AND POLITICAL BACKGROUND

Quintilian described an educational program created for a small, homogeneous population of Latin-speaking males free to concentrate on a single purpose: becoming eloquent public speakers and political leaders who could guide the civic life of Rome and the cities of her empire. It was a brief moment of comparative tranquility before the illusory unity expressed by "Romania" yielded to the ethnic and linguistic patchwork of nations now known as Europe.

Parts of this chapter appeared in different form in "Freshman Composition in the Early Middle Ages: Epistolography and Rhetoric before the *Ars dictaminis,*" *Viator* 23 (1992) 115–34. Translations are my own unless noted otherwise.

From the late second century onward, all across the lands that correspond, more or less, to modern Europe and North Africa, Germanic tribes—"barbarians"—migrating westward in search of land and food provoked wars, devastation, and movements of displaced people. The first wave of great invasions reached its peak after the middle of the fifth century. (Long before then, the Roman empire had split into two main parts; the eastern, Greek-speaking part would have a longer but hardly more tranquil existence as the Byzantine empire.) Meanwhile, the new Christian religion had spread steadily, provoking other kinds of turmoil and sporadic persecutions even after the emperor Constantine declared it the official religion of the empire in 323.

Remarkably, the essence of Quintilian's educational program survived the fragmentation and decay of civic life and the painful transition to a multiplicity of Christian societies in which the imperial system of publicly supported schools and teachers deteriorated and in some places apparently disappeared altogether. For a time, classical learning hung by a frayed thread. At its lowest point, perhaps in the first half of the seventh century, education seems to have been available only within monasteries or from scattered private tutors.

Whatever education did take place was conveyed in Latin. The teaching of Latin had spread early to Rome's provinces,[1] where it would evolve into the Romance languages, and Latin remained the dominant language for centuries, overwhelming local vernaculars as the universal medium of instruction, worship, and public discourse. The first references to the need to communicate in a language other than Latin appear early in the ninth century, by which time Latin was a second language for everyone. How did teachers educate the increasing numbers of non-Romance speakers for whom Latin was totally foreign?

Instruction to a minimal level of what is now called functional literacy cannot begin to account for the sustained explosion of literary creativity that accompanied the spread of Christianity across Europe from the fourth century on. The Anglo-Saxon, Irish, and Germanic peoples had to devote great effort—more than the French, Spanish, and Italians—to learning the forms and syntax and vocabulary of Latin, but they all were apt pupils and were soon displaying their accomplishments abundantly in writing. Although it may be going too far to claim that it was principally the Bible that gave sixth- and seventh-century Merovingian scribes the "possibility" of expressing themselves in Latin,[2] there is no denying that the heritage of classical Latin literature was vastly enlarged and enriched by Christian Latin.

---

[1]Suetonius, *De grammatibus et rhetoribus* §3.

[2]Alf Uddholm, *Formulae Marculfi: Etudes sur la langue et le style* (thesis, Uppsala, 1953) 209.

As a religion of the book, Christianity brought new words, concepts, and imagery to the Latin language, new purposes to education, and renewed vigor to rhetoric. Christian grammar teachers recognized the suitability of the classical education's analytic methods for penetrating the Bible's linguistic mysteries and embraced them readily—at the cost of including their pagan content—and added Christian poetry to their pupils' reading. Pagan rhetoric was a harder sell. Christians long remained uneasy about using rhetoric's arsenal of persuasive techniques, even though they acknowledged the need for able speakers and writers to explain and interpret Scripture and to debate controversial theological issues. St. Augustine, by showing in his *De doctrina christiana* (completed in 427) how to redeploy rhetoric for the purposes of Christian oratory and writing, made possible a Christian theory of rhetoric[3]—and, by his own voluminous writings, encouraged an ever-growing flood of treatises arguing points of Christian teaching.

Thanks in part to a sea change in the quality of Latin writing starting after the middle of the eighth century, the ninth century is often called the Carolingian renaissance. Charlemagne sought not only to vanquish his political foes and enlarge the territories under his rule but also, by ordering the founding of schools, to improve the education of clerics and the Latinity of documents produced in his realm. The copying of manuscripts in monastic scriptoria exploded, and interest in secular classical Latin literature reawakened. Although internecine warfare resumed not long after Charlemagne's death, secure foundations had been laid for a lasting revival of schools and education.

By the twelfth century, the landscape of Europe had changed dramatically. Increasing commerce and trade stimulated the growth of towns and cities in the tenth and eleventh centuries. Urban cathedral schools appeared, and students traveled far to study under famous teachers. From Rome, a powerful papal bureaucracy directed the parish and episcopal structures that had grown into a Europe-wide network. Secular and ecclesiastical powers alike needed educated chancery clerks and lawyers; the study of Roman law and canon law revived, and the first universities were founded.

This chapter in the history of writing instruction must attempt to survey more than a thousand years of European history—centuries marred by loss and destruction and by marvels of preservation and achievement, centuries that can be called "dark ages" only in the sense that too much about

---

[3]See Averil Cameron, *Christianity and the Rhetoric of Empire: The Development of Christian Discourse* (Berkeley: U of California P, 1991); Michael Roberts, *Biblical Epic and Rhetorical Paraphrase in Late Antiquity*, ARCA Classical and Medieval Texts, Papers and Monographs 16 (Liverpool: Francis Cairns, 1985) 62–63.

them is still obscure. To borrow a topos of medieval Latin prefaces, it is a vast and turbulent sea, and my vessel is but a frail coracle. It would be misleading if not impossible to attempt a linear chronological account of writing instruction over this vast space and time. The fundamental continuity of content and method from Roman times onward is clear, however, and strikingly confirmed by the far better documented curriculum of the sixteenth-century English grammar school—still taught in Latin—that Don Paul Abbott describes in chapter 5. Looking backward, Quintilian's *Institutio oratoria*, with its wealth of precious and vivid detail, supplies an essential foundation for my survey of this later period, and to minimize repetition, I shall assume that the reader has digested James J. Murphy's account in chapter 2. Because they are so various, and likely to be unfamiliar, I begin by cataloging the several kinds of extant original source materials that can shed light on how writing was taught in the early Middle Ages. Although I occasionally refer to Greek sources, it is only instruction given in Latin that I discuss.

A SURVEY OF THE SOURCES

Two generalizations can be made about the history of education in the thousand years or so after Quintilian's death: relevant source materials are hard to find, and most of the documentation is indirect and therefore subject to differing interpretations. For every kind of primary source, scholars are at the mercy of manuscript transmission, and considering how much has been lost, we must be doubly grateful for what survives.[4] Since most teaching was oral, the numerous grammar and rhetoric textbooks that do survive (chiefly from the fourth century and later) tell us almost nothing about how, or indeed if, they were actually used in the classroom. Of the preserved Greek and Latin papyri and wax tablets that represent students' classroom notebooks, nearly all contain only grammar and penmanship exercises.

In what follows, I attempt to identify and briefly describe the various late antique and early medieval source-types that pertain to writing instruction. I have arranged them on a rough sliding scale from direct evidence to indirect; some kinds of sources, such as glossed manuscripts, can reside in either category. In this section, I concentrate on describing con-

---

[4]In *Scribes and Scholars: A Guide to the Transmission of Greek and Latin Literature*, 3rd ed. (Oxford: Clarendon, 1991), L. D. Reynolds and N. G. Wilson tell with marvelous clarity the epic story of how "classical literature has been transmitted from the ancient world to the present day" (1). As they say, "The history of texts cannot be separated from the history of education and scholarship" (v).

tent; in the following sections, I draw further from these materials to suggest how they were used to teach writing.

Two caveats should always be kept in mind when dealing with medieval Latin texts. First, a particular danger lurks in judging postclassical and medieval Latin writing not on its own terms but by comparing it to the "golden age" styles represented by Cicero and Vergil.[5] Second, medieval Latin authors often borrowed older material and turned it to their own purposes without giving any indication of the original source, leaving it to modern editors to play detective. Writing three centuries after Quintilian, St. Jerome appropriated his advice for teaching a child to read and write (ep. 107.4, 9, 12); but he concentrated on her reading program in the Bible and Christian authors, and—perhaps because the child in question was a girl?—said nothing about how she might use the ability to write. Whole pages of Julius Victor's *Ars rhetorica* (fourth century?) would disintegrate if his borrowings from Cicero's *De inventione* and Quintilian were removed. Martianus Capella took his sections on rhetorical figures from Aquila, who had gotten them from a Greek text. Cassiodorus stitched together his rhetoric section (*Institutiones* 2.2) from *De inventione* and Fortunatianus, and Isidore in turn relied chiefly on Cassiodorus for his compendium of rhetoric in *Etymologies*, book 2.[6]

School Textbooks

After learning how to read and write the alphabet, a Roman child went to the school of the *grammaticus*, or teacher of literature, whose job (according to Quintilian 1.4.2) was to teach "the art of speaking correctly and the interpretation of the poets." Probably only the teacher had access to any textbooks, and lectured or dictated to pupils from them. This pattern continued at least until the rise of universities in the thirteenth century.

1. *Grammar*.   Fairly complete Latin grammar texts are extant from the third century on. Most popular by far, throughout the Middle Ages, was the little introductory grammar in question-and-answer format by St. Jerome's teacher Donatus; in the eighth and ninth centuries it attracted numerous commentaries, chiefly by Irish and Anglo-Saxon scholars for whom Latin was a totally foreign language. The educational reforms initiated by Charlemagne to improve the level of literacy among the clergy

---

[5]Michael Roberts argues forcefully for the more open-minded approach to late Latin literature in the introduction to his *The Jeweled Style: Poetry and Poetics in Late Antiquity* (Ithaca: Cornell UP, 1989).

[6]For my caveat about such borrowings, see footnote 67. The "borrowing" texts mentioned are edited by Karl Halm, *Rhetores latini minores* (Leipzig: Teubner, 1863). On Isidore's sources in book 2, see Peter K. Marshall, ed. (Paris 1983) 5–7.

also stimulated keen interest in grammar: about thirty manuscripts written in the late eighth century and the first third of the ninth are collections
of grammatical texts, most dating from the fourth and fifth centuries, and
together they represent about three-fourths of the Roman and early medieval grammars extant.[7] Their core is uniformly the eight parts of speech
(the brief *Ars minor* of Donatus contains nothing else); their method, to explicate at dizzying length pronunciation, syllable and word formation, de-
clension, and conjugation. Some grammars also address the special requirements of poetry by cataloging the complex rules of word accent and
metrics. Priscian's monumental advanced grammar, written early in the
sixth century, did not come into widespread use until the ninth; the last
two of its eighteen books, treating syntax, then sometimes circulated separately. Grammatical theory developed much more slowly than rhetorical
theory, and we cannot discern any real theory of Latin grammar before
the twelfth century.[8]

In addition to teaching correct speech, the grammar teacher was responsible for instilling correctness in writing. He began with the faults
(*vitia*) to be avoided, divided into barbarisms (faults within a single word,
e.g., a misspelling or mispronunciation) and solecisms (faults involving
two or more words, e.g., lack of agreement between subject and verb). His
second main task, "interpretation of the poets," naturally included introducing students to the ornaments of style, the figures or *colores*. Book 3 of
Donatus's larger *Ars maior*, which often circulated separately under the title *Barbarismus*, briefly describes the *vitia* and defines a modest selection of
figures (*metaplasmi*, *schemata*, *tropi*) found in literature.

2. *Verse Composition.* From antiquity until the tenth century, reading
at the grammar school level consisted almost entirely of poetry. A number
of self-contained texts on metrics, often associated in manuscripts with
grammars, describe the many meters of classical poetry (as with grammatical terms, Latin borrowed both meters and terminology from Greek). Vast
quantities of Latin poetry, both good and bad, survive; some of it is almost
certainly student exercises on set themes. Because there is nowhere any
explicit discussion of how pupils learned to compose poetry, some scholars maintain—with, I think, excessive caution—that no school instruction
was given in this complicated subject, at least not in antiquity.

---

[7]Bernhard Bischoff, "Libraries and Schools in the Carolingian Revival of Learning," in
Manuscripts and Libraries in the Age of Charlemagne, trans. Michael Gorman (Cambridge: Cambridge UP, 1994) 99. The major grammar texts are edited by Heinrich Keil, *Grammatici latini*
(hereafter *GL*), 7 vols. + suppl. (Leipzig: Teubner, 1857–80). For an overview of Latin grammar from its beginnings through Priscian, see "Grammar, grammarians, Latin" in the *Oxford
Classical Dictionary,* 3rd ed. (1996).

[8]James J. Murphy, *Rhetoric in the Middle Ages: A History of Rhetorical Theory from Saint Augustine to the Renaissance* (Berkeley: U of California P, 1974) 140–46, 152–56.

3. Progymnasmata. Murphy has outlined, in chapter 2, the graded composition exercises subsumed under this name and has noted the significant amount of extant material in Greek. In Latin, the only complete set known is Priscian's *Praeexercitamina*, a translation and adaptation of a work traditionally attributed to Hermogenes, a second-century Greek rhetorician. Since at least twenty-four manuscripts from the late eighth through the twelfth century survive, it seems to have been widely used for a long time.[9] From one Emporius (sixth century?), we have *progymnasmata* sections on *Ethopoeia*, commonplaces, and encomium. Book 1 of Isidore's *Etymologies*, on grammar, ends with sections on fable and history (1.40–44), and book 2, on rhetoric, includes sections on *sententia*, confirmation and refutation, *prosopopoeia*, and *Ethopoeia* (2.11–14).

Probably the most famous witness to the practice of these exercises is St. Augustine, who describes being made to impersonate an angry goddess Juno in an exercise of ethopoeia as he paraphrased the poet's words in prose (*Confessions* 1.17). Augustine also mentions the exercise of encomium, *laus*, and lists several possible subjects for praise, ranging from heaven to a rose.[10] The extremes to which the latter exercise could be carried—only hinted at by Augustine—appear in two fragmentary letters of Fronto (d. c. 166) as encomia of smoke and negligence.[11]

4. Rhetoric. A number of postclassical rhetoric texts, most stemming from the fourth and fifth centuries, were edited by Karl Halm in *Rhetores latini minores*. As his source notes make clear, their authors made much use of Cicero's speeches and his *De inventione* (indeed, the longest work in the book is Victorinus's commentary on the latter), and of Quintilian, but not of the *Ad Herennium*. That work, which was attributed to Cicero throughout the Middle Ages, is first cited by St. Jerome; then there is almost total silence until the tenth century, when the number of manuscripts multiplies rapidly. Although Cicero's reputation as master of eloquence never faltered, it was not until the twelfth century that new commentaries on his rhetorical works began to appear.[12] In the interval, rhetorical figures at-

---

[9]Halm 551–60; Maria Passalacqua, ed., *Prisciani Caesariensis opuscula*, vol. 1: *De figuris numerorum, De metris Terentii, Praeexercitamina* (Rome: Edizione di Storia e Letteratura, 1987) n. 43; trans. Joseph Miller in *Readings in Medieval Rhetoric*, ed. Joseph H. Miller, Michael H. Prosser, and Thomas W. Benson (Bloomington: Indiana UP, 1973) 52–68.

[10]*In Ps.* 144.7, quoted by Roberts 64.

[11]*The Correspondence of Marcus Cornelius Fronto*, ed. and trans. C. R. Haines, Loeb Classical Library, 1.39–49 (Cambridge: Harvard UP, 1928).

[12]For the *Ad Herennium*, see Harry Caplan's introduction to his Loeb Classical Library edition, xxxiv–xxxv (Cambridge: Harvard UP, 1954); and *Texts and Transmission: A Survey of the Latin Classics*, ed. L. D. Reynolds (Oxford: Clarendon, 1983) 98–100. The Ciceronian commentary tradition is exhaustively treated by John O. Ward in *Ciceronian Rhetoric in Treatise, Scholion and Commentary*, Typologie des sources du Moyen Age occidental 58 (Turnhout: Brepols, 1995); see especially chapter 2, "Evolution of the Genre."

tracted much interest; Halm includes several brief treatises devoted to rhetorical figures, and many more are lost (Quintilian mentions some).

Occasional fragments from unidentified rhetorical works offer tantalizing glimpses of other losses: Julius Victor's *Ars rhetorica*, after drawing heavily throughout on Cicero and Quintilian, ends with two remarkable sections from unknown sources, offering rules for conversation (*sermocinatio*) and letters (*epistolae*); an important late eighth-century manuscript of school texts includes a substantial paragraph of untraceable epistolary theory.[13]

Auxiliary Instructional Materials and Reference Works

To help students understand what they read, the teacher discussed the meanings of words and their etymologies, explained syntactical difficulties and mythological and historical allusions, and pointed out rhetorical figures. Surviving collections of such words and of notes that are arranged by letter of the alphabet or by lemmas taken in sequence from a literary work must have originated as teaching or reference books. Longer independent texts, such as collections of historical anecdotes, could be read for their intrinsic interest or used as sourcebooks for composition topics. Did students have direct access to such reference books? It is not known for certain, but probably they did not.

1. Glossaries.   A *gloss*, in its simplest form, represents an effort to explain an unusual or unknown word by a common, familiar one. Numerous surviving glossaries, both Greek–Latin, Latin–Latin, and Latin–vernacular, are traceable from about the sixth century, but some contain material that may be centuries older.[14] Although interest in etymology and rare words goes back at least to Varro, a prodigious Roman scholar of the first century BC, what we think of as dictionaries did not begin to develop until after the middle of the eleventh century, as an outgrowth of glossaries. Michael Lapidge describes a glossary's stages of growth:

> [F]irst, various (perhaps random) interpretations or *interpretamenta* are copied into a manuscript above or alongside particular difficult words (or *lemmata*); secondly, the various *lemmata* and their accompanying *interpretamenta* are collected and copied out separately in the order in which they occur in the text (we refer to these as *glossae collectae*); thirdly, the various *glossae collectae* are sorted roughly into alphabetical order, with all items be-

---

[13]Halm 446–48, 589. I describe the contents of the eighth-century manuscript on p. 105 ("The Progymnasmata and Prose Composition").

[14]For a brief overview and bibliography, see the entry "Glossa, Glossary" in the *Oxford Classical Dictionary*, 3rd ed. (1996).

ginning with the same letter being grouped together (*a*-order); finally, the entries under each letter are resorted into more precise alphabetical order, taking account of the first two letters of each lemma (*ab*-order). A surviving glossary may (and usually does) include materials or batches of words treated in any of these ways, though it will be obvious that when one is trying to identify the text on which the glosses were based, *glossae collectae* offer the clearest evidence.[15]

The first stage represents the teacher's writing into his copy of the work being studied a brief note—which might concern meaning, etymology, pronunciation, or syntax—about a word or words in the text under study, as an *aide-mémoire* for his oral explication of the text; additional bits of information tended naturally to accumulate. Modern historians of education are extracting valuable information about curriculum and teaching methods from glosses attached to texts in manuscripts and from the collections of glosses abstracted from manuscripts and organized into glossaries.[16]

2. Differentiae.   Common from the fourth century on, these collections (which may also be titled, misleadingly, *De orthographia*) take their name from semantic distinctions between partial synonyms, but also may include spelling and pronunciation notes and what might be called usage notes—all, of course, aimed at teaching correct speech and writing.[17] One such compilation, Bede's *De orthographia*, has been felicitously compared to Fowler's *Modern English Usage*;[18] here are two examples of *differentiae* from it:

> *Accidunt* mala, *contingunt* bona, *eveniunt* utraque. (Bad things *befall* one, good things *come to pass*, both *happen*.)

---

[15]Michael Lapidge, "The School of Theodore and Hadrian," *Anglo-Saxon England* 15 (1986) 53–54.

[16]See, for example, Suzanne Reynolds, *Medieval Reading: Grammar, Rhetoric and the Classical Text* (Cambridge: Cambridge UP, 1996); and Gernot R. Wieland's work on glossed manuscripts in Anglo-Saxon England: "The Glossed Manuscript: Classbook or Library Book?" *Anglo-Saxon England* 14 (1985) 153–73, and *The Latin Glosses on Arator and Prudentius in Cambridge University Library MS GG.5.35* (Toronto: Pontifical Inst. of Mediaeval Studies, 1983).

[17]Carmen Codoñer surveys the genre in "Les plus anciens compilations de Differentiae. Formation et évolution d'un genre littéraire grammatical," *Revue de philologie* 59 (1985) 201–19.

[18]By Helmut Gneuss, "The Study of Language in Anglo-Saxon England," *Bulletin of John Rylands University Library of Manchester* 72 (1990) 9–10. For the second example quoted, compare Theodore M. Bernstein, *The Careful Writer: A Modern Guide to English Usage* (New York: Atheneum, 1977) 231: "INCREDIBLE, INCREDULOUS: *Incredible* means unbelievable; *incredulous* means unbelieving, skeptical. From these definitions the error in the following not uncommon misuse should be obvious: 'The incredulously rude Khrushchev. . . .' " I quote Bede's text from Keil, *GL* 7.264.20, 275.25.

Incredibile quod credi non potest, *incredulus* qui credere non vult. (*Incredible* of what cannot be believed, *incredulous* of one who does not want to believe.)

The same impulse to differentiate produced *Exempla elocutionum*, an alphabetized collection made by the grammarian Arusianus Messius around 400. He used the works of four standard school authors (two poets, Vergil and Terence, and two prose writers, Cicero and Sallust) to illustrate words that have more than one grammatical construction.[19] Cassiodorus cites it (*Institutiones* 1.15.7) as an authority under the title *Quadriga* (literally, 'a team of four horses') and Priscian uses some of the same examples in book 18.

3. Scholia and Commentaries. The grammar teacher's task included, in addition to *enarratio poetarum* (explication of the literary work in all its aspects), *iudicium* or critical evaluation. Scholia are isolated bits of explanatory or critical comment found in medieval manuscripts; free-standing commentaries that move sequentially through a work provide the best picture of how this kind of classroom instruction probably proceeded. One of the largest and most important such commentaries is that of Servius (c. 400) on the works of Vergil. It was clearly designed for use in teaching and was quarried in later centuries for the same purpose. Servius marches "word by word and line by line through the text, remarking on punctuation, meter, uncertain readings, myth or other *Realien*, and especially on the language."[20] A few examples show Servius at work:

> (on *Aeneid* 3.16) *litore curvo* 'the curved shore': "curved" is the constant epithet of shores; for when he says in the sixth book, "then he is borne straight along the shore [*recto . . . litore*] to the harbor of Caieta," it means that he sailed in such a way as not to leave the shore.

> (on *Aeneid* 4.582, of the speed with which Aeneas's men obeyed his command to board their ships and leave Carthage): *litora deseruere* 'they deserted the shore', a wonderful description of haste.

> (on *Aeneid* 4.638, when Dido declares her plan to sacrifice to Jove) *Iovi Stygio* 'to Stygian Jove': that is, to Pluto. You should know that the Stoics say that god is one being whose names vary according to his acts and duties. This is also why the divinities are said to be of dual sex, so that when they are in action they are males, but females when they have the nature of being passive. . . .[21]

---

[19]Text in Keil, *GL* 7.449–514. According to *Texts and Transmission* 54, he quotes most of Cicero's extant speeches as well as four lost ones.

[20]Robert A. Kaster, *Guardians of Language: The Grammarian and Society in Late Antiquity* (Berkeley: U of California P, 1988) 170; chapter 5 is devoted to Servius.

[21]Quoted from vol. 3 of the "Harvard Servius," *Servianorum in Vergilii carmina commentariorum*, ed. A. F. Stocker, A. H. Travis, et al. (Oxford: Oxford UP, 1965).

Explication of the text was early transferred to the Bible and other Christian works, but since the text of the Bible was considered divinely inspired its quality was not subject to criticism. An outstanding example of biblical commentary is that of Cassiodorus on the Psalms (mid-sixth century). He made a significant addition to the usual format: a set of thirteen marginal reference marks designating specific topics discussed, such as scriptural idioms, interpretations of names, and rhetorical figures, as well as arithmetic and music.[22]

4. *Sententiae*.   Latin literature abounds with proverbial sayings and moral maxims. The briefest, used to teach children to read, are the two- to four-word injunctions found in the first section of the ancient *Dicta Catonis*, such as *Mundus esto* 'Be tidy' and *Alienum noli concupiscere* 'Do not covet what is another's'. An alphabetically arranged anthology that derives from Publilius Syrus, a mid-first-century BC mime, contains longer sayings, such as *Homo semper aliud, Fortuna aliud cogitat* 'Man's plans and Fortune's are ever at variance'. The *Liber scintillarum*, a large collection drawn from the Bible and Christian writers, was assembled around 700 by a monk named Defensor. Its contents are arranged under 81 headings (e.g., humility, justice, lying, pity, drunkenness, etc.), and the extracts range from a few words to several sentences in length. Its topical arrangement would have made the *Liber scintillarum* very useful (especially for preachers?) and surely contributed to its great popularity: at least 361 manuscripts are known. All of these adages could serve as commonplaces for writing exercises or to ornament longer compositions.[23]

5. *Exempla*.   Latin literature is filled with illustrative anecdotes drawn from mythology or history, used to point a moral. The animal fables that supplied children's earliest extended reading and writing exercises are self-contained exempla about behavior, good and bad. The handbook *Memorable Deeds and Sayings*, composed on an equally condensed scale in the first century AD by Valerius Maximus, supplied to the Middle Ages nine books' worth of canned Roman history and sententious observations, conveniently arranged under such perennially useful headings as chastity and bravery. As with the *Liber scintillarum*, its topical arrangement marks it as a potential sourcebook for speakers and writers.[24]

---

[22]James J. O'Donnell, *Cassiodorus* (Berkeley: U of California P, 1979) 160; James W. Halporn, "Methods of Reference in Cassiodorus," *Journal of Library History* 16 (1981) 71–91.

[23]Both the *Dicta Catonis* and Publilius Syrus are in *Minor Latin Poets*, trans. J. W. Duff and A. M. Duff, Loeb Classical Library, 585ff. and 15ff. respectively (Cambridge: Harvard UP, 1935). *Liber scintillarum*, ed. H. M. Rochais, 117, Corpus Christianorum Ser. latina (Turnhout: Brepols, 1957).

[24]For a study of the work's original purposes and intended audience, see W. Martin Bloomer, *Valerius Maximus and the Rhetoric of the New Nobility* (Chapel Hill: U of North Carolina P, 1992).

6. Colloquies.   Colloquies, or dialogues, were used to teach the vocabulary and grammar of a foreign language. They normally concentrate on daily life, including the routines of dressing, meals, and school, and perhaps sections on various trades or other subjects. The earliest one known was written for Greeks learning Latin, and the latest Latin colloquies were composed by Erasmus for English schoolboys; all are fascinating and often amusing for modern readers.[25]

What might be called a monologic variation on the colloquy form is Isidore of Seville's *Synonyma*. This curious (and popular) work in two books later lent its name to the *stilus Isidorianus*, one of four writing styles first described and named in the twelfth century.[26] It is in essence an extended set of variations arranged into a narrative sequence. Scholars still debate whether Isidore (d. 636) wrote it for educational purposes or for private meditation and spiritual edification. At least one teacher, the eleventh-century Englishman Ælfric Bata, used it for educational purposes in a colloquy.[27] His colloquy (which has an interlinear Anglo-Saxon version) proceeds in the usual way, until the stylistic register changes abruptly at the climax of a scene between the master and a wayward pupil who is being flogged by his fellow pupils at the master's command. Begging for mercy (*Iam moriturus sum* 'I'm about to die'), the student breaks out into a page-long variation on *Synonyma* 1.5–21 in which he laments his wretched state: surrounded by evils, scorned and hated by all, it would be better to die, and so on. It must be intended as a demonstration of how to vary and expand an existing text; I quote parallel sections below when discussing the compositional techniques of paraphrase and imitation.

7. Formula and Letter Collections.   Earlier I mentioned traces of epistolary theory in the fourth-century rhetoric of Julius Victor, and I return to the theory of letter-writing later. Latin letters are a phenomenally rich resource for study and were during the Middle Ages as well. Collections of real letters by the hundreds were formed and published from Cicero onward, by their authors and by others, and were copied and imitated even

---

[25]A good overview of the form, with an edition of a very interesting fourth-century colloquy plus translation and commentary, is A. C. Dionisotti, "From Ausonius' Schooldays? A Schoolbook and Its Relatives," *Journal of Roman Studies* 72 (1982) 83–125. See also Scott Gwara, ed., *Anglo-Saxon Conversations: The Colloquies of Ælfric Bata*, trans. with intro. by David W. Porter (Woodbridge, Eng.: Boydell, 1997). A fully annotated translation of Erasmus's Colloquies appeared in 1997 as volumes 39 and 40 in the *Collected Works of Erasmus*, University of Toronto Press.

[26]See Douglas Kelly, *The Arts of Poetry and Prose*, Typologie des sources du Moyen Age occidental 59 (Turnhout: Brepols, 1991) 83–84, with bibliography.

[27]Scott Gwara, ed., *Latin Colloquies from Pre-Conquest Britain*, Toronto Medieval Latin Texts (Toronto: Pontifical Inst. of Mediaeval Studies, 1996) 15–16.

centuries later.[28] Late in the tenth century, Gerbert modeled his epistolary style on that of Symmachus (fourth century), and letters of Symmachus turn up in twelfth-century handbooks of letter-writing instruction, the *artes dictaminis*.

A related category is the so-called formula collections, most of which were assembled in the eighth and ninth centuries. Various kinds of legal documents (such as wills and donations) predominate, but they also include real letters and model letter salutations, and are characterized by having *Ille* or *N.*, the equivalent of "So-and-so," in place of proper names. One early formula collection, the mid-seventh-century *Formulae Marculfi*, was made specifically for purposes of instruction, according to the author's own preface.[29]

Teaching Manuals and Anthologies; Manuscript Transmission

Gernot Wieland (see footnote 16) has sought to develop criteria by which to distinguish manuscripts used for actual classroom teaching from library reference books, for example, patterns and content of glossing within related manuscripts, accent marks for reading aloud, and "Why this?" notations for oral questioning. Or the collective contents of a medieval manuscript may mark it as a teaching manual: typically, such a manuscript brings together works on grammar, metrics, and rhetorical figures; perhaps works related to numerical calculation, calendar-reckoning, and weights and measures; and sometimes exemplary texts as well. *Florilegia*, or anthologies of literary texts (often, extracts), provide yet another kind of evidence for what was studied in schools and thought worthy of imitation.

Analysis of the manuscript transmission of classical Latin literary works yields information about their changing popularity and use in the Middle Ages. Birger Munk Olsen has published several studies on this topic, concentrating on the period before the twelfth century.[30] In one article, for

---

[28]For an excellent overview of the genre, see Giles Constable, *Letters and Letter-Collections*, Typologie des sources du Moyen Age occidental 17 (Turnhout: Brepols, 1976). For Gerbert and Symmachus: Jean-Pierre Callu, "Gerbert et Symmaque," *Haut Moyen Age: Culture, éducation et société; Etudes offerts à Pierre Riché*, ed. Claude Lepelley et al. (La Garenne–Colombes: Erasme, 1990) 517–28.

[29]*Marculfi formularum libri duo*, ed. Alf Uddholm (Uppsala: Eranos Förlag, 1962) 10: "Sed ego non pro talibus viris [i.e., rethores et ad dictandum peritos], sed ad exercenda initia puerorum, ut potui, aperte et simpliciter scripsi."

[30]Birger Munk Olsen, *L'Etude des auteurs classiques latins aux XIe et XIIe siècles* (Paris: CNRS, 1982–87); "La popularité des textes classiques entre le IX et le XII siècle," *Revue d'histoire des textes* 14–15 (1984–85) 169–81; "Les classiques latins dans les florilèges médiévaux antérieurs au XIIIe siècle," *Revue d'histoire des textes* 9 (1979) 47–121 and 10 (1980) 47–172.

example, he examines classical texts preserved in more than five manuscripts that were copied in the tenth century. Most such manuscripts seem to have been school texts: they contain interlinear and marginal glosses, Lives of the authors, and introductory or explanatory notes. Although works in prose were still the exception among these school texts, a growing interest in history—Livy and Sallust—suggests that prose was moving into the curriculum.[31] This kind of careful quantitative analysis confirms that the "renaissance of the twelfth century," marked by a revival of classical Latin literature, was rather a gradual growth with its roots in the tenth century if not the ninth.

Narrative Sources and Incidental Testimonia

Inevitably, there is an "et cetera" category. For this period, it forms a large haystack, from which the occasional needle can be recovered, but one must work hard to find it and often fall back on speculation.

Incidental remarks in unexpected places may yield significant information. Toward the end of the seventh century, Julian of Toledo wrote an *ars grammatica* based on Donatus. In two separate places, he uses letters to illustrate a point of grammar:

> [On the adverb] Name an adverb that comes from a pronoun. *Meatim, tuatim.* How <is it used>? For example, if I am composing a letter, and you compose one like it, I say, "You did it my way"; if another boy composes a letter like yours, "he did it your way."

> [On metonymy] Likewise, the agent for the effect, as we say "a happy letter" to mean the happiness of those whom the reading of it makes happy.[32]

How vivid the scene of two boys comparing their wax tablets on which each has laboriously composed his own version of, say, an abbot's letter of recommendation for a monk who must travel abroad: "You did it my way!" Because Julian uses letters so casually to make his points, we can infer that practice in letter-writing took place in his schoolroom.

Biographies of saints were immensely popular with medieval readers and writers, and *Vitae* by the hundreds survive. Their format tends to be stereotyped; the saint's education, for instance, is usually passed over with

---

[31]Birger Munk Olsen, "Les classiques au Xe siècle," *Mluellaleinisches Jahrbuch* 24–25 (1989–90) 341–47.

[32]*Ars Iuliani Toletani Episcopi: Una gramática latina de la España visigoda*, ed. Maria A. H. Maestre Yenes, Publicaciones del Instituto Provincial de Investigaciones y Estudios Toledanos Ser. II: Vestigios del Pasado 5 (Toledo 1973) 80.37–39 and 206.116–18.

"He was steeped in letters as a child."[33] More interesting for my present purpose, many early Lives later came to be viewed as factually or stylistically inadequate, and were rewritten, prefaced by criticism of the version being replaced. I think it likely that this kind of revision was also done as a school exercise to practice paraphrase, narrative, and ethopoeia; the topic certainly deserves study.

Information about schools and teaching is more likely to surface in secular biographies, letters, and histories, but it rarely includes details about techniques of instruction. Richer's history of France, written at the end of the tenth century, describes the education of his own teacher, Gerbert of Reims (later Pope Sylvester II), and the liberal arts curriculum Gerbert designed. At first sight it looks promising for this topic, as Richer enumerates the texts Gerbert assigned for study of dialectic and the classical poets—but after mentioning rhetoric as next in the sequence, he skips right over it with *qua instructis* 'after they had been instructed in it'!

John of Salisbury wrote his *Metalogicon* (1159) as a defense of the arts of the trivium. After relaying with approval Quintilian's advice to grammar teachers, John describes how the famous teacher Bernard of Chartres taught grammar in the early twelfth century. Since his portrait stands almost alone in its wealth of detail, it is worth quoting at length.

> This method was followed by Bernard of Chartres. By citations from the authors he showed what was simple and regular; he brought into relief the grammatical figures, the rhetorical colours, the artifices of sophistry, and pointed out how the text in hand bore upon other studies; not that he sought to teach everything in a single session, for he kept in mind the capacity of his audience. He inculcated correctness and propriety of diction, and a fitting use of congruous figures. Realizing that practise strengthens memory and sharpens faculty, he urged his pupils to imitate what they had heard, inciting some by admonitions, others by whipping and penalties. Each pupil recited the next day something from what he had heard on the preceding. The evening exercise, called the *declinatio*, was filled with such an abundance of grammar that anyone, of fair intelligence, by attending it for a year, would have at his fingers' ends the art of writing and speaking, and would know the meaning of all words in common use. But since no day and no school ought to be vacant of religion, Bernard would select for study a subject edifying to faith and morals. The closing part of this *declinatio*, or rather philosophical

---

[33]See Martin Heinzelmann, "Studia sanctorum: Education, milieux d'instruction et valeurs éducatives dans l'hagiographie en Gaule jusqu'à la fin de l'époque mérovingienne," in *Haut Moyen Age* 105–38 at 108–12 and 133–34: early hagiographers, distrusting secular education, often suppressed or downplayed information about a saint's secular education—as indeed did such prominent religious figures as Gregory of Tours concerning their own education.

recitation, was stamped with piety: the souls of the dead were commended, a penitential Psalm was recited, and the Lord's Prayer.

For those boys who had to write exercises in prose or verse, he selected the poets and orators, and showed how they should be imitated in the linking of words and the elegant ending of passages. If anyone sewed another's cloth into his garment, he was reproved for the theft, but usually was not punished. Yet Bernard gently pointed out to awkward borrowers that whoever imitated the ancients (*maiores*) should himself become worthy of imitation by posterity. He impressed upon his pupils the virtue of economy and the values of things and words: he explained where a meagreness and tenuity of diction was fitting, and where copiousness or even excess should be allowed, and the advantage of due measure everywhere. He admonished them to go through the histories and poems with diligence, and daily to fix passages in their memory. He advised them, in reading, to avoid the superfluous, and confine themselves to the works of distinguished authors [. . .]. But since in school exercises nothing is more useful than to practise what should be accomplished by the art, his scholars wrote daily in prose and verse, and proved themselves in discussions.[34]

Several of these points are echoed in two letters that St. Anselm wrote to his nephew, for whose education he was responsible, at about the same time. In both, he urges the youth to study *grammatica* diligently and to practice writing, especially in prose; the second letter, written a year or two later, advises him in more specific detail to develop the habit of daily writing practice (*dictare cotidie assuesce*) and not to write in a complicated, elaborate style but in a straightforward, "reasonable" style.[35] Anselm's letters nicely illustrate how evidence from one kind of source can corroborate that from another, very different kind—in this case, private, personal letters not intended for publication confirm the portrait drawn in a very public, formal document.

---

[34] Trans. Henry Osborn Taylor, *The Medieval Mind*, 4th ed., 2 vols. (Cambridge: Harvard UP, 1949) 2.157–58 (more fluent and readable than Daniel McGarry's *The Metalogicon of John of Salisbury: A Twelfth-Century Defense of the Verbal and Logical Arts of the Trivium* [Berkeley: U of California P, 1962] 67–70).

[35] The first letter also mentions *declinatio*, which according to Gillian Evans "implies the systematic parsing and analyzing of passages of exemplary writing": "St. Anselm's Technical Terms of Grammar," *Latomus* 38 (1979) 413–21. Anselm's letters are edited by F. S. Schmitt, O.S.B., in vols. 3–5 of *S. Anselmi, Cantuariensis Archiepiscopi, Opera omnia* (Edinburgh 1946–51), ep. 290 and 328 (dated 1103 and 1104–05 respectively). It is clear from John's description and from how Anselm uses forms of *declinare* elsewhere (ep. 64, ed. Schmitt 3.180) that it does not mean the grammatical exercise of changing the construction of a chreia to vary the cases of the nouns it contains (Diomedes gives samples of this type: Keil, *GL* 1.310). It sounds rather like the kind of microscopic analysis performed in Priscian's *Partitiones* (see below, "Creating the Child's Mind-Set").

WRITING INSTRUCTION: STRUCTURE, CONTENT, AND METHODS

As John of Salisbury's account suggests, most features of the Roman educational program outlined by Quintilian and analyzed in chapter 2 by Murphy lived on in the Middle Ages: "microscopic" analysis of texts studied; for each kind of speaking and writing exercise, sequencing by length and by degree of difficulty; imitation, paraphrase, and transliteration of what was read; and, from the beginning, memorization—of syllables, adages, fables and myths, reams of poetry (especially Vergil), the Psalms—to an extent that we can scarcely imagine. Of these processes I need only add some medieval examples. Certain other features, and some changes of emphasis, call for closer inspection.

Creating the Child's Mind-Set

First, consider how this kind of education in the verbal arts established the child's "mind-set," which ever after would inform how he or she read and wrote. Of its earliest stage, E. J. Kenney says:

> The methods used [. . .] were slow, thorough, and relentlessly pedantic. Under his elementary schoolmaster (*litterator, magister ludi litterarii*), from about the age of seven, the child practised writing and reciting the letters of the alphabet in every possible combination before repeating the procedure with syllables and then complete words. No short cuts were permitted. "There is no short way with syllables," says Quintilian. "They must be learned thoroughly, and the difficult ones must not (as usually happens) be left until they are encountered in actual words" (1.1.30). That is to say, attention to form is to precede attention to sense. . . .[36]

Even a brief extract from a Latin grammar text on syllables will suggest the deadening force of this approach, which one is tempted to call mindless. To begin his treatment of the noun, Sacerdos (late third/early fourth century) proceeds through the entire alphabet by last letter of the nominative singular and, within that scheme, through all possible combinations of letters into syllables, whether or not such combinations are actually found in any Latin nouns. His treatment of nouns whose nominative singular

---

[36]E. J. Kenney, "Books and Readers in the Roman World," in *The Cambridge History of Classical Literature: Latin Literature* (Cambridge: Cambridge UP, 1982) 6. The process is well described by Stanley F. Bonner, *Education in Ancient Rome* (Berkeley: U of California P, 1977) 165–77.

ends in *-r* covers seven printed pages; it begins thus (I have abbreviated slightly):

> Many nouns end in the letter *-r*. They are of all three genders; neuters belong only to the third declension. Nouns ending in plain [i.e. unbound] *-ar*, none. In plain *-er*, masculine nouns of the second declension, feminine nouns of the third. In plain *-ir*, one, indeclinable, contrary to the rule I just gave that neuter nouns ending in *-r* belong to the third declension and have their genitive in *-is*. In plain *-or*, masculine and feminine nouns of the third declension with the genitive in *-ris*, the *-o-* being short in the nominative and long in the genitive. I have found no noun ending in plain *-ur*.

He then starts over with three-letter syllables: *-bar*, *-ber*, *-bir* (none), *-bor*, *-bur*; *-car*, . . . all the way through the null sets of *-xur*, *-zar*, *-zer*, *-zir*, *-zor*, and *-zur*.[37]

All this—which is confirmed by written exercises preserved in papyri and wax tablets—before the child ever experienced the thrill of learning to read and write whole words, not to mention the two-word sentences of the *Dicta Catonis*! (Martianus Capella hints at its mind-numbing nature in *De nuptiis Philologiae et Mercurii*, book 3: the goddess Minerva cuts off Lady Grammar's presentation of her topic at about this point, just as she is really warming to her task, because the gods have become bored!)[38] This fatigue-march progression from letters to syllables to words to short sentences persisted for centuries; these four distinct stages of grammar study are named by St. Ambrose and St. Jerome and in the ninth century by Remigius of Auxerre.[39]

What Paul Saenger calls the physiology of reading Latin makes this early focus on syllables and words more comprehensible.[40] The lack of a fixed word order and the absence of word separation and punctuation in written texts made reading a matter of decoding, even for the experienced reader. (The beginnings of fixed word order, which would be generalized in Latin's Romance descendants, are visible by about the second century,

---

[37]Quoted from Keil, *GL* 4.11ff. (attributed by the text to Probus, but see Kaster 348–50 and 352–53).

[38]*Martianus Capella and the Seven Liberal Arts*, vol. 2: *The Marriage of Philology and Mercury*, trans. W. H. Stahl and Richard Johnson (New York: Columbia UP, 1977) 105.

[39]François Dolbeau, "Deux manuels latins de morale élémentaire," in *Haut Moyen Âge* 195, and Pierre Riché, "Apprendre à lire et à écrire dans le haut Moyen Age," *Bulletin de la Société nationale des Antiquaires de France*, 1978–79, 195; and, referring to poetry, Marjorie Curry Woods, "Medieval Progymnasmata: Basic Texts, Basic Techniques," paper read at March 1995 meeting of the 4Cs.

[40]Paul Saenger, "Physiologie de la lecture et séparation des mots," *Annales E.S.C.* 44/4 (1989) 939–52, and "The Separation of Words and the Order of Words: The Genesis of Medieval Reading," *Scrittura e civiltà* 14 (1990) 49–74. See now his *Space Between Words: The Origins of Silent Reading* (Stanford: Stanford UP, 1997).

first in texts that reflect spoken Latin; Jerome introduced the arrangement of text by sense units—*per cola et commata*—in his Vulgate Bible translations; word separation and punctuation in manuscripts spread gradually
from the ninth century on.) Harry Gamble prints five lines of a familiar
biblical text with no word separation, and comments, "If a familiar text is
surprisingly difficult, an unfamiliar one would present a far greater challenge. The relentless march of characters across the lines and down the
columns required the reader to deconstruct the text into its discrete verbal
and syntactical components."[41] Even the small surface area and clumsiness
of the waxed tablets normally used for drafting compositions must have
encouraged thinking in small sense units.[42]

Earlier I quoted samples of Servius's commentary on Vergil's *Aeneid*,
and in the same vein Murphy cites what is surely the best example of the
"micro-analysis" practiced in *praelectio* and *enarratio poetarum*: Priscian's
Partitiones on the first line of each book of the *Aeneid*. From it, Murphy
quotes the first six questions on the first word of the poem, *Arma*; in fact,
the commentary inspired by this one word consumes three full pages in
print, and the commentary on the first line alone covers ten and a half
pages (Keil, *GL* 3.459.23–469.12). None of it concerns the line's content
or significance, such as its echoing the first line of the *Iliad*.

This approach to literature mapped neatly onto the Christian ideal of
lectio divina. By a process called *meditatio* or *ruminatio*, patristic exegetes
sought to peel back from the divinely inspired biblical text every layer of
its significance, factual, metaphorical, allegorical, tropological. The
blending of secular and religious methods of analysis can be seen in
Cassiodorus's commentary on the Psalms; it is clearest, though, in a commentary on a nonbiblical religious text such as the *Benedictine Rule*, the
rule book for Benedictine monasteries that all Benedictine monks learned
by heart and from which they heard daily readings: a ninth-century commentary on the Rule (whose author was or had been a teacher) takes
eighty pages to explicate its prologue and chapter 1, which comprise
about four modest pages in print. Isidore's *Synonyma* offers another kind
of *ruminatio*, with its catena of variations slowly drawing the reader on
through a finely calibrated sequence of thoughts.

Quintilian's stricture about memorizing all possible syllables, at one extreme, and Christian *meditatio* at the other, reflect a second fundamental
aspect of what I have called the mind-set inculcated by Roman education
and its medieval heirs: the role of memory. An educated Christian, one

---

[41]Harry Y. Gamble, *Books and Readers in the Early Church: A History of Early Christian Texts*
(New Haven: Yale UP, 1995) 203.
[42]A preference for the small unit of composition was still lively in the twelfth-century *artes
poetriae*: Franz Quadlbauer called it a "Tendenz zur kleinen Einheit " (cited by Kelly 38–39
and 85–88).

raised on adages, Aesop, and the *Aeneid*, who spent years memorizing and reciting the Bible, meditating on its layers of meaning, paraphrasing its stories, had acquired the "habit," the *copia* that Quintilian wished the finished orator to have ready to supply the words for any occasion. Allusions, paraphrases, and quotations from the Bible and the Fathers of the church inhabit most medieval texts, and few medieval writers do not at least occasionally betray their early acquaintance with classical literature as well.

Perhaps an "ordinary" person of no literary renown can exemplify this routine use of memory best. In the mid-ninth century, a Gallic noblewoman named Dhuoda wrote a handbook of moral instruction for her teenage son. Dhuoda was a well-educated, deeply religious layperson. Except for Donatus and other elementary school texts (e.g., glossaries, computus), she cites only religious writings, often adapting them to her own context: all but about a dozen of the 150 Psalms, Augustine, Gregory the Great, Isidore's *Synonyma*, and a few Christian poets.[43] Although it seems unlikely that she had received any instruction in rhetorical theory, she strives (with no great success) for elegant effects. How did she learn to construct sentences, paragraphs, whole compositions; to choose a suitable style, apply appropriate ornaments? The obvious answers are "from the Bible" and "by imitation." She would have been hearing and memorizing those 150 Psalms orally and absorbing their style, even before she learned to read. And it may well have been her readings in Augustine that impelled her to reach for his eloquence by stringing together five gerunds in a row.

Classical and Medieval Verse Composition

Because the principles that governed the writing of Latin verse, though complex, are easier to trace in operation than those for prose, I touch just briefly on poetry. Some modern scholars argue, ex silentio, that formal instruction in verse composition was not part of the ancient Roman school curriculum but rather was a medieval development.[44] This seems to me highly improbable, given the widespread evidence that poetry formed the heart of the grammar curriculum. Students certainly had to learn how to scan and read the various meters of quantitative verse correctly, and their composition exercises likely included verse paraphrases of poetry.[45] The inclusion of metrical material in grammars and the association of gram-

[43]Pierre Riché, ed., *Dhuoda, Manuel pour mon fils*, Sources chrétiennes 225 (Paris 1975) 32–37.

[44]E.g., M. L. Clarke, "Quintilian on Education," in *Empire and Aftermath: Silver Latin II*, ed. T. A. Dorey (London: Routledge & Kegan Paul, 1975) 111; and Roberts 70–71.

[45]One example is a third/fourth-century papyrus line-for-line verse paraphrase of *Aeneid* 1.477–493; Roberts 52 cites it, but only to illustrate paraphrase, rather than as new composition for which knowledge of metrical principles was required.

mar and metrics texts in manuscripts strengthen the assumption, as does the unbroken practice of writing quantitative verse in the Middle Ages and the discussion in twelfth-century *artes poetriae* of metrical and rhythmic versification.[46]

The interplay between Latin syllable formation, word accent, and the meters of classical Latin poetry is not easy to grasp.[47] First, we as speakers of English with its strong stress accent lack sensitivity to the metrical considerations that shaped both Latin poetry and artistic word order in Latin prose. Second, poets borrowed their meters from Greek, which had a different linguistic structure from Latin. Third, because Latin writers on pronunciation and metrics also adopted their terminology from Greek, their analyses are sometimes opaque.

Briefly, then, spoken Latin had a stress accent, the position of which was determined by the length (*weight* is Allen's better term) of each word's penultimate syllable. In order to compose quantitative verse correctly, it was not enough to know which syllables carried the stress accent: you had to know the quantity, or weight, of every syllable (here is the justification for memorizing every possible combination of letters into syllables).[48] A "short" syllable equaled one beat; a "long" syllable, two beats. Gradually, classical poets met the challenge of fitting Latin words into the quantitative Greek metrical forms; the general tendency, brilliantly represented by Ovid, was to make the metrical accent, or *ictus*, coincide with the word accent.

Awareness of syllable length was fading by St. Augustine's lifetime, however, and new stress-based rhythmic verse forms were emerging, to exist in great variety side-by-side with the ancient quantitative meters throughout the Middle Ages.[49] A twelfth-century tour de force is Bernard of Cluny's poem *De contemptu mundi*, some 3,000 lines of strongly rhythmic "leonine" dactylic hexameters, with internal and end-rhyme throughout. It begins:

Hóra novíssima, témpora péssima súnt, vigilémus. . . .

---

[46]Kelly 82–85.

[47]Highly recommended, as a brief, clear, and sensible introduction: W. Sidney Allen, *Vox Latina: A Guide to the Pronunciation of Classical Latin*, 2nd ed. (Cambridge: Cambridge UP, 1978).

[48]Diane Warne Anderson has prepared a detailed diachronic survey of medieval texts for teaching syllable quantities, to appear in a volume of essays I am editing on Latin grammar and rhetoric.

[49]The basic handbook is Dag Norberg, *Introduction à l'étude de la versification latine médiévale* (Stockholm: Almqvist & Wiksell, 1958). Janet Martin surveys the production of both kinds of poetry (as well as prose) in the twelfth century, "Classicism and Style in Latin Literature," in *Renaissance and Renewal in the Twelfth Century*, ed. Robert L. Benson and Giles Constable (Cambridge: Harvard UP, 1982) 537–68.

The principle of fitting stress-based rhythms into originally quantitative metrical forms is familiar to us from Shakespeare's accentual iambic pentameters:

The quá | li tíe | of mér | cy ís | not stráined;
It dróp | peth ás | the gén | tle ráin | from heáv'n. . . .

The Influence of Poetry on Prose

Given the central position of poetry in schooling, it is not surprising to find widespread traces of poetic forms and practices in Latin prose, from the classical period on. What may surprise, given the equally central emphasis on the close study of language, is that Latin writers, Cicero excepted, show little interest in exploring the defining differences between poetry and prose.

1. Rhythm. Prose was often defined negatively by the absence of meter, as *oratio soluta*, speech freed from the constraints of meter, and the use of rhythm in each form is the single area to attract close analysis. Cicero wrote in thoughtful detail about the nature and long history—reaching back to Gorgias and Isocrates—of rhythm in oratorical prose (especially *Orator* §168 ff.). Aristotle, he says (§172), "forbids the use of verse *in oratione* [*oratio* can mean "prose" as well as "oration"], but requires rhythm," *numerus*. Nevertheless, as he demonstrates, poetry and prose share the same metrical patterns. The trick in prose is to keep them from turning into verse.

Quintilian deals with rhythm in the context of *compositio* (the technical term for sentence-level composition) and periodic structure (9.4.1–147). Although he twice declares that the three essentials for artistic *compositio* are *ordo, iunctura, numerus* 'order, connection, rhythm' (9.4.22, 9.4.147), for him the three are not equal: considerations of rhythm govern decisions about order and connection. As the translator notes at the beginning of this discussion (506), "*Compositio* in its widest sense means 'artistic structure.' But in much of what follows it virtually equals 'rhythm.'" Like Cicero, Quintilian discusses metrical feet appropriate for use in prose.

There is ample evidence that later writers and audiences remained sensitive to rhythm in prose, if not to syllable length. St. Augustine, a keen observer of early fifth-century linguistic change, contrasts people's diligence in observing "the rules of letters and syllables received from former speakers" with their neglect of God's covenants of salvation (*Confessions* 1.18); pondering the nature of time, he notes that a long syllable takes longer to say than a short one (*Confessions* 11.22, 23). Rufinus (late fifth century?), writing "on word arrangement and the rhythms of orators," takes Cicero as his chief authority and also quotes approvingly another grammarian's scornful observation that some fools think prose should not use metrical feet, that is, be rhythmical.[50]

By the early sixth century, the characteristic forms of the medieval accentual *cursus*, rhythmical patterns of clause and sentence endings, are visible in Latin prose texts; these are the "elegant ending of passages" that John of Salisbury says Bernard of Chartres recommended to his pupils. By the twelfth century, the overwhelmingly dominant cursus forms would be (using English mnemonics to indicate preferred word divisions):

planus	méns wear | de párt ment
tardus	(a) góv ern ment | súb si dy
	(b) mód ern | phi lós o phy
velox	líb er al | èd u cá tion

Not all medieval writers employ cursus, and modern scholars looking for it in medieval texts sometimes disagree about what they have found; it is particularly risky to use the results of cursus analysis to identify an anonymously transmitted text as having been written by an author whose characteristic cursus patterns have been established.[51]

2. Diction and Style.   If prose too used rhythm, we may ask again, what distinguished poetry from prose? Cicero, after noting that "It once seemed to be a matter of rhythm and verse, but now rhythm has become common in oratory" (*Orator* §66–68), says merely that poets are both constrained by meter and freer to form and arrange words. Quintilian writes at length in book 1, and again in book 8, about correctness in choice and arrangement of words, but offers no systematic discussion of differences between poetic and prosaic diction; he says only that, because the poet is the servant of his meter, "poetic license" excuses in poetry what would be faults in prose (1.5.11–13, 6.2, 8.14). Surveying rhetorical figures in books 8 and 9 (in which he draws his examples of stylistic ornament from both poetry and prose), he observes of nine figures that poets have greater freedom to use them: simile, metaphor, synecdoche, metonymy, antonomasia,

---

[50]Keil, *GL* 6.572.18–23; trans. Ian Thomson in Miller, *Readings* 45. For his date see Kaster no. 130.

[51]The literature on cursus is enormous, difficult, and sometimes contentious. For a general introduction, see the index to Murphy. The period of transition is well explained by Harald Hagendahl, *La correspondance de Ruricius* (Göteborg: Wettgren & Kerbers Förlag, 1952). In *Prose Rhythm in Medieval Latin from the 9th to the 13th Century* (Stockholm: Almqvist & Wiksell, 1975), Tore Janson developed statistical methods of cursus analysis that have been widely adopted.

catachresis, epithet, periphrasis, and tmesis.[52] In book 10.1.27–29, discussing the kinds of reading that contribute most to maintaining and improving the finished orator's skills (he recommends poetry, but with reservations), he repeats that poets enjoy greater freedom of language and use
of figures and explains that metrical necessity compels them to use cir-
cumlocutions and to substitute, lengthen, shorten, or transpose words.
Other writers on style make similar remarks, often using "poetic license"
or "metrical necessity" as a kind of shorthand for whatever characteristics
of poetic diction they have in mind.

At the same time, in the first century AD, literary fashions were changing to favor, among other things, greater use of those rhetorical *colores* recorded as especially poetic by Quintilian. "The adornment of the poet is demanded nowadays also in the orator," says the "modernist" Aper in the
Dialogue on Oratory (§20) by Quintilian's contemporary Tacitus, the dramatic date of which is about 75 AD. Whatever distinctions had once separated prose and verse diction and stylistic conventions were fading rapidly,
and many prose texts acquired a poetic coloring. An egregious example of
this bland statement is Apuleius's romance *Metamorphoses* (after c. 160 AD),
the florid style of which does full justice to its picaresque contents.[53]

The tendency continued in the next few centuries, aided unwittingly by
the effort to reduce Latin grammar to a system, because Donatus and
other grammarians who discuss rhetorical figures took their examples almost entirely from poetry, chiefly Vergil. The confusion of diction and stylistic levels is especially noticeable in Insular (Anglo-Saxon and Irish) writers and those influenced by them, to whom all classical Latin words and
texts were equally foreign and who thought that Donatus, *the* authority on
Latin, was not merely classifying but also commending.[54] A modern Latin
dictionary, in contrast, can tell us by its citations whether a given word was
used exclusively in prose, or label it as, for example, "poetic and post-
Augustan prose." Possibly some collections of *differentiae* attempted something similar. Although the *Exempla elocutionum* of Arusianus Messius illustrates syntactical constructions from two poets and two prose authors, it
makes no perceptible distinctions between prose and verse usage.

In short, I know of no ancient or medieval Latin treatment comparable
to Axelson's *Unpoetische Wörter*,[55] which (among other things) reminds us
that many Latin words were excluded from quantitative verse simply by
their metrical structure, their sequence of long and short syllables. We are
left to assume that when students were introduced to prose texts, their

---

[52]Roberts 72 n. 42.

[53]Known to St. Augustine (*De civ. Dei* 18.18) and ever since as *The Golden Ass*: P. G. Walsh,
The Roman Novel (Cambridge: Cambridge UP, 1970) 143 n. 1.

[54]Michael Winterbottom, "The Style of Aethelweard," *Medium Aevum* 36 (1967) 114–15.

[55]Bertil Axelson, *Unpoetische Wörter. Ein Beitrag zur Kenntnis der lateinischen Dichtersprache*
(Lund: Gleerup, 1945).

teachers may have pointed out various ways in which prose differed from the poetry they were used to studying.

The *Progymnasmata* and Prose Composition

To put it very crudely, in the Roman education of Quintilian's time, poetry was grammar's domain, and prose was rhetoric's. But if reading in the grammar school consisted entirely of poetry, how, and when, did pupils learn to write prose? It was in the *progymnasmata*, the series of graded exercises originally designed to introduce students to rhetoric, that any study of prose writers and instruction in prose composition took place. The classical curriculum made no provision for the systematic study of prose genres outside the *progymnasmata*.

Scholars have sometimes portrayed the *progymnasmata* as a self-contained intermediate stage, a preprofessional curriculum for future orators and advocates studying with a special rhetoric teacher. We should rather understand the *progymnasmata* as a general introduction to rhetoric, for even the most elementary exercises could teach the basic techniques of invention, arrangement, and style that are applicable to any kind of planned discourse, oral or written. It seems obvious that lower-school teachers of language and literature, the *grammatici*, would invoke these principles when teaching poetry: surely they could not be postponed until the advanced course in rhetoric, when the students analyzed famous speeches and practiced declamation. And indeed, Quintilian indicates (2.1–3, 4) that by his time the rhetoric teachers had abandoned most or even all of the *progymnasmata* to the *grammatici*. Responsibility for teaching the rhetorical figures was also assumed by grammar teachers, the division between figures of speech (grammar) and figures of thought (rhetoric) being impossible to maintain in practice.[56]

While grammar teaching continued to emphasize poetry, then, it is clear that the formal study of prose at the elementary level had begun to expand in Quintilian's time or shortly after. Already in place, that is, were the outlines of the "grammar school" curriculum that would live on into the British six-form structure. When new Latin translations of Aphthonius's *progymnasmata* appear in sixteenth-century Europe, they are used in the grammar school.[57]

---

[56]Louis Holtz, "Grammairiens et rhéteurs romains en concurrence pour l'enseignement des figures de rhétorique," in *La rhétorique à Rome*, Calliope I (Paris, 1979) 207–20; Marc Baratin and Françoise Desbordes, "La 'troisième partie' de l'*ars grammatica*," *Historiographia linguistica* 13.2/3 (1986) 215–40.

[57]See chapter 5 by Don Paul Abbott in this volume. The translation of Aphthonius by Ray Nadeau in *Speech Monographs* 19 (1952) 264–85 has been revised by Patricia P. Matsen, *Readings from Classical Rhetoric*, ed. Patricia P. Matsen, Philip Rollinson, and Marion Sousa (Carbondale: Southern Illinois UP, 1990) 266–88.

That structural change originated within the schools. From without, powerful forces of social, political, and religious upheaval that would eventually break up the Roman Empire reinforced it. First, the nature of deliberative and forensic oratory was changing—again, by Quintilian's time—under an increasingly bureaucratic imperial government that favored technical legal skills, streamlined procedural exactitude, and written documents over extended oral presentation.[58] The new atmosphere is palpable in Tacitus's *Dialogue on Oratory*; contrasting the expansive, leisurely style of the Ciceronian era with the modern courtroom, the speaker says:

> [W]hat we need is novel and choice methods of eloquence, by employing which the speaker may avoid boring his hearers, especially when addressing a court which decides issues, not according to the letter of the law, but by virtue of its own inherent authority, not allowing the speaker to take his own time, but telling him how long he may have, and not waiting patiently for him to come to the point, but often going so far as to give him a warning, or call him back from a digression and protest that it has no time to spare.[59]

Second, public oratory did not, as is sometimes assumed, decay or die out in late antiquity. Although Quintilian deplored the current excesses of declamation (2.10), it long remained popular, together with panegyric—both, public showpieces of epideictic speechmaking. Two Greek treatises on panegyric and other forms of epideictic, probably from the late third or early fourth century, have parallels in extant Latin speeches as late as the sixth century (the last recorded Latin panegyric was delivered by Cassiodorus in 536).[60] Long before then, however, a new Christian public had emerged, to provide eager audiences for other kinds of speakers and writers.

It fell to grammar, strengthened by the additional tasks it had already taken over from the rhetoric curriculum, to construct a new rhetoric curriculum: one that would be less singlemindedly devoted to litigation and display, and flexible enough to meet the new needs of new kinds of societies. Nearly all of the rhetorical *progymnasmata* would be not merely useful

---

[58]Michael C. Leff (following John Ward's suggestion), "The Material of the Art in the Latin Handbooks of the Fourth Century A.D.," in *Rhetoric Revalued*, ed. Brian Vickers, Medieval & Renaissance Texts & Studies 19 (Binghamton, NY: Center for Medieval & Early Renaissance Studies, 1982) 75–76.

[59]Tacitus, *Dialogus* §19, trans. William Peterson, 65, Loeb Classical Library (Cambridge: Harvard UP, 1914).

[60]For the Greek treatises, see *Menander Rhetor*, ed. and trans. D. A. Russell and N. G. Wilson (Oxford: Clarendon, 1981) xi. On the popularity of panegyric in the West, see Sabine MacCormack, "Latin Prose Panegyrics: Tradition and Discontinuity in the Later Roman Empire," *Revue des études augustiniennes* 22 (1976) 29–77 (for the speech of Cassiodorus, 73 n. 173).

but essential for educated persons participating in a culture increasingly dependent on writing. What more natural stimulus for Priscian—*Priscianus grammaticus*, a teacher of Latin grammar and literature, not a rhetorician—to translate a Greek *progymnasmata* text into Latin, early in the sixth century?

Other evidence for the survival of Latin *progymnasmata* is easy to overlook, because their content duplicates (or rather, prefigures) that of rhetoric proper. Certain texts usually seen as rhetorics are, or incorporate, *progymnasmata* collections. The thirteen pages in Halm's *Rhetores latini minores* of Emporius, a shadowy figure perhaps contemporary with Priscian, come from a *progymnasmata* text. Book 1 of Isidore's *Etymologies*, on grammar, ends with transitional sections on *fabula* and *historia*, and the epitome of rhetoric that opens book 2 contains four sections of *progymnasmata* exercises, including *ethopoeia*. On a larger scale, I have already alluded to an important manuscript of school texts written at the end of the eighth century that reflects the new curriculum in its choice and arrangement of texts:[61] after 250 folia containing texts devoted to metrics, grammar, and rhetoric, there comes a group of excerpts from various sources that together form a *progymnasmata* sequence. They include anonymous paragraphs on encomium and epistolary theory and the partial text of Emporius (which starts in the middle, with *prosopopoeia*), followed by Priscian's *Praeexercitamina*. Then—most revealing, from the perspective of the later *artes dictaminis*—come rules for composing *litterae formatae*, the coded letters issued by episcopal chanceries: many dictaminal texts, starting with Alberic of Monte Cassino's *Breviarium*, contain similar instructions. (The final ten texts in this manuscript are a miscellany of dialectic, computus, calender reckoning, glosses, etc.)

Techniques of Prose Composition

Writing somewhat later than Priscian, Cassiodorus defined grammar thus:

> Grammar is the knowledge of speaking attractively [*pulchre loquendi*], gathered from distinguished poets and authors; its duty is to teach faultless composition [*sine vitio dictionem*] in prose and verse; its end, to give pleasure through flawless skill in refined speech or writing. (*Inst.* 2.1.1)

Note that grammar has by now, the sixth century, explicitly assumed the task of teaching composition in both poetry and prose. While "faultless"

---

[61]Louis Holtz, "Le Parisinus Latinus 7530, synthèse cassinienne des arts libéraux," *Studi medievali* 3rd ser. 16 (1975) 97–152. I follow Holtz's analysis and numbering of the manuscript's contents.

and "flawless" refer to basic grammatical correctness, the mention of attractiveness and pleasure implies the addition of rhetorical considerations, especially style. (Cassiodorus defines rhetoric in the following section simply as speaking persuasively in civil cases.) Priscian's *progymnasmata* address the first two parts of rhetoric, invention or content and arrangement—each exercise contains a definition and at least one sketchy example of how to construct it—but ignore that fountain of pleasure, style and rhetorical ornament. Where did the students find the matter for their compositions, and learn how to organize and ornament it?

1. Imitation, Paraphrase, and Variation.   Reading and learning to compose proceeded hand in hand from grammar school on. Murphy has analyzed above how imitation, "the deliberate modelling of an existing artifact or text," informed the entire Roman educational program—practiced from the child's first efforts at learning the shapes of the letters through the most advanced composition exercises of the *progymnasmata*. St. Augustine even upheld the power of imitation alone to teach eloquence (*De doct. chr.* 4.3.5). Paraphrase too was thought to have sovereign powers: Michael Roberts similarly extends its reach in his invaluable survey of classical and late antique paraphrase, observing, "In a sense, then, the *progymnasmata* could be subsumed under the genus paraphrase, since they all involved the stylistic elaboration of a predetermined subject."[62]

Paraphrase at the level of word and sentence is *variatio*, and its practice was encouraged by the microanalytic approach to literature, by the glossaries and *differentiae*, by the catalogs of rhetorical figures, by such masters of Latin style as St. Augustine, and perhaps even by Isidore of Seville's paradigmatic *Synonyma*. To teach vocabulary, one of the Anglo-Saxon colloquies offers five ways to say "What do you want?": *O frater! Quid vis? Quicquid queris? Quid aspicis? Quid cupis? Quid optas?* Aethelweard, writing a chronicle early in the eleventh century, found several different ways to express the passage of time (as his subject repeatedly required him to do) beyond a simple *post annum* 'after a year', such as *post decursum anni unius* and *impleta serie anni unius*, and similarly varied ways to express victory in battle.[63] Aethelweard's technique was not novel; in fact, it pales beside the fourth-century historian Ammianus Marcellinus (a Greek writing in Latin), who invented 29 expressions for dying, 35 for daybreak, and 16 for a river flowing into the sea or another river.[64] (The all-time champion of *variatio* is Erasmus, who in *De copia* produced 147 variations on "Your let-

---

[62] Roberts 23.

[63] Winterbottom 115–16.

[64] Harald Hagendahl, *Studia Ammianea* (Uppsala Universitets Årsskrift, 1921) 100–103; the first two are cited by Roberts 151 n. 116.

ter pleased me very much," and 203 variations on "Always, as long as I live, I shall remember you.")[65]

A spectacularly extended example of all three practices—imitation, paraphrase, and variation—occurs in the eleventh-century colloquy by Ælfric Bata mentioned earlier. A brief excerpt highlighting the parallels will show how the speaker in the colloquy, a schoolboy being punished, weaves in and out of his source, Isidore's *Synonyma*, like a modern jazz musician:

Isidore, *Synonyma*:

Nullus mihi protectionem praebet, nullus *defensionem* adhibet, *nullus adminiculum tribuit, nullus malis meis succurrit, desertus sum ab omnibus* hominibus; *quicunque me aspiciunt, aut fugiunt, aut* fortasse *me persequuntur*, intuentur me quasi infelicem, et nescio quae *loquuntur mihi in dolo verbis pacificis; occultam* malitiam *blandis sermonibus* ornant, et *aliud ore promunt, aliud corde volutant.* (1.7)

Ælfric Bata's colloquy:

Nullus mihi protectionem prebet nec *defensionem* prestat, *nullus adminiculum tribuit, nullus malis meis succurrit. Desertus sum ab omnibus* amicis meis et proximis et notis et propinquis. *Quicumque me aspiciunt aut fugiunt aut me* ubique *persequuntur*, et non quiescunt falsa testimonia contra me preparare et dicere [this clause is taken from three paragraphs further on in the Synonyma]. *Loquuntur mihi in dolo uerbis pacificis* et nequitiam *occultant* suam *blandis sermonibus. Aliud ore promunt, aliud corde uolutant* (id est cogitant).[66]

2. Compilatio. To modern eyes, this kind of "variation" looks more like rampant plagiarism. It is, however, endemic among late antique and medieval Latin authors, even though some paid lip service to the modern concept of intellectual property (copyright, of course, did not exist).[67] The usual attitude is expressed by Symmachus, writing to a friend who had reproached him for circulating the friend's poem to others: "Once the poem left you, you lost all rights over it; a work that has been made public is a free object [*Oratio publicata res libera est*]."[68] Once published, a literary work

---

[65]Thomas O. Sloane, "Schoolbooks and Rhetoric: Erasmus's *Copia*," *Rhetorica* 9.2 (1991) 119.

[66]Gwara, *Latin Colloquies* 15–16 and 86–87 lines 66–74. "(id est cogitant)" 'i.e., they think' is a gloss on *volutant* that has crept into the text; the sentence means, "They say one thing with their mouth, [and] turn over [*volutant*] another in their heart."

[67]See the informative survey by Neil Hathaway, "Compilatio: From Plagiarism to Compiling," *Viator* 20 (1989) 19–44.

[68]Ep. 1.31.2, cited by Harald Hagendahl, "Methods of Citation in Post-Classical Latin Prose," *Eranos* 45 (1947) 118.

became common property, available for imitation, paraphrase, and appropriation by subsequent writers.

"Adaptive reuse" of another's work can be detected in any number of medieval Latin works, sometimes simply because the borrowing is inept, the adaptation unsuited to the new context. Bernard of Chartres surely would have reproved for theft the late eighth-century letter-writer who inserted into his different context several phrases taken, in order, from two letters of St. Jerome (himself a notorious borrower) and attributed to the Old Testament prophet Malachi a quotation he had stitched together from three biblical sources, *not* including the book of Malachi; the equivalent but unattributed quotation in Jerome's letter in turn echoes a letter of Cyprian.[69] Did the author of this letter learn his compositional technique in the classroom? Impossible to say, but he had plenty of distinguished company in the practice.

3. *Compositio (Structure).* For the grammar teacher, *compositio* meant chiefly considerations of correctness in word choice, order, arrangement, and syntactical construction within the sentence. Priscian is the first Latin grammarian to treat syntax, in the final two books (*De constructione*) of his magisterial grammar; he includes helpful comments about semantics and usage along the way (for instance, the difference in meaning between the demonstrative pronouns *hoc, iste,* and *ille,* 17.58).

The rhetoric teacher moved beyond the basics of speaking correctly at the sentence level to consider artistic structure—how to speak *well*—and the characteristics of different sentence styles and their appropriate use. Quintilian discussed grammatical *compositio* in book 1. In book 9, his rhetorical treatment, he identifies two kinds of sentence style: one is markedly hypotactic, "closely welded and woven together [*vincta atque contexta*], while the other is of a looser texture [*soluta*]" (9.4.19). (Some rhetorics add a third, paratactic style, *oratio perpetua.*) The first is what we know as the periodic style, "composed of three elements: the *comma,* or as we call it *incisum,* the *colon,* or in Latin *membrum,* and the *period*" (9.4.22).

The third-century rhetor Aquila Romanus included a segment on these styles (three, for him) and their use in his handbook on the figures of speech and thought (Halm 27–28), and Martianus Capella took it over for his survey of rhetoric in book 5 (sects. 526–529; trans. Stahl and Johnson 198–99). *Oratio soluta,* which does not require rhythm or hypotaxis, is used for ordinary speech and for letters, and in judicial speeches when one

---

[69]Bernhard Bischoff, ed., *Salzburger Formelbücher und Briefe aus Tassilonischer und Karolingischer Zeit,* Sitzungsberichte d. Bayerische Akademie d. Wissenschaften, Phil.-hist. Kl., 1973 Heft 4 (Munich 1973) 56. I have studied these letters in "Formulaic Parallels and Epistolary Style," part 2 of an article published jointly with Bengt Löfstedt under the title "Zu den neugefundenen Salzburger Formelbüchern und Briefen," *Eranos* 63 (1975) 69–100 at 83ff.

wants to adopt a conversational tone. *Oratio perpetua* connects clauses paratactically in the normal sequence of thought, and is appropriate for history and narrative. Aquila gives examples of a period and its parts, but does not indicate what kind of writing it is best suited for. He concludes by declaring that a mixture of all three styles is best, because any one alone becomes tiresome. Augustine makes the same point in analyzing biblical examples of periodic structures (*De doct. chr.* 4.7.11ff.).

As its terminology indicates, the theory of the period is Greek, first formulated by Aristotle.[70] It is essentially a theory of prose rhythm, and the centrality of rhythm to Latin prose guaranteed its continued vitality through the development of the cursus and into the High Middle Ages of Latin literature.

4. *Dispositio (Arrangement)*.   Rhetoric texts analyzed the sources of arguments and methods of handling them under invention, the first part of rhetoric. *Dispositio*, the second part, covers the arrangement within each part of the work and of the work as a whole. When discussing it in book 7, Quintilian declines to generalize: he says, in effect, that you must learn by doing, by working on one case at a time, because the circumstances of each individual law case will determine the best arrangement of your material. Therefore, his precepts (which are in any case specific to litigation) are not transferable to instruction in composition.

Two very different kinds of rhetorical practice documents display one aspect of how arrangement was taught. The 145 "Minor Declamations" attributed to Quintilian are (if not actually by him) "fragments . . . from a practising teacher's workshop," and each speech is carefully signposted to make its divisions and succession of arguments clear. "It is just the same impulse, to make the shape of the speech intelligible *in advance*, that causes the frequent use of such phrases as 'postea videbo' [afterwards I shall see], answered by 'interim . . .' [meanwhile]."[71] I found exactly the same impulse at work in Merovingian and Carolingian formula collections comprising students' practice letters: sentence is linked to sentence by *and so, therefore, hence, for this reason*, and so on; larger divisions are set off by *in the first place, next, finally*. Aristotle laid down the principle of using connecting words between sentences (*Rhetorica* 1407a19), and medieval *artes dictandi* advise letter-writers to mark off the divisions of the letter with appropriate introductory words.[72]

---

[70]See George Kennedy, *The Art of Persuasion in Greece* (Princeton: Princeton UP, 1963) 109–11.

[71]Michael Winterbottom, "Schoolroom and Courtroom," in *Rhetoric Revalued* 64, 66.

[72]Carol Dana Lanham, *"Salutatio" Formulas in Latin Letters to 1200: Syntax, Style, and Theory*, Münchener Beiträge zur Mediävistik und Renaissance-Forschung 22 (Munich: Arbeo-Gesellschaft, 1975) 60–63.

ARS DICTAMINIS: THE MEDIEVAL ART
OF LETTER-WRITING

The *Progymnasmata* and Epistolography

From Cicero's time onward, letters were a major literary genre. Thousands of Latin letters survive (and thousands more in Greek), evincing every conceivable subject and style. For Christians, the genre carried special significance: as George Kustas notes, "Christianity had introduced itself to the world in the form of a letter; most of the earliest Christian documents are letters."[73] Christian writers quickly recognized a chief advantage of the format: "The great variety of types and functions of early Christian letters illustrates the flexibility of the genre."[74] I believe that, as part of the centuries-long shift from an oral culture to one dependent on writing, the written letter replaced the spoken declamation of classical antiquity as the primary vehicle for practice in prose composition.

Letters were the only form of elementary composition that was, by definition, written. An ancient, partly traceable theory of letter-writing illuminates epistolary practice and suggests that the letter provided an excellent framework for teaching prose composition.[75] A letter was viewed as half of a conversation, intended to represent the spoken word and the character of the writer, and, therefore, simple vocabulary and an informal style were considered appropriate. Beginners could manage the informal diction, akin to that of ordinary speech, which was recommended for letters. Letters were supposed to be brief; "epistolary brevity" is often invoked to end a medieval letter. Best of all, letters had no fixed subject matter. The letter format was therefore ideal for schoolroom practice on circumscribed themes, and yet for a mature writer, the genre was elastic and accommodating, even inviting. This broad applicability of the letter form, and its informal and elastic nature, made it an attractive vehicle for teaching the *progymnasmata* exercises in rhetoric.

But where is the link between epistolography and *progymnasmata*? Kustas again: "From the point of view of rhetorical theory, it [epistolography] falls under the heading of *ethopoeia*, the progymnasma par excellence which gave the freest scope to the expression of personality traits"; he cites an anonymous scholion on Aphthonius that *ethopoeia* is the perfect kind of *progymnasma* (59). This exercise, the speech in character, was con-

---

[73] George L. Kustas, "The Function and Evolution of Byzantine Rhetoric," *Viator* 1 (1970) 59.

[74] Gamble 37.

[75] I argue this point in detail in "Freshman Composition in the Early Middle Ages: Epistolography and Rhetoric before the *ars dictaminis*," *Viator* 23 (1992) 115–34.

sidered to be among the more difficult, and many examples of it survive, especially of the type using figures from poetry or history that students would have read. St. Augustine recalled having as a schoolboy to deliver a version of Juno's speech in the *Aeneid* (*Confessions* 1.17), and the works of Ennodius (early sixth century), offer several examples, such as what Thetis said when she saw her son Achilles dead, or what Menelaus said when he saw Troy burning. The larger rhetorical principle being stressed in this exercise is *decorum*, suiting one's words to the speaker's age, rank, and fortune, as well as to the situation.

Establishing an authorial voice, an *ethos*, is a central task for any speaker or writer, but character portrayal addresses the very essence of the letter, which is, after all, a substitute for one's physical presence. Two Greek *progymnasmata* texts mention letter-writing in their treatment of *ethopoeia*. Theon (thought to be approximately contemporary with Quintilian) observes that this exercise is useful not only for panegyric and protreptic oratory but also for letters; he explains that a young man should speak differently from an old man, a farmer from a soldier, and so on. Nicolaus (fifth century) recommends practicing the exercise of *ethopoeia* in letter form because one must take into account the character (*ethos* again) of both the sender and the recipient of the letter. Priscian does not mention letters under this exercise, which he calls *allocutio*, but his treatment is otherwise similar.

Splendid literary examples of fictional letters created in accordance with the rhetorical rules for *ethopoeia* are Ovid's *Heroides* and, in Greek, the second- and third-century letters of courtesans, fishermen, and farmers by Aelian and Alciphron. The fourth-century invented correspondence between Seneca and St. Paul is best explained as a classroom exercise in style and characterization; constructed as an exchange between a pagan philosopher and a Christian, the letters also had to employ simple argumentative techniques of confirmation and refutation. Its example suggests an image of schoolboys, perhaps even working in pairs, composing such letters as a variation on the orally delivered speech in character—like the students Julian of Toledo used to illustrate the adverbs *meatim* and *tuatim*.

One might also look for evidence of other *progymnasmata* exercises in letters, singly or in combination with *ethopoeia*. The equally important exercise of *narratio*, for example, was begun early in the sequence. The principles of judicial rhetoric required that the narrative section of a speech should normally be composed in a plain style, akin to that of ordinary conversation; it should be brief; and it should be clear (see, e.g., *Ad Herennium* 1.9). Exactly the same prescriptions of clarity, brevity, and simplicity governed letter style, and so an assignment that combined *narratio* with *ethopoeia* can be readily envisioned. Again, moral maxims abound in letters, accompanied by paraphrase and exegesis; likewise for commonplaces. Neither is it hard to find set-piece descriptions (*ecphrases*) in letters.

To turn the question around, what other forms besides the letter might the study and practice of prose take? A clue is found in book 1 of Isidore's *Etymologies*, where he sketches a grammar curriculum that includes the study of narrative prose of all kinds. Starting with Donatus and his eight parts of speech, Isidore discusses thirty components of *ars grammatica* (1.5). The last four have no analogue either in Donatus or (according to Jacques Fontaine) in any grammar text before Isidore: they are *prosa, metra, fabulae,* and *historiae*.[76] Fontaine calls this "the central addition of Isidorian grammar" (56). Isidore treats all four at length before turning to rhetoric with book 2. He associates *fabula* with *res fictae*, and *historia* with *res factae*—fiction and fact, in modern terms, a distinction made by the classical rhetoric texts in discussing *narratio* (e.g., Cicero, *De inventione* 1.19.27; *Ad Herennium* 1.8).[77] In short, although Quintilian thought that the *progymnasmata* exercise of *narratio* should be the first one taught by the rhetoric teacher (2.4.1), in Isidore's scheme, grammar has effectively claimed *narratio* from rhetoric, and with it *fabula* and *historia*, the practice of artistic prose of all kinds.

There is some evidence that by the ninth century "epistola" could mean simply "prose." Writing to a bishop, Alcuin recommends dividing the pupils in an episcopal school into three levels: the first group learns the elements of Latin morphology and grammar, the most advanced students study Scripture, and the middle group reads *epistolas et parvos libellos* 'letters and little books'.[78] *Libelli* must represent the standard fare of poetic texts customarily read at the grammar school level; by 800, this included not only the *Disticha Catonis*, moralized fables in verse, and Vergil, but also Christian poets such as Juvencus and Prudentius. Alcuin's letter specifies where in the curriculum the study of letters/prose occurred, but does not confirm that the pupils practiced composing letters (or anything else, for that matter) themselves. That can be glimpsed in Notker's Life of Charlemagne when the emperor, returned to the palace after a long stint on the battlefield, summons the boys he had entrusted to the Irish teacher Clemens, so that they might show him *epistulas et carmina sua* 'their letters and poems'.

The Life of Burchard, bishop of Worms 1000–1025, describes his teaching methods at the cathedral school in similar terms:

> In addition, he firmly instructed each pupil, according to his ability, to present to him every day a carefully prepared recitation or written work. Then indeed, because they saw that the servant of God was devoted to study and

[76]Jacques Fontaine, *Isidore de Séville et la culture classique dans l'Espagne wisigothique*, 2 vols. (Paris: Etudes Augustiniennes, 1959; rev. ed. 3 vols. 1983) 1.54.
[77]Fontaine 1.174–85.
[78]Alcuin, ep. 161, MGH Epistolae 4, ed. Ernst Dümmler (Hanover 1895) 260.13–15.

learned in the pages of holy Scripture and filled with the wisdom of God, they were not afraid to offer him their speeches and letters and various [written] questions (*sermones et epistolas quaestiunculasque varias*).[79]

The passage continues with an example of a *quaestiuncula*, which may have been a specific kind of prose composition exercise: in the mid-1060s, Alberic of Monte Cassino, apparently as a novice monk, addressed at least two sets of *quaestiunculae* on scriptural topics to Peter Damiani in letter form (only Peter's answers are preserved).[80] Later, *artes dictandi* often begin by dividing *dictamen* into verse and prose composition and then specifying letters as a subdivision of prose. An early one warns, "There is a great difference between *prosa* and *epistola*, although one is very often put for the other";[81] Conrad of Mure (c. 1275) even declares that all artistic prose is either *sermo* (spoken face to face) or *epistola* (written to absent persons).[82]

The Worms letter collection (dated to the second quarter of the eleventh century, just after Burchard's tenure as bishop) contains numerous exchanges between students and teachers; others sound like school exercises on a set theme. One pair (ep. 20–21) offers an excellent example of letter-writing instruction carried on in letter form. A student has written to the cathedral schoolmaster seeking career advice; the master's reply contains an extended rhetorical analysis of the student's letter, beginning with its salutation. Significantly, the teacher observes that the student has employed a rhetorical *captatio benivolentiae* in his salutation, even though he has not yet studied that subject, that is, rhetoric.

The Rise of *Ars Dictaminis*

With the better schools and renewed interest in classical literature that characterize the Carolingian era, the study of rhetoric began to revive in the eighth and ninth centuries. Toward the end of the tenth century, Gerbert included dialectic and rhetoric in his curriculum at Reims, and new treatises on rhetorical figures appeared in the eleventh century. Worms was almost certainly not the only cathedral school in which letter-writing was taught early in the eleventh century; at exactly the same time, Fulbert of Chartres—to name but one of several outstanding figures—an

---

[79]Walther Bulst, ed., *Die ältere Wormser Briefsammlung*, MGH Briefe der deutschen Kaiserzeit 3 (Weimar 1949) 5.

[80]*Die Briefe des Petrus Damiani*, ed. Kurt Reindel, MGH Briefe der deutschen Kaiserzeit 4, vol. 3 (Munich 1989), nos. 126, 127 (= PL 145.621–34).

[81]Franz Josef Worstbrock, "Die Anfänge der mittelalterlichen Ars dictandi," *Frühmittelalterliche Studien* 23 (1989) 34.

[82]*Die Summa de arte prosandi des Konrad von Mure*, ed. Walter Kronbichler (Zurich, 1968) 30.

influential teacher, a leader in the church, and a fine literary stylist, was writing letters that would be collected and used as school models by the second half of the century.[83] If it is true that the letter form had, at some earlier point, become the primary vehicle for instruction in prose composition, it is hardly surprising that the eleventh and twelfth centuries were a great age of Latin letter-writing, in both quantity and quality.

I. S. Robinson, arguing that "The letter was the form of composition *par excellence* in which eleventh-century scholars could display their training in the *artes*,"[84] has shown what rich opportunities the second half of the century gave them to do so. Long-festering problems within the church, including its relations with secular powers, produced a widespread reform movement that culminated in the investiture contest between papal and imperial factions, sparked by the election of Pope Gregory VII in 1073. Polemical tracts flew around Europe. Regardless of their length and the complexity of their contents, they were cast in the form of letters, with conventional epistolary formulas of salutation and closing; "epistolary brevity" was sometimes adduced to excuse omitting even more argumentation. The twelfth century would, in turn, collect these polemical works and use them as models of style.

Although the verb *dictare* and the noun *dictamen* have the general sense "to compose, composition" and so designate any kind of writing, the *ars dictaminis* 'art of composition' that began to blossom after 1100 concerns only letter-writing.[85] Scholars used to ignore the traces of epistolary theory that antedate the appearance of *dictamen*. They explained the rather swift rise of the new specialized art as a response to the growth of bureaucracy in the eleventh century: royal and ecclesiastical chanceries needed trained scribes to handle their increasingly large and complex correspondence, for which the old formula collections, dating from the sixth century to the ninth, no longer sufficed.[86] There were indeed new markets for instruction in epistolary technique, but, as the scholarly work of the last few decades has shown, they grew out of a much more organic and widespread process of development.[87]

---

[83]A. Clerval, *Les écoles de Chartres au Moyen Age, du Ve au XVIe siècle* (Paris, 1895; rpt. Frankfurt am M. 1965) 114.

[84]I. S. Robinson, "The 'Colores Rhetorici' in the Investiture Contest," *Traditio* 32 (1976) 231.

[85]Martin Camargo gives a concise but thorough introduction to *ars dictaminis*, with rich bibliography, in *Ars dictaminis, ars dictandi*, Typologie des sources du Moyen Age occidental 60 (Turnhout: Brepols, 1991).

[86]See, for example, E. R. Curtius, *European Literature and the Latin Middle Ages*, trans. Willard R. Trask, Bollingen Ser. 36 (New York: Pantheon, 1953) 75–76.

[87]William D. Patt, "The Early 'ars dictaminis' as Response to a Changing Society," *Viator* 9 (1978) 133–55, with additional bibliography.

Dictaminal manuals typically begin by distinguishing prose from verse and then subdivide prose into two or more kinds, one of which is *epistolae* 'letters', before declaring that they will treat only letters. Since the medieval letter permitted a great variety of form and content, however, the restriction is more apparent than real. As Martin Camargo concludes, "The *ars dictaminis*, then, may be defined as that department of medieval rhetoric which taught the rules for composing letters and other prose documents" (20).

The manuals devote vastly disproportionate attention to the salutation—the only part peculiar to the letter form. To it they apply the classical rhetorical theory of the exordium, emphasizing its function of *captatio benivolentiae*. Numerous sample salutations, arranged by rank of addressee, are usually included. Adjectives and phrases appropriate to various categories of sender and addressee (abbot, bishop, king, pope, etc.) and the relationship between them are offered, sometimes in great numbers. In modern America, one rarely encounters a formal letter salutation other than "Dear So-and-so," to which the simple *salutem* of Cicero's letters is comparable. By the twelfth century, however, a continuous tendency to elaborate the opening greeting had so overloaded it that theorists divided salutation and *captatio benivolentiae* into separate components.

A second important task of dictaminal manuals is to define the parts and proper organization of the letter, and classical *dispositio* is found to govern the letter's organization, just as it did that of the speech. In the body of the letter, the narrative receives the most attention, probably because it shared with the letter form brevity and simplicity as defining characteristics. Advice about *elocutio* 'style' is sprinkled throughout, together with examples of ornamentation; rules for cursus are given, and various kinds of letters may be defined and exemplified. Epistolary brevity is almost certain to be mentioned. A collection of model letters, real or invented or both and (like the sample salutations) arranged by rank of addressee, concludes the handbook; some such collections also circulated independently.

For a sense of the (mostly hidden) tradition of epistolary theory that underlay the *ars dictaminis*, compare the following extracts from (1) the section of epistolary theory at the end of Julius Victor's rhetoric (fourth century); (2) an anonymous paragraph of epistolary theory in the late eighth-century collection of school texts I described earlier; and (3) the *Flores rhetorici* (alternatively titled *Radii dictaminum*) by Alberic of Monte Cassino, written about 1075:[88]

---

[88]*Alberici Casinensis Flores Rhetorici*, ed. M. Inguanez and H. M. Willard, Miscellanea Cassinese 14 (Monte Cassino 1938); trans. Joseph M. Miller (unreliable and misleading) in Miller et al. 131–61. I say "about 1075" simply for convenience: nothing in the *Flores* or in what is known about Alberic's life permits a more precise dating. The passage quoted as (3) below is found in Inguanez and Willard 38; my translation.

(1) If you are writing to a superior, your letter should not be facetious; if to an equal, it should not be discourteous; if to an inferior, not haughty. Do not write carelessly to a learned man, nor negligently to one who is uneducated [. . .]. The openings and closings of letters should be reckoned with an eye to differences in friendship or rank—after taking account of customary usage. (Halm 448)

(2) In letters one must consider who is writing to whom and about what. With regard to who is writing to whom, the attributes of the persons must be noted. These are ten: birth, sex, age, upbringing, education, profession, character, disposition, reputation, and rank. For it makes a great difference whether we are writing to a nobleman, an old man, a magistrate, to a father or a friend, to one who is prospering or one who is sad, and so forth. (Halm 589)

(3) The first consideration should be the nature of the sender and that of the person to whom <the letter> is sent: whether, that is, he is of high rank or low, a friend or an enemy, and finally, what his background and situation are [. . .]. If he is of high rank, it should be written in an elevated style; if humble, in a simple style [. . .]. If a learned man writes to one who is of middling or no learning, you will adapt the words to the powers of the recipient. You will represent a prelate in one way, a subordinate in another.

All three passages assume a knowledge of rhetorical *ethopoeia* and *decorum*, of how to suit one's words and style to sender and recipient and to the occasion. And all three antedate the earliest dictaminal texts. (But anyone who has studied *dictamen* will recognize in each its characteristic preoccupation with the minute differentiation of rank and social position that were of paramount importance in constructing twelfth-century letter salutations).[89]

Alberic of Monte Cassino was a pivotal figure. In the *Flores rhetorici*, he discusses letter-writing in considerable detail, but in the larger context of rhetoric. He begins by treating the parts and structure of a speech and of a letter in exactly parallel fashion and then offers five sample salutations and three model letters before devoting the largest part of the work to rhetorical figures, *colores*. Significantly, he says that people are eager for instruction in how to write letters. A second, longer (and less coherent) work called the *Breviarium* contains not only "letter-specific" material (sample salutations, instructions for and models of papal and imperial letters, including *litterae formatae*) but also material appropriate for general instruction in writing: on synonyms and *variatio*, figurative ways to express praise and blame, ornate ways to express simple thoughts, proverbial ex-

---

[89]See especially Giles Constable, "The Structure of Medieval Society According to the *Dictatores* of the Twelfth Century," in *Law, Church, and Society: Essays in Honor of Stephan Kuttner*, ed. Kenneth Pennington and Robert Somerville (Philadelphia: U of Pennsylvania P, 1977) 253–67.

pressions, and so on. (Alberic's own style ran to the ornate, and so it was child's play for him to convert "Have you eaten?" into "Has your collector [*exactor*, usually 'tax collector'] received his daily debt today?" or "Have you paid the collector his daily debt?" or "Have the rumblings of your gut been extinguished by a sufficient abundance?") Since neither of Alberic's works concentrates exclusively on letters, neither is yet a true *ars dictandi*; but both contain the necessary ingredients.

A rivulet of dictaminal manuals began to appear about 1115, first in northern Italy, and soon swelled to a flood. By the last quarter of the twelfth century the art had spread to France, whence it traveled to England.[90] Hundreds of *artes* are extant, in some 3,000 manuscripts and early printed books from the twelfth through fifteenth centuries, but the enormous task of identifying, cataloguing, describing, and editing them is far from finished.[91] Handbooks of letter-writing instruction and model letters in the vernacular continued to appear throughout Europe for centuries— and indeed, the genre lives on even today, both in print and in computer software offering hundreds of instantly customizable model letters "for all occasions!"

CONCLUSION

The five parts of rhetoric were codified in Hellenistic times as invention, arrangement, style, memory, and delivery; its goal was to speak persuasively. By the end of the first century AD, the grammar curriculum included stylistic ornament (i.e., the study of rhetorical figures) as well as grammatical correctness, and at least some of the *progymnasmata* exercises in composition. Writing exercises required invention and arrangement even when the goal was merely paraphrase of a given subject; memory training was an integral part of all education, and students learned the basics of delivery through presenting their composition exercises orally.

---

[90]Martin Camargo has recently edited five English *artes*, with introductions: *Medieval Rhetorics of Prose Composition: Five English "Artes Dictandi" and Their Tradition* (Binghamton, NY: Medieval & Renaissance Texts & Studies, 1995).

[91]Volume 1, *Von den Anfängen bis um 1200*, of a *Repertorium der Artes dictandi des Mittelalters* prepared by Franz Josef Worstbrock, Monika Klaes, and Jutta Lütten was published in 1992 (Munich: Wilhelm Fink Verlag), and two more volumes are planned. Emil J. Polak has published two of a projected four volumes recording dictaminal manuscripts in libraries worldwide: *Medieval and Renaissance Letter Treatises and Form Letters*, vol. 1: *A Census of Manuscripts Found in Eastern Europe and the Former USSR*; vol. 2: *A Census of Manuscripts Found in Part of Western Europe, Japan and the United States of America*, Davis Medieval Texts and Studies 8, 9 (Leiden: Brill, 1993, 1994). Camargo, *Ars dictaminis* (n. 85 above) records many printed editions both in his notes and in chapter 5, Editions, but comments, "A large proportion of those printed [. . .] are in need of new, modern editions" (51).

(Surely the youth Augustine was expected to do more than "Stand up straight!" and "Don't mumble!" when he delivered his speech in the persona of the goddess Juno.) Already, that is, the dividing line between grammar and rhetoric had shifted to enlarge grammar's mandate very substantially.

Quintilian could almost be said to have outlined in his book 10 (summarized in chapter 2 of this volume) what I have ventured to call a new grammar school curriculum, already taking shape in his own time. There, he advised the now-trained orator how to keep his speaking skills honed by assiduous practice in reading, writing, and speaking. Wide reading, including a certain amount of poetry, history, and philosophy, will, by furnishing one with a rich stock of words and phrases, a variety of figures, and a method of composition (*copia verborum, varietas figurarum, componendi ratio*, 2.1), instill the ability to imitate, which forms a large part of art. One will practice writing, for "It is in writing that eloquence has its roots and foundation" (3.3). One should write slowly and critically at first, revising often. But what to write? For subjects, Quintilian refers the reader back to the sequence of studies prescribed in books 1.9 and 2.4; now, concerned only with acquiring copiousness and the habit or facility (*facilitas*, Greek *hexis*), he recommends translation from Greek, paraphrase of various kinds, theses, proofs and refutations, commonplaces, declamations, history, dialogues, and even (for amusement) verse. Composition teachers should enjoy Quintilian's comments on the writing and revision process (10.3.19–33), which include sensible remarks on the environmental conditions conducive to concentration and the recommendation to write on wax tablets because it is easier to erase.

Since Quintilian's program of education and lifelong practice was designed for professional public speakers, the last two chapters of book 10 are strictly confined to speaking skills. He could not know that classical rhetoric's classical purpose would change with the times. By the fourth century, rhetorical theory had begun to divide into specialized subsets that favored written discourse over oral, and the *ars dictaminis* would later be one of these subsets. After analyzing how the fourth-century rhetorical handbooks "depart from the conceptual framework of earlier Latin theory," Michael Leff describes a trajectory linking them in kind to the rise of *ars dictaminis* some seven hundred years later:

> [W]e have reason to believe that some of the characteristics of medieval rhetorical theory already begin to surface as early as the fourth century, e g : the shift in focus from oral to written discourse, the decline of a holistic conception of the art in favor of a loose borrowing of particular elements of the classical system, and an implicit assumption that rhetoric is something to be used for specialized purposes, that it is not the main organizing force in the liberal education of a citizen. By the fifth and sixth centuries, we can recog-

nize conscious attempts to redefine the subject of rhetoric. Augustine, for example, rejects the civil issue entirely [. . .]. The Middle Ages dispersed the elements of rhetoric into a vast number of learned and practical disciplines, and subsequent attempts to reestablish its integrity have stressed the unity of the art as process, not as substance.[92]

For a diachronic study such as this one, where some of the dots are missing from the lines to be connected and one must rely on drawing inferences, the retarding weight of tradition is a helpful ally. When change comes with glacial slowness, we can safely extrapolate from the known to the unknown. Two examples from letter-writing practice can suffice.

Certain topoi and formulaic expressions, such as the language of conversation and the theme of friendship, recur century after century in real letters and then reappear in the *artes dictandi*. A very common epistolary motif, expressing the essence of the letter's purpose, is *absens praesens* 'absent [in body], present [in spirit]'. This is blended with the biblical injunction (Matt. 19.6, Mark 10.9), "Whom God has joined, let not man separate" to produce "Although a great distance separates us, we are nevertheless joined in spirit." When we then encounter this topos in a model letter in an early twelfth-century *ars dictandi*, the dots almost connect themselves.[93]

Almost miraculously, throughout all those turbulent centuries, the exchange of letters connected and reassured friends and religious communities separated by vast distances. I believe that the enormous popularity of letters and letter collections and the existence of a theory of letter-writing prompted the introduction of school instruction in letter-writing, perhaps even before the fourth century. Hundreds, even thousands, of late antique and early medieval letters preserved in collections reflect acquaintance with traditional epistolary topoi and instruction in proper letter-writing practice. Many such letters read very much like practice compositions, and the extant ninth-century collections of salutation formulas were certainly made for instructional purposes.

Similarly, the link between the study of proverbs in school and their use in letters is established; it remains to find *artes dictandi* recommending the use of proverbs, and indeed they do. I noted earlier that Latin literature is filled with adages and moral *sententiae*, which, gathered into collections, supplied children with their first reading (the *Dicta Catonis*) and writers with material (Publilius Syrus, the *Liber scintillarum*). One *progymnasmata* exercise was to elaborate on a proverb, and it was common in the twelfth century to use a proverb or similar sententious saying to begin a letter, as a

---

[92]Leff 74, 76. Leff's article is followed in the same volume by R. R. Bolgar's highly condensed (7 pages) but masterly survey of "The Teaching of Rhetoric in the Middle Ages."
[93]Lanham, "Freshman Composition" 132–33.

way of announcing its theme. John of Garland's *Parisiana Poetria de arte prosaica, metrica, et rithmica* (c. 1220–1235) is an unusual and very interesting work that attempts, as its title indicates, to combine *ars dictaminis* with *ars poetriae* into a universal art of composition.[94] Under the heading of invention, John offers a collection of about sixty *sententiae* suitable for various epistolary situations (12–19); some of his topical headings, and many more of the sayings, echo those in the *Liber scintillarum*. Further on, he instructs how to begin a letter by announcing its theme with a proverb.

Of late medieval England, Camargo points out that:

> the teachers of grammar in both the universities and the lower schools shared many pedagogical methods with the professional *dictatores*, including the composition of models for letters, the most important prose form. Nicholas Orme quotes from the 1309 statutes of St. Albans School, for example, the requirement that those who wished to attain the dignity of Bachelor "take a proverb from the master and compose verses, model letters and a *rithmus* on the subject [i.e., exercises in the three types of *dictamen*], as well as carrying on a disputation in the school."[95]

We know that a new Latin translation of Aphthonius's *progymnasmata* became very popular in Europe from early in the sixteenth century. If my reconstruction of the early medieval grammar curriculum to include rhetorical instruction in the *progymnasmata* and letter-writing is correct, the continuity from Quintilian to the Tudor grammar school curriculum, described by Don Paul Abbott in chapter 5 of this volume, is seamless. The one missing ingredient was the declamation, the pinnacle of the classical rhetorical curriculum. The humanist scholars of Renaissance Italy restored the oration to popularity, and thence it was imported into the Tudor curriculum, for a (temporary) return to dominance of an oral rhetoric.

Finally, then, what had changed by the end of the eleventh century? Coloring all else, ever since the disintegration of the Roman public schools in the fifth or sixth century, education had been in the hands of a church that sought to spread the Word of God. Second, since about the eighth century, Latin had been a second language for everybody, to be learned systematically in school (by those who went to school) and usually in preparation for a clerical career. For the rest, the content of education changed remarkably little before the twelfth century, except in the early structural shift which transferred some of rhetoric's traditional tasks to

---

[94] Traugott Lawler, ed. and trans., *The "Parisiana Poetria" of John of Garland* (New Haven: Yale UP, 1974) xvi–xvii.

[95] Camargo, *Medieval Rhetorics of Prose Composition* 29, quoting Nicholas Orme, *English Schools in the Middle Ages* (London 1973) 101. Camargo notes ad loc. that lists of proverbs occur in association with several *artes dictandi*, including John of Garland.

grammar. The heritage of classical (i.e., profane or secular) Latin literary texts survived, however precariously (some, in a single manuscript), to be recopied for new readers and imitators during the Carolingian renaissance and later, and the secular content of schooling began to increase. Slow but insistent pressures of social, political, and religious change created a demand for specialized bureaucracies—and what bureaucracy has not needed professional, trained personnel: clerks, letter-writers, document processors? The *ars dictaminis* was the first big change, a pragmatic creation that answered a specific need. As the next chapter of this volume shows, more general innovations in writing instruction were on the way.[96]

---

[96]James J. Murphy discusses the implications for instruction of Latin's "second language" status in the twelfth century, in "The Teaching of Latin as a Second Language in the 12th Century," *Historiographia linguistica* 7.1/2 (1980) 159–75.

Chapter 4

The Teaching of Poetic Composition in the Later Middle Ages

Marjorie Curry Woods

Key Concepts. Artes poetriae • *Matthew of Vendôme* • *Basic school reading texts* • *Gervase of Melkley* • *Suggestiveness of language* • *Descriptive methods* • *Memorization and imitation of poetic texts* • *Detail in small units* • *Attributes of persons* • *Extreme and memorable images* • *Retention of classical rhetoric* • *Student reworking of texts* • *Amplification and abbreviation* • *Geoffrey of Vinsauf* • *Medieval classroom pedagogy* • *Change in teaching order of five parts of rhetoric* • *Tropes and figures* • *Exercises in memory and delivery* • *Connected discourse using figures of words* • *A medieval exercise for modern classrooms* • *Rethinking* letteraturizzazione

---

SETTING THE STAGE

In the last quarter of the twelfth century, Matthew of Vendôme, a prolific poet and pedagogue, wrote a treatise on basic aspects of verse composition for young students. Matthew's *Art of Versifying* was the first example of a new, popular genre of treatise that appeared in Europe at the end of the twelfth century, the *artes poetriae*.[1] While this phrase literally means "arts of poetry," Douglas Kelly in his superb recent study of genre argues rightly that we should refer to these works as *The Arts of Poetry and Prose*.[2] Carol Dana Lanham's detailed study (chapter 3 of this volume), while focusing on the earlier period, gives the reader sufficient information about the following centuries to construct an adequate introductory outline to the teaching of prose composition during the later Middle Ages.[3] But in this essay, I focus on how medieval students were taught verse composition, since poetic composition was a distinctive genre of academic and literary experience for the later Middle Ages when the *artes poetriae* flourished.[4] This foregrounding is made necessary by the humanist and post-humanist emphasis on prose composition and because post-romantic literary tastes and standards run counter to an appreciation of the craft of rhetorical poetry. I want to emphasize what is most distinctive, if perhaps counterintuitive, about the medieval compositional tradition. Besides a focus on verse texts, these medieval principles include the use of shockingly memorable imagery, a concentration on very small units of composition, and a shift in order of the five parts of rhetoric—all for pedagogical effect.

BASIC READING TEXTS

In an age when writing materials were scarce, verse texts were a boon to the teacher because they could be memorized more easily than works in prose.[5] What we would consider prodigious amounts of memorization

---

[1]Although not as popular as Geoffrey of Vinsauf's *Poetria nova*, a similar text written a generation or so later, Matthew's *Ars versficatoria* has survived in nineteen manuscripts, a respectable number (Franco Munari, ed., *Matthei Vindocinensis Opera*, vol. 1: *Catologo dei manoscritti* (Rome: Edizioni di Storia e Letteratura, 1977) 141. The best study of this genre is Douglas Kelly, *The Arts of Poetry and Prose*, Typologie des sources du moyen âge occidental 59 (Turnhout: Brepols 1991); see also James J. Murphy, *Rhetoric in the Middle Ages* (Berkeley: U of California P, 1974) 135–93; and William M. Purcell, *"Artes poetriae": Rhetorical and Grammatical Invention at the Margin of Literacy* (Columbia: U of South Carolina P, 1996).

[2]Besides Kelly, *Arts* 39–40, see on this point James J. Murphy, "Poetry without Genre: The Metapoetics of the Middle Ages," *Poetica: An International Journal of Linguistic-Literary Studies* 11 (1979): 1–8.

[3]Other essays, cited in my notes, describe specific developments in this period, and see Ronald G. Witt, *"In the Footsteps of the Ancients": The Origins of Italian Humanism from Lovato to Bruni* (Leiden: E. J. Brill, 2000).

[4]For a discussion of the teaching of prose composition in England during the period covered in this essay, see Martin Camargo, *Medieval Rhetorics of Prose Composition: Five English "Artes Dictandi" and Their Tradition* and footnote 67.

[5]That it was in verse rather than in prose is probably one of the reasons that Geoffrey of Vinsauf's *Poetria nova* so eclipsed Matthew's work in popularity, surviving in two hundred manuscripts.

were commonplace, and recent scholarship has demonstrated that internalizing textual data was integral to medieval monastic and academic life.[6] The rise of the cathedral schools and the universities and the shift from parchment to paper led to the production of cheaper books, and yet the basic medieval schoolbooks continued to consist of texts that could be easily memorized.

Like their classical counterparts, medieval students wrote composition exercises based on texts that they read in school. From the twelfth century on, there was an extraordinary coherence in the readers on which verbal training was based. One introductory reader, called the *Liber Catonianus*, was a collection of late antique and early medieval short texts that took shape during the tenth through the twelfth centuries and continued in popularity throughout the last centuries of the Middle Ages and, in a slightly different form, well into the Renaissance.[7] In its most widely used configuration it comprises the following books:[8]

1. *Distichs* of Cato (third century).[9]
2. *Eclogue* of Theodulus (tenth century).[10]
3. *Fables* of Avianus (fourth century).[11]

---

[6]See Mary J. Carruthers, *The Book of Memory: A Study of Memory in Medieval Culture* (Cambridge: Cambridge UP, 1990).

[7]The classic study of the evolution of this collection is Marc Boas, "De librorum Catonianorum historia atque compositione," *Mnemosyne* 42 (1914): 17–46. George Hamilton's study, "Theodulus: A Medieval Textbook," *Modern Philology* 7 (1909): 1–17 is still useful, as is the short overview of "Curriculum Authors" in Ernst Robert Curtius, *European Literature and the Latin Middle Ages*, trans. Willard R. Trask (New York: Harper, 1953) 48–54. See also Paul Grendler, *Schooling in Renaissance Italy: Literacy and Learning, 1300–1600* (Baltimore: Johns Hopkins UP, 1989) 111–17 and the introduction by Ian Thomson and Louis Perraud to *Ten Latin Schooltexts of the Later Middle Ages: Translated Selections*, Mediaeval Studies 6 (Lewiston: Edwin Mellen Press, 1990) 1–48. For the versions used in Great Britain, see Nicholas Orme, *English Schools in the Middle Ages* (London: Methuen, 1973) 103–06, and Marjorie Curry Woods and Rita Copeland, "Classroom and Confession," *The Cambridge History of Medieval English Literature*, ed. David Wallace (Cambridge: Cambridge UP, 1999) 376–406.

[8]The specific grouping that I take as exemplary here is from Paul Clogan, ed., *The Medieval "Achilleid" of Statius, Edited with Introduction, Variant Readings, and Glosses* (Leiden: E. J., 1968) 3. Sometimes the order of the last two works was reversed.

[9]Translated in Thomson and Perraud, *Schooltexts* 49–85. See also two articles by Richard Hazelton: "The Christianization of 'Cato': The *Disticha Catonis* in the Light of Late Mediaeval Commentaries," *Mediaeval Studies* 19 (1957): 157–73 and "Chaucer and Cato," *Speculum* 35 (1960): 357–80.

[10]Translated in Thomson and Perraud 110–57. See also Hamilton (cited in footnote 7) and R. P. H. Green, "The Genesis of a Medieval Textbook: The Models and Sources of the *Ecloga Theoduli*," *Viator* 13 (1982): 49–106.

[11]J. Wight Duff and Arnold M. Duff, trans., *Minor Latin Poets* (Cambridge: Loeb Classical Library, 1934) 2: 680–749.

4. *Elegies* of Maximianus (early sixth century).[12]

5. *Achilleid* of Statius (first century).[13]

6. *Rape of Proserpine* of Claudian (fl. c. 400).[14]

This is the reader that students used after mastering the basics of Latin grammar from Donatus. All of the texts are divided into verse units of increasing length that were easy for students to memorize, discuss, and imitate in composition exercises.[15]

A different kind of reading list is outlined by Gervais of Melkley in the preface to his early thirteenth-century *ars poetriae*, *The Art of Versifying*.[16] As Gervais tells us, his work was written for young boys, "the rough ones" (*rudium*).[17] His numerous citations from the *Cosmographia* of Bernardus Silvestris show that such complex, and one would have thought, adult works as this one (more below) could be introduced to beginning students in small units illustrating particular rhetorical techniques. Gervais recommends that older students consult the *Barbarismus* of Donatus, Horace's *Ars poetica*, and the *Rhetorics* of Cicero.[18]

Gervais then praises a group of classical and medieval Latin literary works that were widely used in the schools. They exerted a powerful effect on students such as Gervais:

---

[12] Translated by L. R. Lind in Gabriele Zerbi, *"Gerontocomia": On the Care of the Aged and Maximianus, "Elegies on Old Age and Love"* (Philadelphia: American Philosophical Society, 1988) 309–36.

[13] Statius, *Works*, trans. J. H. Mozley (Cambridge: Loeb Classcial Library, 1969) 2: 508–95. A version of the text with medieval commentary is edited in Clogan, *Medieval Achilleid*.

[14] Translated by Harold Isbell in *The Last Poets of Imperial Rome* (1971; New York: Penguin, 1982) 75–106. See also R. A. Pratt, "Chaucer's Claudian," *Speculum* 22 (1947): 419–29.

[15] For a postulated sequence of medieval exercises based on this reader and resembling the classical series of exercises called *progymnasmata* or *praeexercitamina*, see Woods, "Quintilian and Medieval Teaching," *Quintiliano: Historia y actualidad de la Retorica*, ed. Thomás Albaladejo, Emilio del Rio, and José Antonio Caballero (Logroño: Inst. de Estudios Riojanos; Calahorra: Ayntamiento, 1998) 3: 1531–40. On classical and medieval imitation exercises in general, see Alexandru N. Cizek, *"Imitatio et tractatio": Die literarisch-rhetorischen Grundlagen der Nachahmung in Antike und Mittelalter* (Tübingen: Max Niemeyer, 1994).

[16] Hans-Jurgen Gräbener, ed., Gervais von Melkley, *Ars poetica*, Forschungen zur romanischen Philologie 17 (Münster: Aschendorffsche Verlagsbuchhandlung, 1965); unpublished translation by Catherine Yodice Giles, "Gervais of Melkley's Treatise on *The Art of Versifying* and the Method of Composing in Prose: Translation and Commentary" (PhD Diss., Rutgers U, 1973).

[17] Giles 2; Gräbener 2.2.

[18] Giles 2; Gräbener, 2.2–5. The term "Rhetorics" (*Rhetoricas*) refers to Cicero's *De inventione*, also called the *Rhetorica vetus* (Old Rhetoric), and the Pseudo-Ciceronian *Rhetorica ad Herennium*, known as the *Rhetorica nova* (New Rhetoric).

Master John of Hanville, the breasts of whose teaching nourished my rough infancy,[19] has indeed invented many elegancies, has handed several on to his hearers. In fact in his little book concerning philosophical pilgrimage, which he calls *Architrenius*, he attended to a great many.[20] Indeed, only looking into [his] little book is sufficient to give form to a rough spirit. The same may be said of Claudian, Dares the Phrygian,[21] Bernardus Silvester. The same [may be said] of the ancients—namely Lucan, Statius, and Vergil. You may also learn very much from the little books of Ovid.[22]

Along with another text praised by Gervais, Alan of Lille's *Anticlaudianus*,[23] these works belong to what Douglas Kelly calls the medieval genre of "masterpiece," which provided examples of style and content for students to use in their own writing.[24] One of the most distinctive and, to a modern reader, unexpected aspects of word play in the texts used to teach style and composition to young students during the Middle Ages is the intense figuration and sexual suggestiveness of the language.[25] This factor is present even in the introductory verse reader discussed above, the *Liber Catonianus*. The last work in this collection, Claudian's *Rape of Proserpine*, was famous throughout the Middle Ages as an example of extended description, particularly for its evocation of the paradoxical coupling, through Pluto's "rape" of Proserpine, of darkness with light, death with life. The conversion of the gloomy inhabitants of the underworld into happy wedding guests is symptomatic of the antithetical, oxymoronic quality of the coupling of Pluto with Proserpine:

[19]For other examples of maternal imagery used for male figures, see Caroline Walker Bynum, *Jesus as Mother: Studies in the Spirituality of the High Middle Ages* (Berkeley: U of California P, 1982) 110–69.

[20]Johannes de Hauvilla, *Architrenius*, trans. and ed. Winthrop Wetherbee, Cambridge Medieval Classics 3 (Cambridge: Cambridge UP, 1994).

[21]The narrator of a Latin work purporting to be an eye-witness account of the fall of Troy written by a Trojan, translated by Richard M. Frazer, Jr., in *The Trojan War: The Chronicles of Dictys of Crete and Dares the Phrygian* (Bloomington: Indiana UP, 1966).

[22]Giles 4. On Ovid's "little books" see Ralph Hexter, *Ovid and Medieval Schooling: Studies in Medieval School Commentaries on Ovid's "Ars Amatoria," "Epistulae ex Ponto," and "Epistulae Heroidum,"* Münchener Beiträge zur Mediävistik und Renaissance-Forschung 38 (Munich: Arbeo-Gesellschaft, 1986).

[23]Alan of Lille, *Anticlaudianus or The Good and Perfect Man*, trans. James J. Sheridan (Toronto: Pontifical Inst. of Mediaeval Studies, 1973).

[24]See Kelly, *Arts* 61–64; see also Martin Camargo, "Beyond the *Libri Catoniani*: Models of Latin prose style at Oxford University ca. 1400," *Mediaeval Studies* 56 (1994): 165–87.

[25]See footnote 41.

The furies lost their wrath and made a bowl of wine from which they drank.
The snakes that live on their foreheads lifted their mouths to the wine and
became happy like all the monsters and fiends of Hell.[26]

The physical union of Pluto and Proserpine is not described, but it is antic-
ipated by Pluto's violent rupturing of the earth in his passion to reach the
surface, "When the island of Sicily felt Pluto's blow / and opened herself,"
and it is echoed later when Proserpine's mother dreams "that a spear
pierced the body of her child."[27]

The *Achilleid* of Statius is more direct. Achilles' mother, fearing the pre-
diction of his death in the Trojan War, dresses him in girl's clothing and
hides him in what is virtually a harem, where he is able to rape with impu-
nity the young girl whom he loves, an accepted form of seduction in many
classical texts.[28] The *Achilleid* encompasses cross-dressing, sexual exploration, the literal taking up of arms, and escape from an anxious and protec-
tive mother—a cornucopia of adolescent male fantasies. Although Statius
died with the text unfinished, it ends with the hero's passing from puberty:
"So much do I remember, friends, of the training of my earliest years, and
sweet is their remembrance; the rest my mother knows."[29] During the
Middle Ages, the unfinished text was redivided into five books and given a
final line that brought Achilles' ship to the Trojan shore and, thus, Achilles to his adult male destiny.

Just as startling is the *Eclogue* of Theodulus, which appears at an earlier
position in the reader. This poem is the story of a composition contest between Pseustis, a pagan shepherd "born in Athens" (because, as one of the
glosses says, "that's where there are clever shepherds"[30]), and a shepherd-
ess named Alithea, a "virgin from the seed of David."[31] In each paired qua-
train Pseustis begins with a vignette from classical mythology, such as
Deucalion's flood, which Alithea matches with one from the Old Testament, such as Noah's. Yet the correspondences sometimes involve an almost lurid sensibility. In one pair of stanzas, for example, Pseustis describes the metamorphosis of Phyllis into a cork tree, and the reaction of
her beloved, Demophon, who, "returning there, moistens the trunk with
upturned mouth." Then Alithea answers with the story of Lot's "Faithless

[26]Isbell 93.

[27]Isbell 89, 96. The plural "spears" (*telis*) in the original Latin of the second example
(3.71) is less explicit than Isbel's felicitous rendering.

[28]See Woods, "Rape and the pedagogical rhetoric of sexual violence," *Criticism and Dissent
in the Middle Ages*, ed. Rita Copeland (Cambridge: Cambridge UP, 1996) 56–86.

[29]*Achilleid* 2.166–67.

[30]Bernard D'Utrecht, *Commentum in Theodulum*, ed. R. B. C. Huygens (Spoleto: Centro
Italiano di Studi sull'alto Medioevo, 1977) 1.13.

[31]*Eclogue* 9.

wife," who is turned "Into an effigy of salt—animals lick the rock-crag."[32] These complementary images of licking are unforgettable, and the capping of the first by the moralizing of the second only heightens the visual effect.

Such suggestive sensuality seems not to have bothered medieval teachers or their young students. Most other medieval reading texts used to teach poetic composition also contain explicit sexual imagery. The *Cosmographia* of Bernardus Silvestris, which Gervais of Melkley quotes constantly in his book for young boys and which Douglas Kelly argues was the compositional masterpiece *par excellence* for medieval teachers, is famous for its celebration of natural sexuality. Near the end of this work, which depicts the creation of man in the image of the cosmos, comes the following description:

> The phallus [. . .] carefully rejoins the vital threads severed by the hands of the Fates. Blood sent forth from the seat of the brain flows down to the loins, bearing the image of the shining sperm. Artful Nature molds and shapes the fluid, that in conceiving it may reproduce the forms of ancestors.
>
> The nature of the universe outlives itself, for it flows back into itself, and so survives and is nourished by its very flowing away. For whatever is lost only merges again with the sum of things, and that it may die perpetually, never dies wholly.[33]

Texts used for instructing older students were sometimes more judgmental; Ovid needed to be "moralized" for adults but not for children learning to read and write from his texts.[34] Alan of Lille's *Plaint of Nature* is a sequel to the *Cosmographia* that, like the *Poetria nova*, was widely used as a university text in central Europe in the fifteenth century.[35] In it, Nature laments the condition of the created world and especially the prevalence of male homosexuality:

---

[32]*Eclogue* 111, 116. Unpublished translation by Harry Butler and Sandra Bernhard. Thomson and Perraud do not convey the image of licking (in which the similarity of the story resides) in the first example. They render line 111, "Ille reversus eo truncum rigat ore," as "He returns to the spot and waters the trunk with tears from his upturned face" (*Schooltexts* 131).

[33]*The "Cosmographia" of Bernardus Silvestris*, trans. Winthrop Wetherbee (New York: Columbia UP, 1973) 126. This description balances the focus on female creativity—dark, chaotic and formless—with which the work opens. I am indebted to Wetherbee for pointing out this complementarity.

[34]Cf. Hexter, *Ovid and Medieval Schooling* 10–11.

[35]For evidence of the teaching of *The Plaint of Nature* in medieval universities, see Jeanne Elizabeth Krochalis, "Alain de Lille: *De planctu Nature*; Studies towards an Edition" (PhD Diss., Harvard University, 1973), esp. 535–42. On the teaching of the *Poetria nova* at universities, see Woods, "An Unfashionable Rhetoric in the Fifteenth Century," *Quarterly Journal of Speech* 75 (1989): 312–30, and "A Medieval Rhetoric Goes to School—and to the University," *Rhetorica* 9 (1991): 55–65.

The active sex shudders in disgrace as it sees itself degenerate into the passive sex. A man turned woman blackens the fair name of his sex. The witchcraft of Venus turns him into a hermaphrodite. He is subject and predicate; one and the same term is given a double application. Man here extends too far the laws of grammar. Becoming a barbarian in grammar, he disclaims the manhood given him by nature. Grammar does not find favour with him; he prefers a trope. This transposition [a pun on *translatio*, or metaphor, and the reversal of the "natural" sexual position], however, cannot be called a trope. The figure here more correctly falls into the category of defects.[36]

But analogies with the correct use of language could also be made on behalf of homosexuality. John Boswell argues that Alan of Lille's diatribe may have been an attempt to counter a devastatingly simple grammatical argument for same-sex love from the "Debate Between Ganymede and Helen," a debate poem on homosexual versus heterosexual sex that "was recited aloud to students and known by heart by many educated persons."[37]

> [. . . T]he right way is like with like.
> Man can be linked to man in an elegant conjunction.
> If you don't know this, look at the gender of adjectives;
> Grammar dictates that masculines go with masculines.[38]

This fascination with connections between the body and language served several pedagogical purposes, as is shown in the next section.

THE ARTS OF POETRY AND PROSE

The *artes poetriae*, too, revel in passages of what could be considered objectionable content. Following, for example, is the first part of a famous description from Matthew of Vendôme's *Art of Versification*:[39]

> Beroe is a mangy cur, a pallid social outcast,
> Horrid in appearance, the work of a nature gone mad.
> She is another Tesiphone, a public disgrace.
> A mere specter, she is weighed down with wasting away.
> Her body is filthy to look at and repulsive to touch.

---

[36]Alan of Lille, *The Plaint of Nature*, trans. James J. Sheridan (Toronto: Pontifical Inst. of Mediaeval Studies, 1980) I, meter 1.

[37]John Boswell, *Christianity, Social Tolerance, and Homosexuality: Gay People in Western Europe from the Beginning of the Christian Era to the Fourteenth Century* (Chicago: U of Chicago P, 1980) 256, 250, n. 60.

[38]Translated by Thomas Stehling and James J. Wilhelm in *Gay and Lesbian Poetry: An Anthology from Sappho to Michelangelo*, ed. Wilhelm (New York: Garland, 1995) 181.

[39]Matthew's work is one of the major medieval sources for J. N. Adams, *The Latin Sexual Vocabulary* (Baltimore: Johns Hopkins UP, 1982).

Her itching neck denies her hand any rest.
The itch covers her head like a close-fitting cap,
And flies complain they find not a scrap of food.
Her head is bald and her parched skin like rust.
Dirt flows down her menacing brow—pale and unsightly.
Bushy brows bristling above bleary eyes make the upper
Half of her face a thicket of grime and filth.
Her eyebrows reaching down to cover her nose
Vainly try to offset a thin and wasted neck.
Her ears are packed with dirt; only the eyes
Do not seem to teem with worms. From them slime drips.
Her pale eyes have bloody matter running from them.
As soon as her bleary eyes seem dry of filth,
They fill up again and about her buzz hungry flies
Which her eyelids like mousetraps imprison in little baskets
Of foul matter. Her fetid flat nose that lies along
Her face at a distorted angle drips pestilential mucus.
This flow keeps her upper lip wet as the thick froth
From her nose returns to its diseased host.
Beroe's wretched cheeks are stiff and cracked with wrinkles;
In this forest of wrinkles one can spot her eyes by
The rheumy sickness welling up in them. Her drooping
Lips grow pale as her Stygian saliva manures her mouth's
Curving lines. A film covers her teeth, which are
Doubly destroyed by her stinking breath and by worms.[40]

Matthew refers to his audience as "listeners"; for the full effect of this set piece the entire passage (the second half is quoted below) should be read out loud. It is particularly effective when read to its intended audience of adolescent boys, for whom descriptions of physical grossness can be peculiarly alluring as well as repelling. Thus, the passages of relentless scurrility in his work are probably a deliberate pedagogical technique meant to intrigue the student.[41] As Mary Carruthers notes about another work,

---

[40]Matthew of Vendôme, *The Art of Versification*, trans. Aubrey E. Galyon (Ames: Iowa State UP, 1980) 1.58.

[41]Cf. Kelly, *Arts* 91–92: "Indeed, the variety of subjects used in the illustrations—from the lofty to the obscene, the holy to the profane—is precisely what might alternately edify or entertain teen-age schoolboys and hold their attention." I concentrate here on the more "entertaining" imagery. On specific kinds of imagery directed at male adolescents during the thirteenth and fourteenth centuries, see Susan Einbinder, "The Voice from the Fire: The Medieval Literature of Jewish Martyrdom": "Among the more educated [members of the audience of lament poems, which were composed for recitation in synagogue settings], a core of adolescent and young adult men would have taken keen pleasure in exercising their wits to complete truncated verses and fill in the exegetical associations evoked by the poetic text. At the same time, images of pollution, with their own range of associations (many sexual) and polemical vulgarity would have had their own appeal." (Essay in preparation, quoted with permission.) For more on male adolescence, see William C. Jordan, "Adolescence and Con-

"[. . .] Prudentius' *Psychomachia* is designedly disgusting and morbid because it is those qualities that make it memorable, particularly for the novice, schoolboy minds for which it was written."[42]

To us, this passage from Matthew's work is noteworthy for its agism and
misogyny. But almost lost in the mass of disgusting detail is the format of
the description. Using the kind of prescriptive structure that medieval
composition teachers favored, Matthew proceeds from head to toe in the
rest of the passage, which follows immediately after the section just quoted:

> Her scabbiness extends down that repulsive mass of knots,
> Sores, and streaming corruption called a neck. Enlarged veins
> Draw and crisscross her chest, while the flabby skin
> Of her breasts makes them look like deflated bladders.
> She is nothing but skin and bones.
> Her stomach swells out with sores which
> The nearby Lethe, the doorway to her lower regions,
> Stirs up. Oh wretched chaos of a woman! Even her
> Height is contracted by a a dreadful hump which,
> To speak briefly, makes her back puff out.
> Her chamber pot bristling with worn-out hairs is
> A turbulent lake, and the waters of that sulphurous whirlpool
> Run red. To gaze on her body is horrible—there
> The underworld lies hidden, a lake brimming with filth.
> The joints of her knees are stiff, yet
> They are steeped in a painful flow of burning pus.
> Her mangy shins are worm-eaten, and her gouty feet so
> Painful that each toe suffers as though it were a foot.[43]

I give Matthew's description of Beroe in its entirety because it conveys,
better than any set piece in a modern composition handbook, the impact
of concrete, specific, seemingly individual detail. Yet, just after this passage Matthew declares:

> Listeners [. . .] should try to bear firmly in mind that in the descriptions
> given above they are to understand the general techniques of descriptions by

---

version in the Middle Ages: A Research Agenda," forthcoming in John van Engen and
Michael A. Signer, eds., *In the Shadow of the Millennium.*

[42]Carruthers continues: "That, at least, was the assumption in ancient pedagogy When
the novice John Cassian [. . .] had trouble forgetting the epic stories which his *pedagogus* instilled in him as a child, he remembered most powerfully *exactly* the disgusting and bloody
parts, the 'images of warring heroes' that turned unbidden before his mental eye as he
prayed the liturgy or tried to meditate on his psalms." *The Craft of Thought: Meditation, Rhetoric, and the Making of Images, 400–1200* (Cambridge: Cambridge UP, 1998) 144; see also
101–102.

[43]Matthew of Vendôme, *Art* 1.58.

means of examples involving specific persons; otherwise their understanding of the material will not be what the writer intends [. . .]. Therefore, those characteristics which are attributed [. . .] to various persons who are described should be understood, not as peculiar characteristics of those particular persons, but as characteristics that may apply to other persons of the same social status, age, rank office, or sex.[44]

Matthew's example and subsequent remarks demonstrate several of the key characteristics of medieval composition pedagogy:

1. a concept of character types organized around principles of behavior appropriate to general classes of persons (the Attributes of Persons, also called Circumstantiae, found in classical composition theory as well);[45]
2. the use of extreme and hence memorable images;[46]
3. a focus on small units of composition (set pieces illustrating a particular technique or approach) compiled by aggregation from even smaller units (lines or images separable from the work at hand and suitable for reuse in other compositions).[47]

Matthew's work, and the other examples of the genre that followed, reformulated—or rather repackaged—compositional doctrine and rhetorical techniques that teachers had been using for centuries. The accretion of commentaries around Horace's *Ars poetica*, Cicero's *De inventione*, and the Pseudo-Ciceronian *Rhetorica ad Herennium* had provided a contextual framework for these works that allowed them to be employed in medieval classrooms very different from the classical environments in which, and for which, they had been composed.[48] The medieval Arts of Poetry and Prose retained the classical figures and tropes, the five parts of rhetoric (Invention, Arrangement, Style, Memorization, and Delivery), and the concept of elaborating character and action according to set types (Attributes or Circumstances). The focus of the medieval treatises was on very small units of composition. This microscopic approach to composition reinforced the style characteristic of much medieval artistic prose and verse:

---

[44]Matthew of Vendôme, *Art* 1.60. Douglas Kelly remarks that "The importance of the proper name among the *loci* suggests strikingly the intention to typify, to generalize, rather than to individualize, that characterizes material style as *descriptio*" (*Arts* 74).

[45]See Woods and Copeland, "Classroom and Confession."

[46]In addition to those works mentioned above in notes 41 and 42, see also Carruthers, *Book of Memory* 133–34.

[47]Kelly, *Arts* 38–39; 85–88.

[48]Kelly, *Arts* 47–50; see also Elza C. Tiner, "Elements of Classical and Medieval Rhetoric in the Teaching of Basic Composition," *Virginia English Bulletin* 41 (1991): 114–20.

repetition and variation of words and phrases as well as of larger structural units that resulted in set pieces clearly divisible into couplets, individual lines of verse, and even half lines. That these same compositional techniques are employed to great effect by modern commercial advertising indicates the psychological insight of such a focus.

MEDIEVAL STUDENT COMPOSITIONS

Surviving manuscripts of medieval school compositions illustrate how students reworked material from the texts that they read.[49] Most are based on the works of Ovid, especially the *Metamorphoses*, whose interwoven narratives provided medieval teachers with perfect topics for short composition assignments, such as the story of Queen Niobe (based on *Metamorphoses* 6:146–312). Bruce Harbert, the most recent editor of a famous manuscript containing medieval rhetorical treatises and student compositions, Glasgow Hunterian MS V.8.14,[50] summarizes Niobe's story as follows: "Niobe, wife of Tantalus, was proud that she had more children than Latona, mother of Apollo and Diana. Apollo and Diana punished her by killing all her children and turning her to stone."[51] A pair of thirteenth-century student compositions on Niobe in the Hunterian manuscript show contrasting methods of reacting to her. The longer of the two is an exercise in using the Figures of Words in which the first three couplets of the poem demonstrate the first three of these rhetorical figures: *repetitio*, repetition of the first words of successive phrases or clauses; *conversio*, repetition of

---

[49]See also the description of Bernard of Chartres's teaching methods quoted by Lanham in chapter 3 of this volume.

[50]This manuscript is an important collection that also contains most of the late twelfth- and early thirteenth-century treatises on verse composition. The collection is analyzed and some of the student poems are described by Edmond Faral in "Le manuscrit 511 du 'Hunterian Museum' de Glasgow," *Studi medievali* n.s. 9 (1936): 18–119. More recently, Bruce Harbert edited all of the poems in the manuscript except the composition treatises in *A Thirteenth-Century Anthology of Rhetorical Poems: Glasgow MS Hunterian V.8.14* (Toronto: Centre for Medieval Studies, 1975). Following Faral, Harbert argues that one and possibly two groups of shorter poems in the manuscript are student compositions (4). The pair of student poems discussed here are nos. 24–25 in Harbert and 23–24 in Faral.

[51]Harbert, *Anthology* 30. Michael Winterbottom on the importance of the theme in the ancient schools: "[W]hat might Niobe say over the bodies of her dead children" was a "regular feature of the Greek progymnasmata or preliminary rhetorical exercises" (*Roman Declamation* [Bristol: Bristol Classical Press, 1980] 52). On another important Art of Poetry and Prose found in this manuscript, the *Documentum de modo et arte dictandi et versificandi*, and its relation to a later treatise of unknown authorship, the *Tria sunt*, see Martin Camargo, "*Tria sunt*: The Long and the Short of Geoffrey of Vinsauf's *Documentum de modo et arte dictandi et versificandi*," *Speculum* 74 (1999): 935–55.

the last words of successive phrases or clauses; and *complexio*, repetition of the first and last words of successive phrases or clauses.[52]

> **How** stupid, **how** insane, **how** wicked it is to vex the gods,
> you teach by your cry, O Daughter of Tantalus.
> You are in heart **swollen**, in speech **swollen**, in deed **swollen**
> as you prepare to surpass Latona's progeny with your own.
> **Why** do you do **this**? **Why** do you affect **this**? **Why** do you believe that
> you can profit in **this**?[53]

The companion piece to this poem, only six lines long, emphasizes in abbreviated form the emotional and dramatic aspects of Niobe's self-absorption:

> Famous Niobe—prolific, powerful, generous—
> scatters wealth, rejoices in offspring, recounts her ancestors.
> With her husband a king, with her face a dowry, with her stock from the gods,
> she holds herself better than her people because of her offspring, and
> she swells with pride.
> Her husband Amphion begins to swell just like the progenitor of his ancestors
> on the genealogical tree—she the granddaughter, he the son of Jove.[54]

Although both poems about Niobe are relatively short, as is appropriate for student composition assignments, Faral notes that they are complementary in length as well as focus and treatment. They constitute a set pair of examples of school exercises in amplification and abbreviation, with appropriately different techniques and approaches.[55] They are also rather judgemental about Niobe, although other evidence indicates that some

---

[52] The Figures of Words are patterns of placing or shaping words, or emphasizing similarities between them, within short units of discourse ranging from a few words to a few sentences.

[53] Harbert, *Anthology* poem 24.1–6 (emphasis mine). Unpublished translation by Cheryl Eve Salisbury and Wilma Wierenga quoted with permission. Edmond Faral, an earlier editor of the manuscript, identified twenty-one figures in this poem of forty-six lines, some of which, as he points out, are also identified in the margin of the manuscript (Faral, "Le manuscrit 511" 34–36).

[54] Unpublished translation by Asa Gopal of Harbert 25.1–6 quoted with permission.

[55] Faral, "Le manuscrit 511" 36. For the compositional techniques of amplification and abbreviation, see *"Poetria nova" of Geoffrey of Vinsauf*, trans. Margaret F. Nims (Toronto: Pontifical Inst. of Medieval Studies, 1967) 24–42. There is a second translation in Ernest Gallo, *The "Poetria nova" and Its Sources in Early Rhetorical Doctrine* (The Hague: Mouton, 1971), and a third, by Jane Baltzell Kopp, appeared in *Three Medieval Rhetorical Arts*, ed. James J. Murphy (Berkeley: U of California P, 1971).

compositional assignments asked students to empathize with characters of different ages, genders, and social status from their own.[56]

Another group of student poems in this manuscript, including some written by Gervais of Melkley himself when he was at school, are based on a story from Ovid with more obvious student appeal: Pyramus and Thisbe (*Metamorphoses* 4.55–167). These adolescent lovers thwart their parents' desire to keep them apart by communicating through a chink in the wall separating their houses; a nighttime tryst under a mulberry tree ends in their deaths.[57] Robert Glendenning notes that the story of Pyramus and Thisbe "occupied a privileged place in the curriculum of a number of important schools in France, Germany, and probably England in the decades before and after 1200 [. . .]." He continues: "Although other pairs of lovers were certainly well known and often treated in medieval literature, I can find no other theme so often attested as a basis for the learning of grammar and rhetoric. The exposure of boys in early adolescence to this morally ambiguous theme, precisely in connection with the use of rhetoric, with its many antithetical devices for exploring irony and paradox, is a subject of considerable interest in itself [. . .]."[58] Matthew of Vendôme wrote a school poem on the same topic in which he elaborated endlessly on the topic of the lovers' "one heart in two bodies"[59]:

> Pyramus and Thisbe are two, and yet not two. One love joins them both, and does not allow their being two. They are two and yet not two, because they are one in mind, one in trust, one in spirit, one in love [. . .]. They are two, they are one. So are they two in body but one in mind, and so does a single love unite the two. Equals in intelligence, they are blessed by an equal beauty, an equal grace of manner, an equal claim to high birth, and equal reputation for piety. Their outward forms are similar; only their sex dares by its difference to make them unequal, equal as they are otherwise in all other ways.[60]

That this image was sufficient to identify the story is clear from a marginal gloss in one of the manuscripts of Geoffrey of Vinsauf's *Poetria nova*. In his example of digression, Geoffrey begins with a reference to two lovers:

---

[56]See Woods, "Weeping for Dido: Epilogue on a Premodern Rhetorical Exercise in the Postmodern Classroom," forthcoming in *Latin Grammar and Rhetoric: Classical Theory and Medieval Practice*, ed. Carol Dana Lanham.

[57]The version of the story best known to modern audiences is, of course, the rehearsal of the play of "Pyramus and Thisbe" in Shakespeare's *A Midsummer Night's Dream*.

[58]Robert Glendenning, "Pyramus and Thisbe in the Medieval Classroom," *Speculum* 61 (1986): 71. See also Thomson and Perraud, *Schooltexts* 217–26; 232 36.

[59]Glendenning, "Pyramus and Thisbe" 60, 62. According to Glendenning, Matthew's poem and one by Gervais on the same subject using the same image are part of the tradition of lyrics, many of which were produced in medieval schools, that helped to convert the topos of "one mind in two bodies" from one describing intense male friendship to one evoking heterosexual love (73).

[60]Thomson and Perraud, *Schooltexts* 227.

"The bond of a single love bound together two hearts; a strange cause divided them one from the other. But before they were parted, lips pressed kisses on lips; a mutual embrace holds and enfolds them both."[61] This description induced a reader of a thirteenth-century copy of the *Poetria nova* in Paris, Bibliothèque Nationale Fonds Latin Manuscript 8171, to identify the story in the margin as that of Pyramus and Thisbe ("[. . .] *fabulam de piramo et tisbe*"; fol. 10v).[62] Thematically related to this image is Matthew's emphasis on the essential equality of the two lovers; that they are a matched pair. The story of Pyramus and Thisbe, with their escape from home, blurring of gender-limited personal traits, and romantic double suicide, was an excellent complement to the more remote topic of Niobe: queen, wife, and mother. Yet both composition assignments focus on the rhetorical development of imagined emotions based on reactions to characters from classroom readings.

After working for some time on short assignments based on single subjects, students learned to appreciate the larger structure of works. For example, the version of a teacher's commentary on the *Poetria nova* intended for older students emphasizes the author's effective transitions from part to part, "like Ovid's from story to story."[63] These transitions in the *Poetria nova* are noteworthy because the work itself is interpreted as having a double structure: it is organized according to both the five parts of rhetoric and the six parts of a rhetorical discourse.[64] When studying narrative poems, too, older students were taught to analyze and, we can assume, imitate rhetorical *dispositio* (arrangement) in terms of both natural and artificial order. They learned that the *Aeneid* displays artificial order by beginning *in mediis rebus*, but it also demonstrates natural order when the first six books are interpreted as an illustration of the six stages of a man's life.[65] Such double structures were particularly prized and emphasized during the later Middle Ages.[66] It was not until university that students

---

[61]*Poetria nova*, trans. Nims 35.

[62]In some manuscripts, however, the pair are glossed as two men.

[63]Woods, ed. and trans., *An Early Commentary on the "Poetria nova" of Geoffrey of Vinsauf* (New York: Garland, 1985) 67, from the gloss on line 737.

[64]"And the book consists, in a secondary of these six parts of a discourse. Primarily, however, it consists of the five parts of rhetoric." Woods· *Early Commentary* 5, from the *accessus*, or introduction, to the commentary.

[65]See the preface and the summaries of each book in *The Commentary on the First Six Books of Virgil's "Aeneid"* by Bernardus Silvestris, trans. Earl G. Schreiber and Thomas E. Maresca (Lincoln: U of Nebraska P, 1979) 3–4, 6, 16, 17, 24, and 28. (The attribution to Bernardus Silvestris has been challenged; see Christopher Baswell, "The Medieval allegorization of the 'Aeneid': MS Cambridge, Peterhouse 158," *Traditio* 41 (1985): 181–237.

[66]See Woods, "*Verba* and *Sententia* and Matter and Form in Medieval Lectures on Poetic Composition," *The Uses of Manuscripts in Literary Studies: Essays in Memory of Judson Boyce Allen*, ed. Charlotte Cook Morse, Penelope Reed Doob, and Marjorie Curry Woods, Studies in Medieval Culture 31 (Kalamazoo: Medieval Inst. Publications, 1992) 19–39.

learned a comparative theory of rhetoric broadly applicable to various kinds of texts.[67] Such polarization of the techniques of teaching rhetoric and composition to older and younger students might seem strange to us, nourished as we are on the humanist tradition, which tries to find means whereby a certain decorous control over language can be maintained. But the polarization of medieval teaching does make possible the fulfillment of the most extreme aspects of the appropriation of codes of discourse.[68]

I would like to suggest, then, that actual medieval classroom practice in composition followed a different order for the five parts of rhetoric from that found in both classical and medieval rhetorical theory. In rhetorical treatises, the parts of rhetoric are treated in the following standard order: (a) elaborating parts of the subject (*inventio* 'invention'), (b) organizing the parts (*dispositio* 'arrangement'), and (c) putting the subject into words (*elocutio* 'style'). These are followed by (d) memorization (*memoria*) and (e) delivery (*pronuntiatio*). But in the medieval classroom, composition exercises for young students began with (c) examples of the tropes and figures, or *elocutio*, accompanied always by exercises in (d) memory and (e) delivery. Then students proceeded to (b) the study of larger structures, or *dispositio*, and only at the end to (a) methods of generating more material for longer and longer works, or *inventio*.[69] Such a sequence is unexpected since we interpret the traditional progression of the parts of rhetoric as chronological rather than programmatic. Nevertheless, the medieval approach was pedagogically sound: recent work in teaching children how to write poetry demonstrates the importance of specific words, word-play, repetition, and performance in their initial creative endeavors.[70]

---

[67]See Woods, "A Medieval Rhetoric Goes to School." When the *Poetria nova* was used to teach composition at university, it was prose composition, specifically the composition of letters, to which it was applied. For the development of the *artes dictaminis*, or arts of letter-writing written specifically for this purpose, see chapter 3 of this volume by Carol Dana Lanham; and Martin Camargo, "Toward a Comprehensive Art of Written Discourse: Geoffrey of Vinsauf and the *Ars Dictaminis*," *Rhetorica* 6 (1988): 167–94. For further information on this genre, consult the works discussed in Camargo, *Ars Dictaminis, Ars Dictandi.* Typologie des sources du moyen âge occidental 60 (Brepols: Turnhout, 1991).

[68]The medieval polarization of learning about discourse seems to me in some ways analogous to Freud's primary and secondary processes; a discussion of Freud that is useful in this context is Kaja Silverman, *The Subject of Semiotics* (New York: Oxford UP, 1983) especially 77–86. Such an analogy becomes especially important when we remember that, after about the eighth century, all medieval students were learning to appropriate a new language in their rhetorical training; see James J. Murphy, "The Teaching of Latin as a Second Language in the Twelfth Century," *Historiographia Linguistica* 7 (1980): 159–75.

[69]See Kelly, "The Scope of the Treatment of Composition in the Twelfth- and Thirteenth-Century Arts of Poetry," *Speculum* 41 (1966): 261–78; and Camargo, "Rhetoric" 107.

[70]See, for example, Elizabeth McKim and Judith W. Steinbergh, *Beyond Words: Writing Poems with Children* (Green Harbor: Wampeter P, 1983).

A MEDIEVAL EXERCISE FOR THE MODERN CLASSROOM[71]

While late medieval teachers may have been surprisingly openminded in their choice of reading material for the classroom, they were extraordinarily rigid in the structural requirements that they demanded of their students in composition assignments. After experimenting with this combination of approaches in my own classrooms, I have come to believe that the medieval practice of employing model texts and composition exercises that combine the retelling of known themes, virtuoso displays of highly figured language, and potentially controversial images can be particularly successful in the modern classroom.

If surviving texts are an indication of degree of attention to a particular technique, one of the most popular medieval writing assignments was to produce a piece of connected discourse in verse using all of the Figures of Words in their traditional order.[72] This exercise, which I call the Display of Figures, is known to us both from extant student exercises, such as the first Niobe poem discussed above, and from models in rhetorical teachers' handbooks. The most famous example of the latter is Geoffrey of Vinsauf's summary in the *Poetria nova* of the Christian Bible's story of man's fall and redemption. Geoffrey's first three figures are rendered in Margaret Nims' translation as follows:

> **Deed** so evil! **Deed** more evil than others! **Deed** most evil of all deeds! O **apple**! wretched **apple**! Miserable **apple**! **Why** did it affect you, that tasting **of Adam**? **Why** do we all weep for the fault of that one man, **of Adam**?[73]

This initial pattern of *repetitio*, *conversio*, and *complexio* is distinctive and highly recognizable at the beginning of this exercise, as we saw in the first of the student compositions on Queen Niobe quoted earlier.

A third example, this time in prose, has recently been discovered by Martin Camargo. Like the excerpt from the *Poetria nova*, it is found in a teacher's manual.[74] Its subject is praise of a certain Bartholomew, and the first three figures are as follows, given first in Latin because I have been unable to reproduce the figures in the English translation.

---

[71]Some parts of this section of the essay are used with permission in "Weeping for Dido."

[72]A case can be made for employing the above-mentioned Pyramis and Thisbe exercise. But the Display of Figures is more widely applicable and useful in the modern classroom, for reasons that I describe below.

[73]Nims, *Poetria nova* 56.

[74]The exercise serves as Part II of an "Encomium Illustrating The Rhetorical Colors," which part has survived in at least five manuscripts; the version quoted here is from an English manuscript copied in the early thirteenth century: Cambridge, Trinity College MS R.14.40. Camargo is in the process of identifying the author and editing the treatise, and I am grateful to him for providing me with his transcription and allowing me to quote from it here.

Tota mens Pyeridum, **tota** Eliconis armonia, **tota** Parnasi prudentia in consecrati gratiam spirent opusculi. Arguto police citharam tangat fidibus fisus **Apollo**. Per tonos et semitona, per concordes uocum discordias sublimis spiret **Apollo**. Ad animandum cohortem musicam in aplausus melicos totus sit **Apollo**. **Quis** aureo Apollinis plectro modificandus? **Bartholomeus**. **Quis** consona trium armoniarum dissonantia intonandus? **Bartholomeus**. **Quis** choreis Elyconiadum psallendus? **Bartholomeus**.[75]

[Let **all** the insight of the Muses, **all** the harmony of the Helicon, **all** the knowledge of Parnassus contribute to the occasion of this devoted little work. May **Apollo**, trusted by the faithful, pluck this lyre with a resonant thumb. May exalted **Apollo** breathe through the tones and the semitoned, through the harmonious dissonances of sounds. May **Apollo** apply himself wholly to moving his musical retinue to lyric applause [measures?]. **Who** is to be molded by the golden instrument of Apollo? **Bartholemew**. **Who** is to be intoned by the concordant dissonance of the three harmonies? **Bartholomew**. **Who** is to be serenaded by the meters of the Muses? **Bartholomew**.]

For more than a decade, I have included this exercise as part of a series of written assignments in two undergraduate courses, one on rhetoric and style and one on medieval literature in translation, at two different universities.[76] It is by far the most structured of any rhetorical exercise—ancient, medieval, or early modern—that I have come across, but much of its suc-

---

[75]Medieval spelling retained: Pyeridum = Pieridum; police = pollice; aplausus = applausus.

[76]The written assignments in the rhetoric class, all adapted from pre- or early modern rhetoric handbooks, are the following:

1. Translate two paragraphs of academic prose taken from one of the class readings into dialogue form, either using characters and setting from an assigned Platonic dialogue or creating new ones.
2. Translate two pages of a Platonic dialogue into academic prose, taking as a model two paragraphs from the source used for the first "translation" assignment. Imitate as closely as possible the construction of the sentences, vocabulary, and diction of the academic piece.
3. Write your own defense of Helen of Troy.
4. Rewrite one of the reading assignments as a fable of no more than one page.
5. Summarize in one page or less one of the longer reading assignments. Summarize the same work in one sentence.
6. [The sixth assignment is the one discussed in this essay.]
7. Using Erasmus's exercise from *De copia* as a model, write one sentence 75-100 different ways.
8. Using as a model one of the Shakespearean passages brought in by each member of the class, imitate the form, structure, and diction as much as possible while creating an original context and characters.

All of the exercises are read aloud in class for comment and reaction.

cess lies in its very rigidity. My modern students must, like medieval students before them, write connected discourse using the Figures of Words in a specific order.[77] An experiment in which I allowed students more freedom in choosing the order was disastrous. Choice produced anxiety, and students rarely were able to find a place for each of the figures: there were always a few left over. When students are required follow a fixed order, however, they have always been able to do so. This structure provides a kind of security, a mask behind which the students can hide while displaying their virtuosity—often focusing on a person of a different age, gender, or status. Significantly, the premodern topic of Niobe discussed earlier incorporates all of these changes, if we can assume that the student who composed it was an adolescent boy.

Like the medieval student, the modern student must choose for the subject a character or situation from one of the works read as a class assignment. The reasons for this become clear when the students share their compositions with each other. First, the extremely structured nature of the exercise generates sentences of dense figuration and heightened emotional content. Since one is literally ornamenting, or "coloring," the chosen text by developing it through the Figures of Words, the audience best perceives and feels the rhetorical development when the story or base line is known to them. That is, the reader or listener re-experiences internally the base text or story at the same time that the ornamented, often much altered version is being read, or preferably heard.[78] Second, this dimen-

---

For the class on medieval literature in translation, students write three papers, for each one of which the student has the choice of a modern analytical or a medieval rhetorical assignment. The three rhetorical assignments are typically the following:

1. Rewrite a passage of two or three pages of one of the assigned works in the style of one of the others.
2. [The second assignment is the one discussed in this essay.]
3. Amplify in the style of Chrétien de Troyes an incident in one of the highly abbreviated texts of Marie de France; or abbreviate in the style of Marie de France one of the amplified romances by Chrétien de Troyes.

[77]Geoffrey of Vinsauf uses the thirty-five Figures of Words in the order established in book 4 of the pseudo-Ciceronian *Rhetorica ad Herennium*, while the author of the Bartholomew exercise uses a slightly shorter list of examples, as does the author of the student exercises on Niobe. (The student's order is also based on magisterial authority, however; see Faral, "Le manuscrit 511" 36.) Rigid order served a mnemonic function for students who would have been expected to know all of the figures of words by heart. I recommend using the order in the *Rhetorica ad Herennium* and the *Poetria nova* because of its historical importance and because I suspect that there may be psychological and pedagogical effects created by this order.

[78] This combination of anticipation and reaction is another reason why each student must follow the same order.

sion of the exercise takes advantage of one of the most problematic aspects of courses that are built around influential texts from the premodern periods: encoded values, relationships, and power structures often personally offensive to modern students.[79] Yet, rewriting a known text demands that the student study intensely the "base" or "shared" (I avoid the term "original" here) version in order to rewrite it successfully.

Nevertheless, the exercise also encourages the student to make radical changes in that version. In order to take advantage of the heightened emotional resonance of the densely figured language that they are required to produce, students usually adopt an intensely emotional—whether serious or not—persona for the point of view being expressed. Their versions often involve changes in age, gender, power, and sexual orientation in the base text—a modern version, perhaps, of the focus on sexual language in the medieval classroom. This modern version of a medieval rhetorical exercise almost always becomes my students' favorite written assignment, and it is the assignment whose products I have come to anticipate most in my courses.

REWRITING THE PAST FOR THE FUTURE

My own experience in the classroom as a teacher who has used medieval methods of teaching composition, albeit with an inevitably modern sensibility, has encouraged me to challenge key issues, values, and judgments in the modern study and appropriation of the classical rhetorical tradition. In an earlier version of this essay, I outlined some of what I consider to be problematic if unintended conclusions to be drawn from an uncritical acceptance of the concept of the *letteraturizzazione*, or decay into literariness, of rhetoric in certain periods and cultures.[80] What is particularly pernicious about this narrative is that the tradition of pedagogy becomes a corrupting influence on the rhetorical tradition. I continue to discover that the insights gained from studying medieval rhetorical composition help me to rethink approaches to both the modern classroom and the "classics" of the Western tradition.

In conclusion, then, I consider that primary rhetorical and poetic artifact of this tradition, the *Iliad*. The part of the *Iliad* most likely to be analyzed in a modern rhetoric or composition class is book 9, the embassy to

[79]I have examined the implications of some of the disturbing content of medieval school texts in "Rape and the Pedagogical Rhetoric of Sexual Violence." As an older woman, I would enjoy recasting Matthew's description of Beroe quoted earlier.

[80]See Woods, "The Teaching of Writing in Medieval Europe," *A Short History of Writing Instruction, From Ancient Greece to Twentieth-Century America*, ed. James J. Murphy (Davis: Hermagoras, 1990) 77–94, especially 79–80, 93).

Achilles, which contains three successive pieces of unpersuasive rhetoric. These are found in the middle of the *Iliad*, that is, in its weakest part rhetorically speaking. Earlier rhetoricians like Plato knew that the beginning of the *Iliad*, as of any text, is far more important than the middle, which is why Plato chose the beginning of the *Iliad* to paraphrase in book 3 of the *Republic* (392e–394a) in a successful pedagogical exercise to demonstrate how to deprive the text of rhetorical effect.[81] There, it is the power of an old man—whose speech is unpersuasive to Agamemnon in its narrative context but moving to audiences of the work—that Plato wants to suppress.

Yet even the beginning of a work, though more important than the middle, is not the most rhetorically significant part. As that deft medieval manipulator of words, Chaucer's Pandarus, knew, "th'end is every tales strengthe" (*Troilus and Criseyde* II.260). The *Iliad* ends, not with the victorious Greeks, but with the defeated Trojans, and those who speak for them are four women and a fallen, shattered old man. The final speakers have power only to praise their dead hero. One speaker is mad, another is going insane, and all are bereft and without hope. But they all can speak and move modern readers.

The unfamiliar and alien aspects of medieval composition theory may make modern readers uneasy, and medieval rhetoric may, indeed, be a perversion of classical rhetoric as we have chosen to define it, but I contend that the compositional rhetoric of the classical era may have been more like that of the Middle Ages than we are comfortable admitting: taught in the classroom, based on the memorization and imitation of poetic texts, and focused as much on those who could not persuade as on those who did prevail.

ACKNOWLEDGMENTS

The author is grateful to Martin Camargo, Gaye Denley, Rosa Eberly, Susan Einbinder, Judith Ferster, Peter Jelavich, Kathleen Kelly, Carol Dana Lanham, and Ronald Witt for specific suggestions for and contributions to this version of the essay, and to Carol Harding, James J. Murphy, and other readers who have communicated their reactions to the earlier version.

---

[81]This is not Plato's only use of a pedagogical exercise. Duff and Duff point out that "In Plato's *Phaedo*, 60–61, Socrates says a dream led him to turn Aesopic fables into verse," as in *Phaedrus* 259, *Symposium* 203, and *Protagoras* 320–21 (*Minor Latin Poets* 2: 681, n. 3). Note the importance of the dialogues containing such exercises to our assessment of Plato's discourse on language—and sexual desire.

Chapter 5

Rhetoric and Writing
in the Renaissance

Don Paul Abbott

> *Key Concepts.* *Revival of classical rhetoric • English grammar schools • Continental Jesuit colleges • Pedagogical practice • Rhetoric and humanism • Importance of Latin and Greek • Grammar as integrated curriculum • Eramus's* De ratione studii *• Erasmus and Quintilian • Knowledge of things and words • Latin as living language • Imitation of texts • "Elementarie" schools • Common grammar school curriculum • Double translation • Domination of rhetoric and Latin • Mechanics of writing • Tyranny of the oration • Union of poetic and rhetoric • Literature as always persuasive • Imitation as principal method of learning • Cicero as model for imitation • Juan Luis Vives's* On Education *• Collections for imitation • Progymnasmata • Student commonplace books • Amplification • Development of copia • Jesuit schools parallel to English grammar schools • Jesuit education described in* Ratio studiorum *• Cypriano Suárez S.J.* De arte rhetorica *• Women and rhetoric • Possible reintegration of rhetoric into modern curriculum*

"Nothing so marked the difference between the Middle Ages and the Renaissance," says Paul Grendler, "as the revival of classical rhetoric." Medieval scholars "dismembered ancient rhetoric" retaining "discreet technical elements such as definitions of rhetorical figures. Medieval writers developed a highly logical intellectual system and a technical, scientific language in which to express it. But they abandoned classical rhetoric's fusion of thought and expression within a unified cultural and ethical vision of society, or at least, Renaissance humanists thought so."[1] The revival of classical rhetoric and its "fusion of thought and expression" came to exercise enormous influence over learning and schooling in the Renaissance. Foster Watson explains: "Indeed, if there is one school subject which seems to have pre-eminently influenced the writers, statesmen and gentlemen of the sixteenth and seventeenth century, in their intellectual outfit in afterlife, probably the claim for this leading position may justly be made for Rhetoric and the Oration."[2]

Rhetoric dominated the thoughts of Renaissance intellectuals and the curriculum of Renaissance schools to an extraordinary degree. So extensive was rhetorical inquiry that James J. Murphy calls Renaissance rhetoric the subject with "one thousand neglected authors."[3] In order to bring into relief the pedagogical aspects of this immense subject I look primarily at two institutions: the grammar schools of England and the Jesuit colleges of the Continent. Scrutiny of these institutions offers a number of advantages for an investigation of the teaching of writing in the Renaissance. First, it was in these schools that rhetoric was most often taught. Although rhetoric was also a university subject, philosophy and theology, broadly defined, frequently overshadowed rhetoric in higher education. Second, an examination of the grammar school insures an emphasis on the pedagogical rather than the theoretical issues. The schoolmasters were intensely interested in how their young students should be taught to write and, fortunately, left considerable testimony as to their methods. Third, a look at these schools maintains an emphasis on the development of the system of writing instruction ultimately inherited by the public and parochial schools of the United States. In particular, by contrasting grammar school and Jesuit college practices with current methods, it may be possible to draw some conclusions that are relevant to current instructional needs. I begin, then, by briefly outlining the nature of the English grammar school.

THE ENGLISH GRAMMAR SCHOOL

The English grammar school is a sixteenth-century invention. Although the term "grammar school" was mentioned in England as early as 1387, Dean Colet's founding of St. Paul's School in 1510 marks the real begin-

---

[1]Paul Grendler, *Schooling in Renaissance Italy: Literacy and Learning, 1300–1600* (Baltimore: Johns Hopkins UP, 1989) 205.

[2]Grendler 205.

[3]James J. Murphy, ed., "One Thousand Neglected Authors; The Scope and Importance of Renaissance Rhetoric," *Renaissance Eloquence: Studies in the Theory and Practice of Renaissance Rhetoric* (Berkeley: U of California P, 1983) 20–36.

ning of a new educational movement. The grammar schools were inspired by the ideals of the European humanists and, in the case of St. Paul's, directly encouraged and assisted by Desiderius Erasmus. These schools, were, in a very real sense, an effort to put the educational theories of the Humanists into pedagogical practice. Thus, the main aim of the schools was also a major goal of Renaissance Humanism: the creation of elegant and eloquent expression. The grammar schools sought to teach the kind of expression known to Cicero, but lost in the Middle Ages. Thus, the art of expression was necessarily conceived in the language of classical rhetoric. In the minds of the humanists and in the grammar school classrooms rhetoric and humanism were intertwined.[4]

The term grammar may be, therefore, slightly misleading to modern readers. In its narrowest sense, grammar meant Latin grammar. Knowledge of Latin gave students access both to the classical masters of expression and to the current scholarly and political communication in the international language. The educational goal, therefore, was to provide something far more than a rudimentary acquaintance with a foreign tongue. What grammar really meant to the masters of the Grammar Schools was what it meant to Quintilian. After a boy has learned to read and write, says Quintilian, he is then turned over to a *grammaticus*, a teacher of literature and language. The concern of this profession, says Quintilian, "may be most briefly considered under two heads, the art of speaking correctly and the interpretation of the poets; but there is more beneath the surface than meets the eye. For the art of writing is combined with that of speaking, and correct reading precedes interpretation, while in each of these cases criticism has its work to perform."[5] Grammar, then, may be best understood as signifying an integrated curriculum of oral and written composition combined with literary criticism.

This literary and Latinate curriculum was advocated by a wide variety of humanists, but it was Erasmus who most directly inspired the English Grammar Schools. In T. W. Baldwin's phrase, Erasmus "laid the egg" of the grammar schools. Baldwin asserts that "anyone who wishes to understand the principles upon which the sixteenth-century grammar school was founded in England would be very unwise to begin anywhere else than with Erasmus."[6] In his small book *De ratione studii*, Erasmus proposes a

---

[4]For an excellent survey of the relationship between rhetoric and humanism see John Monfasani, "Humanism and Rhetoric," *Renaissance Humanism: Foundations, Forms, and Legacy*, ed. Albert Rabil, Jr., vol. 3: *Humanism and the Disciplines* (Philadelphia: U of Pennsylvania P, 1988) 171–235. For a discussion of the educational practices of the humanists see Anthony Grafton and Lisa Jardine, *From Humanism to the Humanities* (Cambridge: Harvard UP, 1986).

[5]Chapter 38 Quintilian, *Institutio oratoria*, trans. H. E. Butler (Cambridge: Harvard UP, 1980) I. IV. 2–4.

[6]T. W. Baldwin, *William Shakspere's Small Latine and Less Greeke* (Urbana: U of Illinois P, 1944) I:77.

course of study which would become the basis of the grammar schools. Although not published until 1512, *De ratione studii* went through any number of earlier versions, including one that Erasmus sent to Colet for the latter's reaction. Colet responded that he read the "epistle about studies" and told Erasmus that "I not only approve it all, but I truly admire your genius, and art, and learning, and copiousness and eloquence. I have often wished too, that the boys at our school could be taught in the way you explain."[7] In due time, the boys at St. Paul's and the other grammar schools would indeed be taught in the way Erasmus had explained. The method of study that Erasmus advances is very much dependent on Quintilian "who has left a very through treatment of these matters, so that it would seem the height of impertinence to write about a subject he has already dealt with."[8] So agreeable is Quintilian to humanists like Erasmus that it is reasonably accurate to say that the grammar school curriculum is a combination of Quintilian and Christianity. So strong is Quintilian's influence that the methods outlined by James J. Murphy in chapter 2 of this volume, could, with slight revision, serve to describe the education of sixteenth-century England.

Erasmus begins *De ratione studii* by concurring with the ancient position that knowledge is "of two kinds: of things and of words," that is, of ideas, truths, and of language.[9] The knowledge of words comes first, but knowledge of things is ultimately more important. Although Erasmus distinguishes two types of knowledge, the two are interdependent, and "a person who is not skilled in the force of language is, of necessity, short-sighted, deluded, and unbalanced in his judgment of things as well."[10] Knowledge of Latin and Greek is essential in the acquisition of knowledge because humankind's greatest ideas are to be found in these two languages. Thus, grammar comes first, but only as a means to an end. Erasmus recommends only enough grammar as is necessary to allow the students to get on with the important tasks of reading, writing, and speaking. As students become increasingly familiar with the classical languages, more complex grammatical matters can be introduced. Erasmus is generally impatient with excessive attention to rules. He wishes Latin to be a truly living language to be used, rather than to be analyzed and systematized. As soon as the basics have been mastered, students should begin to read increasingly complex classical and Christian sources. These texts become the objects of imitation; students are expected to imitate both the el-

---

[7]Cited in Baldwin I:78.

[8]Erasmus, *Collected Works of Erasmus*, ed. Craig R. Thompson, vol. 24: *Literary and Educational Writings: De copia / De ratione studii*, trans. Betty I. Knott (Toronto: U of Toronto P, 1978) 672.

[9]Erasmus 666.

[10]Erasmus 666.

oquence of the "words" and the morality of the "things." Thus, the educational program of Erasmus is at once both literary and moral. So confident is Erasmus of his approach that he makes this promise: "given youth who are not totally incompetent intellectually, I would with less trouble, and within fewer years, bring them to a credible degree of eloquence in each language than those notorious instructors who force their charges into their own stammering form, or rather lack, of expression."[11]

Precisely how the followers of Erasmus would bring students to "a credible degree of eloquence" can be seen from the records of what was taught in the grammar schools. That curriculum is particularly remarkable because the grammar school was intended to educate boys from about the ages of seven to fifteen. Before attending a grammar school, students would likely have gone to a "petty" or "elementarie" school. Richard Mulcaster, in *The Elementarie* (1582), says that such a school should consist of five activities: "reading, writing, drawing, singing, & playing."[12] The first two of these activities were typically the most important. The primary accomplishment of most petty schools was probably the teaching of the alphabet and basic vernacular literacy. The grammar school thus served as a kind of middle school between the *elementarie* and the university. Yet the grammar school was, in many ways, the heart and soul of English education: students attended it longer than any other stage of education and in the sixteenth century, at least, the grammar school was at the forefront of educational innovation.

The humanistic curriculum of the grammar schools was predicated upon the recommendation of Erasmus that students be given a grammatical introduction followed by increasingly complex reading and writing accompanied by additional grammar when necessary. The schools were divided into five to eight classes, or "forms." These forms were in turn divided into two broad groupings according to the instructor. The lower forms usually presented the rudiments of Latin grammar and were taught by an "usher." Beginning typically with the third form, a more accomplished teacher, the "master," took over to teach advanced Latin grammar, Greek grammar, and, especially, rhetoric. The following specimen of a late sixteenth-century grammar school timetable illustrates the thoroughness and complexity of the teaching methods. The numbers in parentheses indicate the days of the week.

USHER'S FORMS

First Form

7–11 A.M.
The Royal Grammar (2; 3; 4; 5).

---

[11]Erasmus 691.
[12]Richard Mulcaster, *Elementarie*, ed. E. T. Campagnac (Oxford: Clarendon, 1925) 59.

Repetition of the work of the week (6).
Examination on the lecture of the previous afternoon (7).

1–5 P.M.
English Testament, or psalms of David in English (2; 3; 4).
Half Holiday (5).
Repetition of the work of the week continued (6).
Lecture on Aesop's Fables (6).
Writing out the catechism in English (7).

Second Form

7–11 A.M.
Lecture on the Colloquies of Erasmus, or on the Dialogues of Corderius (2; 3).
Lecture on the Cato senior, or Cato junior (4; 5).
Repetition of the week's lectures (6).
Examination of the lectures of the previous afternoon (7).

1–5 P.M.
Translation from English into Latin. Home lessons and exercises given out and prepared (2; 3; 4).
Half Holiday (5).
Repetition of the week's lectures continued. Lectures on Aesop's Fables (6).
Writing out the catechism in English. Arithmetic (7).

MASTER'S FORMS

Third Form

7–11 A.M.
Lecture on the Letters of Ascham, or Sturm's Cicero's Letters, or Terence. Paraphrase of a sentence (2).
Lecture on Ascham, etc., as on Monday. Vulgaria in prose (3).
Lecture on Palingenius, or the Psalms of Hess. Paraphrase of a sentence (4).
Lecture on Palingenius, or the Psalms of Hess (5).
Vulgaria in prose, and repetition of the week's lectures (6).
Examination in lecture of the previous afternoon (7).

1–5 P.M.
Latin syntax, or Greek grammar, or the figures of Sysenbrote [Susenbrotus].
Home lessons given out and prepared (2; 3; 4).
Half Holiday (5).
Repetition of the week's work continued Lectures on Erasmus' Apothegms (6).
Catechism and New Testament (7).

Fourth Form

7–11 A.M.
Lecture on Cicero de Senectute, or de Amicitia, or on Justin (2; 3).

Lecture on Ovid's Tristia, or de Ponto, or Seneca's Tragedies (4: 5).
Verse Theme, and repetition of the week's lectures (6).
Examination on the lecture of the previous afternoon (7).

1–5 P.M.
Prose Theme (2; 4).
Latin Syntax, or Greek Grammar, or Figures of Susenbrotus. Home lessons
and exercises given out and prepared (2; 3; 4).
Half holiday (5).
Repetition of the week's lectures continued, and lecture on Ovid's Fausti (7).
Catechism and New Testament (7).

Fifth Form

7–11 A.M.
Prose Theme (2; 4).
Lecture in Cicero or Sallust or Caesar's Commentaries (2; 3).
Verse Theme (3; 6).
Lecture in Virgil or Ovid's Metamorphosis, or Lucan (4; 5).
Repetition of the week's lectures (6).
Examination of the lecture of the previous afternoon (7).

1–5 P.M.
Latin Syntax, or Greek Grammar, or Figures of Susenbrotus. Home lessons
and exercises given out and prepared (2; 3; 4).
Half Holiday (5).
Repetition of the week's lectures continued, and lecture on Horace, or
Lucan, or Seneca's Tragedies (6).
Declamation on a given subject by several senior scholars. Catechism and
New Testament (7).[13]

This timetable presents a reasonably complete view of what an English
grammar school student would be expected to endure. While there was
some variation in texts and assignments, the pattern of teaching was remarkably constant throughout England. Students at St. Paul's, Eton, Win-
chester, Rotherham, and the other grammar schools could expect to engage in much the same grammar, reading, lectures, examinations,
themes, and declamations. What the timetable does not fully reveal are the
exact methods used to teach the attainment of elegant expression in
Latin. Teaching methods, however, were remarkably consistent from
school to school.

With this brief sketch of the English grammar school curriculum, we are
now in a position to look more closely at the nature of writing instruction
in sixteenth-century England. The remainder of this chapter concentrates

---

[13]Appendix P. A. Monroe Stowe, *English Grammar Schools in the Reign of Queen Elizabeth*
(New York: Teachers Coll., Columbia U, 1908) 185–88.

on the master's forms, that is, the "upper division," of the grammar school where composition, literature, and rhetoric were most fully taught. A closer look at the master's forms makes clear certain critical features of the grammar school approach to writing—features which, for better or for worse, separate so much of current practice from humanist tradition.

Perhaps the most fundamental aspect of the grammar school curriculum was that it was in its entirety a linguistic and literary curriculum. The original and fundamental purpose of the institution was to make the students eloquent in Latin. This intent is clearly revealed in the complete title of Roger Ascham's educational treatise of 1570: *The Scholemaster, Or plaine and perfit way of teachyng children, to understand, write, and speake, the Latin tong, but specially purposed for the private brynging up of youth in Jentlemen and Noble mens houses, and commodious also for all such, as have forgot the Latin tonge, and would, by themselves, without a scholemaster, in short tyme, and with small paines, recover a sufficient habilitie, to understand, write, and speake Latin.*[14] In order to ensure that children would indeed understand, write, and speak the Latin tongue, grammar school statutes commonly required both masters and scholars to speak Latin at all times while on school premises. The instruction in Latin was to be so complete and unremitting that the ancient language could not help but become as familiar as the vernacular. Thus, Charles Hoole, in *A New Discovery of the Old Art of Teaching Schoole* (1660), has his scholars in the fifth form translate an oration or a passage from Sallust, Livy, or Tacitus every day and then recite these efforts in Latin and English each week. In the sixth form, Hoole requires that the students "continue to make *themes* and *verses*, one week in Greek and another in Latine; and ever and anon they may contend in making Orations & Declamations."[15]

This intensive instruction in Latin was not designed to teach the vernacular, but of course a second language can only be taught by employing the native tongue of the students. Consequently, the grammar schools also taught composition in English. The process of translating from English to Latin and back into English began early and continued throughout the forms. Juan Luis Vives, who, like his mentor Erasmus, exercised considerable influence on English education, recommends that "as soon as they have learned syntax, let the pupils translate from the mother-tongue into Latin, and then back again into the mother-tongue."[16] Ascham enthusias-

---

[14]Roger Ascham, *The Scholemaster*, ed. John E. B. Mayor (1863; New York: AMS, 1967).

[15]Charles Hoole, *A New Discovery of the Old Art of Teaching Schoole*, English Linguistics 1500–1800, 133, ed. R. C. Alston (Menston, Eng.: Scolar, 1969) 173, 200.

[16]Juan Luis Vives, *On Education* [*De tradendis disciplinis*], ed. and trans. Foster Watson (1913; Totowa: Rowman, 1971) 114. Although born in Spain in 1493, Vives spent most of his adult life in the Low Countries and England where, for a time, he lectured in Greek, Latin,

tically endorses this "double translation" as far superior to a single translation from one language to another. Invoking the authority of Pliny the Younger, Ascham claims that

> this exercise of double translating is learned easily, sensiblie, by litle and litle, not onlie all the hard congruities of Grammar, the choice of aptest wordes, the right framing of wordes and sentences, cumlines of figures and formes, fite for every matter and proper for everie tong, but that which is greater also, in marking dayly and folowing diligentlie thus the steppes of the best Authors, like invention of argumentes, like order in disposition, like utterance in Elocution is easelie gathered up: whereby your scholar shall be brought not only to like eloquence, but also to all trewe understanding and right judgement, both for writing and speaking.[17]

For these reasons, says Ascham, "I am moved to think this way of double translating, either onlie or chiefly, to be the fittest for the spedy and perfit atteyning of any tong."[18] The act of translating from English to Latin and back again, all the while attending to the principles of rhetoric, could not help but perfect the student's ability to compose in English. Moreover, the vernacular made steady inroads into the province of rhetoric in the late sixteenth and seventeenth centuries. Many vernacular textbooks' authors simply adapted, with little alteration, the methods of teaching Latin composition and applied them to English.[19] The program of the grammar school might best be thought of, then, as a kind of bilingual education. Latin was the primary language, but English was never far behind.

So complete was the domination of rhetoric and Latin in this curriculum that there was simply very little room for anything else. For example, what science was taught was often subservient to literary demands. In *De ratione studii* Erasmus recommends wide knowledge in order to facilitate the literary explication of ancient poets and other writers. Geography, says Erasmus, "which is useful in history, not to mention poetry, must also be mastered [. . .]. Here the main object is to have observed which of the vernacular words for mountains, rivers, regions, and cities correspond to the ancient."[20] Similarly, says Erasmus:

---

and rhetoric at Cardinal College, Oxford. Vives died in Bruges in 1540. For an account of Vives's contributions to Renaissance rhetoric see Don Paul Abbott, "Juan Luis Vives: Tradition and Innovation in Renaissance Rhetoric," *Central States Speech Journal* 37 (1986) 193–203.

[17]Ascham 103–104.

[18]Ascham 104.

[19]David Thomson demonstrates that late medieval grammar masters in England simply translated the Latin grammars of Priscian and Donatus into English. See *A Descriptive Catalogue of Middle English Grammatical Texts* (New York: Garland, 1979) esp. 1–49.

[20]Erasmus 24:673.

astronomy must not be passed over, especially that of Hyginus, since the poets liberally sprinkle their creations with it. The nature and essence of everything must be grasped, especially since it is from this source that they are accustomed to draw there similes, epithets, comparisons, images, metaphors,
and other rhetorical devices of that kind. Above all, however, history must be
grasped. Its application is very widespread and not confined to the poets
[. . .]. In short, there is no branch of knowledge, whether military, agricultural, musical, or architectural which is not useful for those who have undertaken an exposition of the ancient poets or orators.[21]

For Erasmus and his followers in the grammar schools, nonliterary
knowledge was useful primarily for its ability to assist in the development
of eloquence.

Language occupied this preferred position in the grammar school curriculum because it is a defining characteristic of the human being. Vives says:

> The first thing man has to learn is speech. It flows at once from the rational
> soul as water from a fountain. As all beasts are bereft of intellect, so are they
> also lacking in speech. Discourse is also the instrument of human society, for
> not otherwise could the mind be revealed, so shut in is it by the grossness
> and density of the human body. Like as we have the mind by the gift of God,
> so we have this or that language, by the gift of art.[22]

Vives continues by noting that "language is the shrine of erudition, and
as it were a storeroom for what should be concealed, and what should be
made public. Since it is the treasury of culture and the instrument of human society, it would therefore be to the benefit of the human race that
there should be a single language, which all nations should use in common."[23] Latin was, of course, just such a "single language" and as such well
deserved its singular place in the schools. Latin made possible, for the Europeans and the English, at least, an international exchange of ideas, commerce and diplomacy. While suited to the needs of the present, Latin,
without any native speakers, inevitably also kept its users cognizant of the
past. Its users were especially cognizant of the literature of the Romans
and were well aware that the oration was the literary form that dominated
Rome. So it was in the grammar school classroom.

THE DOMINATION OF THE ORATION

The technological advances of the Renaissance made the teaching of writing more possible and practical than ever before. The printing press ar-

---

[21]Erasmus 674–75.
[22]Vives 90.
[23]Vives 91.

rived in England in 1477, and paper production began in the first years of the sixteenth century. The use of books, that is, textbooks for students to read and copybooks in which to write, made the act of writing far more central to the educational endeavor. Thus Richard Brinsley in *Ludus Literarius: or, The Grammar Schoole . . .* (1612) devotes an early chapter to a discussion of how the act of writing might be facilitated:

1. The schollar should be set to write, when he enters into his Accidence; so euery day to spend an hour in writing, or very neere.

2. There must be special care, that every one who is to write, haue all the necessaries belonging thereunto; as penne, inke, paper, rular, plummet, ruling-pen, pen-knife, &c.

3. The like care must be, that their inke be thin, blacke, cleere; which wil not run abroad, nor blot: their paper good; that is, such as is white, smooth, and which will bear inke, & also that it be made in a book. Their writing books would be kept faire, strait ruled, & each to haue a blotting paper to keep their books from soyling, or marring under their hands.

4. Cause euery one of them to make his own pen; otherwise the making, and mending of pens, will be a very great hinderance, both to the Masters and to the Schollars. Besides that, when they are away from their Masters (if they have not a good pen made before) they wil write naught; because they know not how to make their pens themselves.[24]

Brinsley then presents an equally detailed account of how a pen is to be made, from the selection of the quill to the cutting of the nub. The remainder of the chapter involves instructions for holding the pen and for perfecting the techniques of writing. All of this detail is, in part, necessary because of the relative newness of writing with pen and ink in the classroom. Yet, despite the obvious importance and practicality of writing in the grammar school, treatises treat writing primarily as a physical activity (*orthographia*), while the mental activities continue to be expressed in oral terms. In other words, the conceptual and expressive functions of composition continue to be expressed in the terminology of classical oratory. Despite the rapid advances in printing, the oration remained fixed as the supreme form of discourse, just as it had been for the Romans. In the opinion of Walter Ong, the oration "tyrannized over ideas of what expression as such—literary or other—was."[25]

---

[24]John Brinsley, *Ludus Literarius*, English Linguistics 1500–1800 62, (Menston, Eng.: Scolar, 1968) 29.

[25]Walter Ong, "Tudor Writings on Rhetoric, Poetic, and Literary Theory," *Rhetoric, Romance, and Technology: Studies in the Interaction of Expression and Culture* (Ithaca: Cornell UP, 1971) 53.

This oratorical "tyranny" is certainly apparent in the four principle composition exercises of the grammar school: letter-writing, verse-making, the theme, and the oration. The oration is invariably the final, and hence presumably the most difficult to accomplish, of these various assignments. Practically speaking, however, the three exercises which preceded the oration followed much the same rules of composition. Letter-writing, the most elementary exercise, provided a convenient introduction to the elements of rhetoric. In *The English Secretorie. Wherein is Contayned, a Perfect Method, for the inditing of all manner of Epistles and familiar letters* . . . (1586), Angel Day indicates that letter-writing may be divided into three parts: invention, disposition, and elocution. Of the five parts of classical rhetoric, Day omits only memory and delivery, the two most fully oral parts of the ancient division.[26] Likewise, Day also directs that the letter be organized precisely as a classical oration: *exordium, narratio, propositio, confirmatio, confutatio,* and *peroratio.*[27] Indeed, any kind of discourse could be, and should be, organized in just this way. Citing Aphthonius, Brinsley says that he gives his students "a Theame to make, following the example in their booke, to prosecute the same parts of the Theame; as *Exordium, narratio, confirmatio, confutatio, conclusio.*"[28] It is no exaggeration to say that the rules of the classical oration were applied to every kind of discourse.

The oratorical domination of poetry is perhaps most surprising today, but it is simply another example of how completely ancient rhetoric governed all expression. There is no very clear demarcation between rhetoric and poetry in the Renaissance and the language of rhetoric is always deemed the appropriate idiom for the analysis of the poetry.[29] Thus Abraham Fraunce's *Arcadian Rhetorike* (1588), is, as the title suggests, a rhetoric which uses Sydney's epic, as well as the poetry of Boscan, Garcilaso, Tasso, and other vernacular poets as a source of rhetorical precepts. A few years later Sydney wrote his *Defense of Poesie* (1595) in the form of an oration.[30]

This union of rhetoric and poetic and all other genres was possible, indeed even essential, because all discourse shared the same end: to speak well and to speak persuasively. The civic and forensic origins of rhetoric are never out of sight in Renaissance literature; that is, literature, like rhetoric itself, is always argumentative and persuasive, never neutral.[31]

---

[26]Angel Day, *English Secretorie*, English Linguistics 1500–1800 29 (Menston, Eng.: Scolar, 1967) 19–20.

[27]Day 22.

[28]Brinsley 172 73.

[29]For a complete treatment of this relationship see Brian Vickers, *Classical Rhetoric in English Poetry* (1970; Carbondale: Southern Illinois UP, 1989).

[30]See K. O. Myrick, *Sir Philip Sydney as a Literary Craftsman* (Cambridge: Harvard UP, 1935) esp. 46–83.

[31]See Ong 65.

There is no conception of a use for language that is merely expository, or merely descriptive, or merely narrative. Such functions existed only insofar as each promoted the ultimate end of persuasion. Nowhere is this more apparent than in the work of John Milton. D. L. Clark has demonstrated that Milton, while a student at St. Paul's School in London, had learned his lessons well. Milton's famous essay on freedom of the press was modeled after an Isocratean oration and is titled "Areopagitica; A Speech of Mr. John Milton For The Liberty Of Unlicensed Printing. To The Parliament Of England."[32] Similarly, "Paradise Lost" is "An Oration to Justify The Ways of God to Men."

IMITATION AND LEARNING

The "Areopagitica" demonstrates the appeal of classical models to even a creative genius like Milton. "That Milton should aspire to such literary and oratorical ideals as moved the orators and poets of antiquity is natural enough," says Clark, "for he had an early education very like their own."[33] In basing his essay on a classical pattern, Milton was simply doing what he had been taught to do. If there is one constant in Renaissance education, it is a belief in the necessity, indeed, the inevitability of *imitatio* as the principle method of learning. Imitation is made necessary by the human condition. Says Vives:

> Although it is natural to talk, yet all discourse whatsoever belongs to an 'art' which was not bestowed upon us at birth, since nature has fashioned man, for the most part, strangely hostile to 'art.' Since she lets us be born ignorant and absolutely skilless of all arts, we require imitation. Imitation, furthermore, is the fashioning of a certain thing in accordance with a proposed model.[34]

Human expression, in particular, requires imitation to perfect. According to Ascham "all languages, both learned and mother tonges, be gotten onlie by *Imitation*. For as ye used to heare, so ye learne to speake [. . .]. And therefore, if ye would speake as the best and the wisest do, ye must be conversant, where the best and the wisest are."[35] The best and the wisest are to be found, more often than not, in classical literature: "in the Greek and

---

[32]Donald Lemen Clark, *John Milton at St. Paul's School: A Study of Ancient Rhetoric in English Renaissance Education* (New York: Columbia UP, 1948). See also Wilbur E. Gilman, "*Milton's Rhetoric: Studies in His Defense of Liberty,*" U of Missouri Studies 14 (1939): 12–13.

[33]Clark 3.

[34]Vives 189.

[35]Ascham 134.

Latin tong, the two onlie learned tonges, which be not kept in common taulke, but in private bookes, we finde alwayes wisdom and eloquence, good matter and good utterance, never or seldom a sonder."[36]

The belief in a literary education that favors imitation over rules naturally requires great authors to imitate. But which great authors? The answer, invariably, was the best writers from the best periods. That, in turn, almost always meant Cicero. There was considerable debate about whether or not Cicero was the only model for imitation, but there was little disagreement that he should be at the very least, one of the models.[37] Says Vives: "There are those who, out of all authors, select only Cicero, whom alone they imitate. Cicero is indeed the best, though he does not contain every merit. Nor is he the only author with good style. When he delights and teaches us he is admirable beyond the rest." The conclusion, says Vives, is that "if Cicero is the best and most eminent stylist, others are not, on that account, bad or contemptible."[38] In other words, Cicero is first among the ancients, but only one of a number of worthy models. Among many others, Vives himself suggests, "for an intellectual and learned circle, the speeches of Demosthenes are suited. So, too, are those to be found in Livy, in whose histories orations are interwoven. For sweetness and rhythm we have Isocrates. Plato has a still higher flight."[39] Each Renaissance educator has a favorite list of authors, but all agree on the need to imitate the greats of antiquity.

Vives suggests how this process of imitation should proceed: "the zealous imitator will study, with the greatest attention, the model he has set up for himself, and will consider by what art, by what method, such and such was achieved by the author, in order that he himself with a similar artifice may accomplish his own intention in his own work."[40] With the assistance of the master, then, the student should first analyze the appropriate model to determine the method of composition and then gradually attempt to apply these methods in their own writing. Naturally, a child needs considerable assistance in analyzing models and generating sophisticated prose and verse. The grammar school sought to facilitate this process by engaging the students in a series of increasingly complicated imita-

---

[36]Ascham 136.

[37]In the *Ciceronianus*, Erasmus rejects the imitation of Cicero to the exclusion of all other models. See *The Ciceronian: A Dialogue on the Ideal Latin Style*, trans. Betty Knott, *Collected Works of Erasmus*, vol. 28. For an account of the debates about Ciceronianism, see Izora Scott, *Controversies over the Imitation of Cicero as a Model for Style and Some Phases of their Influence on the Schools of the Renaissance* (New York: Teachers Coll., 1910). For a thorough discussion of Cicero's place in the schools of the Renaissance, see Joseph S. Freedman, "Cicero in Sixteenth- and Seventeenth-Century Rhetoric Instruction," *Rhetorica* 4 (1986) 227–54.

[38]Vives, 191–92.

[39]Vives 194.

[40]Vives 195.

tive exercises. Ascham discusses five such exercises. Although the fifth is explicitly called "imitation," all five are predicated on the emulation of models. The five are: (a) translation, especially double translation; (b) paraphrase, "not onlie to expresse at large with more wordes, but to strive and contend (as Quintilian saith) to translate the best latin authors into other latin wordes";[41] (c) metaphrase, the translation of prose into verse and verse into prose; (d) epitome, the distillation of classical works into their essences. This is an exercise Ascham much "mislikes" for it emphasizes only matter and disregards expression and it can cause students to lose sight of the original model. Finally, after much translation, paraphrase, metaphrase and perhaps epitome, the student is ready for (e) imitation proper: the careful scrutiny and creative emulation of an approved model.

This emphasis on imitation naturally meant that there must be sufficient material to imitate. While the models of imitation were to be found in the ancient masters, the Renaissance educators also devised various devices to make the words and ideas more readily accessible to young minds. Thus there are innumerable books of lists which serve as guides for composition. These collections, compendia, and anthologies of adages, apothegms, commonplaces, and figures all provide handy sources of the wisdom of the ancients. Thus, Erasmus's *Adagia* began as a collection of 818 proverbs and ultimately grew to include 4,151 adages. These proverbs, which Erasmus culled from classical sources, contributed, he says, four things to discourse: "philosophy, grace and charm in speaking, and the understanding of the best authors."[42] Thus the proverbs contained in this collection should be studied for their merits and then applied where appropriate in a composition. A similar work is Robert Cawdrey, *A treasvrie or Storehouse of Similes: Both pleasaunt, delightfull, and profitable, for all estates of men in general. Newly collected into Heades and Common places* (1600). Cawdrey's 858-page book contains similes arranged alphabetically from "Accusation" to "Zeale." Much like the apothegms of Erasmus, these similes serve as a ready source of philosophically sound illustrative material for composition. The term *commonplace* in the title is indicative of Cawdrey's purpose. As Joan Lechner explains, the commonplace, in this sense, may be thought of "as a little oration or as a 'speech within a speech.' "[43] These "little speeches which were regularly inserted in longer orations for purposes of amplification, exposition, persuasion, and description were thought of as 'commonplaces' because they provided ready-made 'argu-

[41]Ascham 106.
[42]Erasmus, *Collected Works of Erasmus*, vol. 31: *Adages*, trans. Margaret Mann Phillips 14.
[43]Sister Joan Marie Lechner, O.S.U., *Renaissance Concepts of the Commonplaces* (1962; Westport: Greenwood Press, 1974) 3.

ments' which in some way magnified (or minimized) a subject."[44] These
collections of commonplaces, figures, proverbs, and all the rest served as a
source of approved material which could be inserted directly or altered to
fit individual needs.

In addition to these collections of "little speeches" and other relatively
short devices, students could also make use of collections of more complete discourses. Angel Day's *English Secretorie*, for example, comprises
"sundry examples of euery Epistle." Day includes at least one example of
deliberative, confirmatory, laudatory, hortatory, dehortatory, suasory,
disuasory, and all the other genres of letters that he identifies. Another
work that provides complete examples of discourse is Richard Rainolde's
A booke called the Foundacion of Rhetorike (1563). *The Foundacion of Rhetorike*
is an English adaptation of Reinhard Lorich's Latin version of Aphthonius's *Progynasmata*.[45] The *Progymnasmata*, or a set of introductory exercises, comprises fourteen progressively more difficult compositional models from simple fables to complex questions of law. Rainolde readily
acknowledges his debt to his ancient source:

> Aphthonivs a famous man, wrote in greke of soche declamacions, to
> enstructe the studentes thereof, with all facilitie to grounde in them, a most
> plentious and rich vein of eloquence. No man is able to inuente a more prof-
> itable waie and order, to instructe any one in the exquisite and absolute per-
> fection, of wisedome and eloquence, then Aphthonius Quintilianus and
> Hermogenes.[46]

Thus Rainolde expresses both his conviction in the efficacy of imitation
and his faith in the ancients whom he is himself imitating. In his enthusiasm for Aphthonius, Rainolde is by no means alone; Aphthonius is one
of the most widely accepted authorities for writing instruction. Brinsley,
for example, bases his instructions for the teaching of themes on Aphthonius.[47]

In addition to the works of Rainolde and Day and all the various "store-
houses" of epitomes, adages, and figures that were printed in the sixteenth and seventeenth centuries, students were also expected to collect
their own commonplaces and enter them in their "copie" books. After recommending a number of authors that students might profitably read,

---

[44]Ibid.

[45]Richard Rainolde, *The Foundation of Rhetoric*, English Linguistics 347 (Menston, Eng.:
Scolar, 1972). Aphthonius's *Progymnasmata* was widely printed in the Renaissance and
Lorich's version, with twenty-eight editions in the sixteenth and seventeenth centuries, was
especially popular. See James J. Murphy, *Renaissance Rhetoric: A Short Title Catalogue* (New
York: Garland, 1981) 22.

[46]Rainolde, "To the Reader."

[47]Brinsley 172–90.

Hoole next advises: "let every one take one of those books forementioned, and see what he can finde in it for his purpose, and write it down under one of those heads in his Commonplace book."[48] The students should then "all read what they have written, before the Master, and every one transcribe what others have collected, into his own book; and thus they may alwayes have store of matter for invention ready at hand, which is far beyond what their own wit is able to conceive."[49] These student commonplace books functioned in concert with the various published collections to insure that the students would have a sufficient storehouse of material for the process of writing.

When grammar school students were finally faced with actually writing a theme, they were at least theoretically well stocked with material that would make the process relatively easy. In actual fact, of course, the process could be painful. In Brinsley's dialogue, *Ludus literarius*, one of the characters admits that the themes that "my children have done hereby for a long time, they have done it with exceeding paines and feare, in harsh phrase, without any inuention, or iudgement; and ordinarily so rudely, as I have been ashamed that anyone should see their exercises. So as it hath driuen mee into exceeding passions, causing me to deale ouer rigorously with the poore boies."[50] Indeed, the grammar school curriculum appears extremely rigorous by any standard, and it is easy to imagine that many of those who experienced it were less than enthusiastic in their studies. Despite the frustrations of the Masters and the recalcitrance of the boys, the grammar schools certainly provided their charges with the opportunity to develop the ability to write comprehensively on virtually any subject.

Grammar school students were rather young, and they were never really expected to write discourse that would exceed the models they were constantly reading. Nevertheless, students in the later forms were expected ultimately to write themes that, while in the spirit of their models, were not simply slavish reproductions of them. Thus, Hoole recommends that the master should not tie the students "to the words of any Authour, but giving them liberty to contract, or enlarge, or alter them as they please; so that they still contend to go beyond them in purity of expression."[51] Ultimately, says Hoole, once the master determines that "they have gained a perfect way of making Themes of themselves, you may let them go on to attain the habit by their own constant practice."[52]

The "perfect way of making themes" was naturally dependent on the accumulation of material for imitation. The actual assembly of this previ-

---

[48]Hoole 183.
[49]Hoole 183.
[50]Brinsley 173.
[51]Hoole 185.
[52]Hoole 186.

ously gathered material was governed by the process of *amplificatio*—the achievement of copiousness or "copie." Amplification was, in effect, the active implementation of imitation. As such, the process combined the classical divisions of invention, style, and arrangement. Although the sixteenth-century educational reformer Peter Ramus had attempted to make invention the sole property of logic, this re-arrangement did little to banish invention from the grammar school, where invention and style combined in the process of amplification.[53] Brinsley and Hoole could, therefore, recommend Ramistic texts and still discuss invention without any sense of anomaly. Brinsley advises that students should "trie what reasons they can inuent of themselves according to the chiefe heads of Inuention" such as causes, effects, subjects, and adjuncts.[54] Later he admits that this approach may be too hard for children "who haue read on Logicke," but he nevertheless continues to advocate the use of these topics.

It is in the work of Erasmus, however, that the union of invention and elocution within the rubric of amplification is most apparent. Ascham calls Erasmus "the ornament of learning in our tyme"[55] and this veneration in large part is due to the Erasmus's *De duplici copia verborum et rerum*. *De copia* may be thought of as the first grammar school textbook; in fact, Erasmus wrote it for that purpose. In a letter to Dean Colet, the founder of St. Paul's school, he says:

> I thought it would be appropriate for me to make a small literary contribution to the equipment of your school. So I have chosen to dedicate to the new school these two new commentaries De copia, inasmuch as the work in question is suitable for boys to read and also, unless I am mistaken, not unlikely to prove helpful to them, though I leave it to others to judge how well-informed this work of mine is, or how serviceable it will be.[56]

De copia was judged very serviceable as a textbook upon its first publication in 1511. Indeed, "so widespread did its use become that it was worth pirating, summarizing, excerpting, turning into a question-and-answer manual, and making the subject of commentaries."[57] The frequency with which *De copia* was reprinted "testifies to the significance of the work and

---

[53] The standard account of "Ramism" is Walter Ong, S. J., *Ramus, Method, and the Decay of Dialogue* (Cambridge: Harvard UP, 1958). For the first modern English translation of a work by Ramus, see *Arguments in Rhetoric Against Quintilian: Translation and Text of Peter Ramus's Rhetoricae Distinctiones in Quintilianum (1549)*, trans. Carole Newlands, with an introduction by James J. Murphy (DeKalb: Northern Illinois UP, 1986).
[54] Brinsley 180.
[55] Ascham 140.
[56] Erasmus 24:285.
[57] Translator's Introduction, Erasmus 283.

to its influence during the first three-quarters of the sixteenth century in both arousing and ministering to a particular stylistic ideal."[58]

That stylistic ideal is captured in the Latin word *copia*, which is rendered "abundance" in the standard English translation of the work.[59] But as Donald B. King explains, there is no entirely suitable English word: "as used by Erasmus, copia encompasses within its meaning the meaning of four English words: variation, abundance or richness, eloquence, and the ability to vary and enrich language and thought."[60] Erasmus believes that the development of *copia* is necessary because "exercise in expressing oneself in different ways will be of considerable importance in general for the acquisition of style."[61] More particularly, "variety is so powerful in every sphere that there is absolutely nothing, however brilliant, which is not dimmed if not commended by variety. Nature above all delights in variety; in all this huge concourse of things, she has left nothing anywhere unpainted by her wonderful technique of variety."[62] Practically speaking, "this form of exercise will make no insignificant contribution to the ability to speak or write extempore, and will prevent us from standing there stammering and dumbfounded."[63] Ultimately, says Erasmus, "if we are not instructed in these techniques, we shall often be found unintelligible, harsh, or even totally unable to express ourselves."[64] *Copia*, then, is the very foundation of style.

After these introductory remarks, Erasmus says that he will now "give some brief advice on the exercises by which this faculty may be developed."[65] The next three hundred or so pages are devoted to this "brief advice" on achieving copiousness in both words and ideas. For the most part, variety in words is achieved by the use of figures and tropes, variety in ideas by the rhetorical topics. There is, however, very little discussion of the theory of figurative or topical language in *De Copia*. Rather, the emphasis in Erasmus's book, as in the grammar school classroom, is on practical application in discourse. This approach culminates in a "practical demonstration" of abundance in chapter 33 of *De copia*. Erasmus promises to "take one or two sentences and see how far we can go in transforming the basic expression into a Protean variety of shapes."[66] As it turns out,

---

[58] Translator's Introduction, Erasmus 283.
[59] Erasmus, vol. 24: *Copia: Foundations of Abundant Style.*
[60] Erasmus, *On Copia of Words and Ideas*, trans. Donald B. King and H. David Rix (Milwaukee: Marquette UP, 1963) 9.
[61] Erasmus, *Collected Works* 24:302.
[62] Erasmus, *Collected Works* 24:302.
[63] Erasmus, *Collected Works* 24:302.
[64] Erasmus, *Collected Works* 24:302.
[65] Erasmus, *Collected Works* 303.
[66] Erasmus, *Collected Works* 348.

Erasmus can go so far as to produce 195 variations on the sentence "your letter pleased me mightily."[67] This demonstration is followed by 200 variations on "always, as long as I live, I shall remember you."[68] In this virtuoso performance, Erasmus is being intentionally extreme. He deliberately takes a "not particularly fertile" sentence and creates some 200 variants to show his readers the infinite fecundity of human language. Erasmus does not recommend going quite this far in the classroom; it is, rather, a dramatic testimony to the plasticity of language to those who might not believe it.

There is nothing terribly original about Erasmus's *De copia*. The work is based on broad reading in the classics, a knowledge of rhetorical theory, and great practice in composition. In short, Erasmus's work is the result of an education much like that he had in mind for young boys. *De copia* and the grammar school curriculum were together a celebration of the centrality of language in human affairs. When a student left the grammar school, he might not be able to generate two hundred versions of the same sentence, but he would certainly be prepared to write on any subject with skill, dispatch, and perhaps even eloquence.

JESUIT EDUCATION

An examination of the Grammar School demonstrates just how thoroughly rhetoric dominated the curriculum and directed the teaching of writing in England. This rhetorical domination was not limited to England but was typical of European education as well. The Jesuit educational system, "undoubtedly the most successful and influential to come out of the Renaissance," is proof of this rhetorical emphasis.[69]

Not long after its founding (the order was sanctioned by Pope Paul III in 1540), the order became deeply involved in education, an association which has, of course, persisted to the present. The founder of the order, Ignatius Loyola, had established both a primary school and a college. By the early seventeenth century, there were nearly 300 Jesuit colleges in existence. These colleges were the backbone of the Jesuit educational mission. They were secondary schools, offering an education between the elementary and university levels. As such, they roughly parallel the English grammar schools. Students in the humanities courses were typically between ten and sixteen years of age.

Beginning in the middle of the sixteenth century and lasting well beyond the Renaissance, the order's schools were guided by the *Ratio*

---

[67]Erasmus, *Collected Works* 348–54.
[68]Erasmus, *Collected Works* 354–64.
[69]Scaglione 51.

studiorum, the Jesuit plan of studies. The educational objectives of the *Ratio studiorum* were being developed as early as 1540, preliminary versions were issued in 1586 and 1589, and the definitive version was promulgated in 1599. The *Ratio studiorum* was derived from the pedagogical precepts of antiquity and, like classical education, it was intended to produce students who were masters of eloquence.[70]

To achieve this goal, the *Ratio studiorum* stipulated that five courses were to be taken over a period of five years: three courses in progressively advanced Latin and Greek grammar, followed by a course in humanities, and culminating in the study of rhetoric. The humanities class acted as a kind of transition between the grammatical studies and rhetorical studies. Edward Lynch summarizes the content of this course:

> The aim of this class is to lay the foundation for eloquence, after the pupils have finished the grammar classes. This is done in three ways: by a knowledge of the language, some erudition, and a sketch of the precepts pertaining to rhetoric. For a command of the language, which consists chiefly in acquiring propriety of expression and fluency, the one orator used in daily prelections is Cicero; among historians, Caesar, Sallust, Livy, Curtius, and others like them; among the poets, Virgil, excepting some of the eclogues and the fourth book of the Aeneid, as well as Horace's *Odes*, and elegies, epigrams, and other works of classic poets.[71]

After completing the class in humanities, the student was ready for the study of rhetoric, the goal of which was to attain

> perfect eloquence, which comprises two great faculties, the oratorical and the poetical. It regards not only the practical but also the cultural. For the precepts of oratory, Cicero may be supplemented by Aristotle and Quintilian. Style is to be formed on Cicero, though help may be drawn from approved historians and poets. Erudition will be derived from the history and manners of nations, and from the authorities of writers and every sort of learning.[72]

The rhetoric text specified in the 1599 *Ratio studiorum* was *De arte rhetorica libri tres, ex Aristotele, Cicerone, et Quinctiliano praecipue deprompti*

---

[70] The literature about Jesuit education is vast. For discussions of rhetoric's place in it see, in addition to Scaglione, Edward Lynch, S.J., "The Origin and Development of Rhetoric in the Plan of Studies of 1599 of the Society of Jesus," PhD diss., Northwestern U, 1968, Jean Deitz Moss, "The Rhetoric Course at the Collegio Romano in the Latter Half of the Sixteenth Century," *Rhetoric* 4 (1986) 137–52, and François de Dainville, *L'education des jésuites* (Paris: Minuit, 1978) esp. chapter 2: "Humanites classiques" 167–307. John W. O'Malley discusses the early importance of an educational program in *The First Jesuits* (Cambridge: Harvard UP, 1993) 200–42.

[71] Lynch 261.

[72] Lynch 262.

(1557?) of Cypriano Suárez, S.J. (1524–93). Although Suárez's *De arte rhetorica* was not required until 1599, it was in use in Jesuit colleges well before that date. Because of its association with the *Ratio studiorum*, *De arte rhetorica* became one of the most widely used of all Renaissance rhetoric textbooks in Europe and, of course, in the New World as well. The *Ratio studiorum* of 1599 was made mandatory in some 245 Jesuit schools in Europe and in Europe's overseas empires.[73] And while Suárez's book was not used at all Jesuit institutions, it was the required text in a great many of these schools.[74]

Suárez's book is well suited to the Jesuit goal of *eloquentia perfecta*—it is a distillation of the precepts from the great rhetorical triumvirate of antiquity: Cicero, Aristotle, and Quintilian. As much as he admires these three authorities, Suárez believes that no single ancient text dealt adequately with the entire art of rhetoric. Suárez proceeds to enumerate the faults of each of the basic treatises written by his three sources.[75]

Because of these inadequacies, Suárez says "our [Jesuit] teachers desired: to collect all the elements of eloquence in some book, method, and plan; to explain these with definitions and to illustrate them with examples from the teaching of Aristotle; in the case of Cicero and Quintilian to include not only their teaching but usually their very words."[76] This is precisely what Suárez does, with the intention of assisting "young men to read the learned books of Aristotle, Cicero, and Quintilian wherein lie the wellsprings of eloquence."[77]

Suárez is committed to the utility of ancient precepts, and sees no reason to tinker with them in the sixteenth century. He is aware, he says:

> that many of the teachings handed down by the ancients are attacked even in
> published books by people who should more reasonably have defended
> them. However, since many persons of exceptional learning have defended
> these teachings, I have decided not to change, without a good reason, what
> the judgment of so many centuries of learning has approved. In fact, I
> strongly urge you, Christian reader, to uproot completely from your mind
> this inordinate desire to contradict ancient writers rashly, so that it does not
> then proceed further towards the undoing of your intellect.[78]

---

[73]Lynch 258.

[74]For a discussion of the Jesuit teaching of rhetoric in Spain's American colonies, see Don Paul Abbott, *Rhetoric in the New World* (Columbia: U of South Carolina P, 1996) 102–20.

[75]Lawrence J. Flynn, "The *De Artes Rhetorica* (1568) by Cyprian Soarez, S.J.: A Translation with Introduction and Notes," PhD diss., U of Florida, 1955, 105–07.

[76]Flynn 108.

[77]Flynn 108.

[78]Flynn 108–09.

Having thus affirmed the superiority of ancient precepts, Suárez proceeds to present a compendium of classical rhetoric. In his introduction, Suárez summarizes *De arte rhetorica* this way:

> In the first book, which concerns invention, sixteen topics for arguments are explained, and at the same time the matter suitable for arousing hearers is extracted from them. Certain rules are also set forth adapted to embellishment and deliberation [demonstrative and deliberative speaking]. The second book which contains rules for arrangement treats the divisions of a speech, the status, judgment, and the kind of dispute which arises over the meaning of a writing. Also, syllogistic reasoning, enthymeme, induction, and example are treated. Besides, since ancient writers frequently refer to the epichereme, sorites, and dilemma, the effectiveness of these is explained. Finally, the third book teaches the embellishment of speech contained in words, either simple or compound. It also discusses rare and new words, tropes, ornaments of words and of thoughts; the origin, cause, nature, and use of well knit metrical prose; and finally, it treats memory and delivery.[79]

Thus, students in Jesuit colleges could expect to be inundated with unadulterated classical rhetoric, whether in Europe, or Mexico, or Peru. What is striking about the Jesuit college curriculum is its similarity with the English grammar school. Pedagogically, at least, the Reformation and Counter-Reformation served to reinforce the need for training eloquent and persuasive advocates for the true Christianity. Thus, despite great theological differences, education in both Protestant and Catholic countries recognized the need for writing instruction based on the precepts of ancient rhetoric.

WOMEN AND RHETORIC

An examination of the curricula of the grammar schools and the Jesuit colleges furnishes a great deal of information about the practice of literary pedagogy in the Renaissance. Such an institutional approach does not, of course, tell us very much about those excluded from these institutions. The grammar schools and the Jesuit colleges were concerned almost exclusively with the education of young boys of the upper class and nobility. English boys of the lower classes had much less opportunity to participate, and girls, of whatever class, had even less opportunity for an institutional education. The Jesuits taught only boys. The exclusion of women from these schools is especially striking in light of the humanists' acknowledg-

---

[79]Flynn 112–13.

ment of the need, indeed the duty, to educate women as well as men. The educational reformers recommended a classical and humanistic education for girls, which was similar in methods and materials to that recommended for boys. Despite the similarity of male and female education, the humanists believed that there must be fundamental differences between the teaching of girls and boys. One of the most striking distinctions between the two programs is seen in the humanists' conviction that, unlike men, women should not be taught rhetoric. Leonardo Bruni, in a letter to Baptista Malatesta written in 1405 or 1406, proposes what an educated lady should study and should not study. Bruni says that the "subtleties of Arithmetic and Geometry are not worthy to absorb a cultivated mind, and the same must be said of Astrology." He adds:

> the great and complex art of rhetoric should be placed in the same category. My chief reason is the obvious one, that I have in view the cultivation most fitting a woman. To her neither the intricacies of debate nor the oratorical artifices of action and delivery are of the least practical use, if indeed they are not positively unbecoming. Rhetoric in all its forms—public discussion, forensic argument, logical fence, and the like—lies absolutely outside the province of woman.[80]

Vives makes much the same point in *The Instruction of a Christian Woman*: "The study of wisdome, the which doth enstruct their manners, and enfourme their lyving, and teacheth them the waye good and holy lyfe. As for eloquence, I have no great care, nor a woman nedeth it not, but she nedeth goodnes and wysedome."[81] Both Bruni and Vives make clear that instructing a woman in rhetoric, the most public of arts, is unproductive because women were, for the most part, excluded from public life. As Margaret King says of the educated women of the Renaissance: "Such women had been educated to do nothing and go nowhere."[82] Girls were educated to participate in the private life of the home, whereas boys were educated to participate in the public life of the Church and the state.

The exclusion of women from public life, and hence from instruction in rhetoric, would have obvious implications for the teaching of writing to women. It is not necessarily the case, however, that excluding women from instruction in rhetoric resulted in a female education entirely separated from the rhetorical tradition. Most humanists agreed that women needed many, but of course not all, of the skills required by men. Thus Richard Mulcaster identifies four subjects that the "young maiden" must master:

[80]"Leonardo D'Arezzo Concerning the Study of Literature," *Classics in the Education of Girls and Women*, ed. Shirley Nelson Kersey (Metuchen: Scarecrow, 1981) 23.

[81]Kersey 40.

[82]Margaret King, *Women of the Renaissance* (Chicago: U of Chicago P, 1991) 213.

"*reading* well, *writing* faire, *singing* sweet, *playing* fine."[83] Mulcaster adds
that the "young gentlewoman" should also "speake the learned languages
[. . .] with some *Logicall* helpe to chop, and some *Rhetoricke* to brave."[84] A
significant portion of a girl's (as well as a boy's) education must be devoted
to reading and writing. Rarely do the humanists make distinctions about
the methods used to impart basic literacy to either boys or girls, but beyond the elementary level the approaches begin to diverge. This is particularly true when it comes to reading material. Bruni says that the gentlewoman has before her "as a subject peculiarly her own, the whole field of
religion and morals."[85] The goal of Bruni and other humanists is to instill
in the young gentlewoman a sense of prudent and chaste behavior appropriate to the good wife and caring mother. This can be accomplished, says
Bruni, not only by the careful reading of Christian texts, but by the "noblest intellects of Greece and Rome."[86] Bruni recommends the ancient historians as especially instructive, but also emphasizes that "the great Orators of antiquity must by all means be included. Nowhere do we find the
virtues more warmly extolled, the vices so fiercely decried" (24).[87] While
there was little need for women to practice oratory, there was every reason
for women to read the speeches of orators past. At least since Isocrates, a
rationale for rhetoric was that it offered moral inculcation, and that rationale obtained in the Renaissance. Indeed, Bruni claims that questions of
morality and virtue be pursued by "men and women alike," but religion
and morals "hold the first place in the education of a Christian lady."[88]
Thus, while there was, therefore, no need to train women to be orators,
there was every reason, literary and moral, that they should be acquainted
with the rhetorical tradition.

Moreover, there were those who ignored the injunction against teaching women rhetoric. Perhaps the most notable exceptions were the education of Mary and Elizabeth Tudor. Vives supervised the education of
Mary, and Roger Ascham taught Elizabeth. Ascham appears to have used
his tutelage of Elizabeth as an opportunity to test the methods recommended in the *Scholemaster*. Mary and Elizabeth are, however, special cases
because, as potential rulers, they were given what was essentially a man's
education. Other women also received classical and humanistic training.
Thomas More ensured that his three daughters, Margaret, Cecilia, and
Elizabeth, together with Margaret Giggs, a relative, were taught the complete humanistic curriculum.

---

[83]Kersey 64.
[84]Kersey 65.
[85]Kersey 23.
[86]Kersey 23.
[87]Kersey 24.
[88]Kersey 24.

Although few households were as enlightened as More's, women were typically educated at home by a tutor or family member. Frequently, initial literacy in the vernacular was the responsibility of the women of the household. Thus, when there emerged in the Renaissance what King calls "the female voice," that voice was typically expressed in the vernacular.

Relatively few girls attended a school beyond the most elementary. This, of course, was true of boys as well. Few children, male or female, were sufficiently privileged to enjoy the benefits of an institutional education. Boys were excluded from education by class and economics; girls were excluded for these reasons as well as gender. Thus, the education of women occurred outside educational institutions; women learned to speak and write in a manner influenced by, but not truly a part of, the rhetorical tradition.[89]

CONCLUSION

Those sufficiently privileged to attend schools, and especially the English Grammar Schools, received an education designed to endow students with eloquence. Furthermore, this eloquence was to be a special kind: the classical eloquence of Cicero's citizen-orator. The theory and practice of Cicero and the pedagogy of Quintilian shaped a curriculum reverential toward the past and yet attentive to the present. These Latin grammar schools could, therefore, teach an ancient language and also prize eloquence in the vernacular. The rhetorical tradition was so persistent that despite the influence of printing, the spoken word of the classical oration remained the dominant pattern for all discourse. Just as the oration remained pre-eminent, so too did the educational methods of antiquity. The inescapable necessity of imitation as the only way to master expression was virtually unchallenged. In these fundamental ways, the teaching of writing in the Renaissance differs from current practices.[90] Yet the differences may be neither as great nor as insurmountable as they appear.

From the writing teacher's standpoint, at least, the grammar school and Jesuit masters had a clear advantage over their successors. The curricula were almost entirely literary; the teaching of reading, writing, and speaking was the sole effort of the master, every day and every form. It is im-

---

[89]For an excellent treatment of women's education in the Italian Renaissance, see Anthony Grafton and Lisa Jardine, *From Humanism to the Humanities* (London: Duckworth, 1986) 29–57. Their account asks the crucial question: "Women Humanists: Education for What?"

[90]Dale L. Sullivan details the "modern inability to appreciate imitation as a serious pedagogical method" in "Attitudes toward Imitation: Classical Culture and the Modern Temper," *Rhetoric Review* 8 (1989): 5–21.

probable that many would want to claim such an advantage and surrender the infinitely more diverse curriculum of modern times. Nor could a technological society ever accept an exclusively literary education. While we cannot return to the Renaissance, we can perhaps approximate some of the best of its cultural aspirations and find in the work of great educational theorists and practitioners inspiration for present efforts.

Perhaps the greatest advantage of Renaissance education was an approach to language instruction that was concentrated and unified, whereas ours has been, in contrast, diluted and diffuse. What Renaissance educators combined, we have fragmented and departmentalized. The Renaissance recognition of the primacy of language and the unity of all acts of expression is, however, beginning to reassert itself. "Writing across the curriculum" is the most obvious but not the only manifestation of this attitude. While we have not approached the Renaissance pervasiveness of language in education, we increasingly recognize that the teaching of writing cannot be restricted to one hour three times a week. While we are unlikely to restore years of instruction in Latin grammar, we increasingly realize that Americans are not well trained in foreign languages, and this neglect disadvantages us in important ways. What the grammar school experience suggests is that the study of languages, native or foreign, should complement each other rather than be thought of as independent or even mutually irrelevant subjects.

Just as a reunion of languages, native and foreign, is endorsed by Renaissance practice, so too is a reintegration of the spoken and written word. The historically recent division of "English" and "Speech Communication" into separate departments would confound any grammar school master or, for that matter, virtually any rhetorician before, say, 1900.[91] The revival of rhetoric has already begun to subvert this division, but the divisions between disciplines are still very potent.

This disunity of the discourse arts is apparent, too, in present approaches to reading and writing. Literary criticism, as we know it, cannot be said to exist in the grammar school. Classroom literary analysis was designed to provide the student with appropriate moral and philosophical ideas for discourse and to demonstrate the possibilities of style which could ultimately be emulated. In other words, reading served writing. To the grammar school master, the reflexive nature of most critical inquiry would be incomprehensible. Reading, writing, and reciting existed as closely correlated activities, but writing and speaking were always the end, and reading and textual analysis were the means to that end.

---

[91]For discussions of the separation of the written and spoken word in American education, see James A. Berlin, *Rhetoric and Reality: Writing Instruction in American Colleges, 1900–1985* (Carbondale: Southern Illinois UP, 1987) and James J. Murphy, *The Rhetorical Tradition and Modern Writing* (New York: MLA, 1982).

The study of language is certainly a major preoccupation of the twentieth century. Yet, that study is dispersed over a wide variety of fields, some of which are oblivious to the practical pursuit of any kind of eloquence. In the Renaissance, that interest in language was concentrated in the study of "grammar," broadly defined, and rhetoric. It is this concentration that gives Renaissance rhetoric much of its effectiveness. Brian Vickers suggests that the Renaissance "reintegrated" the study of rhetoric after the "fragmentation" of the art following the fall of Rome.[92] Perhaps it is not too much to hope that histories such as this one might further the reintegration of rhetoric into the twentieth-century curriculum, helping to restore rhetoric to its historical mission of teaching writing and speaking and, ultimately, eloquence.

---

[92]Brian Vickers, *In Defence of Rhetoric* (Oxford: Clarendon, 1988) chapter 5: "Renaissance Reintegration," 254–93.

Chapter 6

Writing Instruction in Great Britain: The Eighteenth and Nineteenth Centuries

Linda Ferreira-Buckley
Winifred Bryan Horner

> ***Key Concepts.*** *Social and political changes* • *Politics and religion* • *English vernacular versus Latin* • *Writing versus oratory* • *Methods of writing instruction* • *Early continuity of medieval pedagogy* • *Imitation and memorization* • *Study of "Belles lettres" as models* • Hugh Blair's Lectures on Rhetoric and Belles Lettres • *Richard Whately's "Argumentative Composition"* • *George Jardine's objection to dictation* • *Dissenting academies* • *Examinations and themes* • *1831 Report of the Royal Commission* • *Introduction of the personal essay* • *Responses to writing* • *Composition favored over literature* • *"Redbrick" universities* • *Writing instruction for working people* • *Writing instruction in Scotland, Wales, and Ireland* • *Scottish universities on continental plan* • *Three Scottish educators: Aytoun, Bain, and Jardine* • *Gaelic and Welsh vernaculars discouraged* • *Improvement of female education* • *University Extension Lecture movement* • *Salons* • *Entrance of women into universities* • *Foundation of women's colleges*

As the preceding chapters have made clear, the reign of classical languages as the medium of scholarship and learning ensured that the study of Latin and Greek would dominate the curricula of schools and universities in Great Britain. During the eighteenth and nineteenth centuries, however, the sovereignty of the classical languages was increasingly challenged, and writing instruction in English evolved in response to social, political, religious, and economic developments. Three related linguistic factors altered the way writing was taught: the gradual abandonment of Latin as the language of education and culture; the shift from an oral culture to a basically literate one, that is, from an emphasis on speaking to an emphasis on writing; and the proliferation of books and periodicals. This essay looks at how such developments affected the teaching of writing and rhetoric in schools and universities in eighteenth- and nineteenth-century Britain, that territory encompassing England, Scotland, Wales, and Ireland. Although the period and society covered is far more complex than the comparatively uniform culture of the preceding chapter, the generalizations offered here should help readers appreciate the diversity of language instruction of the period. Because of the geographic and cultural breadth of this essay, neither chronology nor topic nor location alone suffices as an organizational principle; thus the exposition deploys all three. The chapter first reviews trends that cut across the period and examines dominant methods of writing pedagogy. It then takes up the educational opportunities particular to each of the British Isles. Finally, it turns to female education since girls did not share most of the privileges enjoyed by boys.

It was a time of great social change. The eighteenth century saw rapid industrialization, and across Britain, the rural agricultural population migrated to cities in large numbers. Between 1700 and 1800, Manchester and Liverpool mushroomed into industrial centers. Between 1800 and 1900, Scotland changed from a poor agricultural society to a relatively industrialized one, whose population increased from 84,000 to 500,000, and Wales became a leading exporter of coal and iron, its population quadrupling. Incensed by the government's economic policies, workers there rioted, contributing to upper-class anxiety about class rebellions. The 1800 Act of Union dissolved the Dublin Parliament, and Ireland came fully under British control. Between 1800 and 1900, Ireland lost half of its population to famine and emigration, with those remaining suffering the hardships of British colonization; Irish nationalists' agitation also increased British attempts at control.

Along with such shifts came economic growth and political reforms that dispersed power beyond the traditional power bases. Preparatory schools and universities were either not available or not adequate to meet the challenges. At the beginning of the eighteenth century, England had only two universities (Oxford and Cambridge), Ireland one (Trinity), Scotland four (Edinburgh, Glasgow, St. Andrews, and Aberdeen), Wales none. By the end of the nineteenth century, dozens had been established. Secondary schools proliferated due to economic stability and the presumption of opportunities. The middle classes, especially the large and powerful merchant class, sought access to education, including training in reading, writing, and speaking the vernacular. A sign of good breeding, "proper

English" was a rung on the ladder of upward mobility for the native English and the provincial alike.

Lectures, coffee houses, clubs, and societies proliferated, providing active forums for such interests. The literary scenes of London, Edinburgh, and Dublin were intellectually lively, giving rise to such journals as the *Spectator*, *Rambler*, and *Edinburgh Review*, all of which helped to standardize and valorize English. They published good prose and celebrated it. Hundreds of other less famous newspapers and periodicals surfaced locally or nationally and encouraged interest in the vernacular. In the middle of the eighteenth century, Adam Smith, Robert Watson, Hugh Blair, and Thomas Sheridan delivered rhetoric lectures at the urging of Henry Homes, later Lord Kames, who believed that such refinements were necessary if Edinburgh professionals were to advance. The lectures were well attended and became part of the regular university curriculum. Just so, in towns and cities across the British Isles, in single and serial lectures, specialists (and a few charlatans) lectured men and women, boys and girls, on the proper uses of spoken and written English.[1]

Never separate after the Jacobite defeat in 1746, religion and politics played important parts in the drama of education and writing instruction in the eighteenth and nineteenth centuries. Since most eighteenth-century teachers were clergymen and many university students were training for the ministry, education was often connected with religion. Poor children received what little education they could from church-sponsored schools or foundations. Secular educational institutions were rare. Religion was considered the rationale for, and basis of, education; proponents argued that education was a path to virtue. Not surprisingly, then, much writing instruction centered on sermon writing, as young men were trained to marshal the wisdom of the scriptures for instruction in daily living. Such instruction varied radically, of course, according to the propensities of Anglicans, Dissenters, and Catholics. Not only do the most famous rhetoricians of the time take up sermon writing, but it also forms the subject of dozens of current manuals. Collections of sermons enjoyed brisk sales; students of all ages might develop their prose style by studying sermons according to the dictates of imitation exercises.

Those who were not members of the Anglican Church faced serious educational obstacles in Great Britain. The 1662 Act of Uniformity required all students and teachers to swear allegiance to the Church of England, prohibiting dissenters from matriculating at Oxford and Cambridge. Other restrictions applied. While uniting the parliaments of England and Scotland, the 1707 Act of Union allowed Scotland to retain independence in educa-

---

[1] D. D. McElroy's *Scotland's Age of Improvement: A Survey of Eighteenth-Century Clubs and Societies* (Pullman: Washington State UP, 1969) remains the best first source.

tion and religion. Its well-established universities—highly respected academically in England and on the continent, and with no religious constraints—attracted multitudes of students. At the beginning of the period, students wishing to remain in England turned to the many dissenting academies run by religious nonconformists, which provided a university-equivalent education; later, they might attend one of the "redbrick" universities founded to provide the middle classes with a practical education. Anglicans serious about education often chose one of these options since Oxford and Cambridge were reputed to have become morally and educationally decadent. It is in these academies and in the Scottish and English redbrick universities that disciplinary innovations took place, where English as an academic subject flourished, where instruction in writing came to mean writing in English instead of writing in Latin, topics discussed next.

THE LINGUISTIC SITUATION

A rise in nationalism also contributed to the growing acceptance of English vernacular language and literature. Although men and women of culture had long read English literature at home, it was still considered popular literature unworthy of formal instruction. But as the demographics of schooling changed, students could no longer be expected to command "proper" English, and thus English became a regular part of the curriculum, English literature serving as, in J. D. Palmer's words, "the poor man's classics," or, we might add, the provincial's classics, gaining full respectability only in the twentieth century.[2] Nationalism also gave rise to a reverence for the past, hence the nostalgia for local vernaculars such as Scots and Gaelic, manifesting itself in the recovery, study, and promotion of folk literature. The Edinburgh literati, for example, sponsored James McPherson's "recovery" of the Ossian poems. They longed for a record of a Scots literary tradition, even as they repudiated "Scotticisms" in their own written prose. Some Irish and Welsh cherished indigenous literature, even as their own use of the vernacular was deemed unlearned, vulgar, and an impediment to British nationalism.[3] Local vernaculars were banished from

---

[2] D. J. Palmer, *The Rise of English Studies* (London Oxford UP, 1965) 78.

[3] The diminishment of Scots, Gaelic, and Welsh has been well documented, including the role played by British educational policies. For example, Parliament's mid-nineteenth-century educational reforms cautioned against allowing Welsh to be used in school; by century's end, only half of the population spoke Welsh, and very few could write it. Gaelic also suffered In 1800, half of the Irish population spoke only Gaelic; by mid-century, only a quarter of the population could even speak Gaelic (of these, only 5% were monolingual). Many families, eager for their children to prosper, supported these early English-only policies. For additional information, see, for example, David Williams's *A Short History of Modern Wales* (London: J. Murray, 1962), and Sean O'Tuama's edited collection, *The Gaelic League Idea* (Cork: Mercier, 1972).

provincial classrooms. Such prejudice no doubt helped to legitimize the study of English. Teachers, elocutionists, grammarians, and lexicographers—with Enlightenment faith in rationality and rules—set out to standardize English, firm in the belief that change indicated deterioration and that Latin grammar was the standard by which all languages should be measured. Such beliefs would be increasingly challenged. The eighteenth century saw the publication of Nathaniel Bailey's *Universal Etymological Dictionary* (1721) and Samuel Johnson's *Dictionary of the English Language* (1755); the late nineteenth of the *Oxford (or New) English Dictionary*, testimony to the growing respectability of the vernacular, even in learned circles.

Interest in national language encouraged reexamination of older English texts stored in libraries such as the British Museum, the Bodleian at Oxford, and the University Library at Cambridge. As Jo McMurtry explains, by the end of the nineteenth century, Victorians "had found, edited, and published virtually the entire canon of English literature" in addition to such scholarly tools as concordances and dictionaries.[4] Early in the eighteenth century, university students would hear about word histories as they were schooled in proper usage; by the end of the nineteenth, they would be examined extensively in philology, that is, historical and comparative linguistics. As scholarship broadened, new guidelines for academic writing were developed and passed on.

During the eighteenth and nineteenth centuries, schools, dissenting academies, and universities shifted to English, but the shift was gradual and contested, and cultured persons in the eighteenth century read and wrote in Latin. Oxford, Cambridge, Trinity, and many of the oldest grammar and public schools clung to the classical languages. In English, Scottish, Welsh, and Irish grammar schools, students learned Latin grammar and wrote extensively—in Latin. Their religious exercises, too, were in Latin, and they sang psalms in the classical languages. At many schools, regulations mandated that all discussions, save those in family groups, were to be in Latin, although it is difficult to determine how steadfastly such rules were observed. What's more, literacy was defined as the ability to read and write Latin. Objections to the dominance of the classical languages were raised as education began to have more utilitarian ends for merchants and other men of business.

Another consequential shift was that from the spoken to the written, from the oral to the literate. Although most writing instruction in the eighteenth and nineteenth centuries drew upon rhetorical theory, available rhetorical theories were diverse. Rhetoric had long privileged the study of

---

[4]Jo McMurtry, *English Language, English Literature: The Creation of an Academic Discipline* (Hamden: Archon, 1985).

oratory. Students had engaged in many and varied written exercises to develop their stylistic virtuosity and had often composed themes, but these had been considered scripts for oral delivery or preparatory training for writing speeches. (Indeed, until well into the nineteenth century, most significant examinations remained oral, precursors of today's PhD dissertation defenses.) For most of our period, writing instruction built explicitly on this rhetorical tradition. Although "rhetoric" long referred to "public *Speaking* alone," Richard Whately explains in *Elements of Rhetoric* (1828), "as most of the rules for Speaking are of course applicable equally to Writing, an extension of the term naturally took place; and we find even Aristotle, the earliest systematic writer on the subject whose works have come down to us, including in his Treatise rules for such compositions as were not intended to be publicly recited."[5]

Whately goes on to observe that

> [t]he invention of Printing by extending the sphere of operation of the Writer, has of course contributed to the extension of those terms which, in their primary signification, had reference to Speaking alone. Many objects are now accomplished through the medium of the Press, which formerly came under the exclusive province of the Orator; and the qualifications requisite for success are so much the same in both cases, that we apply the term "Eloquent" as readily to a Writer as to a Speaker [. . .] because *some part* of the rules to be observed in Oratory, or rules analogous to these, are applicable to such compositions. Conformably to this view, therefore, some writers have spoken of Rhetoric as the Art of Composition, universally; or, with the exclusion of Poetry alone, as embracing all Prose-composition. (2–3)

Other theorists, he later notes, confine the term to "Persuasive Speaking" (4) or extend the discipline more widely to include discourses in art, law, logic, ethics, and politics. Indeed, in the eighteenth and nineteenth centuries, theorists and teachers variously defined rhetoric and writing instruction narrowly or broadly, necessitating that generalizations about language theories of the period be grounded in particular cases.

Prior to the eighteenth century, writing instruction per se had centered upon oratory, letters, and sermons, but as people's interests were increasingly served by government representatives and the legal profession during the eighteenth century, the dominance of oratory decreased as writing became the medium of communication and record. Oratorical exercises lost favor in some schools, yet "elocution"—a truncated rhetoric of delivery (rhetoric's fifth canon or office)—enjoyed great popularity, even as

---

[5]Richard Whately, *Elements of Rhetoric*, ed. D. Ehninger (Carbondale: Southern Illinois UP, 1963) 2.

critics decried its limitations and excesses.[6] The oral uses of language continued to draw the attention of school and university students, as it did George Drummond, a student in John Stevenson's logic course at Edinburgh, whose theme "Rules of Conversation," dated 25 April 1740, is one of many on such topics currently housed in university archives across Great Britain. Manuals and essays celebrated the virtues of conversation and proffered advice on how to engage in its practice. Thomas De Quincey's "Conversation," which first appeared in 1847 in *Tait's Magazine*, maintained that "[w]ithout an art, without some simple system of rules, gathered from experience of such contingencies as are most likely to mislead the practice when left to its own guidance, no act of man nor effort accomplishes its purposes in perfection."[7] Facility in conversation, it was assumed, was linked to facility in writing. To be sure, interest in the oral uses of language changed but did not disappear.

Another factor in the changing linguistic scene was the rapid increase in the reading public, which, in turn, created a large class of writers who wrote specifically for this populace. Spirited exchanges ensued in the numerous printed publications of the period—books, pamphlets, and periodicals. Public and private libraries increased in number and size. Accordingly, more readers wished to write proficiently, if not expertly. Writing manuals and textbooks became more and more numerous to serve this reading and writing public, helped by new printing technologies that cheapened production costs.[8] At the beginning of the eighteenth century Latin was still favored for textbooks; by the end of the nineteenth the trend was reversed. (Lectures follow suit.) At first English and Latin texts were used side by side, since good English textbooks were not available. At some of the academies, Latin textbooks "were abridged and translated by students before being used by them" (McLachlan 22). Often instructors wrote their own; more of-

---

[6]Wilbur Samuel Howell emphasizes the reductive nature of elocution by quoting the opening line of an elocutionary manual—"Always breathe through the nostrils"—alongside that of Aristotle's *Rhetoric*—"Rhetoric is the counterpart of dialectic." See Wilbur Samuel Howell, *Eighteenth-Century British Logic and Rhetoric* (Princeton: Princeton UP, 1971) 145–256. Howell's criticisms notwithstanding, elocution sometimes constituted a rich component of rhetorical education.

[7]Thomas De Quincey, *Selected Essays on Rhetoric by Thomas De Quincey* (Carbondale: Southern Illinois UP, 1967) 264.

[8]Ian Michael's *The Teaching of English: From the Sixteenth Century to 1870* (London: Cambridge UP, 1987) documents three centuries of British textbooks dedicated to the study of English and thus serves as an invaluable reference. Although Michael devotes only a dozen pages (303–16) to those texts explicitly teaching "written expression," other sections also pertain to composition instruction. Also see Louis G. Kelly's *Twenty-Five Centuries of Language Teaching: An Inquiry into the Science, Art, and Development of Language Teaching Methodology, 500 B.C.–1969* (Rowley: Newbury, 1969).

ten still their dictated lectures served as textbooks for the class. By the end
of our period, textbook publishing was big business.

METHODS OF WRITING INSTRUCTION

Though we can draw some generalizations, writing curriculums varied.
Scottish Common Sense Philosophy proved especially influential, while
classical rhetoric waned in the course of the nineteenth century. It is difficult to document the ways writing was actually taught during this period,
since much instruction was oral and since instruction in writing was to
some degree integrated into every course, the acknowledged responsibility of every instructor. When classics dominated the curriculum, pupils
practiced their language skills as they studied the geography, history, and
arts of the ancient world; so too, as English became the language of instruction for studies across the curriculum, students wrote in the vernacular as never before. In the following discussion, we draw from textbooks,
lectures, student notes, books on education, and university calendars. Of
course, such sources are not infallible because, in some cases, they indicate
what individuals felt ought to be done, not what was actually done.

Language Exercises

Medieval pedagogy lasted well into the period. The trivium of grammar,
logic, and rhetoric provided solid, if somewhat tired, training in communication skills during much of the eighteenth century. Texts such as John
Holmes's *The Art of Rhetoric Made Easy* (London, 1739), John Lawson's *Lectures Concerning Oratory* (Dublin, 1758), and John Ward's *A System of Oratory*
(London, 1759) reveal typical pedagogical approaches. Instructors believed that in order to learn to read, one first had to learn to spell and that
the study of grammar was basic to writing instruction. Thus, students progressed from words to sentences to paragraphs to themes and finally to
lengthier compositions or orations. Memorizing and modeling were common methods of improving student writing. Well into the twentieth century, grammar and writing instruction remained inextricably bound.
    As earlier noted, at the start of our period, grammar was the grammar
of Latin since writing instruction was writing Latin; however, as part of this
instruction, students were required to translate "into a good English stile"
(Michael 274), and as late as the end of the nineteenth century, proficiency in English was often tested by translation from Latin. Writing and
speaking, English and Latin were likely to be taught side by side, instruction in one reinforcing instruction in the other (making the commonplace
that classical languages prevailed somewhat misleading). For example, a

master might dictate a letter for the student to write out in Latin, then transpose into English (Michael 308). Whether in Latin, or English, or Latin and English, medieval exercises comprised an integral part of writing instruction. Eventually, as modern foreign languages came into the curriculum, studying them was also considered a viable means of improving English. In 1867, for instance, a master at Eton urged that French or another modern language be substituted for Latin as a means of improving English (Michael 311). The redbrick universities and academies often taught such languages as German, French, Arabic, and Punjab, alongside the classical ones, all of which contributed somewhat to the students' abilities in English. True, not everyone approved, since Latin had long been considered paradigmatic, and arguments about what language ought to be primary in school continued throughout our period.

What we today call basic English was sometimes part of writing instruction. Unlike the elitist and exclusive Oxford and Cambridge, the more democratic Scottish universities and redbrick universities served many students who were not proficient speakers and writers in the standard received British dialect. Eradicating provincialisms fell within their educational mission. Language instruction covered fundamentals.

Grammar was considered a necessary part of all composition instruction of the period and was therefore stressed at all levels. Based on the assumption of a universal grammar common to all languages, the Latin system was at first adapted without change to English. In the grammar schools, the students were often expected to know their grammar books by heart; instruction might then proceed in catechetical fashion. Grammar exercises associated with the old rhetoric were also widely used by students at all levels: imitation; varying (which involved changing a sentence into all of its possible forms); paraphrasing; and prosing (turning verse into prose). Transposition, a common exercise, entailed "the placing of Words out of their natural Order, to render the Sound of them more agreeable to the Ear" (cited in Michael 283). Elliptical exercises were sentences with some omitted words that the student was expected to supply. These exercises were used in the nineteenth century, though perhaps less frequently; translation from Latin into "correct English" and later from a modern foreign language continued to be used well into the twentieth century.

The practical benefits of ridding these students of their "rusticisms" and in training them in mechanics of a written standard cannot be overestimated, even as we lament cultural biases. Usage lessons, designed especially for students trying to eradicate traces of a provincial dialect, supplemented textbooks and instruction in writing. In addition to their notetaking, in whatever form practiced, university students often continued the preparatory school exercises, inherited from the medieval universities and the Latin tradition.

Memorizing books and literary passages was common practice even at the university level, for students were expected to have patterns of good writing in their head. Parsing sentences and correcting "false English" were also widely practiced. Students were expected to correct sentences that had errors of spelling, syntax, or punctuation and to cite the rule that had been violated. The master then corrected the exercises orally and returned them to the students, who, with the help of classmates, made their own corrections in writing. Since paper was expensive, students often wrote their first versions on slates and copied the corrected version into their notebooks.

Reading and writing remained closely associated with literature, broadly defined. Literary texts, both classical and English, served the rhetoric course as models for good oratory and writing, what McMurtry describes as a sort of "window display, to be taken in snippets [. . .] as illustrations for rhetorical techniques" (122). Although there was little attempt to explore or critique, literature served rhetoric in a very real way since students were often required to imitate models. As examples were more frequently drawn from English rather than from classical literature, interest shifted during the nineteenth century from rhetorical effect to an emphasis on the literature itself. Nevertheless, the early teachers of literature considered instruction in writing part of their mission until newer, more "efficient" methods of evaluating proficiency in English (e.g., testing knowledge of philological and historical fact) came to eclipse essay and oratorical forms. English literature came to dominate newly formed English departments, but writing instruction remained a distinctive part of courses. Communication skills, written and spoken, were recognized as central to the entire educational endeavor.

Although classical rhetorical approaches had always relied upon literary examples, belletristic rhetoric foregrounded the study of the belles lettres. Drawing upon continental theorists and upon his own training in classical rhetoric at the University of Edinburgh, Hugh Blair compiled a broad and accessible guide to reading and writing, *Lectures on Rhetoric and Belles Lettres* (1783). Steeped in classical theory, for which he professes much respect, but determined to revise it for modern use in view of Enlightenment thinking, Blair has been variously characterized as the British Quintilian and as a bridge between Enlightenment and Romantic theories of writing.[9] For Blair and his followers, all humane writing—whether oratory, philosophy, poetry, drama, science—shared fundamentals and thus might all be usefully studied in the rhetoric course. The teaching of oral and written skills were closely linked. (Not until late in the nineteenth cen-

---

[9]See, for example, George A. Kennedy, *Classical Rhetoric and Its Christian and Secular Tradition from Ancient to Modern Times* (Chapel Hill: U of North Carolina P, 1980) 235.

tury did oral and written skills begin to be separated into different courses and different departments.) What's more, such study profited equally the writer or speaker, and the reader or hearer. Blair's text, in full and abridged form, sold well throughout Great Britain in the late eighteenth and nineteenth centuries. It also inspired such other books as William Barron's *Lectures on Belles Lettres and Logic* (London 1806) and Alexander Jamieson's *A Grammar of Rhetoric and Polite Literature* (London 1818). Although the full extent of belletristic rhetoric's reach cannot yet be determined, Blair, along with fellow Scots George Campbell and Henry Homes, Lord Kames, influenced the course of writing instruction in nineteenth-century Britain, broadening the range of texts studied and linking it with literary appreciation. (The work of these Scots was also strongly felt in North America, as Elizabethada Wright and Michael Halloran make clear in chapter 7 of this volume.)[10]

In his "Preface," Richard Whately recalls that *Elements of Rhetoric* (1828) originated for "private use of some young friends" (xxxiii). It went on to serve many boys and young men (and we speculate not a few sisters and wives). Whately was especially interested in student composition, as a tutor at Oriel College, Oxford, as principal of St. Alban's Hall, and when, as Archbishop of Dublin, he worried about cultivating new generations of ministers. Despite Whately's observation that the book was "designed principally for the instruction of *unpractised* writers" (xxxvi), the book was used in colleges as well as in schools, its practical orientation a welcome relief from more theoretical treatments. He revised and expanded *Elements*, each edition attending more to pedagogical concerns, culminating in the seventh edition of 1846.

Whately restricted writing instruction exclusively to "Argumentative Composition," "considering Rhetoric (in conformity with the very just and philosophical view of Aristotle) as an off-shoot from Logic" (*Elements* 4). Whately's popular treatise lays out rules necessary to "*establish*" or "prove" notions "to the satisfaction of *another*" (5). Whately's concern with written rhetoric is often as a script for spoken rhetoric, but his work formed the bases of much nineteenth-century writing instruction. Along with its companion volume, *Elements of Logic* (1826), it guided teaching practices into the twentieth century.

By the time *Elements of Rhetoric* was published, many writers and teachers were loathe to admit studying "rhetorical" precepts, so excessive had been earlier dependence on detailed artificial systems of rhetoric. While deploring such excess, Whately observes: "The simple truth is, TECHNI-

---

[10] The essays collected in Lynee Lewis Gaillet, ed., *Scottish Rhetoric and Its Influences* (Mahwah: Erlbaum, 1998) examine the far-reaching dominance of the Scots in America.

CAL TERMS ARE PART OF LANGUAGE" (19, emphasis in original).
He presents philosophical and practical principles both general and specific to guide understanding. Despite its limitations—its rejection of a full
rhetorical art of invention, its rejection of probable truths, its preference
for inference and neglect of empirical knowledge, its relative neglect of forensic and deliberative topics, its embrace of faculty psychology, and so
on—the textbook and its author taught generations of students to argue
convincingly, if not persuasively. His student John Henry Newman recalled how the prose and reasoning abilities of his Oxford classmates
benefited from Whately's unstinting attention. Indeed, Newman emulated
many of his mentor's methods when teaching school and university in
England and Ireland.

The Lecture System and Writing

There were significant differences between the tutorial system in place at
Trinity and Oxbridge (as Oxford and Cambridge were called) and the lecture system favored by the Scottish and English redbrick universities and
by the dissenting academies. In the latter, lectures were augmented by the
catechetical system whereby the professor lectured for an hour a day and
spent an additional hour or two questioning students about the material
covered in the lecture. The custom of "dictates," where the professor
spoke slowly enough so that the student could take down the lecture word
for word, provided accurate textbooks for the student and practiced him
in composition. But there were abuses. In a moral philosophy course, one
student complained that the professor was dictating "fast enough in all
conscience to keep 20 persons writing" and that he "does not feel very
morally philosophical."[11] Student notes from David Masson's course, for
example, vary little over thirty years. Robert Schmitz tells the story of students who were following Masson's lecture from an earlier set of student
notes. Objecting to changes when Masson deviated from their copies, they
would shuffle their feet in protest, whereupon Masson, rising, would remark, "Gentlemen . . . as I have been in the habit of saying" and would return to his previous years' notes.[12] But more significant, dictation was a
component of writing instruction: it familiarized students with the physical practice of writing and instilled codes of formal English. The methods
employed at the dissenting academies are characteristic:

[11](EUL Ms. Gen. 850). We include manuscript references within the text, employing the
following abbreviations: U of Edinburgh Library, EUL; Glasgow U Library, GUL; and National Library of Scotland, NLS. We also include each library's catalogue numbers.
[12]Cited in Robert Morrell Schmitz, *Hugh Blair* (Morningside Heights: King's Crown) 67.

Some of the later tutors dictated word by word. Others like Doddridge and Priestley read their lectures and then handed over the MSS. to be copied by their pupils at leisure. Belsham spoke from brief hints and imperfect notes. Pye Smith provided pupils with an outline of his principal course.[13]

Working from the broad outline, students then wrote out the details. Sometimes students were given printed lectures, as by Priestley at Hackney College and Warrington. Aided by their small size and in contrast to the ancient English universities, the dissenting academies fostered free discussion. They departed from the traditional lecture course, which, in their case, usually consisted of comment on a text and instead fashioned their courses to suit their own and their students' needs (Smith 263). Students often used their course notes as their text after the medieval fashion. Some embellished their notes with drawings and bits of humor; one set contains scenes from Glasgow in the margins and a reference to Aristotle as the "Rev. J. G. Aristotle" (GUL BC 28–H.3.). Some bound the notes into book form.

Textbooks were expensive, students often poor. Students who could not afford textbooks used their professors' personal libraries although poorly paid academy professors had few to lend. And few dissenting academies had libraries, although university libraries fared better. The redbricks and provincial libraries housed both classical and contemporary guides to writing, as did the better high school libraries. (The work of Hugh Blair, George Campbell, Lord Kames, Lindley Murray, and Richard Whately served as textbooks for almost a hundred years in Britain and elsewhere and were usually available in multiple copies in libraries.)

Some students developed a shorthand in which they took notes (e.g., EUL Ms. Gen 49D), while others used phonetic spellings, a popular movement in the nineteenth century (e.g., EUL Ms. Gen. 700). The professorial practice of dictating notes was indeed common and might well be considered part of writing instruction, drawing on one facet of classical imitation exercises. The extent to which dictates contributed to students' skill in composition undoubtedly varied radically from classroom to classroom. At Glasgow, Jardine objected to this procedure since the student "is constantly occupied with the mechanical operation of transferring the words of the lecture to his note-book." Consequently, his mind is not engaged, and "when he leaves college, accordingly, his port-folio, and not his memory, contains the chief part of the instruction he carries away." He suggested that after leaving the classroom, students immediately review the lecture in their minds and "commit to writing in their own composition,

---

[13]Herbert McLachlin, *English Education under the Test Acts: Being the History of Non-Conformist Academies 1662–1820* (Manchester: Manchester UP, 1931) 23.

whatever they judge to be of leading importance."[14] In this way, he asserts, "The students have to remember,—to select and arrange the materials furnished to them, and to express, on the spur of the occasion, their ideas in plain and perspicuous language" (Jardine 289). Jardine's suggestion of summarizing the lectures in a written composition proved invaluable as a productive exercise in selecting and organizing a body of information. (The only extant set of notes of Adam Smith's rhetoric lectures appear to be from two students collaborating in like manner.)[15] Jardine's observations shaped teaching practices elsewhere in the British Isles.

Examinations and Themes

The catechetical system, whereby students were quizzed on lecture materials, was initially oral, but toward the middle of the nineteenth century the written examination began to replace the oral question-and-answer format. In the description of his course on moral philosophy, Professor Calderwood at the University of Edinburgh asserted that class time was devoted "partly to examinations, written and oral." He added that "subjects are also prescribed for elaborate Essays, as well as for briefer occasional exercises" (EUL Calendar 1859–60). In the same calendar, Fraser, professor of logic and metaphysics, wrote that class hours were devoted to lectures and "also to discipline, by means of Conversations, short Exercises, and Essays, meant to train the members to logical habits and a reflective life. General Examinations, at which answers are returned in writing to questions proposed by the Professor, are held at intervals the course of the Session" (Bryce 4). In general, the practice of writing instruction followed the recommendation of the *1831 Report of the Royal Commission*: "In addition to Examinations, Exercises and Essays should be required from all the regular Students in each class, and ought to be criticized by the professor" (35). Consequently, instruction in writing was never confined to any single course, though language arts instructors sought to develop students' prose style in particular ways.

Giving evidence before the Commission in 1827, Professor Robert Scott described his class in moral philosophy, which met for two and a half hours during the day. The first half hour was spent in oral examination of the preceding day's lecture "with the students reading aloud their written answers to questions assigned the day before." A considerable part of the afternoon hour was spent "in the practice of composition"; subjects were

---

[14]George Jardine, *Outlines of Philosophical Education Illustrated by the Method of Teaching Logic, or First Class of Philosophy in the University of Glasgow* (Glasgow: Printed by Andrew & James Duncan, Printers to the University, 1818) 278. See Gaillet (1997) for a fuller discussion of Jardine's instructional practices.

[15]J. C. Bryce, "Introduction" to *Adam Smith Lectures on Rhetoric and Belles Lettres*, gen. ed. A. S. Skinner (Indianapolis: Liberty Classics, 1985) 4.

prescribed "and a time fixed, before which the essays must be left by the authors at the Professor's house" (Royal Commission 40). Jardine's approach at Glasgow is described in his 1825 *Outlines of a Philosophical Education*. Themes should be "prescribed frequently and regularly," and the subjects should be "numerous and various." In a four-ordered sequence, he described his assignments. In the first order, during the first two months, there was a theme almost every day, "the subject proposed in the form of a question." The second order used analysis and classification: "How may books in a library be arranged?" The third order suggested a proposition that the student was to prove: "The hand of the diligent maketh rich," "Do holidays promote study?" or "Personal talents and virtues are the noblest acquisition." The fourth and final order engaged the student "in the higher processes of investigation," which "may be said to constitute the envied endowment of genius" (Jardine 291–360).

Whately's pedagogy was student centered, as he reminded teachers to assign relevant writing topics that engage the learner. The young writer "must be encouraged to express himself (in correct language indeed, but) in a free, natural, and simple style; which of course implies (considering who and what the writer is supposed to be) such a style as, in itself, would be open to severe criticism, and certainly very unfit to appear in a book" (*Elements* 23). He goes on: "the compositions of boys *must* be puerile," but "to a person of unsophisticated and sound taste, the truly contemptible kind of puerility would be found in the other kind of exercises": those "*dried specimens*" "on any subject on which one has hardly any information, and no interest; about which he knows little, and cares still less" (23). Thus dismissing the traditional subjects of declamations and other composition exercises, Whately urged the teacher instead to

> Look at the letter of an intelligent youth to one of his companions, communicating intelligence of such petty matters as are interesting to both—describing the scenes he has visited, and the recreations he has enjoyed during a vacation; and you will see a picture of youth himself—boyish indeed in looks and in stature—in dress and in demeanour; but lively, unfettered, natural, giving a fair promise for manhood, and, in short, what a boy should be. Look at a theme composed by the same youth, on 'Virtus est medium vitiorum,' or 'Natura beatis omnibus esse dedit,' and you will see a picture of the same boy, dressed up in the garb, and absurdly aping the demeanour of an elderly man. (*Elements* 23–24)

Whately and those who follow him ushered in a new kind of writing in Britain: the personal essay (although Whately's goal was argumentative writing).

Specifically, he recommended drawing up an outline, or "skeleton [. . .] of the substance of what is to be said," one from which the writer could freely deviate, "a *track* to mark out a path for him, not as a *groove* to confine him" (25). He also offered detailed guidance for discovering and arranging propositions and arguments"[16] and for forming a natural prose style and delivery.

Responses to Writing

How teachers responded to student writing is difficult to discern since such evidence tends to be ephemeral. Extant evidence suggests that practices varied and that teachers at both the secondary and university levels paid close attention to student work. Teachers checked traditional writing assignments, like those requiring students to translate from Latin into English, for correctness. Such exercises were intended to inculcate correctness, form a writer's style, and extend a student's stylistic range. The instructor's markings were suited to those ends: sometimes the instructor marked the work; other times students were expected to self-correct it. Exercises and themes were frequent.

Edinburgh University Library has in its manuscript library a collection of twelve essays written by John Dick Peddies for William Spalding's course in Rhetoric and Belles Lettres in 1844–45 (EUL Ms. Gen. 769D). Written during his last year in the university, the themes vary from twelve to forty-two pages and cover such topics as "Remarks on Harris' Treatise on Music, Painting, and Poetry" and "Remarks on different points in the Association Theory of Beauty." Professor Spalding's comments, brief and complimentary, were likely augmented by oral comments. It was common for teachers to read the themes, either in class or after, and to discuss the student's work with him. Spalding, for example, corrected errors in agreement and the use of "will" for "shall." Other papers displayed common confusions like "principle" for "principal," "their" for "there." (Popular textbooks of the period reviewed such matters.)

Throughout the eighteenth and nineteenth centuries, then, with few exceptions, responding to student writing was a matter of correction rather than appraisal, and more often than not it was oral. In the lower schools, it was largely correction of mechanical errors, as described in John Walker's "Hints for correcting and improving juvenile composition":

> The pupil writes a draft on loose paper. Next day he copies it, with amendments, on the lefthand side of the paper of an exercise book. He reads the theme, without interruption, to the teacher, who then takes it sentence by sentence and shows the pupil where he has erred, either in the thought, the structure of the sentence, the grammar of it, or the choice of words. (cited in Michael 222)

---

[16]It dealt with methods of proof, not methods of inquiry. The philosopher seeks, the rhetor communicates.

The pupil then made a fair copy on the righthand page of his exercise book. Walker urged that course enrollment be kept as low as possible (cited in Michael 222).

Often students read their work aloud so that it might be criticized publicly either by the professor or classmates or both. In describing his course to the Royal Commission in 1831, Professor Robert Scott reported: "After being examined in private by the Professor, and the inaccuracies, whether of thought or composition, carefully marked, they are returned to the authors, by whom they are read publicly in the class; their inaccuracies are pointed out, and commented on, and an opinion as to their merits or defects publicly expressed" (*Royal Commission* 40). The first sct of essays "is generally read by the Professor, without mentioning the names of the authors [. . .] to save the feelings of individuals," Scott added (*Royal Commission* 40).

Jardine's method of responding to themes, outlined in a chapter titled, "On the Method of Determining the Merits of the Themes," sounds remarkably modern and influenced many British teachers during the nineteenth century. Faced with a class of nearly two hundred students, he contended that "experience and habit enable the teacher to execute his work more expeditiously than might at first be believed" (364). He further suggests for large classes the use of "examinators," ten or twelve students from the class who read other students' written work with the professor selecting works that "abound with defects" for his own inspection, which he returned with remarks "most likely to encourage, and to direct future efforts" (371). (Indeed, he urged that "the professor must touch their [students'] failings with a gentle hand" [365].)

In notes from David Masson's class in 1881, the student jots down the assignment and instructions on the last page of volume four: "Attend to neatness of form, expression, and pointing, as well as the matter" (EUL Ms DK. 4.28–30). Masson, who taught first at University College, London, and subsequently at Edinburgh, commented on both form and content. Somewhat unusually, John Hoppus, a professor at University College, London, for nearly forty years, determined prize essays by student vote.

EDUCATION IN THE BRITISH ISLES

Eighteenth-century grammar schools, which developed out of a variety of cathedral, abbey, collegiate, parish, and song schools from the fifteenth and sixteenth centuries, aimed to turn out students who could read and write Latin. As the name grammar school suggests, students embarked on an intensive course of Latin grammar. They went on to study Greek and rhetoric while continuing to improve their proficiency in Latin by writing verse. After attending the equivalent of high school, a privileged few entered university. British students in the eighteenth century who sought out higher education might attend one of the universities—Oxford, Cambridge, Trinity, St. Andrews, Aberdeen, Glasgow, or Edinburgh—or one of the dissenting academies. In the nineteenth century, they might also attend Catholic University, Dublin, the University of Wales, or any of the new English redbrick universities.[17] Students' choices depended largely on religious affiliation, economic status, and the region in which they lived.

England

By the eighteenth century Oxford and Cambridge had degenerated into a "preserve for the idle and the rich."[18] Their cost—between 200 and 300 pounds per annum in the 1830s—was prohibitive to most citizens. They were also elitist institutions: undergraduates of noble birth wore embroidered gowns of purple silk and a college cap with a gold tassel, which distinguished them from poor students, who donned simple attire. What's more, such students were excused from all examinations leading to a degree (even though test standards were dismally low) and were required to be in residence only thirteen weeks out of the year. "[A]ll the leading men of the eighteenth century—Bentham, Butler, Gibbon, Adam Smith, Vicesimus Knox and many lesser lights," Nicholas Hans points out, "condemned the two Universities from their personal experiences as students."[19] Knox, headmaster of Tonbridge School from 1778 to 1812, called the requirements for the Oxford degree a "set of childish and useless exercises" which "raise no emulation, confer no honour and promote no improvement." Fellows "neither study themselves nor concern themselves in superintending the studies of others" (cited in Barnard 25–26). Scholar R. L. Archer describes Oxford of the time as "a university in which professors ceased to lecture, and where work was the last thing expected." Students "entered the University not to feed on solid intellectual food, but to enjoy a costly luxury." Indeed, Oxford was marked by "extravagance, debt, drunkenness, gambling, and an absurd attention to dress."[20] While

---

[17]Because females of means were eligible for few of the educational opportunities enjoyed by boys and men of means in the eighteenth and nineteenth centuries, our discussion here refers to male students only, unless we indicate otherwise. We devote a later section to female education.

[18]H. C. Barnard, *A History of English Education from 1760*, 2nd ed. (London: U of London P, 1961) 24.

[19]Nicholas Hans, *New Trends in Education in the Eighteenth Century* (London: Routledge and Keegan Paul, 1955) 42. Hans attempts to refute charges commonly made against eighteenth-century Oxford and Cambridge, especially that poor students had deserted them. His arguments are not convincing against substantial evidence to the contrary.

[20]R. L. Archer, *Secondary Education in the Nineteenth Century* (Cambridge: Cambridge UP, 1921) 7.

Cambridge did not fare quite so badly, both southern universities were preserves of the cultural elite.

In the late eighteenth century, class attendance was low. At Oxford in 1850, "out of 1500 or 1600 undergraduates, the average annual attendance at the modern history course was 8; at botany 6 and at Arabic, Anglo-Saxon, Sanskrit and medicine, none" (Barnard 82). Lectures were dubbed "wall lectures" because the lecturers had no audience but the walls. Oxford and Cambridge offered little for students who came well prepared. Preparatory school students beat out university students to capture many of the universities' classical prizes. Reform came slowly in the middle of the nineteenth century under the Oxford University Act and the Cambridge Reforms of 1854–56. Founder's Kin scholarships were opened to competition, and for the first time University business could be carried out in English instead of Latin (Barnard 123). Life fellowships were abolished, and celibacy was no longer required for college fellows. In 1871, religious tests for the degree were finally abolished. New professorships were established, the curriculum was broadened, and examinations were made more stringent.

In spite of these nineteenth-century reforms, however, Oxford and Cambridge continued to be aristocratic and conservative. Under the direction of their college tutor, Oxford and Cambridge students were instructed first in Latin and then in Greek composition. Tutors varied greatly in expertise and commitment, and some colleges offered quite a strong classical education. Both Matthew Arnold (at Balliol) and John Henry Newman (at Trinity) were schooled in classical language studies, going through language exercises like those described by Don Paul Abbott in chapter 5 of this volume. Translation exercises not only developed students' command of Latin and Greek but of English as well. When the tutor was qualified (as the tutors of Arnold and Newman apparently were) and his charges studious, writing instruction was well served. More often, it seems, studies were unfocused, with the student dabbling in Latin and Greek, never understanding the relevance of the classics, never understanding how rhetoric might draw connections between education and life. It was left first to the Scottish universities and English dissenting academies, then to the English redbricks to inspire educational innovations, including the establishment of English vernacular as an academic study. Under pressure and with reluctance, Oxford and Cambridge institutionalized English studies only at the end of the nineteenth century, long after the dissenting academies, the provincial universities, and redbrick universities had done so.

Dissenting Academies. Dissenting academies, sponsored by Protestants who opposed the prevailing Anglican-controlled education, were innovative and strong in the eighteenth century. As Thomas P. Miller has established, as early as the last quarter of the seventeenth century, English composition and literature were taught to college-age students in purposeful, systematic ways.[21] The academies had begun as a response to the 1662 renewal of the Act of Uniformity, originally passed in 1559, by which all schoolmasters and students were required to take the oath of conformity and to renounce the Scottish covenant. On August 24 of that year, nearly 2,000 rectors and vicars resigned (McLachlin 1). The early academies were illegal, but after the Act of Toleration in 1689, the English grammar schools and high schools were opened to all comers, though the universities maintained religious restrictions. The academies filled the gap by offering education equivalent to that of the universities, but distinguished themselves by being the first to offer modern subjects, including English composition and literature. Founded by fine scholars who were themselves often educated in Scotland or on the continent, the academies were marked by a seriousness and a political activism lacking at the two ancient universities. Originally designed to educate ministers, in the eighteenth century the academies broadened their scope and took on utilitarian purposes. English studies served the dissenters' economic and political reform agendas (see Miller and McMurtry).

In general, the academies were superior to the colleges of Oxford and Cambridge, for they boasted much stricter curriculums. Terms were longer, vacations shorter. Students were as young as fourteen since preparatory opportunities were limited: freed from religious restrictions, these institutions served the brightest eighteenth-century British youth, turning out a generation of brilliant men of letters as well as an avid reading public. Students often began to study in early morning, hearing lectures at six and seven, and they continued through the evening (McLachlin 25). Nonconforming academies, which proliferated during the eighteenth century, tended to be small in faculty and students. Students moved from one school to another, taking advantage of each institution's academic strengths. One student attended five academies and studied under five tutors (McLachlin 23–25).

As Miller explains, dissenters embraced a comparative method of instruction, in which "conflicting views of controversial issues were presented, and then students researched and composed essays arguing their positions," a method "consistent with the dissenters' belief that free inquiry would advance political reform and economic and moral improvement" (86). In so doing, they rejected the conservative approaches to classical language instruction then dominant. At John Jennings's early

---

[21]See chapter 3 ("Liberal Education in the Dissenting Academies") of Miller's *The Formation of English Studies* (Pittsburgh: U of Pittsburgh P, 1997) for a discussion of how dissenters taught English. Our account draws upon Miller's work.

eighteenth-century academy, for example, students were ordered not to draw upon the received truths of tradition but rather, as Philip Doddridge remembered, to focus on "such subjects as are discoverable by the light of nature" (qted. in Miller 89). Liberal reformers, they marshaled the power of language instruction in "the progress of reason toward a utopia of free trade, scientific innovation, and rational religion" (Miller 88). Writing instruction helped to fulfill the pedagogical goals of such teachers as Isaac Watts, Philip Doddridge, Joseph Priestley.

In *The Compleat English Gentleman*, written in 1728, Daniel Defoe recommends studying English along the lines his teacher Charles Morton promoted: each week students, under the guise of public figures, wrote an oration and two compositions. "Thus he taught us to write a masculine and manly stile, to write the most polite English, and at the same time to kno' how to suit their manner as well to the subject they were to write upon as persons or degrees of persons they were to write to; and all equally free and plain, without foolish nourishes and ridiculous flights of jingling bombast in stile, or dull meanness or expression below the dignity of the subject or the character of the writer" (cited in Miller 90). Differences with classical traditions notwithstanding, these new approaches to writing instruction remained strongly rhetorical. Though writing instruction varied by individual teacher, some practices were common. Students often debated orally as preparation for writing, critiqued discourse (including sermons), rejected dependence upon traditional invention and syllogistic reasoning, favored empiricism, promoted enlightenment values like individualism, encouraged student discussion, respected the vernacular, and favored plain styles and practical forms and genres likely to be useful in public life and future employment.

Part of the curriculum at all levels, writing instruction took its place variously alongside the study of elocution and belles lettres, as well as alongside mathematics, geography, classical and modern languages, history, political economy, and science. The practical was valued over the aesthetic, composition over literature. In fact, Joseph Priestley, who taught at Warrington Academy, pioneered forms of scientific and political writing (see Bazerman). Miller credits thinkers like Smith and Priestley with developing "a modern philosophy of public education" (105). During the first quarter of the nineteenth century, however, the academies lost much of their vitality as they became more narrowly practical and abandoned the working classes and the poor.

The New Universities.   Another development in the nineteenth century was the founding of the "redbrick" universities, whose facades contrasted markedly from the stone characteristic of the ancient universities. The first of these, London University (later University College, London), was founded in 1828. Not only was there no religious test for admission and degree, theology was pointedly excluded from the curriculum. Although classical studies found an honored place, science, medicine, and other modern, practical studies, including the vernacular, were favored. Indeed, it was here that the first formal professorship explicitly devoted to English was established. In the earliest years, writing instruction in the English courses was modeled after Scottish belletristic pedagogy.[22] Under the Rev. Thomas Dale, college students at University College took "Principles and Practice of English Composition," in which they studied the philosophy of language and the fundamentals of speaking and writing. Earlier as tutor to John Ruskin and other children, and later as professor of English at University College, London, and at King's College, London, Dale drew upon Blair's *Lectures on Rhetoric and Belles Lettres*, an edition of which he later produced. In Dale's literature course, students also applied these principles to works of English letters and to their own compositions on polite subjects. Decades later when David Masson assumed the English professorship at University College, Lonon, he paid more attention to great literary traditions, to philology, and to classical rhetoric, confirming that classical rhetoric was esteemed by at least some new literature professors. Successors taught much the same way, although as the century wore on philology and English literature came to occupy more course time, composition less.

Although professors of English worked from different philosophies of composition, they all required that students compose frequently. What's more, students wrote in most courses since professors of other disciplines recognized the role of writing in learning and the importance of writing in professional life. Not only did students write constantly in their foreign language courses (ancient and modern), where translation and style exercises sharpened their command of both languages; they wrote in courses like moral philosophy, where for nearly forty years John Hoppus, a dissenting minister, drew explicitly upon the writing-to-learn theories promoted by his mentor George Jardine. Indeed, courses taught by Hoppus and others employed the range of exercises practiced today under the rubric of writing across the curriculum and collaborative pedagogy.

Upset that London was served only by a secular institution, Anglicans founded King's College, London, in 1831. Due largely to opposition from Oxford and Cambridge, neither college was at first allowed to grant degrees, but beginning in 1836, the University of London was chartered to grant degrees, with students from University and King's among those sit-

---

[22]See Linda Ferreira-Buckley, "Scotch Knowledge and the Formation of Rhetorical Studies in 19th-Century England," *Scottish Rhetoric and Its Influences*, ed. Lynee Gaillet (Mahwah: Hermagoras, 1997) 163–75.

ting for examinations. From this beginning, other nonsectarian and non-residential institutions were founded during the second half of the nineteenth century as instructional rather than degree-granting colleges, among them, the University of Manchester (1871), Liverpool (1881), Leeds (1877), and Newcastle (1871). Many institutions evolved from colleges of various types, originally supported by funds from private individuals and business and civic institutions. Not until 1898 were these institutions permitted to grant degrees, all such credentialing until that time being through the University of London. All of these institutions departed from purely classical education since proficiency in writing English was now considered an indispensable component of education.

Writing Instruction for Working People. Writing instruction figured in diverse adult working-class education in the nineteenth century: public lectures, scientific, philosophical, and literary societies, mechanics institutes, book clubs, reading rooms and libraries, and the like. All sought the mutual improvement of members, most usually middle-class or skilled working men, though unskilled laborers and women sometimes benefited as well.[23] Most often such efforts were led by volunteers (often middle-class men and woman or clergy). Sometimes funded by wealthy donors, the organizations and institutions charged small fees (not insignificant to working people, who suffered poor salaries) to cover expenses. Procedures varied: volunteers taught groups; members formed study groups; individuals engaged in self-study, sometimes guided by another.

Though the diversity of adult education needs to be stressed, some generalizations hold. Liverpool and Manchester boasted large mechanics institutes that drew many of their members from the middle class. Subjects such as English language and literature, botany, history, music, and art were included in the afternoon offerings at Manchester, which attracted older middle-class "ladies" with the opportunity to acquire the "intellectual culture" befitting their station in life, while day offerings attracted daughters of the lower-middle class with the "knowledge and skills" suitable for a "young lady."[24] In the latter especially, English skills were stressed: "considerable attention was given to the spoken word and art of conversation and writing, which included not only letter writing but also writing bills, keeping cash accounts, sealing letters and penmaking," for "[s]uch skills," June Purvis observes, "might help young women become

---

[23]Historical inquiries have not yet yielded detailed accounts of writing instruction at such locations. Local histories provide a useful beginning point for primary work: see, for example, W. S. Porter, *Sheffield Literary and Philosophical Society* (Sheffield 1922) and E. K. Clarke, *History of the Leeds Philosophical and Literary Society* (Leeds 1924).

[24]June Purvis, *Hard Lessons: The Lives and Education of Working-Class Women in Nineteenth-Century England* (Cambridge: Polity Press, 1989) 134.

competent in middle-class rituals of "calling" as well as in managerial skills as a future mistress of a household" (135). At Manchester, the superintendent, a Miss Wood, took responsibility for the English Department and taught English reading, grammar, and writing, a sign of the respect accorded the vernacular. Miss Askew assisted. These studies occupied three hours each day. Mr. Daniel Stone taught Biography and Criticism of English literature on Thursdays from 4 p.m. to 5 p.m.[25] Despite gains in adult education, literacy remained under guard: "controversial" literature was banned in the reading rooms and from the curriculum for both men and women. Class anxiety could not be dispelled—those running the institutes did not want to incite the working class men and women (Purvis 160). Studies for men focused on rudimentary language skills that might foster the technological expertise useful for their livelihood. Defying the many who believed that the poor should remain illiterate, the evangelical Hannah More pioneered efforts to teach reading to the poor (typically, the aim was to make the Bible accessible), but she refused to teach writing on the grounds that such skill might make them ungovernable.[26]

Working men's colleges were another influential component of adult education. The People's College in Sheffield (1842) and the London Working Men's College (1854) were the first of dozens that would spread throughout Britain. Unlike the institutes, whose focus was practical, the colleges valued "humane culture," "democratic comradeship," and "enrichment of personality" (Purvis 164). Admission was open to any working man who could read and write, the skills upon which their studies were to build. The study of English (including essay writing) flourished—Thomas Kelly compares their curriculums to those offered earlier at dissenting academies.[27] When women were finally admitted, they were refused the composition and elocutionary instruction offered men since such skills were appropriate to the public sphere, not the domestic sphere.

Scotland

More democratic and with fewer religious restrictions for admission or degrees, the Scottish philosophy of education differed considerably from that of the English and Irish. While the ancient English and Irish universities restricted higher education to a tiny percentage of the population,

---

[25] *Twenty-Second Annual Report of the Directors of the Manchester Mechanics' Institution* (Manchester: Johnson, 1846) cited in Purvis 135.

[26] On the positive side, her *Cheap Repository Tracts*, published between 1795 and 1798, sold millions of copies, and in so doing, "pioneered female writing for the mass market of the lower classes" (Anderson and Zinsser 126).

[27] Thomas Kelly, *History of Adult Education in Great Britain*, 3rd ed. (Liverpool: Liverpool UP, 1992) 182.

Scottish universities admitted all able students who sought an education. Because preparatory schools were scarce, allowance was always made for the "lad o'parts"—usually a gifted young man tutored by the local parson in a parish school who then went early to university, sometimes as young as fourteen (Findlay 9–10). Thomas Carlyle, the eldest of five children, walked eighty miles from his home in Ecclefechan to the University of Edinburgh at age fourteen.[28] University courses were designed to fill in deficiencies.

Scottish universities attracted students from the families of merchants, farmers, and factory and land workers, for in the north education was considered a public and state responsibility in addition to an individual and voluntary one. Thus throughout our period all Scottish children received a primary education that stressed basic literacy skills in English (or occasionally the local vernacular). The Scots felt strongly that basic education should be available to all and that the talented student should also have access to higher education.[29] Some Scottish students proceeded to university with no Latin, though with some proficiency in English composition. Those fortunate enough to attend schools like Edinburgh High School came steeped in classical rhetoric, much like their counterparts in England, having gone through style exercises as preparation for writing orations, the pinnacle of their high school experience.[30] So firm was the faith in the universal applicability of classical study that English was not officially made part of the curriculum at Edinburgh High School until 1827, when it was made one of four optional "General Knowledge" classes available to students who paid additional fees, and then largely because the institution feared losing students to other more "modern" programs. Not until midcentury was a regular English master employed.

The Scottish universities of Glasgow, St. Andrews, and Aberdeen, all founded in the fifteenth century, were modeled on the continental rather than the English pattern, a fundamental difference that became particularly significant during the eighteenth century. During that century, their universities attracted students not only from the surrounding regions but also from England and the continent. Scottish universities retained their more broadly democratic flavor and their philosophically based education.[31]

---

[28]See Ian Campbell, *Thomas Carlyle* (New York: Charles Scribner's Sons, 1974) for details of Carlyle's education.

[29]Hans 31. For a different perspective, see McElroy, who has challenged claims of Scottish superiority in education.

[30]See Linda Ferreira-Buckley and S. Michael Halloran, "Introduction," *Hugh Blair's Lectures on Rhetoric and Belles Lettres* (Carbondale: Southern Illinois UP, 2001).

[31]George Elder Davie, *The Democratic Intellect: Scotland and Her Universities in the Nineteenth Century* (Edinburgh: Edinburgh UP, 1961).

The Scottish universities had offered a more general education, ordered by the regent system in which a single professor stayed with one
group of students during their entire program. He was expected to teach
all the subjects in the arts curriculum: Latin, Greek, mathematics, chemistry, natural philosophy, and in the final year, logic, moral philosophy, and
rhetoric. Practice in composition—Latin composition—came under the
regents' purview and thus did not differ fundamentally from other universities following the dictates of ancient rhetoric. Regenting was abolished in
Edinburgh in 1708, at Glasgow in 1727, and at St. Andrews in 1747 but
persisted in King's College in Aberdeen until 1798 because of the influence of Thomas Reid. The students seemed not to suffer since professors
often had quite able assistant lecturers, who conducted classes, lectured,
and commonly assumed their positions upon the chairholder's death.

To be sure, during both the eighteenth and nineteenth centuries, Scottish universities and dissenting academies were distinguished by able professors who wrote widely in the journals of the day and were innovators in
philosophy and rhetoric, among other fields. Although Adam Smith is
better known today for *Wealth of Nations* (1776) than for his course in rhetoric, for example, his influence in language education was consequential.
The importance of Hugh Blair and George Campbell, whose books were
used on both sides of the Atlantic in the eighteenth and nineteenth centuries, has been well documented.[32]

In the nineteenth century, Scotland had less well known but nonetheless influential educators who had a profound effect on the future of
English studies and writing instruction at both British and American universities. Three deserve special note: Edward Edmondstone Aytoun, Alexander Bain, and George Jardine. The following brief sketch underscores
the range and variety of writing instruction in nineteenth-century Scotland and should thus caution against overgeneralizations.[33] Edward Edmondstone Aytoun, who held the chair of Rhetoric and Belles Lettres at
Edinburgh from 1845 to 1865, did not believe in instruction in classical
rhetoric: "I believe the ancient systems to be unsuited to the circumstances

---

[32]See the critical introductions to British rhetoricians provided in Michael Moran, ed.,
Eighteenth-Century British and American Rhetorics and Rhetoricians (Westport: Greenwood, 1994)
and the description of nineteenth-century Scottish educators and curriculum in Horner's
Nineteenth-Century Scottish Rhetoric (Carbondale: Southern Illinois UP, 1993). Also see the essays collected in Gaillet.

[33]Our characterizations of Scottish universities are based on lecture notes taken by students, which are housed in the manuscript sections of Scottish libraries. These notes are "dictates" and represent, in many cases, word-for-word representations of a professor's lectures.
For a more detailed account see Winifred Bryan Horner, "Rhetoric in the Liberal Arts: Nineteenth-Century Universities," *The Rhetorical Tradition and Modern Writing*, ed. James J.
Murphy (New York: MLA, 1982); and, especially, Horner, *Nineteenth-Century Scottish Rhetoric*,
which documents the archives in the Scottish universities.

of our time" (NLS MS 4913, fol. 29v).[34] Aytoun covered the principles of vernacular composition with an examination of style as exhibited by eminent English authors, along with the rules of spoken discourse. He also offered a critical review of British literature and occasional lectures on ancient and medieval literature. His course did come to include more and more English literature, however, a trend popular with students, who paid course fees directly to Aytoun. At his request, the title of his chair was altered to Professor of English and Literature. The study of English literature was an increasingly significant part of the curriculum. In fact, when in 1861 a Royal Commission recommended that English be offered by all four Scottish universities, and since none but Edinburgh had a course at the time, writing instruction was assigned to professors of logic. At the outset, the "English" course might well include English history and geography, itself reminiscent of the way such disciplines comprised classical studies. At the time, the concept of literature was broad enough to include historical and scientific essays as well as "works of the imagination" and students usually wrote themes, with varying degrees of instruction. In writing to a friend about his teaching, Aytoun complained that he had enough themes to read to "roast an ox," wry testimony that his students did write frequently.

Professor of Logic and Rhetoric from 1860 to 1880 at Aberdeen, Alexander Bain moved writing instruction in a markedly different direction. His 1864 course description indicates his emphasis. The Professor of Logic, the Calendar reads, "has two classes, one in English Language and Literature, and the other in Logic." The English class would include "the higher Elements of English Grammar; the Principles of Rhetoric, applied to English Composition, and some portion of the history of English literature."[35] Drawing students from northern districts, Bain faced problems different from those of his Edinburgh colleagues. The students who went to Aberdeen were in general younger, less well prepared, with dialects marked by rusticisms. The perceived duty of the universities became to teach such students to speak, read, and write "cultivated" English (at the time the London received standard). Coming from just such a background, Bain took as his own the responsibility of educating these students. An immensely popular psychology teacher now recognized as a leader in the discipline, he was

---

[34]According to the *Dictionary of National Biography*, thirty students were enrolled in his classes in 1846; an astonishing 1,850 by 1864. Aytoun's lectures in his own hand are contained in manuscripts 4897-4911 in the collection of the National Library of Scotland. These manuscripts attest that Aytoun was constantly changing and updating his lectures and was a lively and informative lecturer. Excerpts from his lectures are published in Erik Frykman, *W. E. Aytoun, Pioneer Professor of English at Edinburgh*, Gothenburg Studies in English 17, Gothenburg, 1963). Also see Horner *Nineteenth*.

[35]Alexander Bain, *English Composition and Rhetoric: A Manual* (London: Longmans, 1866) n.page.

an immensely unpopular rhetoric teacher, for he conceived of the rhetoric course largely in terms of grammar and basic composition, a remedial course in English. Many characteristics of early twentieth-century rhetoric can be traced directly to his influence: the modes of discourse, which he delineated as narration, description, exposition, argument, and poetry; the topic sentence; and the organic paragraph. His textbook, *English Composition and Rhetoric* (1866), went through six editions in ten years; his several grammar books also sold well. Bain felt strongly that the way to good English, written and spoken, was primarily through a knowledge of grammar, which he conscientiously drilled into his students. His pedagogy reduced composition to the teachable forms that are his legacy.

Like Bain, George Jardine recognized Scottish students as ones "who are not qualified, either in respect to age or previous acquirements," but he approached this challenge in a very different way, his enlightened teaching methods prefiguring those of modern composition.[36] During his long tenure as Professor of Logic and Rhetoric at the University of Glasgow from 1774 to 1824, Jardine was deeply involved in the educational issues of the day, a strong champion of the Scottish system. While formerly education was preparation for church and state, he recognized that modern Scottish universities were designed for young men "destined to fill various and very different situations in life" (Jardine 31). He understood that knowledge was not enough and admonished his students that "a man may be capable of great reflections but if he cannot communicate it to others, it can be little use" (GUL Ms. Gen. 737, vol. 2, 157). His remarkably enlightened teaching methods, described in his book *Outlines of Philosophical Education Illustrated by the Method of Teaching Logic, or First Class of Philosophy in the University of Glasgow*, urged peer evaluation, promoted writing as a way of learning, and made frequent sequenced writing assignments. Writing instruction was necessarily dispersed throughout the curriculum. The extent of his influence is only beginning to be understood.

Wales and Ireland

Irish and Welsh students had fewer options open to them. Wales had a few grammar schools but no universities; Ireland, with its largely Catholic population, did not fare much better. Illiteracy was pervasive in Wales. The Registrar-General reported in 1864: "In south Wales, an average of 64 per cent of men and 48 per cent of women were able to write their

---

[36]George Jardine, *Outlines of Philosophical Education Illustrated by the Method of Teaching Logic, or First Class of Philosophy in the University of Glasgow* (Glasgow: Printed by Andrew & James Duncan, Printers to the University, 1818) 427. See Lynee Lewis Gaillet, "George Jardine's Outlines of Philosophical Education: Prefiguring 20th-Century Composition Theory and Practice," *Scottish Rhetoric and Its Influences* (Mahwah: Hermagoras, P 1997), 193–208, for a fuller discussion of Jardine's instructional practices.

names. In North Wales, the corresponding figures were 64 per cent of men and 48 per cent of women."[37] As in Scotland, much Welsh education issued from provincial linguistic anxiety. Middle-class parents often wished their sons and daughters to lose telltale signs of Welsh in written and spoken language, the well-off sometimes sending their children to England to "finish" their schooling. As W. Gareth Evans remarks, "as elsewhere, the ethos of the middle-class girls' schools was English rather than Welsh" (Evans 60). By the middle of the nineteenth century girls studied French, the only language permissible, on designated weekdays at the best schools. Welsh was strictly forbidden. H. M. Bompas, who authored the eighth volume of the Taunton Report, expresses the common view that the native language "interferes with education": "It would appear that it is beginning in some parts to be considered unfashionable for girls to know Welsh, and this feeling is likely to make the language die out rapidly, at least among the middle classes."[38] Since boys, at least those of means, were also expected to acquire the classical languages, they were even less likely to study Welsh in school.

Not until the end of the nineteenth century did some citizens reclaim the right to study their home language. In her prize-winning essay on the set topic, "The Higher Education of Girls in Wales with practical suggestions as to the best means of promoting it," student Elizabeth Hughes argued for the study of Welsh in schools and colleges.

> Let us have a national education to preserve and develop our national type [. . .]. An ideal Welsh education must be national. It must differ from an ideal English education primarily because of the difference of race [. . .]. Difference of race, far from being a subject for regret, as far as possible should be deepened and perpetuated. The differences of race found within the bounds of the British Empire can become a source of strength and completeness.[39]

The language spoken by a million people was not to be so honored until well into the following century, however. The University of Wales in Aberystwyth was not founded until 1872.

Irish education also suffered under colonial control. Irish or Gaelic, the indigenous language, was not a school or official language and languished correspondingly. Well-off Protestants founded so-called "English schools" to promote British education, not least of which was a command of the King's English. As Miller points out, such efforts affected not only schools but university study as well. John Lawson, professor in oratory and history,

---

[37]W. Gareth Evans, *Education and Female Emancipation: The Welsh Experience, 1847–1914* (Cardiff, Wales: U of Wales P, 1960) 53.

[38]*Report of the Taunton Commission*, vol. 8, cited Evans 61.

[39]*Transactions of the Liverpool National Eisteddfod*, 1884, 40–62, 49–50; cited in Evans 137.

whose *Lectures Concerning Oratory* (1758) draws upon classical precepts in discussing rhetoric and poetry, was the first university professor in Ireland to publish language lectures in English, Miller notes.[40] In this regard, Lawson typified Protestant educators in Ireland of our period who felt the pressures of residing in a cultural province and thus sought to "meet the Irish gentlemen's need to know the language and literature of England" (Miller 118). Anglicans in Ireland continued to attend Trinity College, Dublin, whose classical curriculum and academic seriousness offered a solid if somewhat old-fashioned education in writing. A full archival record documents instruction in rhetoric and writing there, including curriculum records and prize essays.[41] Founded in 1592, Trinity College introduced students to rhetoric in a variety of contexts, including in the lectures of the "Professor of Theological Controversies," and, beginning in 1724, in the lectures given by the holder of the Erasmus Smith Chair of Oratory and History. In formulating instruction in rhetoric, holders of the chair, John Lawson beginning in 1750, but especially Thomas Leland beginning in 1761, drew upon classical rhetoric but sought to correct and enrich it in light of the new rhetoric. Both Lawson's *Lectures Concerning Oratory* (1758) and Leland's *Dissertation on the Principles of Human Eloquence* (1765) suggest the coming together of the old and new rhetorical principles and eloquence's broadening to include both oratory and poetry.

Students practiced classical language exercises, written and oral, as part of their formal study, but, just as important, they fostered those language skills in extracurricular societies. In 1747, for example, Edmund Burke founded the "Academy of Belles Lettres" at Trinity, a forum for lively debate (it would lead to the Historical Society and the College Historical Society, the latter for the expressed purpose of the "Cultivation of History, Oratory, and Composition" (qtd. in Moss 407). Students longed for "practical experience." Jean Dietz Moss, quoting from the club's early minutes, makes clear that its "business" was "speeching, reading, writing and arguing, in Morality, History, Criticism, Politicks, and the useful branches of philosophy" (403). In *Chironomia* (1806) Gilbert Austin writes that "The speaking societies set up at various times in London and in Dublin, and perhaps in other cities, have had the practice of declamation for their object. Imaginary subjects have been discussed and debated with all the interest of real occasion, and with all the efforts of declamation; and not infrequently with considerable powers of eloquence. These societies operated as incentive to oratory, and awakened love of eloquence, if they

----

[40]Our discussion of Irish education draws upon the helpful accounts offered by Thomas Miller in *The Formation of College English* (1997) and by Jean Dietz Moss in "Discordant Concensus': Old and New Rhetoric at Trinity College, Dublin," *Rhetorica* 13.4 (1996): 383–411.

[41]See Moss's rich account.

did not teach it" (212). (At various times and places, however, anxious administrators banned student debate about controversial contemporary issues.) About such efforts at the University of Dublin, Austin writes that they are "flourishing in all the acquirements of classical knowledge, classical eloquence, morality, loyalty, and religion; a nursery of oratory, learning, and taste" (212).

The Irish Catholic population did not fare as well. Some risked punishment by relying on illegal "hedge" schools, which educated students in Gaelic culture and the classics (Moss 385). Catholic aristocracy in Ireland employed private tutors and sent their children to continental universities. As government restrictions eased in the nineteenth century, Catholics were permitted to attend state schools (Trinity had begun admitting Catholics in the 1790s), but as John Henry Newman argued, British Catholics needed an institution of their own. "Robbed, oppressed, and thrust aside, Catholics in these islands have not been in a condition for centuries to attempt the sort of education which is necessary for the man of the world, the statesman, the landholder," he observed. "Only advanced and rigorous study"—liberal education that aimed at "cultivation of the mind" and thus fostered thinking, speaking, and writing—would politically empower Catholics.[42] When, in the 1850s, Newman helped to found the Catholic University in Dublin, he insisted that students be immersed in classical language study, much like that which he had enjoyed at Trinity College, Oxford. Grammar and rhetoric were central in writing instruction in Latin and Greek. They studied English language and literature as well, a sign of the vernacular's acceptance in higher education.

FEMALE EDUCATION

No matter what their class affiliation, British girls were not permitted the level of education afforded boys of their class.[43] A few eighteenth-century girls attended grammar schools, but those fortunate enough to receive an education usually received it at home, often under the tutelage of their

---

[42]John Henry Cardinal Newman, *The Idea of a University* (Garden City: Image Books, 1959) 12.

[43]Although literacy statistics are not wholly reliable (not least because definitions of what constitutes "literacy" differ radically) historians have arrived at rough estimates: "While women's ability to read and write trailed behind men's (by twenty to twenty-five percentage points in this era), literacy became standard for girls above the working class. By 1750, 40 percent of Englishwomen and 27 percent of French women could sign their names—not an adequate test of literacy, but one of the few ways of assessing it before the nineteenth century." Bonnie S. Anderson and Judith P. Zinsser, *A History of Their Own: Women in Europe from Prehistory to the Present*, vol. 2 (New York: Harper & Row, 1988) 139.

mother or governess. Boys could go away to school—a move toward intellectual and social independence. "School parted us," lamented George
Eliot, looking back on her own brother's exodus.[44] The distance was both
physical and psychological, of course, for the boy would be immersed in
Latin and eventually Greek, in reading, speaking, and writing—intellectual activities made to foster in him a public sense of self. Indeed, traditionally the purpose of secondary and higher education was to train young
men for service to church and state, roles then unthinkable for women.
Some girls might study from a brother's books, but most parents discouraged the practice. Some might go to an academically weak finishing
school, where writing instruction would be limited to discursive forms suitable for social occasions or to composing light verse. Very early on, Quak-
ers and a few nonconformist schools defied cultural mores to offer girls
serious academic educations and deemphasize "accomplishments."[45] Although some men became advocates of women's education—Daniel Defoe
decried the "barbarous custom of denying the advantages of Learning to
Women" as early as the seventeenth century, observing, "We reproach the
Sex everyday with Folly and Impertinence, while I am confident, had they
the advantages of Education equal to us, they wou'd be guilty of less than
ourselves"[46]—the Defoes were few, and their arguments went largely un-
heeded until the end of the nineteenth century.

Prohibitions against female education were made on both biological
and cultural grounds. One commonly held fear was that rigorous study led
to infertility and insanity—a woman thus defying her God-given limitations would be unsexed, dehumanized.[47] Medical officials warned that females were ill-equipped to handle the rigors of study: overtaxed by the demands of learning the classical languages, for instance, a female might be
driven insane. Even Darwin and Herbert Spencer believed that scientific
evidence confirmed such lore (Anderson and Zinsser 151–52). Society
feared that educated women would be "argumentative wives" who would
undermine the institution of marriage. They "would join in discussions of
public affairs and disturb the household by challenging the opinions of
their husbands and sons." Accordingly, learned women were undesirable,

---

[44]Ruby V. Redinger, *George Eliot: The Emergent Self* (New York: Knopf, 1975) 61.

[45]Gillian Avery, *The Best Type of Girl: A History of Girls Independent Schools* (London: Andre
Deutsch, 1991). Also see 159–66.

[46]Quoted in D. P. Leinster-Mackay, *The Educational World of Daniel Defoe* (U of Virginia,
1981) 37.

[47]Carol Dyhouse, *Girls Growing up in Late Victorian and Edwardian England* (London:
Routledge & Kegan Paul, 1981) and "Good Wives and Little Mothers: Social Anxieties and
the School Girls' Curriculum 1890–1920," *Oxford Review of Education* 3.1: 21–35. Showalter,
Elaine, "Victorian Women and Menstruation," in *Suffer and Be Still: Women and the Victorian
Age*, ed. Martha Vicinus (Bloomington, IN: Indiana UP, 1972) 38–44.

destined to become "old maids."[48] Would a man be happier "if he were mated with a 'being' who, instead of mending his clothes and getting his dinner cooked, had a taste for a literary career upon the subject of political economy?" asked a *Saturday Review* writer in 1864. Decidedly not. "There is a strong, an ineradicable male instinct, that a learned, or even an over-accomplished young woman is one of the most intolerable monsters in creation."[49] High-level literacy—especially the skills of rhetorical educa-tion—endangered the domestic ideal.

Even advocates of female education disagreed on its end: some, like Emily Davies, argued that females must have a liberal education identical to that enjoyed by males in order to avail themselves of professional op-portunities. Others, like Hannah More and Dorothea Beale, argued for a distinctly female education that prepared them to fulfill the special role God ordained for "the fairer sex." Still others, like Frances Mary Buss, un-der whose leadership the North London Collegiate School and Camden Girls' School flourished, emphasized modern subjects likely to help women find full employment.[50] All of these orientations specified a type of writing instruction.

Given the state of female education, it is remarkable that the eighteenth and nineteenth centuries produced so many strong female writers. Many were self-taught, using manuals such as those by Hugh Blair, Alexander Jamieson, and Lindley Murray. Many wrote prolifically in diaries and let-ters, two discursive forms readily available to them. Harriet Martineau rose early to write in secret.[51] The woman who dared write publicly risked censure.

As capitalism expanded the middle classes and increased free time, women became more avid readers and writers. For the first time, large numbers of women could distance themselves from the physical work nec-essary to running a household (a lower-middle-class woman would have a servant, an upper-middle-class woman might have a dozen), and polite learning marked class membership.[52] Girls of means deigned not prepare

---

[48]Joan Burstyn, *Victorian Education and the Ideal of Womanhood* (London: Croom Helm, 1980) 42.

[49]"Feminine Wranglers," *Saturday Review* 18 (1864) 112; cited in Burstyn 42.

[50]Dale Spender, *Women of Ideas* (London: Pandora, 1988) 449.

[51]Francois Basch, *Relative Creatures: Victorian Women in Society and the Novel*, trans. An-thony Rudolf (New York: Schocken, 1974) 106.

[52]In 1746, Eliza Haywood advised readers of *The Female Spectator* to learn only enough housekeeping to supervise the servants; more, she warned, might earn her "The reputation of a notable housewife, but not of *a woman of fine taste*, or in anyway qualify her for polite con-versation, or of entertaining herself agreeably when she is alone" (qtd. in G. E. Fussell and K. R. Fussell, *The English Countrywoman: A Farmhouse Social History* (London: Andrew Melrose, 1953] 106, emphasis mine). Not long after, Hugh Blair would preach similar virtues for his young male students at Edinburgh.

themselves for the workplace but rather for their role at home and in society. In such households, literacy and manners were closely linked, and girls studied courtesy manuals and language books that taught them the conventions of letter writing and other appropriate forms. Periodicals (some now edited and written by women) catered to the female at home, offering advice and entertainment, often in essay form. Less expensive periodicals (priced at about sixpence in 1800) targeted the women of the working class (Anderson and Zinsser 139).[53] Such entries served as models to be absorbed and emulated. One among many such organizations was the Edinburgh Essay Society (founded in 1865), "a galaxy of youthful maidens, eager for self improvement."[54] For all of the eighteenth century and most of the nineteenth, girls received a poor primary education that favored the domestic arts over academic ones—some girls received none at all. Even girls from well-off families received an inadequate education, for, as Joan Burstyn observes, "Schooling was considered a way for girls to obtain social rather than intellectual skills." Parents chose schools accordingly, paying more attention to the other pupils' social backgrounds than to curricular matters (22). Girls were trained "to behave as contenders in the marriage market, and as social hostesses" (Burstyn 22). Any writing instruction they received—from their mother, governess, private tutor or private school—was suited to these purposes: letters of all kinds, meditations, and the like.

Girls of the lower classes, who attended the public elementary schools (as did six-sevenths of the working class, male and female) did not fare well (Avery 65). According to Annmarie Turnball, before the 1870 Education Act, working-class children suffered much the same education: basic reading, perhaps some rudimentary writing, religion; they often left school at a young age, as soon as they could work or mind younger siblings. At those schools not under the auspices of the state—including dame schools (run by women) and charity schools—curriculums were more gendered, with most of the girls' time spent on sewing, needlework, and cleaning, the activities presumed to be most useful in their adult life (Turnball 84). During the closing decades of the nineteenth century, girls of all classes in England, Wales, and Ireland received free primary education from the state (Scottish girls had long benefited from such). For most of the poor, working, and lower-middle classes, the education was still inadequate and included only minimal instruction in reading and writing. A significant portion of "writing" time was devoted to penmanship and to

---

[53]See also Alison Adburgham, *Women in Print: Writing Women and Women's Magazines from the Restoration to the Accession of Victoria* (London: Allan, 1972).

[54]Quoted in Gillian Avery, *The Best Type of Girl: A History of Girls' Independent Schools* (London: Andre Deutsch, 1991), 64.

the most basic dictation skills; very little was given to composing original themes. Women philanthropists also recognized that their poorer sisters needed to be educated if they were to secure an honorable living. Some, like Jessie Boucherette, founded institutions like the Society for Promoting the Employment of Women (1859) to offer "a solid English education to young girls and teach older women to write a letter grammatically" (qted. in Anderson and Zinsser 185). While poorer girls might be taught to read, they were rarely taught to write more than their name. If, after 1870, attention to academics increased somewhat for all children, the reading and writing assignments given girls and boys were gender-specific. Boys were to be independent (although obedient to authority) and brave; girls, submissive and meek.

The middle class did not fare much better. In response to Frances Buss's 1865 testimony, the Schools Inquiry Commission (i.e., the Taunton Committee) concluded:

> It cannot be denied that the picture brought before us of the state of middle-class female education is, on the whole unfavourable [. . .] want of thoroughness and foundation; want of system, slovenliness and showy superficiality; inattention to rudiments; undue time given to accomplishments, and these not taught intelligently or in any scientific manner; want of organisation [. . .] a very small amount of professional skill, an inferior set of school books, a vast deal of dry, uninteresting work, rules put into the memory with no explanation of their principles, no system of examination worthy of the name [. . .] a reference to effect rather than to solid worth, a tendency to fill rather than to strengthen the mind.[55]

Change came slowly.

Many girls of the upper-middle classes studied under governesses before being sent off to a finishing school. Girls were educated according to the changing whims and fortunes of their family. "Girls changed schools often, but the progression from one establishment to the next was not logical except in the social sense," writes historian Joyce Senders Pederson.[56] Toward the end of the century, the education of female elites improved markedly. Pederson writes: "The public schools and colleges prepared women for public life most obviously in transmitting many of the intellectual skills required for effective functioning in the public sphere. In the

---

[55]Frances Buss, "Evidence to the Schools Inquiry Commission (1865)," *The Education Papers: Women's Quest for Equality in Britain, 1850–1912*, ed. Dale Spender (New York & London: Routledge & Kegan Paul, 1987) 140–41

[56]Joyce Senders Pederson, *The Reform of Girls' Secondary and Higher Education in Victorian England: A Study of Elite and Educational Change* (New York: Garland, 1987) 48. Also see Margaret Bryant, *The Unexpected Revolution: A Study in the History of Women and Girls in the Nineteenth Century* (Windsor, Eng.: NFER, 1979.

old-fashioned, private schools even elementary skills often had been either badly taught (as with arithmetic) or taught so as to be of little use in public life (as was the case with the spiked, illegible handwriting favored by some school mistresses for its supposedly decorative effect). In the new public schools, on the other hand, the children routinely acquired at least the basic arithmetic and literary skills required in the conduct of virtually all sorts of public business, while in the upper school forms and in the women's colleges they were introduced to more arcane disciplines which they had to master were they to compete with men in academic and professional pursuits" (350–51). In order for women to participate effectively in public, they had to reject the affective ploys they had been taught to rely upon. Reforming headmistresses and college heads worked to instill independence in their charges (352). Types of writing and topics for writing changed accordingly—from social forms to the professional, from the personal or light moral topics to serious often historical, economic, or political topics. At Kensington High School in 1873, girls were asked to write an essay on the following question: "Which does more for the promotion of industry and commerse, he who expends a given amount of wealth on his own direct personal enjoyments, or he who profitably invests the same, and why?" At Shrewsbury High, students competed every year for best essay on the British Empire. The first issue of North London Collegiate's *Our Magazine* contained essays on the Irish question (Pederson 354). Schools also formed debating and literary societies to foster the writing and speaking talents of their charges. Thus schooled, the female graduate of a public school thirsted for further academic training and showed a distinct interest in public affairs.

Thanks to the pioneering efforts of the Girls' Public Day School Trust, the education of upper-middle-class girls improved markedly in England and Wales.[57] Its standards were rigorous: schools under its supervision were staffed with teachers and a headmistress trained in high academic standards and teaching methodology; their curriculum was comparable to boys' public schools, although in addition to Latin, modern studies like French, German, and English (composition, grammar, and literature) were deemed important. The schools were inspected regularly. Its girls sat successfully for examinations, including the Oxford and Cambridge Local Examinations.

But not until the end of the century when two sisters, Emily Shirreff and Maria Shirreff Grey, "laid the foundation of a national education system for girls at the secondary level, a valid teacher-training pattern for that level of education, a revamped, in fact a new national system of early childhood education and the teacher-training structure to sustain it" did all

---

[57]Josephine Kamm, *Indicative Past: A Hundred Years of the Girls' Public Day School Trust* (London: George Allen & Unwin Ltd., 1971) 50.

British girls receive regular instruction in writing (Spender 454–55). Until then the language education of girls and women was spotty, varying greatly by class and family. Of course, the pattern of improvement in female education was erratic and differed within a given city, and, of course, many women and men not mentioned here contributed to those efforts. In *The Best Type of Girl: A History of Girls' Independent Schools*, Avery observes that "English was traditionally a woman's subject and was despised on that account by boys' public schools, who would not recognize as a serious discipline something that they felt was part of the heritage of any well bred gentlemen" (251). Avery maintains that "until there was an abundance of specialist teachers for other subjects, it was probably the best one taught." Instruction was given in literature, composition, and in grammar, the latter being "the girls' substitute for the Latin complexities with which their brothers wrestled." The result, she maintains, was that "girls often emerged as far more fluent on paper than boys, though the content of their essays may not have been particularly apt or informative" (Avery 251). They learned to recite literature, and they frequently listened to it being recited. Arguably, as students acquired an ear for the language, they became more able crafters of the vernacular. The institutionalized study of vernacular literature often required students to compose essays.

In the latter half of the nineteenth century, higher education gradually became available to women.[58] At North London Collegiate in 1883, students were drilled in French, which they had to translate painstakingly. Doing so was thought to improve their command of standard English. The teaching of English language was similarly uninspired: students "had to be word-perfect in the footnotes given in their texts, these consisting of the paraphrasing of lines thought to be obscure" (Avery 247). They also parsed, analyzed clauses, memorized poetry and prose, all in the service of mind training (Avery 248).

In the nineteenth century, the gradual influx of women, first to instruction in universities, then to examinations, and finally at the end of the period to degrees, was perhaps inevitable and helped to bring political and economic recognition to women. The first women's college was Queen's, founded in 1848 thanks to the lobbying of the Governesses' Benevolent

---

[58] In 1848–49, Queen's College and Bedford College for Women were founded in London, although examinations and degrees were still denied them. In 1865, Cambridge, Edinburgh, and Durham opened their local examinations to women, and the University of London followed in 1868. It was not until 1871, however, that a house of residence was opened for women at Cambridge, and, although in 1874 the University of Edinburgh issued a certificate for women, it was not until 1887 that Victoria University, formed from the union of colleges at Manchester, Liverpool, and Leeds, admitted women to degrees. The four Scottish universities followed suit in 1892 and the Federated University of Wales in 1893. Not until 1920 did Oxford grant women students full university status.

Institution, which recognized the grave need for competent teachers. Institutions like the Ladies' College (Bedford) followed soon after, mostly to provide teacher training. In 1858, Dorothea Beale, a graduate of Queen's College for Women, became principal of Cheltenham Ladies' College, founded several years earlier to provide middle-class women a rigorous education (but not one equal to that boys received in the public schools). Instruction in female "accomplishments" was replaced by serious training in language and science.[59] Other institutions followed the bold example. Beale also helped to found St. Hilda's College, Oxford, in 1893. Such institutions offered serviceable if not rigorous instruction in writing.

Another advancement in womens education came with the University Extension Lecture Movement, inspired by Anne Jemima Clough, born in Liverpool but receiving her childhood education in South Carolina before returning to her country of birth to teach, first in Ambleside, then London and Liverpool. Frustrated by the poor quality of female education, she organized what became the University Extension Lecture movement and the North of England Council for Promoting the Higher Education of Women. The circuit ensured that girls from dozens of schools enjoyed high quality lecturers (Spencer 449–50). Training in the vernacular—appreciation of the belles lettres, practice in elocution, instruction in composition—was featured.

Salons

A consideration of women's writing instruction would be incomplete without a glance at salons.[60] Importing a tradition begun by the Marquise de Rambouillet in France (not unrelatedly, the birthplace of belletristic rhetoric), British city dwellers took to the salon as "a space in which talented and learned women could meet with men as intellectual equals." "By insisting on tastefulness, courtesy, and polite behavior," Rambouillet shaped "a genteel environment where aspiring authors of both sexes were encouraged to share their work, comment on each others' productions, and participate in elaborate discussions and conversational games" (Anderson and Zinsser 104). The woman orchestrating such a circle did much to nurture the literary aspirations of the intellectual and social elites who met in their salon or drawing room. One such woman in mideighteenth-century London was Elizabeth Montagu, who, tired of trivialities like card playing, organized a salon at her home. Such groups became known as "Bluestock-

---

[59]Dorothea Beale, *History of the Ladies College, 1853–1904* (London, 1905).

[60]Peter Quennell, ed., *Affairs of the Mind: The Salon in Europe and America from the 18th to the 20th Century* (Washington, DC: New Republic, 1980) provides a useful overview of the salon movement.

ings," an appellation that played off the white and black stockings that were de rigeur for Englishmen attending formal events (Anderson and Zinsser 109).[61]

Indeed, women's entrée to writing was often through training in arts, either through manuals in rhetoric and belles lettres or courtesy manuals, which schooled them in the necessary social forms of writing, just as it taught them to discern and appreciate the moral virtues of beautiful style. The patroness of the salon, the "salonieres," also sponsored poor women like Elizabeth Carter, whose literary talents would have otherwise gone unrecognized and unsupported. The majority of women received no such opportunities, however, and society continued to deem them intellectually inferior. What's more, as hotbeds of culture, learning, and politics, salons became suspect in nineteenth-century Britain, especially for women (Anderson and Zinsser 114). Accordingly, "bluestocking" became a derogatory epithet for learned women who violated the norms of female domesticity.[62]

Middle-class women (viewed as guardians of culture by scholars from Cicero to modern linguist William Labov) constituted a significant portion of the audience in the popular city lectures in the eighteenth and nineteenth centuries. English literature was accessible to them as the classics were not. Their interest contributed to the illegitimacy of literature as an academic discipline, for as they filled lecture halls and (later) classes, women became, as Jo McMurtry points out, "an implicit liability when it came to demonstrating how hard the subject was" (McMurtry 13). Such forums did expand women's participation in literate culture and thus precipitated opportunities for writing.

One final note: the charitable activities of Victorian women also contributed to their literacy skills. True, many women simply dabbled in philanthropy, but for others these projects became serious work. Letters of solicitation had to be written, as did speeches, reports and records. Such activity constituted a form of professional writing that merits further study.

CONCLUSION

Clearly, writing instruction in Great Britain varied greatly in the eighteenth and nineteenth centuries. Indeed, although this essay draws broad

---

[61]Feminist Mary Wollstonecraft observed, "[W]omen seem to take the lead in polishing the manners everywhere, that being the only way to better their condition" (*Letters Written during a Short Residence in Sweden, Norway, and Denmark* (Lincoln: U of Nebraska P. 1976) 181; qted. in Anderson and Zinsser 110).

[62]In 1825, *Ladies Magazine* opined, "Magazines, journals, and reviews abound with sarcastic comments upon the blue-stockings and their productions. Intellectual acquirement, when applied to a woman, is used as a term of reproach" (Cynthia L. White, *Women's Magazines: 1693–1968* [London: Michael Joseph, 1970] 39; qted. in Anderson and Zinsser 116).

generalizations, we do not mean to suggest that the period's instructional practices were limited to those discussed here; we hope that this chapter has suggested the range and diversity of writing instruction.

Some generalizations can be safely drawn, however. At most eighteenth- and nineteenth-century schools, academies, and universities, writing was taught by precept reinforced by intensive practice. Students wrote frequently in all courses and at all levels. In the grammar and high schools, in addition to exercises, students wrote fables and stories and composed verse. At the university level the students wrote essays and orations on a variety of subjects in addition to summaries of and responses to the lectures.

Precept guided intense practice in the form of examinations, exercises, and essays. Instruction in writing and speech continued side by side within the same courses. Since Oxford, Cambridge, and Trinity Universities and most grammar and public schools preserved the classical tradition until the end of the nineteenth century, and thus taught writing through the old rhetorical and grammatical methods, it is to the dissenting academies, to the Scottish universities, and to the redbrick universities that we must look to see the beginnings of the modern tradition in English studies.

Chapter 7

From Rhetoric to Composition: The Teaching of Writing in America to 1900

Elizabethada A. Wright
S. Michael Halloran

> **Key Concepts.** *John Brinsley's Latin-based writing program for boys • Catharine Beecher's English vernacular curriculum for girls • Imitation and practice common to both • Modern neglect of primary sources • Conservative oral vernacular curriculum • Rhetoric and "compositions" • Writing exercises at Princeton and Harvard • Orations and debates in literary societies • Movement from scripted speech to silent prose • Belletristic rhetoric: Blair, Jamieson, Newman • "Taste" as new aesthetic criterion • Shift toward personal writing topics • Improved technologies for writing • Rise of the middle class • Larger numbers of university students • Writing as aid to social credentialing • New importance of "correct" English • Exposition versus persuasion • Discourse as a mechanism • Education for girls and non-whites • Writing as bypasser of oratory forbidden to women • Women as teachers • Current-traditional rhetoric • Emerging status of rhetoric as composition • Literature versus rhetoric • The social purpose for writing instruction*

One would expect to find major differences between the school curricula developed by seventeenth-century minister and schoolmaster John Brinsley and that developed by nineteenth-century minister's daughter and schoolmistress Catharine Beecher. The two planned for schools centuries apart, in sharply differing environments, and serving vastly different students. Brinsley planned a school for white boys in the new British colony in the Virginia wilderness; Beecher developed a school in the populous city of New Hartford, Connecticut, in the thriving young nation of the United States. Yet, there are noteworthy similarities, as well as differences, between Brinsley's and Beecher's curricular plans, and they can begin to tell us about the evolution of the teaching of writing in America.

In his work outlining his plans for his colonial grammar school and college, *A Consolation for Our Grammar Schools* (1662), Brinsley sets out 34 specific purposes for the grammar school. Here are a few that give a sense of how the teaching of "writing" was treated in the curriculum:

1. To teach scholars how to be able to read well, and write true orthographie in a short time.

4. In the severall Fourmes and Authors to construe truly, and in proprietie of words and sense, and also in pure phrase; to parse of themselves, and to give a right reason of everie word, why it must be so and not otherwise; and to deliver the English of the Lectures perfectly out of the Latine.

5. Out of an English Grammaticall translation of their Authors, to make and to construe anie part of the Latine which they have learned, or do presently learne; to prove that it must be so, and so to reade the Latine out of the English, first in the plaine Grammaticall order; after as the words are placed in the Author, or in other good composition. Also to parse in Latine, looking onely upon the translation; and in all their Poets which they so learne: to do all this without booke, which is farre the surest, viz. to repeate, construe, and parse with their booke under their arme.

20. To write Theames full of good matter, in pure Latin and with judgement, and how to invent matter of themselves.

22. So to imitate and expresse Ovid or Virgil, as you shall hardly discerne, unlesse you know the places, whether the verses be the Authors or the Scholars: and to write verses extempore of any ordinarie theame.

23. To translate forth of English or Latin into Greeke. Also to write theames or verses in Greeke.

23. To come to that facilitie and ripenesse, as not onely to translate leisurely and with some meditation, both into English and Latin [. . .] but more also, to read anie easie Author forth of Latin into English, and out of English to reade it into Latin againe, as Corderiius, Terence, Tullies Offices, etc. To do this in Authors and places which they are not acquainted with, and almost as fast as they are able to reade the Author alone.

33. To grow in our owne English tongue, according to their ages, and growth in other learning: to utter their minds in the same both in propriety, and purity; and so to be fitted for divinity, law, or what other calling or faculty soever they shall be after employed in.[1]

---

[1]John Brinsley, *A Consolation for Our Grammar Schools* (1622; New York: Scholars, 1943). Brinsley had previously written the *Ludus Literarius* referred to by Don Abbott in chapter 5 of this book. Unfortunately, Brinsley's Virginia school never came to be a reality; the project was halted by an Indian massacre.

Similarly, Beecher wrote of her plans for teaching reading and writing at the Hartford Female Seminary in the 1831 annual catalogue for the school:

[I]t is found that making good readers out of poor ones, is a work of time, and is not to be accomplished in the period which can be devoted to it. . . .

In *writing* much difficulty has always been experienced in curing bad habits. The system of Carstair, lately adopted, has been found more efficacious than any other [. . .]. For even when a good hand is once formed, it is soon lost again, unless practice forms it into habit.

The art of Composition, is one of the most laborious and difficult to a teacher [. . .]. But a regular course may be pursued, adapted to the degree of advance in maturity and knowledge, which will eventually enable almost any young persons to write with ease and elegance, on any subject with which they are acquainted.

In teaching this art, various methods have been adopted. The first thing done is, to endeavor to furnish the pupils with *words* to use [. . .]. This has been most effectually secured by the following method.

The teacher takes some writer of easy and elegant style—such for example as Washington Irving—and selects a passage in which some description is given, or some character portrayed, or some incident related. This is read over two or three times, to accustom the ear to the measurement of the sentences and the peculiar turns of expression. Then the meaning of all the most uncommon words is explained; finally a *memorandum* of the *principal words* is given, to all the class [. . .].

The pupils are then to bring, the next day, an imitation of the piece read, using the words given, and aiming to catch the style and turn of expression. By continuing this exercise, and changing the *subjects* and the *authors*, it will be found that scholars will soon acquire a ready command of language and easy modes of expression [. . .].

Another exercise has been employed to teach *unity* and *method*. Such a work as Foster's Essays has been taken, and one of the essays selected with the requisition that the *general plan* shall be discovered and drawn out by reading over the essay [. . .].[2]

Both Brinsley and Beecher are concerned that their students learn the basic mechanics of writing quickly and that they retain these skills through frequent practice. Both stress the need for their students' maturity, knowledge of vocabulary, skills with invention, understanding of texts. Both state that study of important authors is an important means to gain some of these skills, Brinsley recommending students study Ovid and Virgil, Beecher recommending Irving and Foster. Both Brinsley and Beecher de-

---

[2]*The Annual Catalogue of the Hartford Female Seminary Together With An Account of the Internal Arrangements, Course of Study, and Mode of Conducting the Same* (Hartford: Olmsted, 1831) 14–16.

scribe methodical procedures of analysis and imitation of the authors read.

Nevertheless, there are equally important differences in their pedagogies. Probably the most obvious is Brinsley's assumption that the ability to write in English was clearly and consistently related to the ability to read and write in the classical languages—indeed, was subordinated to it. For Brinsley, "purity" in English was to be attained through the practice of emulating classical models and internalizing the grammatical and rhetorical forms of the classical languages. Beecher was concerned primarily with the development of "purity" in English, and she expected her students develop it through examination and analysis of writers in English.

The most crucially important difference is one that goes unexpressed. While Beecher's school was for young women, the school Brinsley envisioned (but never actually developed) was to serve white males. Though many female and nonwhite residents of the colonies did receive some form of education, formal schooling was clearly for white boys during the seventeenth and early eighteenth centuries. If girls and nonwhites received an education, they attended schools after-hours or during the summer, when the schools had finished giving boys their lessons. Similarly, nonwhites and girls were often taught informally by educated neighbors who wanted some extra money or simply felt the desire to teach. Thus, for a woman or a nonwhite to receive an education such as that outlined by Brinsley, she or he needed to be very lucky or very well-off, but such an education was certainly possible.

That Brinsley was concerned with teaching boys and Beecher with girls may be a partial explanation of the differences between their pedagogies, but it must also be recognized that Brinsley's views were typical of formal English education in the early seventeenth century. Writing English was closely connected with study of the classical languages, and with oral performance. Translation, imitation of models, reading aloud, copying dictated material and printed texts, and recitation both catechetical and disputational were standard classroom activities. The primacy of the classical languages is ironically suggested by the fact that when Harvard students formed their first extracurricular literary and debate society near the end of the second decade of the eighteenth century, they established a rule *against* the use of Latin.[3] Such literary and debate societies would eventually play a role in supporting a curriculum of oratorical and literary studies in English. For more than a century after the founding of the first American college, however, students learned to write English through learning to write and speak the classical languages. The methods of instruction had been in use

[3]David Potter, "The Literary Society," *History of Speech Education in America. Background Studies*, ed. Karl R. Wallace (New York: Appleton, 1954) 238–58.

since classical times (when the classical languages were vernacular) and have been described in previous chapters of this book.[4]

There is a less obvious but equally important difference between the assumptions of the two scholars, centuries apart. For Brinsley, texts were meant to be read aloud. For Beecher, much reading was done aloud, yet much was done silently. During the seventeenth century and the centuries prior to it, the primary medium of instruction was speech, and the translation, imitation, or composition a student wrote, whether in English or in one of the classical tongues, was understood as a script for oral performance. While seventeenth-century culture was highly literate, it still relied heavily on oral communication for day-to-day business and used writing and print as means of scripting and recording oral communication. Paper was relatively expensive and would continue to be for at least two centuries. Books were likewise scarce and expensive. To reserve a written or printed text for a single, private reader was a considerable extravagance, so texts were commonly shared by the expedient of reading aloud. During the nineteenth-century, texts were still somewhat of a luxury, but they were becoming increasingly common. Among the more common ones were "readers," some of which included systems of notation to indicate patterns of intonation and prose meter that testify to the strong residue of the primarily oral emphasis of earlier curricula.[5]

While the move from classical to vernacular can be placed roughly in the eighteenth century, and the move from oral scripting to silent prose in the nineteenth, it would nonetheless be a considerable oversimplification to characterize these as two discrete steps completed at fixed dates in the past. Writing in English was well established in American schools by the closing decades of the eighteenth century; yet, as recently as the 1930s, Bliss Perry could offer the opinion that the best way to learn to write English is to study the classical languages.[6] And while "composition," in the sense of a course in the writing of silent prose, was probably the sole common denominator in American colleges by the close of the nineteenth century, reading papers aloud has always been a more or less commonly used pedagogical practice, more common now than at the end of the nineteenth century, as it happens. And while they are overshadowed by courses in "English composition," meaning the writing of silent prose, courses in formal speech continue to flourish in many colleges today, particularly in the midwest.

---

[4]For an excellent discussion of writing instruction in this period, see Porter Gale Perrin, "The Teaching of Rhetoric in the American Colleges before 1750," diss., U of Chicago, 1936.

[5]See, for example, Ebenezer *Porter's The Rhetorical Reader, Consisting of Instructions for Regulating the Voice, with a Rhetorical Notation, Illustrating Inflection Emphasis, and Modulation* (1835). A copy from an antique shop claims on its title page to be the 220th edition.

[6]Bliss Perry, *And Gladly Teach: Reminiscences* (Boston: Houghton Mifflin, 1935) 254–55.

The movements from classical to vernacular and from scripted speech to silent prose are nonetheless both sufficiently distinct in historical fact and sufficiently distinguishable in concept to be useful in organizing the history of writing instruction in America. The remainder of this chapter, therefore, considers the oral-vernacular curriculum of the late eighteenth and early nineteenth centuries and the development of a "compositional" curriculum, meaning a curriculum emphasizing the writing of prose meant for silent reading, in the nineteenth century. First, the chapter examines some of the implications of this compositional curriculum on who received an education and how.

What we have to say throughout should be regarded as provisional. History is, of course, always subject to revision, since it is always written from the perspective of a particular moment in history. However, in this case, the provisionality of the story goes beyond the simple fact of being rooted in a historical perspective. What primary materials exist—textbooks, student manuscripts, diaries, lecture notes, college calendars and catalogs—have not been given the attention they deserve. Even less attention has been given to those primary materials that tell us about important writing instruction that went on outside the formal classroom. Writing has been a virtually invisible topic in the material history of modern culture, and the teaching of writing has been similarly neglected in the history of education. Much scholarship remains to be done on the story of writing instruction in America; this chapter merely provides an overview of the beginning of such an understanding.

THE ORAL VERNACULAR CURRICULUM

During the course of the eighteenth century, the writing of formal English gradually established itself as a primary concern in American colleges. In the period immediately preceding the Revolution and extending into the early decades of the nineteenth century, writing instruction was governed by assumptions and methods drawn from the English derivation of classical rhetoric. Oratory of the deliberative, forensic, and ceremonial kinds was assumed to be the most important mode of discourse. Students learned the conceptual material, the techne or "art" of rhetoric, by transcribing dictated lectures and engaging in catechetical or disputational recitations, though topical invention and deductive argument were de-emphasized under the influence of the new empirical philosophy.[7]

---

[7]Wilbur Samuel Howell, *Eighteenth-Century British Logic and Rhetoric* (Princeton: Princeton UP, 1971) 441–45 and passim.

The two most characteristic surviving examples of the art as taught in this period are John Witherspoon, "Lectures on Eloquence" and "Lectures on Moral Philosophy" (1802) and John Quincy Adams, *Lectures on Rhetoric and Oratory* (1810).[8] Also significant were John Ward's *A System of Oratory* (1759) and Hugh Blair's *Lectures on Rhetoric and Belles Lettres* (1783).[9] Ward's *System* was taught at Harvard and used there to draw the statutes for the Boylston Professorship of Rhetoric and Oratory and by this means became a model for Adams' Lectures.[10] Blair's *Lectures* eventually became the most widely used rhetoric text in America; more is said of its significance later on in this chapter. Witherspoon's lectures were read at Princeton, where he served as president from 1768 until his death in 1794. Adams presented his lectures as the first Boylston Professor of Rhetoric and Oratory at Harvard from 1805 to 1809. We call Witherspoon and Adams the two most characteristic American rhetorics of the late eighteenth and early nineteenth centuries because they represent deliberate efforts to appropriate classical rhetoric for use in America. Ward and Blair were British writers whose works happened to be used here.[11]

In addition to learning the art (or what we would call the theory) of rhetoric, students wrote "compositions" of various kinds, including orations that were supposed to exhibit the full range of techniques described by the theory. Witherspoon demanded his students be eloquent in the vernacular (as teachers of the early part of the eighteenth century did not) and similarly expected students know the classical languages, building their command of formally composed English upon that knowledge.[12]

---

[8]Witherspoon's Lectures were first published in *The Works of the Rev. John Witherspoon, D.D. L.L.D. Late President of the College at Princeton, New Jersey III* (Philadelphia: W. Woodward, 1802) 367–592; they have also been published under the title *Lectures on Eloquence and Moral Philosophy* (Philadelphia: Woodward, 1810) and *The Selected Writings of John Witherspoon*, ed. Thomas P. Miller (Carbondale: Southern Illinois UP, 1990). For Adams's lectures, see John Quincy Adams, *Lectures on Rhetoric and Oratory* (1810; New York: Russell, 1962).

[9]John Ward, *A System of Oratory* (1759; Hildesheim: Georg Olms Verlag, 1969). Hugh Blair, *Lectures on Rhetoric and Belles Lettres* (London and Edinburgh: Strahan & Cadell and Creech, 1783; Philadelphia: Robert Aitken, 1784; also numerous American editions through the nineteenth century; and *Landmarks in Rhetoric and Public Address*, ed. Harold E. Harding (Carbondale: Southern Illinois UP).

[10]Ronald E. Reid, "The Boylston Professorship of Rhetoric and Oratory, 1806–1904: A Case Study in Changing Concepts of Rhetoric and Pedagogy," *Quarterly Journal of Speech* 45 (Oct. 1959): 241.

[11]Warren Guthrie's series of articles under the collective title "The Development of Rhetorical Theory in America" remains dependable as a bibliographical guide to the rhetorical works used in America during the period through 1850. See *Speech Monographs* 13 (1946): 14–22; 14 (1947): 38–54; 15 (1948): 61–71; 16 (1949): 98–113; 18 (1951): 17–30.

[12]In this he is in agreement with Quintilian, who prescribed translation as one means of making Roman students eloquent in Latin.

Witherspoon also included the study of English grammar in the Princeton curriculum—an important innovation for the time—and took the relatively modern and nonprescriptive view that the grammar of a language is "fixed" by its best writers. Among models of English prose, he particularly recommends Addison, Swift, and Pope. He especially recommends imitation as a compositional exercise, but cautions against devoting too much time to the imitation of any one author.

In practice, the writing exercises done at Princeton during the period of Witherspoon's presidency seem to have fallen into two broad categories: compositions and orations. The former were relatively brief pieces done on the short notice of no more than a few days for presentation in a recitation period, during which the class tutor and sometimes the other students would offer critical comments. A student diary from 1786 suggests that writing compositions (which category probably included Witherspoon's translation, narration, imitation, and description) did not inspire much enthusiasm. The student diarist (identified in the Princeton Library catalogue, but not the diary itself, as John Rhea Smith) dithers over these assignments and not infrequently completes them after the due date. Yet, this same student exhibits considerable enthusiasm and diligence in working on orations. In an entry for Jan. 6, he records writing out an oration due to be presented one week later, then going to bed without having begun to write a composition due the next day.[13] "Smith" is habitually tardy and uninterested when working on compositions, yet seeks out opportunities to practice his orations before tutors and fellow students. The difference may have been a matter of audience and may have been peculiar to this student. The primary audience for his compositions was a class presided over by a tutor named Greene (most likely Ashbel Greene, later president of Princeton) for whom "Smith" obviously has neither respect nor affection. The audience for orations was the entire college assembled in the main hall.

In keeping with the emphasis of the current rhetorical theory on civic life, the topics on which students wrote tended to be political. Here is a list of some questions disputed at Harvard College commencements in the decades leading to the Revolution, illustrating the increasing focus on contemporary political affairs:

Is unlimited obedience to rulers taught by Christ and his apostles? (1729)
Is the voice of the people the voice of God? (1733)
Does Civil Government originate from compact? (1743, 1747, 1761, and 1762)
Is civil government absolutely necessary for men? (1758)

---

[13][John Rhea Smith], A Journal at Nassau Hall (photostatic copy of an unpublished manuscript dated 1786, held in the Princeton U Library).

Is an absolute and arbitrary monarchy contrary to right reason? (1759)
Are the people the sole judges of their rights and liberties? (1769)[14]

The period spanned by this list coincides with the shift at Harvard from
Latin to English as the primary focus of rhetorical instruction. When they
were first introduced, the English language disputations and orations
were assigned to the duller students, but starting in the 1740s, they were
more and more often assigned to the brighter ones. The question listed
above for 1743 was argued in the affirmative by Samuel Adams, that listed
for 1758 by John Adams.

Appendix A to this chapter illustrates the kind of speech a student of
the time would have composed in responding to such a question. This one
was delivered at the commencement of Princeton (then called the College
of New Jersey) in 1772 by Philip Vickers Fithian, defending the thesis that
"Political jealousy is a laudable passion." This being a commencement
oration, we can assume that Fithian lavished his best efforts on it, and yet
it is somewhat murky in thought, flat and pedantic in style, and erratic in
punctuation and other mechanical elements. For all its flaws, this oration
has in it a detectable hint of the persuasive logic that would characterize
the writings of Fithian's contemporary at Princeton, James Madison (class
of 1771), and of many others who studied the neoclassical rhetoric taught
during this period. It illustrates the traditional rhetorical form characteristic of most of the student writing done in this period and, likewise, the
concern with civic problems.

In addition to their assigned work, students spent considerable effort
on composing orations and debates for the student literary societies. Orig-
inating with the Spy Club founded at Harvard in 1719, the movement for
literary and debate societies gathered momentum quickly around mid-
century. By the closing decades, the typical college had at least two, and ri-
valry between them was a powerful motive for hard work on writing.[15] The
Princeton diarist "Smith" writes with obvious enthusiasm of his own activities with the Cliosophic Society. Anne Ruggles Gere correctly notes that
activities of the societies included a great deal of what we now call "peer response": students would critique each others' work within the society in
preparation for a contest or other public performance, then receive criticism of their public performance from the college at large.

On the evidence of the Smith diary, peer response was important for assigned work as well. Smith frequently seeks out classmates as well as tutors
to practice his assigned orations on, and he clearly values the criticism of

---

[14]Samuel Eliot Morison, *Three Centuries of Harvard 1636–1936* (Cambridge: Harvard UP, 1936) 90–91.

[15]Potter, op. cit. See also Anne Ruggles Gere, *Writing Groups: History, Theory, and Implica-tions* (Carbondale: Southern Illinois UP, 1987) 9–16.

his peers equally with that of the tutors. Indeed, the tutors seem to have stood in such a relationship to the students that their criticism would have as much, perhaps more in common with peer response than with a modern composition teacher's critique of a student's paper. Smith records, with no sense of its being a remarkable event, that the tutor Greene "attempted an extempory discourse but did not shine very brilliantly" in a meeting of the Cliosophic Society (Mar. 19 entry). The tutors participated more or less as equals with the students in the rich oratorical activities of the college and could expect the same sort of criticism of their own efforts as the students received from the tutors and each other. Neither the tutors nor anyone else graded students' work in the way we do today; the work was not done in the context of courses and credit hours and grade point averages. The audiences for which a student wrote regularly were his own class, his literary society, and the entire college assembled. It was the approval of these audiences that mattered, and the critical response of the tutor was valuable insofar as it helped a student achieve that end. Examination for purposes comparable to what we call grading was done infrequently, usually in the form of oral disputation with the college president and perhaps the trustees judging the students' performance.

FROM SCRIPTED ORALITY TO SILENT PROSE

Gerald Graff writes of an "oratorical culture" that provided some rationale and support for literary study in colleges during the first half of the nineteenth century.[16] By an oratorical culture, he means the activities of the literary and debate societies and the formally required speaking exercises in English that pervaded college life from roughly 1750 up to around 1875, when the theory and practice of American discourse had been transformed by seemingly apolitical ideals of individualism and professionalism.[17] Equally important, and perhaps more clearly, this oratorical culture provided an appropriate and supportive context for writing instruction in a period when writing was primarily the scripting of an oral performance.

While students participated enthusiastically in this collegiate oratorical culture up through the opening decades of the nineteenth century, Graff argues that the system was weak and in the process of an inevitable collapse. Sharon Crowley agrees that the system was weak but largely due to eighteenth-century theorists' attempts to integrate contemporary devel-

---

[16]Gerald Graff, *Professing Literature: an Institutional History* (Chicago: U of Chicago P, 1987) 35–51.

[17]For more on this transformation, see Gregory Clark and S. Michael Halloran, eds., *Oratorical Culture in Nineteenth-Century America: Transformations in the Theory and Practice of Rhetoric* (Carbondale: Southern Illinois UP, 1993).

opments in philosophy, psychology, and logic. The results of these ambi-
tious efforts, though, were the creation of a theory that privileged the
authorial mind rather than a communal knowledge. Nan Johnson also differs from Graff in that she sees this oratorical culture as strong but evolving toward a pragmatic hybridization of oratory, composition, and critical
analysis.[18] While participation in this debate is beyond the scope of this
chapter, we want to focus on three aspects of the change from oratory that
can shed light on the nature of the new modes of writing instruction that
came into use during this period. First, there was a new emphasis, both in
the colleges and in the society at large, on *belles lettres*—poetry, fiction,
drama, essay—that had occupied a less prominent place in the older oratorical culture. Second, certain technological developments facilitated a
heavier reliance on writing as an independent medium in both the society
at large and the schools. Third, the emergence of a middle class and the
professions altered the curriculum and student population in ways that
placed new burdens on academic writing. We take these three topics up in
order of their mention.

Belletristic Rhetoric

The increased interest in belletristic writing is reflected in the textbooks
used through the early decades of the nineteenth century. The most popular was Hugh Blair's *Lectures on Rhetoric and Belles Lettres*, published in
Scotland in 1783 and adopted at Yale and other American colleges shortly
thereafter, but the belletristic trend is equally evident in the first commer-
cially successful American text, Samuel P. Newman's *A Practical System of
Rhetoric* (1827).[19] Some belletristic notions are also present in John Witherspoon's primarily neoclassical *Lectures on Eloquence*, particularly in the final lecture, which is devoted to principles of taste and criticism that
Witherspoon no doubt learned as a classmate of Hugh Blair at the University of Edinburgh. According to Warren Guthrie, Blair's *Lectures* had become the most popular work on rhetoric in American colleges by 1803,
and its continuing influence is suggested by the numerous editions that

[18]Sharon Crowley, *Methodical Memory: Invention in Current-Traditional Rhetoric* (Carbondale: Southern Illinois UP, 1990); Nan Johnson, *Nineteenth-Century Rhetoric in North America*
(Carbondale: Southern Illinois UP, 1991).

[19]Newman devotes two of his five chapters to the belletristic notion of "taste" and in other
ways exhibits the belletrists' tendency to foreground aesthetic considerations in writing. *A
Practical System of Rhetoric*, 10th ed., (New York: Dayton, 1842). For a compelling analysis of
Newman's work that attempts to explain the reasons for this text's extraordinary success, see
Beth L. Hewett, "Samuel P. Newman's *A Practical System of Rhetoric*: An American Cousin of
Scottish Rhetoric," *Scottish Rhetoric and its Influences*, ed. Lynee Lewis Gaillet (Hillsdale:
Hermagoras, 1998) 179–92.

appeared to and beyond the middle of the nineteenth century.[20] Guthrie records that it was in use at Yale and Williams as late as 1860. Another important Scottish belletristic rhetoric, Alexander Jamieson's *A Grammar of Rhetoric and Polite Literature* (1818), appeared regularly in American editions from 1820 until about 1880 and was established as a regular text for sophomores at Yale by Chauncey Allen Goodrich.[21] At Wesleyan and Amherst, Jamieson was used for a while and then replaced by Newman's *A Practical Stystem of Rhetoric*.[22] Belletristic rhetoric thus became popular at the peak of the oral-vernacular period in writing instruction. Much has been written recently about this popularity. For example, Winifred Bryan Horner and Thomas Miller observe that this trend was strongly influenced by similar economic and political factors in Scotland and the United States.[23]

In Blair, Jamieson, and Newman, belletristic rhetoric incorporates some of the traditional concern for oratory in the classical genres, and includes a classical pedagogy based upon the use of models, imitation, and graded practice, including translation into English from other languages. But the emphasis shifts somewhat from eloquence to the new ideal of "taste." As Barbara Warnick has illustrated, this shift can be understood as belletristic rhetoricians incorporating the empirical work of their contemporaries with their own.[24] Replacing the traditional form of invention, a psychophysiological understanding of humans was formed by these rhetoricians as they attempted to illustrate ways the aesthethic appeal of a discourse could influence its persuasive effect. A second implication of belletristic rhetoric's substitution of taste for eloquence is that it tends to make rhetoric an art of the audience more than of the speaker or writer. Taste is a quality that distinguishes readers of texts. Eloquence is a virtue of the speaker or writer who makes them. Belletristic rhetoric thus set the stage for the elevation of interpretation and reading over invention and writing that would characterize the discipline of English studies.

Perhaps owing to their elevation of aesthetic concerns and the role of the reader, belletristic rhetorics offered analyses of prose style more detailed and meticulous than anything in the neoclassical texts. Blair and

---

[20]"The Development of Rhetorical Theory in America, 1635–1850, 111," *Speech Monographs* 15 (1948): 62.

[21]A. Craig Baird, "Introduction" to *Essays from Select British Eloquence* by Chauncey Allen Goodrich (Carbondale: Southern Illinois UP, 1963) xvi.

[22]"The Development of Rhetorical Theory in America 1635–1850, IV," *Speech Monographs* 16 (1949): 102.

[23]Winifred Bryan Horner, *Nineteenth-Century Scottish Rhetoric: The American Connection* (Carbondale: Southern Illinois UP, 1993), and Thomas P. Miller, *The Formation of College English* (Pittsburgh: U of Pittsburgh P, 1997).

[24]Barbara Warnick, *The Sixth Canon: Belletristic Rhetorical Theory and Its French Antecedents* (Columbia: U of South Carolina P, 1993).

Jamieson, in particular, are still worth reading for their stylistic analyses.[25] They differ from classical treatises on style, emphasizing the genius of the individual author as a source of the material of discourse. And in keeping with the emphasis on the individual, they presented a more individualistic view of style. Alongside the classical ideal of plain, middle, and grand styles, which, in Cicero, were treated not as distinct kinds but as stylistic registers that might all be present in the same speech,[26] belletristic rhetoricians developed longer catalogues of stylistic characters that distinguished the qualities of particular writers. Witherspoon, for example, gives primary emphasis to the traditional categories of plain, middle, and grand styles (calling them "plain," "mixed," and "sublime"), but also describes "more personal" characters of style—including the simple, smooth, sweet, concise, elegant, ornate, just, nervous, chaste, and severe styles—and illustrates each with one or more references to specific authors. The new belletristic practice of distinguishing multiple styles represents an early step toward our own emphasis on the need for each writer to articulate a distinct personal "voice."

Robert Connors points to a more direct consequence of the belletristic emphasis on the individual, realized in late nineteenth-century composition pedagogy: a strong shift to more "personal" topics for assigned writing.[27] Connors shows that many of the topics for writing assignments advocated in late nineteenth-century composition texts focused more sharply on the students' personal experience and feelings than had the writing assignments typical of earlier times. In the traditional rhetoric, students might have been asked to develop a broad and general topic such as "patriotism;" a late nineteenth-century text such as Reed and Kellogg's *Higher Lessons in English*[28] would urge students to narrow the subject to something like "How Can a Boy Be Patriotic?" and consult their own experiences and feelings in developing it. This shift reflects the same concern with private, individual experience that marks imaginative literature, particularly that of the romantic and postromantic period in contrast to traditional oratory's focus on culturally sanctioned commonplaces. The shift to more personal writing assignments thus fits with the rise of literary study as the

[25]Jamieson offers what we believe is the earliest published discussion of anticlimax as a deliberate rhetorical effect, giving an astute analysis of the sinking sound and sentiment in Horace's line, "Parturient montes, nascetur ridiculus mus." *A Grammar of Rhetoric and Polite Literature* (New York: Armstrong, n.d.): 182.

[26]For this reading of Cicero on the plain, middle, and grand styles, see S. Michael Halloran and Merrill D. Whitburn, "Ciceronian Rhetoric and the Rise of Science: The Plain Style Reconsidered," *The Rhetorical Tradition and Modern Writing*, ed. James J. Murphy (New York: MLA, 1982) 61.

[27]Robert J. Connors, "Personal Writing Assignments," *College Composition and Communication* 38 (May 1987): 166–83.

[28]Alonzo Reed and Brainerd Kellogg, *Higher Lessons in English* (New York: Clark, 1878).

central focus of the new departments of English that were the locus of instruction in rhetoric.

Technological Developments

Discussions of the connection between technology and writing usually focus on one or more of three revolutions: the development of alphabetic literacy in ancient Greece; the invention and diffusion of the printing press during the Renaissance; and the development of electronic media, the word-processing computer especially, in our own time. Another revolution in writing technology occurred during the nineteenth century, one less dramatic perhaps than these three, but nonetheless important in its consequences for writing and writing instruction. Pens, ink, and pencils improved significantly, making it possible for people to write with less fuss and mess, and fewer pauses for blotting the ink and sharpening pens. Paper decreased substantially in cost, making it economically feasible for people to write more, to use writing freely as a medium of exploration, to discard drafts and revise more extensively. Book and periodical production increased dramatically, making printed material available to everyone.[29] Other dramatic changes occurred within the postal system, making it easier and less expensive to conduct both business and personal affairs in writing. While post-riders and stagecoaches had given way to an official postal service (with Benjamin Franklin its first postmaster-general in 1753), the cost of this service was prohibitive to all but the very wealthy. Not until the middle of the century were the rates reasonable enough for the average person to consider sending writing through the mail.[30]

---

[29] Two excellent sources on the development of technology during the eighteenth and nineteenth centuries are Scott Bennett, "The Golden Stain of Time: Preserving Victorian Periodicals," *Investigating Victorian Journalism*, eds. Laurel Brake, Aled Jones, and Lionel Madden (New York: St. Martin's, 1990) 166–183; and Cynthia White, *Women's Magazines 1693–1968* (London: Michael Joseph, 1970). An interesting insight into the complexities of the fuss and mess of even the advanced nineteenth-century writing technologies can be found in chapter 3 of Susan Warner's 1850 bestselling novel, *The Wide, Wide World* (New York: Feminist, 1987), which notes a young girl's extensive purchases of communication technologies so she can write letters to her mother in Europe.

[30] A rich source of this information and much on changing technology is John W. Moore, compl., *Moore's Historical, Biographical, and Miscellaneous Gatherings, In The Form Of [Sel]ected Notes Relative To Printers, Printing, Publishing, and Editing of Books, Newspapers, Magazines, and Other Literary Productions, such as the early Publications of New England, the United States, and the World, from the Discovery of the Art, or from 1420 to 1886: With Many Brief Notices of Authors, Publishers, Editors, Printers, and Inventors* (1886; Detroit: Gale Research, 1968) 23–24. The importance of this change in postal rates to nineteenth-century Americans can be noted today in Cambridge, Massachusetts' Mount Auburn Cemetery where people and their families comment on what they want posterity to remember them for: on the gravestone of one man, Barnabas Bates, is the inscription, "Father of Cheap Postage."

What prompted these nineteenth-century revolutions was, of course, none other than the Industrial Revolution, seen from the perspective of writing and written communication. Its consequence was a society more radically literate in the sense that public and private affairs could rely on prose meant for silent reading only rather than as a script for oral performance. Curiously, this aspect of the Industrial Revolution seems not to have been very much commented on, perhaps because it has been so successful.[31] We find it difficult to recall that the physical act of writing, of inscribing words on a surface, was once hard and costly work quite apart from the intellectual effort of inventing the words to inscribe. Yet for medieval monks copying manuscripts, it was exactly that. Elizabeth Larson notes, in an excellent brief study of the relationship between writing implements and the composing process, that scribal work was for monks considered a "reasonable substitute for physical labor," and that analogies between writing and such work as ditch digging were common in the medieval period. She notes further that the clumsy implements used by medieval scribes were not significantly improved until the nineteenth century.[32] The late eighteenth-century Princeton diarist quoted earlier most likely wrote with a quill pen that needed constant mending.

The physical recalcitrance of old-style writing tools necessitated a two-stage composing process: first think out very carefully what to say, then write it down, ideally getting it exactly right the first time. Within this framework, "invention" occurs entirely in the mind rather than "at the point of utterance," and memory becomes a key inventive resource. Larson shows how our own, very different view of writing as "a continuing process of revision" depends radically on convenient writing implements and relatively cheap paper. With pens that do not require constant sharpening, ink that requires little or no blotting, and cheap yet serviceable paper, it becomes possible to write in the free, exploratory manner advocated by Peter Elbow, for example. But while the potential for such a composing process was developed during the nineteenth century, it remained for later generations of teachers to exploit it. Current-traditional texts in this period continued to treat thinking and inscription as distinct acts. What little advice the nineteenth-century texts have to offer on the subject of revision remains grounded in the old two-stage composing

---

[31]A notable exception is Marshall McLuhan, *The Gutenberg Galaxy* (Toronto: U of Toronto P, 1962). Other recent scholarship has explored more subtle changes in technology (see, e.g., James W. Chesebro and Dale A. Bertelsen, *Analyzing Media: Communication Technologies As Symbolic and Cognitive Systems* (New York: Guilford Press, 1996) and David S. Kaufer and Kathleen M. Carley, *Communication at a Distance: The Influence of Print on Sociocultural Organization and Change* (Hillsdale, NJ: Erlbaum, 1993)).

[32]Elizabeth Larson, "The Effect of Technology on the Composing Process," *Rhetoric Society Quarterly* 16 (1986), 43–58.

process. G. P. Quackenbos, for example, tells the student to write a draft, then let sufficient time pass "so that the writer may, in a measure, forget the expressions he has used, and criticise his work as severely and impartially as if it were the production of another."[33] The criticism is to be accomplished through reading the draft carefully aloud, after which another clean copy is written with full attention to "neatness of chirography." Like the rhetoricians of the eighteenth century, Quackenbos assumes a sharp distinction between the acts of thinking and inscription.

This development of technology also allowed for an important new development in the art of rhetoric. With writing communicated through the eyes of readers rather than through the ears of an audience, visual metaphors had to be invented for understanding style and structure. Important among these were words, sentences, and paragraphs understood as "elements" of discourse; the outline format (which was an inheritance of Peter Ramus's earlier move in the direction of a visualized rhetoric); and the very notion of *structure*, which suggests a quasi-architectural three-dimensional ordering of parts. An influential effort to elaborate this notion of structure in discourse was the sentence-diagramming system invented by Alonzo Reed and Brainerd Kellogg and established as a standard element of pre-college work in English through their *Graded Lessons in English* (1875) and *Higher Lessons in English* (1878). This system was essentially a representation in abstract spatial terms of the grammatical relationships among words, phrases, and clauses in a sentence; as such, it constituted a step in the direction of modern linguistic techniques of representing syntactic relations, such as Chomskyan and immediate constituent diagramming. Unlike these later developments, the Reed and Kellogg diagramming system failed to preserve the natural order of words in the sentence. Nonetheless, the system represented an advance in the effort to understand the structure of discourse at the sentence level. In addition, Reed and Kellogg's work responded to the shift from an oratorical to a literary and professional culture. The inclination to represent discourse visually is likewise evident in Kellogg's independently authored *A Text-Book on Rhetoric* (1880), which did not make use of the diagramming system but did present numerous exercises based on close analysis of syntactic structure. In one instance, in which Kellogg extended the approach of spatial diagramming to semantic relationships as well as syntax, he seems to be groping toward a modern view—which is to say a "visualized" view—of semantics. Yet he seems unaware that he is operating at a frontier in a developing field of knowledge. He treats rhetoric as a body of common knowledge to be recorded in a textbook for high school and college students.

---

[33]G. P. Quackenbos, *Advanced Course of Composition and Rhetoric* (New York: D. Appleton and Company, 1859), 334.

One of the most important influences of these developments in technology, an influence increasingly recognized by nineteenth-century educators, was that the advances in communication technologies enabled more and more people to communicate at a distance. As David Kaufer and Kathleen Carley have observed, material components of writing can dramatically influence how and to what extent the average person could both send and receive messages.[34] Egerton Ryerson, president of Canada's Victoria College, comments on the transformative power of these developments in his 1842 inaugural address:

> In an age of printing and writing—in all its varieties—to write well is of the last [i.e., most] importance. The power which an eloquent orator exerts over an assembly, an able writer exerts over a country. The "pen of a ready writer" has frequently proved an instrument of more potent power, than the sword of the soldier, or the sceptre of the monarch. The "heavens are his sounding board," and a nation, if not the world, his audience; and his productions will be listened to with edification and delight, by thousands and millions whom the human voice could never reach.[35]

The Rise of the Middle Class

The many improvements in writing technologies coincided with the century's new emphasis on the individual, which was, of course, not peculiar to literature or the teaching of writing. The seventeenth and eighteenth centuries saw a growth of individualism that manifested itself, for example, in the American Declaration of Independence. Through the eighteenth century, individualism was, in this country, chiefly a matter of political rights, but during the nineteenth century, the idea that everyone has a "right" to rise socially and economically took root. People came to see the socioeconomic status of their birth not as a place they ought to occupy for life, but as a starting point from which to climb upward in competition with their fellows. As Burton Bledstein shows, this new middle-class ethos, which developed during the first half of the nineteenth century, was crucial to the emergence of the apparatus of professionalism during the sec-

---

[34]David S. Kaufer and Kathleen M. Carley, *Communication at a Distance: The Influence of Print on Sociocultural Organization and Change* (Hillsdale, NJ: Erlbaum, 1993).

[35]Cited in Henry A. Hubert, *Harmonious Perfection: The Development of English Studies in Nineteenth-Century Anglo-Canadian College.* (East Lansing: Michigan State University Press, 1994). Hubert's book also creates an interesting comparison between the teaching of writing in Canada and that in the United States, arguing that Canadian colleges' writing instruction has almost always come under the auspices of literature classes. Reading Ryerson's words, one cannot help but wonder what he would have thought of today's technologies which allow rhetors to reach millions instantaneously.

ond half of that century.[36] The middle-class spirit made people competitive strivers; professionalism created arenas for striving and a currency of exchange in the form of "professional expertise." While the changes in technology certainly did not create this individualism and professionalism, they certainly contributed to their creation.

The growth of the middle-class spirit placed a new burden on the colleges both in sheer numbers of students and in new responsibilities. Students who came to college as a means of rising on the socioeconomic ladder swelled classes far beyond anything known in the seventeenth and eighteenth centuries.[37] Without cheap paper and ink, colleges would never have been able to meet these demands, and less affluent students would never have been able to have such lofty goals. With the increasingly large numbers of students, the grades that Smith did not receive from his tutor became a reality; credentialing became a function of schools, one they had perhaps always had in theory, but had never had to take quite so seriously before. As Sharon Crowley acknowledges, the larger numbers of students made the old system of oral recitation and disputation unworkable. Composition courses provided a means to teach larger numbers of students at once, assessing their success by measuring their adherence to prescribed standards. The new competitive spirit of the society gave a much greater importance to the business of sorting students, that is, of determining which were superior and which merely adequate, and here too writing recommended itself as a means. Because written work could be evaluated more precisely, it allowed for a more meticulous sorting of the students.[38] Credentialing also became important because with books more available to everyone, even people outside schools, anyone could learn. As Anne Ruggles Gere has shown, women and nonwhites learned a great deal outside the walls of a school.[39] Credentialing, then, became a way of stating whose learning came from a recognized classroom and whose from outside it. The possession of credentials in the form of a diploma distinguished those whose knowledge carried the social imprimatur of a college from those who were merely knowledgeable.

---

[36]Burton J. Bledstein, *The Culture of Professionalism: the Middle Class and the Development of Higher Education in America* (New York and London: W. W. Norton & comDanv. 1976).

[37]At Harvard, class size first reached 100 in 1860, then went to 200 in 1877, to 300 in 1892, to 400 in 1896, to 500 in 1904, and to 600 in 1906 and remained at about that level until shortly before World War 1. Morrison, *Three Centuries of Harvard*, 415–16.

[38]Francis Wayland, then president of Brown, argued for a shift from oral to written examination in *Thoughts on the Present Collegiate System in the United States* (1842; rpt. New York: Arno Press and The New York Times, 1969) 99 ff.

[39]Anne Ruggles Gere, *Intimate Practices: Literacy and Cultural Work in U.S. Women's Clubs, 1880–1920* (Urbana: University of Illinois Press, 1997).

Credentialing also created a growing emphasis on correctness of grammar and usage. As Sterling Andrus Leonard showed more than seventy years ago, the ideal of "correctness" in English was essentially an eighteenth-century invention.[40] Some evidence of this development can be seen in American colleges during the late eighteenth century, particularly in the views of John Witherspoon, who inveighed on aesthetic grounds against the use of contractions and invented the term "Americanism" as a pejorative for forms of expression peculiar to this side of the Atlantic.[41] However, by the standards that would become current in the closing decades of the nineteenth century, Witherspoon was permissive, advising his students not to worry, for example, about punctuation.

In the competitive middle-class society of the nineteenth century, speaking and writing "correct" English took on new importance as a sign of membership in the upper strata. The new reliance on writing as a medium of evaluation lent further importance to correctness, and such current traditional rhetoricians as John Franklin Genung, Barrett Wendell, and Adams Sherman Hill consequently gave heavy emphasis to usage and grammar.[42] Many of them, Hill in particular, developed standards of correctness far more subtle than the actual practice of elite speakers and writers, and thus beyond anything requisite to give students the social mobility they sought. And by attempting to impose a "hyper-correct" dialect on the generally privileged students at Harvard and the other established liberal arts colleges, Hill and others may actually have strengthened the linguistic obstacles to upward mobility, ensuring that those students formally studying the dialect could overcome the obstacles while those informally studying would not. The relationship between the middle-class ethos and the rhetoric of correctness was thus a complex one. This relationship also reveals how, as James Berlin states, "English studies is a highly overdetermined institutional formation, occupying a site at the center of converging economic, social, political, and cultural developments at the end of the nineteenth century, developments that continue to affect it today."[43]

[40]Sterling Andrus Leonard, *The Doctrine of Correctness in English Usage, 1700–1800* (Madison: University of Wisconsin Press, 1929; rpt. New York: Russell and Russell, 1962).

[41]Witherspoon's diatribe against contractions is contained in the "Lectures on Eloquence," lecture number three. According to H. L. Mencken, *The American Language: An Inquiry into the Development of English in the United States*, 4th ed., (1919; New York: Knopf, 1960), Witherspoon invented the term "Americanism" in papers called "The Druid," which appear in Witherspoon's *Works*, vol. 4. (Mencken 4–6).

[42]A standard work on what happened to rhetoric during the move toward written composition is Albert Raymond Kitzhaber, "Rhetoric in American Colleges 1850–1900," diss., U of Washington, 1953. It is Kitzhaber who dubbed Genung, Wendell, Hill, and Fred Newton Scott "the big four."

[43]James Berlin, *Rhetorics, Poetics, and Cultures: Refiguring College English Studies*. (Urbana: NCTE, 1996) 22.

The coincidence of the middle-class ethos with advances in science, commerce, and industry produced a new cultural ideal: professionalism. According to Bledstein, at least two hundred learned societies were formed in this country during the 1870s and 1880s, formalizing a professional ethos in areas ranging from chemistry to folklore, political science to ornithology. Even sports began to take on the trappings of "professionalism" during this period, underscoring the power of the new ethos.[44] To be a professional was a new ideal representing what the culture most valued, as Quintilian's citizen orator had represented what classical culture most valued. Unlike the citizen orator, a version of which was central to the vernacular neo-classical rhetoric of the late eighteenth century, the professional was a specialist whose service to society took the form of applying arcane, scientifically-based knowledge to "the common purposes of life."[45] One gained this knowledge in the credentialing college, but as Cheryl Geisler observes the college also worked to persuade the public to legitimize this specialized knowledge while delegitimizing the public's knowledge.[46] Thus, the knowledge of the professional was in marked contrast to the communally sanctioned wisdom that had been the province of the citizen orator. Another difference between the culture of the professional and that of the orator was that the knowledge of the professional was morally neutral—in essence, a commodity that could be exchanged for money, and thus a means of advancing one's personal fortune while also serving the public good. As Katherine H. Adams and David R. Russell illustrate, professional knowledge or "expertise" was rooted in methods of inquiry particular to the profession, a point which helps to account for the often noted decline of invention in nineteenth-century rhetoric.[47]

The most appropriate rhetorical form for expression of the professional's expertise was clearly not the morally tinged persuasion of the old-style orator, but dispassionate exposition and argumentation. With reason and imagination separated, the new ideal of professionalism thus appears in rhetoric as a tendency to emphasize the last two of the four "modes of discourse"—description, narration, exposition, and argumentation. In

---

[44]*The Culture of Professionalism* 80 ff.

[45]This expression is taken from a frequently quoted statement by Stephen Van Rensselaer of his purpose in founding what would eventually become Rensselaer Polytechnic Institute, one of the pioneer institutions in the development of the new profession of engineering: "the application of science to the common purposes of life." See Samuel Rezneck, *Education for a Technological Society: A Sequicentennial History of Rensselaer Polytechnic Institute* (Troy: RPI, 1968).

[46]Cheryl Geisler, *Academic Literacy and the Nature of Expertise: Reading, Writing, and Knowing in Academic Philosophy.* (Hillsdale: Erlbaum, 1994) 80.

[47]Katherine H. Adams, *A History of Professional Writing Instruction in American Colleges: Years of Acceptance, Growth, and Doubt* (Dallas: Southern Methodist UP, 1993) and David R. Russell, *Writing in The Academic Disciplines, 1870–1990: A Curricular History* (Carbondale: Southern Illinois UP, 1991).

the current-traditional method, the approach to teaching writing most dominant in the late nineteenth- and early twentieth-centuries, persuasion became a minor aspect of argumentation, serving only to supplement substantive appeals with some appeal to the passions. Within the ethos of professionalism, passion would ideally be eliminated altogether, and so persuasion, once the overarching purpose of all rhetoric, became a concession to the weakness of the audience.

The ethos of professionalism is reflected also in the common organizational scheme for current-traditional textbooks: from words, to sentences, to paragraphs, and finally to the whole discourse. The underlying metaphor is of the discourse as something constructed carefully from parts, much as a machine is assembled from its parts, or as science in the Baconian inductive mode assembles discrete observations into general principles. Seen in this way, discourse is not so much the moral and political engagement with an audience of classical rhetoric, as the construction of a knowledge-bearing object, a mechanism by which professional expertise can be made available for use.[48]

EDUCATION FOR GIRLS AND NON-WHITES

As we mentioned at the beginning of this chapter, most of the formal rhetorical education discussed in this history, such as that outlined by John Brinsley for the Virginia Company, was reserved for white boys. White boys were the ones whose ability to earn a livelihood would depend on an education, and allowing others to use the precious resources of paper and ink was an extravagance.[49] Nevertheless, many girls and nonwhite residents of the colonies did receive a education. E. Jennifer Monaghan's convincing analysis of the colonies' documents shows that although most girls did not know how to write, laws demanded that parents teach their sons *and daughters* to read, and parents suffered serious consequences if they did not abide by these laws.[50] To meet these educational requirements, wealthy parents often sent their children to "dame" or "adventure"

---

[48]A notable exception to the tendency of nineteenth-century rhetoricians to treat discourse as a mechanism is Fred Newton Scott, who preferred the organic view developed by Plato in the *Phaedrus*.

[49]For an interesting discussion of other reasons girls were kept outside the rhetorical tradition, see Miriam Brody, *Manly Writing: Gender, Rhetoric, and the Rise of Composition* (Carbondale: Southern Illinois UP, 1993).

[50]"Literacy Instruction and Gender in Colonial New England," *Reading in America: Literature and Social History*, ed. Cathy N. Davidson (Baltimore: Johns Hopkins UP, 1989) 53–80. Related to this rich but frequently overlooked history, Susan Miller, in *Assuming the Positions: Cultural Pedagogy and the Politics of Commonplace Writing* (Pittsburgh: U of Pittsburgh P, 1998), makes the excellent point that we must resist the temptation to glorify nineteenth-century reformers of women's education by creating a mistaken history of education that ignores the extensive educational systems for women that existed before these women's reforms began.

schools. Frequently run by single women who supported themselves with students' tuitions, these schools had a curriculum that depended entirely on the interests of the students and the background of the dame in charge. According to Thomas Woody, these schools sometimes provided little more than babysitting services and sometimes they specialized in teaching dancing or a craft or even offered both sexes extensive lessons in the classical languages. Yet one element almost always excluded from a girl's education was practice in public speaking.[51] On the other hand, some parents chose to educate their daughters themselves. While home education was a financial necessity for families unable to afford the rather expensive dame or adventure schools, even wealthy parents frequently chose to educate their daughters themselves, as the example of Margaret Fuller attests. Some slaves and other black residents of the colonies were also able to learn to read and write, though their access to lessons was even more limited than that of white girls. Nevertheless, many African Americans gained an education, often through their own determination to learn, as in the case of Frederick Douglass, and sometimes because slave owners took it upon themselves to teach some or all of their slaves, as in the cases of Phillis Wheatley and Harriet Jacobs.[52] With the change from an oral-vernacular curriculum to a compositional one, educational opportunities for women and nonwhites changed radically.

Women's education seems to have benefited from the three aspects of the change from oratory to composition that we previously discussed (i.e., the emphasis on belletristic writing, technological developments, and the emergence of a middle class and the professions). Belletristic rhetoric's focus on taste and literary style rather than eloquence fit well with the nineteenth-century's notions of womanhood.[53] Theories of belletristic rhetoric

---

[51]Thomas Woody, *A History of Women's Education in the United States* (New York: Science Press, 1929).

[52]See Frederick Douglass, *Narrative of the Life of Frederick Douglass, An American Slave, Written by Himself* (New York: Norton, 1997) 29, 31–35 and Harriet A. Jacobs, *Incidents in the Life of a Slave Girl Written by Herself* (Cambridge: Harvard UP, 1987) 8. Phillis Wheatley's education is widely known through her poetry and documented eighteenth-century controversy over whether or not she was in fact the author of her own poetry.

[53]For an extensive discussion on the changing perceptions of womanhood and how these perceptions fostered women's education see Ruth H. Bloch, "American Feminine Ideals In Transition: The Rise Of The Moral Mother, 1785–1815," *Feminist Studies* 4 (June 1978): 101–27; Janet Carey Elred and Peter Mortenson, " 'Persuasion Dwelt On Her Tongue': Female Civic Rhetoric in Early America," *College English* 60 (Feb. 1998): 173–88; Catherine Hobbs, "Introduction: Culture and Practices of U.S. Women's Literacy," *Nineteenth-Century Women Learn To Write*, ed. Hobbs (Charlottesville: UP of Virginia, 1995) 1–33; JoAnn Campbell, " 'A Real Vexation': Student Writing in Mount Holyoke's Culture of Service, 1837–1865," *College English* 59 (Nov. 1997): 767–88; Sara Delamont, "The Contradictions in Ladies' Education," *The Nineteenth-Century Woman: Her Cultural and Physical World*, ed. Delamont and Lorna Duffin (London: Croom Helm, 1978), 134–165; and Barbara Welter,

considered women's conversation to provide models of excellent prose, providing educators of young women with an additional justification for arguing that rhetoric was consistent with womanhood.[54] Technological developments made cheap paper and ink available, thus eliminating extravagance as an argument against teaching girls to write. The availability of inexpensive paper also encouraged letter-writing, an art applauded by theorists of belletristic rhetoric and considered very appropriate for the female sex. In addition, the change in class structure created an increasing number of middle-class families who were eager for their daughters to gain an education and help the family rise financially. For one thing, teaching was perceived to be an acceptable profession for women, and for a daughter to be able to help support the family through teaching, she would have to have an education herself. An older sister contributing to the family income through teaching could help make it possible for a younger brother to pursue his own education, and hence the social and economic advancement of the family. Such was the logic of the new middle-class ethos.

The effects of these changes on nonwhites were far more complex. As Susan Miller notes, it was not until several decades into the nineteenth century that laws against teaching African Americans to write were enacted, a time coinciding with the evolution from scripted orality to silent prose. The coincidence of laws being enacted just as large numbers of African Americans had access to a writing education was most likely no coincidence at all. Instead, the accessibility of texts and the ability of the masses to communicate at a distance were probably factors in the legal exclusion of African Americans from education.[55] Such laws may have been a reaction of white citizens, anxious about the power African Americans could gain from the advances in writing technologies, an anxiety very similar to that felt by the elite in ancient Greece who feared the power that the sophists gave to others.[56] The race- and class-conscious white population was probably equally anxious for the opportunities literate African Americans might "take" from them. Accessibility of texts and a rising middle class may have had very different effects on Native Americans. As Mike Jackson's work on the literacy in the Cherokee Nation suggests, such changes

---

Dimity Convictions: The American Woman and the Nineteenth Century (Athens: Ohio UP, 1976); Linda K. Kerber, *Women Of The Republic: Intellect And Ideology In Revolutionary America* (New York: Norton, 1980).

[54]See Adam Smith, *Lectures on Rhetoric and Belles Lettres*, ed. J. C. Bryce (Oxford: Clarendon, 1983).

[55]*Assuming the Positions* 59–60.

[56]For example, Frederick Douglass' acknowledgment of the influence of the *Columbian Orator*, a text he "got hold of," illustrates the power the printed word could provide an individual.

allowed white missionaries to advance their own goals while depriving Native Americans of their culture.[57]

Despite these negative impacts on nonwhites, the changing notions of class and advances in technology allowed for the increasing acceptance of formal schooling for girls. Advocating for more complex and standardized education, women such as Catharine Beecher, Emma Willard, and Mary Lyon argued that women were best suited to supply the increasing demand for teachers, since teachers dealt mostly with children and women were innately talented in this area. Yet, with this social acceptance of education for girls, many old prescriptions and restrictions remained. For example, though girls were to learn, they were not to learn too much. In addition, though the curriculum was becoming increasingly compositional, elements of oratory that remained were still forbidden to women. As Robert Connors observes, while Beecher's seminary taught rhetoric, it appeared not to include actual speaking.[58] Nevertheless, as can be seen in the catalogues to her school cited at the beginning of this chapter, Beecher's lessons in rhetoric were very rich. Though these extensive instructions do not include any provisions for her students to engage in the traditional modes of public address, Beecher did provide many opportunities for her students to read aloud. In his memoir to his wife who was a student at Beecher's school, James Parton tells of his wife's participation in one of the school's annual exhibitions in which students read their works.[59]

The 1831 catalogue's seeming omission of mention of these annual exhibitions is far from surprising. To provide women with an advanced education without running afoul of the many prohibitions still in place, educators adopted many Janus-faced strategies to legitimize their curriculum.[60] For example, while women could not deliver orations, it was considered socially appropriate for them to read aloud—so they did. P. Joy Rouse cites a story of a female student cooperating with this dictate by carrying her essay book to the stage, politely holding the written text, and boldly delivering it as an oration without glancing at it.[61] Schools such as Cathar-

[57]Mike Jackson, "Reading Sequoyah's Invention of the Cherokee Syllabary," unpublished conference paper presented at Forty-Ninth Annual CCCC Convention, April 1998.

[58]Robert J. Connors, *Composition-Rhetoric: Backgrounds, Theory, and Pedagogy* (Pittsburgh: U of Pittsburgh P, 1997).

[59]James Parton, "Memoir" in Fanny Fern, *Fanny Fern: A Memorial Volume Containing Her Select Writings And A Memoir By James Parton* (New York: Carleton, 1873) 37–42.

[60]Almost all scholars of women's nineteenth-century education have observed these strategies. For example, Eldred and Mortensen call the strategy "rhetoric of use," Delamont "double conformity," and JoAnne Campbell "culture of service."

[61]"Cultural Models of Womanhood and Female Education: Practices of Colonization and Resistance," *Nineteenth-Century Women Learn To Write*, Catherine Hobbs ed. (Charlottesville: UP of Virginia, 1995) 230–47.

ine Beecher's alma mater, the Litchfield Academy, could also provide women with the skills necessary for oratory by making school plays part of the curriculum, thereby forcing these women to work on various elements of delivery.[62] Martha Osborne Barrett, a student at the Massachusetts normal school, observes another important way women gained oratorical skills when she records in her diaries her formal school's association with a Lyceum where women and men participated in debate, arguing such topics such as "Advantages of Education and Disadvantages of Ignorance" and "Shall we be justified in assisting Ireland if she declares herself independent?"[63]

While Catherine Hobbs states that women's increasing access to education is not what caused the transformation of rhetoric, Robert Connors argues women's inclusion in education reshaped a competitive and confrontational forum into a nurturing and personal one. We would have to agree and disagree with both Hobbs and Connors. Certainly women's access to education was not the sole factor involved in the transformation from an oratorical curriculum to a compositional one, but there is much to suggest it was *a* factor. In addition to the decorous and calming effect women had on education, as cited by Connors, women's influence on the transformation of oratory was integrally tied to their socially sanctioned education and their changing role in the educational process. As the middle class grew and more and more men attempted to gain access to the professions, the demand for boys' education grew. As we illustrated, pioneers of women's education argued that women were better suited to be teachers of children than were men. Therefore, the demand for girls' education grew, fueled by the growing need for teachers. However, since women were seen as ill-suited orators, they could not very easily teach public speaking. Similarly, women were not seen as social leaders; therefore, they could not easily use rhetoric as a tool for developing social policy. What women were perceived as being able to do, in addition to providing nurturance and moral habits, was to teach formulaic, unimaginative lessons and enforce rigid grammatical prescriptions, lessons and prescriptions that were very much a part of Current-Traditional Rhetoric. Women such as Catharine Beecher, then, are much more implicated in the move toward the disempowering composition course. The irony in women's involvement in the development of Current-Traditional Rhetoric is that without this truncation of the rhetorical tradition, women might have had even less of a possibility of participating within the educational systems and the rhetorical forum.

---

[62]See Emily Noyes Vanderpoel, compil., *Chronicles of a Pioneer School From 1792 to 1833 Being the History of Miss Sarah Pierce and Her Litchfield School* (Cambridge: Cambridge UP, 1903).

[63]F. Mss. 13274. Env. 2, Fdr 2. Phillips Library, Peabody Essex Museum, Salem, MA.

THE EMERGING STATUS OF RHETORIC
AS COMPOSITION

The course in English composition that evolved in the late nineteenth century was an attempt to adapt rhetoric to dramatically changed conditions both inside and outside the academy, conditions produced by the industrial revolution, the new middle-class and professional mores, and changing women's roles. The task facing nineteenth-century educators and theorists was thus an opportunity for scholarly work of the highest order, an opportunity of which they do not seem to have been able to take advantage. While some textbooks show flashes of originality and careful thought, there is little effort to develop a historical context or probe underlying principles and no sense that the subject is intellectually challenging and socially important. However, as Andrea Lunsford notes regarding Alexander Bain, their intention for serious scholarship may have been genuine.[64] Good intentions have a way of drying up, however, under the harsh reality of overwhelming numbers of students and the consequent grinding work load. Thus, as Sharon Crowley and Robert Connors illustrate, textbooks became simplistic compilations of beliefs and prescriptions, departing from texts of a few decades earlier that probed underlying principles and stressed the subject's intellectual challenge and social importance.[65]

Donald Stewart attributes this unfortunate limitation of late nineteenth-century rhetoric to the influence of Francis James Child, fourth Boylston Professor of Rhetoric and Oratory at Harvard.[66] Child held a largely undisguised contempt for rhetoric in both its traditional and more purely literate modes throughout his 25-year tenure as Boylston Professor. When relieved by A. S. Hill in 1876, Child became a driving force in establishing literary study as the central focus of the Harvard Department of English. Stewart contrasts Child's view of the emerging profession of English studies with that of Fred Newton Scott of the University of Michigan, one of the few late nineteenth-century scholars who saw rhetoric as an intellectually challenging subject and took a more balanced view of the English department as comprising scholarly work in rhetoric and linguistics as well as literary study. Stewart sees in the origin of professional English studies a struggle between the Harvard model of Child and the broader model advocated by Scott, a struggle in which the view of Child

---

[64]Andrea A. Lunsford, "Alexander Bain and the Teaching of Composition in North America," Scottish Rhetoric and its Influences, ed. Lynee Lewis Gaillet (Hillsdale: Hermagoras, 1998) 219–27.

[65]Crowley, Methodical Memory, and Connors, Composition-Rhetoric.

[66]Stewart, "Two Model Teachers and the Harvardization of English Departments," The Rhetorical Tradition and Modern Writing, ed. James J. Murphy (New York: MLA, 1982) 118–29.

prevailed and the new discipline was effectively "Harvardized" by the early years of the twentieth century.

Documentary evidence assembled by John C. Brereton as well as Gerald Graff and Michael Warner shows that the notion of a two-sided struggle between Harvard literati and Michigan rhetoricians giving shape to the profession of English studies is oversimplified.[67] Harvard and Michigan were by no means the only influential schools, nor were they necessarily the most influential ones. Further, among the early advocates of English literary study, there were numerous sharp differences, for example between the scientifically oriented philologists and proponents of an older belletristic approach. And of course the importance of a "belletristic" view should remind us that the shift of emphasis from writing to reading, and the consequent demotion of "rhetoric" to the status of a low-level service course, has roots in the rhetorical tradition itself. Stewart is nonetheless correct in his conclusion that *something like* Francis Child's vision came to dominate English studies, and the term "Harvardization" can perhaps serve as a useful synechdoche for what happened in the closing years of the nineteenth century. The discipline of English became primarily the study of literary texts, not in Stewart's catholic sense of "includ[ing] everything from a seventh grader's paragraph on fishing, to a graduate student's term paper on Chaucer's Pardoner, to *Moby Dick*,"[68] but in the narrow sense of classics understood to be fundamentally different from anything the student might write. Rhetoric became a secondary concern, largely unrelated to the study of literature and thus free to lay down "rules" for composition in total disregard and sometimes direct violation of the example set by those classic texts.

CONCLUDING REMARKS: THE SOCIAL PURPOSE FOR WRITING INSTRUCTION

Much of great value was lost in the evolution from the neoclassical rhetoric of the late eighteenth century to the composition course of the late nineteenth. Heuristic theory and procedures virtually disappeared, and the sense of audience was narrowed. In place of a rich array of stylistic forms and techniques was the flat voice of mechanical correctness. The greatest loss was of the sense of a large social purpose for writing, a social role for which rhetorical art was necessary equipment. Neoclassical rhetoric had

---

[67]John C. Brereton, *The Origin of Composition Studies in the American College, 1875–1925: A Documentary History* (Pittsburgh: U of Pittsburgh P, 1995); Gerald Graff and Michael Warner, eds., *The Origins of Literary Studies in America* (New York: Routledge, 1989) 39.

[68]"Two Model Teachers," 125–26.

focused on an updated version of Quintilian's citizen orator as the role for which students were being educated. They were supposed to become virtuous leaders of their communities, and effective writing was one of the key abilities they would need to fulfill this responsibility. The new course offered little in place of this ideal. Composition skills were important for success in the new middle-class, professional culture, but there is no evidence that even this somewhat narrow and functionary purpose was made clear to students. The larger purpose of social leadership through discourse that had been both central to, and explicit in, neoclassical rhetoric had no equivalent in the rhetoric of English composition.

One can question whether the Quintilianic ideal or anything like it could or should have survived. For one thing, it was aristocratic, perhaps fundamentally so, and excluded all but white men. It assumed as audience a *mobile vulgus* needing the intelligent and moral leadership of a skilled orator. For another, it assumed a stable and readily compassable body of common knowledge. The first assumption was in conflict with the ideology of populist democracy, the second with the rapid advance of specialized, arcane knowledge and its applications to "the common purposes of life."

Our own view is that aristocratic assumptions about speaker and audience were accidental to the theory and practice of classical rhetoric, and that it could have been adapted quite readily to the needs of a widening democracy. Frederick Antczak shows persuasively that there was a need, and it was not fulfilled by the schools. Christine Oravec's study of political criticism suggests democratic theories of rhetoric stressed the importance of presenting information clearly to an audience to ensure the audience's participation.[69] Classical rhetoric might have been adapted to the needs of the changing American culture and served as an art of political competency for the widening enfranchised public. Instead, it was virtually abandoned by the colleges in favor of a socially and politically unaware rhetoric of composition. Simultaneously, and perhaps in consequence, our political discourse grew increasingly artless and irrational.

One can also question traditional rhetoric's assumption that knowledge is stable and compassable by the individual. The problem of this assumption is at the heart of much extraordinary debate, both academic and public, that has surrounded such books as E. D. Hirsch's *Cultural Literacy* and Allen Bloom's *The Closing of the American Mind*. The growth of specialized knowledge in the nineteenth century was directly related to the development of English composition. The new disciplines and professions left a

---

[69]Frederick Antczak, *Thought and Character: the Rhetoric of Democratic Education* (Ames: Iowa State UP, 1965) 12–54. Antczak's primary focus is on non-academic efforts, particularly the lyceum and chautauqua movements, to "reconstitute" the democratic audience as politically competent. Christine Oravec, "The Democratic Critics: An Alternative American Rhetorical Tradition of the Nineteenth Century," *Rhetorica* 4 (1986): 395–421.

smaller and smaller place in the curriculum for "rhetoric," which at the beginning of the nineteenth century had occupied as much of the students' time as the major discipline does for most of our students today. "Composition," as understood by Hill, Genung, Wendell, Kellogg, and Scott was simply a course in our sense of that term, competing for the students' time and attention with an ever growing array of other courses, some of which bore ironic traces of the rhetorical tradition they were displacing. Composition also provided a means by which women could begin to participate within a rhetorical forum, albeit a much deprived forum. The much maligned current-traditional rhetoricians had to adapt to the new reliance on silent prose and yet accomplish their work in a narrow corner of the curriculum. This narrow corner also provided an opening for some people to enter the academy.

Perhaps they deserve more credit than they have had. The social and technological changes of the nineteenth century were profound. The new course in English composition, which, by the turn of the twentieth century, was probably the sole common element in American college education, was itself an important invention, an educational "technology" to deal with dramatically changed circumstances and problems. If not giants on whose shoulders we now stand, the current-traditional rhetoricians are nonetheless significant contributors to the tradition of writing instruction. Seen in the context of the time, their accomplishments are deserving of some attention and respect.

APPENDIX A

An Example of Student Writing in the Revolutionary Period

September 10th 1772

Nassau Hall

Princeton University

An Exercise at the Public Commencement

It is altogether needless, to detain this respectable assembly only for two or three minutes, with any introduction to the following Subject, further than by just telling them it is my design to prove that "*political jealousy is a laudable passion.*"

Jealousy is a strange temper in the human mind, & like several other of our passions, it has various effects when its subjects are different; it is also of many kinds, as political, domestic, & ecclesiastic Jealousies, Jealousy in

Friendship, and between the Sexes; each of which has a different effect on the mind from all the others, & several of them, if carried to any considerable length, are generally attended with dangerous consequences: especially the two kinds last mentioned, Jealousy in Friendship, & between the Sexes; for in friendship when two persons of agreeable tempers, have by long acquaintance proved each others fidelity, so as to communicate all their secret intentions to each other, & have contracted a particular esteem between themselves, if by any means, whether false or true, the one becomes suspicious that the regard, or the faithfulness of the other is diminished, he is then watchful of every action, & misapplies every unmeaning expression, which at once destroys their quiet, & is seldom removed, but most usually terminates in open hatred. But it is said by some that a small degree of Jealousy between those of different Sexes improves, & increases mutual Esteem, because esteem is said to be the foundation of Jealousy; but when it arrives at a certain pitch, it then turns the other way, & rages with ungovernable violence; like attraction in small bodies, which ceases to act at a certain distance, & then repulsion separates them with a double force; I am, however, quite unable to comprehend what can be a cause for this mysterious limitation, & as no valid reasons have been brought to support it, but innumerable Examples which operate against it, we conclude that wherever Jealousy between the sexes takes place, it destroys the comfort & happinessof the parties, in proportion to its Strength, & Duration. It is therefore mischievous in its nature in both these kinds, & neither desirable, nor laudable; perhaps the same things or worse might be said of domestic & eclesiastic Jealousies, but I pass them by, & proceed to observe that political Jealousy differs from them all in these respects; it is rational, & uniform, & necessary.

Any person who considers the importance of a free State, of how great value the lives the liberties, & the property of a nation are, & considers that the surrounding nations are envious of their neighbours happiness, & therefore always desirous of reducing them to subjection, will see at once & readily confess, that it is most just, that those who have the ruling power, should keep a watchful eye upon the whole conduct of those in whose power it is to disturb & injure them; & this observation is Jealousy of their designs, which is the first & surest step to self-preservation, because it is the simplest, & most safe method that can be taken to preserve the state, as it does not suffer mischief to take place & the safety of every individual in a state depends entirely upon the Security of the whole, consequently this kind of Jealousy is a first principle of Nature, which never goes contrary to reason; & which always directs to something needful & for our good, political Jealousy is therefore rational & founded in unerring nature.

It is like wise uniform, for it only excites politicians to a constant attention to those things which are likely to keep the state in safety, but when public hostilities are committed against the state there is nothing then that can be called Jealousy for the resentment is open and common: Political Jealousy, then in this view, is of great importance in two respects, it is first the most easy and effectual way to keep a nation in peace, or make them successful in war, as it urges to constant readiness for the greatest danger; & likewise its natural tendency is to unite the people; for when they see the Rulers of the nation inattentive to the national welfare, they immediately become dissatisfied, because their own lives and property are in danger, & often in this case they rebel against the government, & unite among themselves to defend their own lives & secure their property; but when a people see their Rulers watchful over the state, & always forward to detect & chastise intruders, if the nation is in peace they are quiet & at ease, and when war commences they cheerfully, & couragiously join with their rulers, to scourge, & subdue the common enemy; now seeing Jealousy of this kind never grows to be a tumultuous, & dangerous passion, it certainly cannot be deny'd but that it is useful; & it is besides a necessary passion for it is the spring that gives life and motion to government, & its force is so powerful that its influence extends throughout the largest State, & so mild that it never injures the weakest subject.

It seems, finally to have been a particular passion, implanted by the supreme God in certain Men, which assists them to rule a state in equity, & to make use of all necessary, & possible means to preserve it in safety; & when those who are destitute of it are set over a nation they seem placed there by providence to chastise the people, & for their own destruction; when private interest is prefered by Politicians to the National welfare, or when *discord* & mischievous factions enter among them, these show at once that instead of being directed by the genuine gentle temper above described they are *possessed* with a spurious, selfish, helborn passion.

Now seeing it has been made appear that this kind of Jealousy tends in general to the good of a Nation; seeing it never promotes feuds, & factions, nor ever grows to be turbulent & excessive; seeing its tendency is to unite a people in friendship among themselves, and make them powerful against their enemies; & seeing its influence is as extensive as the most populous state, & at the same time mild & gentle, who can deny; I ask, who can deny but that it is laudable, lovely, desirable, & most excellent? did I ask who can deny? It is a confessed truth, & admitted by all;   It therefore only remains that I implore the great *Genius* which presides over our nation, to inspire our *king* & his *council*, & all our *Rulers* with this noble spirit. Oh! inspire them mighty Goddess, with a temper like to thine; suffer them not we first intreat thee to be swayed from their duty by sordid interest; make them always consider that upon their consultations depends the safety of a vast empire! let them therefore be all men of integrity, & unquestionable sincerity; take from them all malice, & revengeful inclinations, & fill them with love & harmony among one another, so that our happy government may be established & flourish, so long as the Sun & Moon endure   But, if it is written in the books of *Fate* that a change in the Government must take place; Oh! transfer it to this *western World*, set up *here* thy royal standard, where ignorance & barbarity lately reigned; may virtue & learning, & Arts be always the subjects of thy particular attention; establish a Government, & set over it such men as shall be ever watchful for the common good, that they may forever rule a brave, a free, & a happy People.

—Philip V. Fithian

From *Philip Vickers Fithian, Journal and Letters, 1767–1774*, ed. John Rogers Williams (Princeton: The University Library, 1900).

APPENDIX B

"In Reading, the Grammar of Elocution, and the mode of instruction pursued by Professor Barber of Cambridge College, have been introduced, but it is found that making good readers out of poor ones, is a work of time, and is not to be accomplished in the period which can be devoted to it, by scholars who come for only one or two terms.

In *writing* much difficulty has always been experienced in curing bad habits. The system of Carstair, lately adopted, has been found more efficacious than any other. But most pupils who write a bad hand, will seldom form a good one, without consenting to practise an hour a day, for two or three months. For even when a good hand is once formed, it is soon lost again, unless practice forms it into habit.

The art of Composition, is one of the most laborious and difficult to a teacher; and is one which cannot be attained in its higher style, except by minds of a certain degree of maturity and of acquired knowledge. But a regular course may be pursued, adapted to the degree of advance in maturity and knowledge, which will eventually enable almost any young persons to write with ease and elegance, on any subject with which they are acquainted.

In teaching this art, various methods have been adopted. The first thing done is, to endeavor to furnish the pupils with *words* to use; for generally children have but a very scanty stock of expressions at their command. This has been most effectually secured by the following method.

The teacher takes some writer of easy and elegant style—such for example as Washington Irving—and selects a passage in which some description is given, or some character portrayed, or some incident related. This is read over two or three times, to accustom the ear to the measurement of the sentences and the peculiar turns of expression. Then the meaning of all the most uncommon words is explained; finally a *memorandum* of the *principal words* is given, to all the class. Occasional *combinations* of expressions also, are sometimes given, that young writers would not be apt to employ; such for example as 'wavy lines of light,' &c.

The pupils are then to bring, the next day, an imitation of the piece read, using the words given, and aiming to catch the style and turn of expression. By continuing this exercise, and changing the *subjects* and the *authors*, it will be found that scholars will soon acquire a ready command of language and easy modes of expression.

Another exercise, which has been found very useful, is one which is designed to give a knowledge and use of *poetic language* and *imagery*. For this purpose, selections are made from he standard poets on a great variety of subjects. Thompson's Seasons furnishes imagery for describing scenery, and changes of nature; his *Castle of Indolence* furnished *drowsy* imagery; Cowper furnishes poetic language for objects in every day life; Pope's translations, and Scott's poems, furnish war-like imagery; and thus by varied selections every important subject can be dwelt upon in the language of poetry. These extracts are given as the exercise in *transposition*, which the poetic imagery also is to be selected, and incorporated into specimens of original composition. In this way the style and beauties of the standard poets are studied, which a ready and elegant command of language is acquired. It has been intended that this exercise should include a course of reading and extracts from all the best English classics. But time has never been obtained for preparing such a course.

Another exercise has been employed to teach *unity* and *method*. Such a work as Foster's Essays has been taken, and one of the essays selected with the requisition that the *general plan* shall be discovered and drawn out by reading over the essay. As this writer does not mark out the divisions of his subjects as prominently as some writers do, it demands more attention to obtain an analysis. After the general analysis of the whole essay has been obtained, a particular analysis of *each chapter* is required. Then the object of each separate *paragraph* is required, and in all it is to be pointed out, how the general plan of the whole essay is kept in view, and at the same time the plan of the chapter and of the paragraph.

After thus learning to trace out and understand how unity is to be preserved in very composition, the mode of *expanding* and *illustrating ideas* in attempted. This is done by taking the *analysis* of a certain portion, containing all the prominent ideas, and attempting to expand and illustrate as fully as the author has done. The efforts of the pupil are to be compared with those of the author. At first it will be found that they fall far short in fullness, and it will not be until after repeated attempts that a young writer will succeed in expanding and exhibiting clearly, just *the same and no other* topics than those embraced by the writer in the part from which the analysis is selected. This exercise has been found particularly useful in teaching *didactic* composition.

Another exercise has been pursued to teach *method* and *order* in the arrangement of ideas. Several subjects are proposed by the teacher to the class and discussed. An example is then given of *forming a plan* or *skeleton*, as the basis of a composition. The pupils are then required to bring in plans of their own, on the various subjects discussed. But as this branch has a great measure fallen under the care of the Principal, the pressure of other duties, and failure of health, have prevented a regular progress through any plan. But all these methods have been tried at different times, and have afforded satisfactory evidence that where *systematically* pursued, they would fully accomplish the object intended." (14–16).

From *The Annual Catalogue of the Hartford Female Seminar Together With An Account of the Internal Arrangements, Course of Study, and Mode of Conducting the Same* (Hartford: George F. Olmsted, 1831).

Chapter 8

A Century of Writing Instruction in School and College English

Catherine L. Hobbs
James A. Berlin

> **Key Concepts.** *Writing instruction at heart of curriculum • Historical neglect of continuity of writing instruction • Writing pedagogy as site of contestation • The new school and college • Morrill Federal Land Grant Act of 1862 and 1890 • Rise in school and university populations • Current–traditional rhetoric and meritocracy • Shift from invention to arrangement and style • Role of inductive method and science • Reduction of social problems to technical problems • Literature and the liberal culture idea • Methods of instruction in the school • English as a new discipline • Social efficiency and English studies • Fred Newton Scott's rhetoric of public service •* **Reorganization of English in Secondary Schools** *(1917) • Self-expression and creative writing • Challenges from behaviorism • Challenges from social rhetorics • An "experience curriculum" • Life adjustment curricula • "Communication" courses • Literature and composition • Linguistics and composition • Historical rhetorics • The New Rhetoric • Writing as cognitive process • Personal and linguistic growth • Social epistemic theories • The spiral curriculum • Teacher initiatives • Cultural studies and composition • Computers and technological change • Composition at century's end*

A PREFATORY STATEMENT

The following chapter builds on the history written by the late James A. Berlin for the first edition of this book. Beginning with the revolution of the 1890s that transformed Greek and Latin language and literature studies into English studies, his chapter never responded directly to the technological revolution taking place at the time of its publication. But his later work on cultural studies did articulate a pedagogical theory and practice for the information age in which the semiotic interanimation of media texts and graphics shapes our social lives. Berlin's historical perspective makes it possible to better understand the current technological revolution and its conflicts, frequently manifested on numerous fronts as different constituencies and alliances struggle over competing versions of literacy to uphold their differing visions of society.

INTRODUCTION

Writing instruction in school and college English programs has been a scene of struggle over the last century. Even before the late-century attention to language as a creator of meaning and experience, educators and policy shapers realized that the study of language and literature was an integral part of learning rather than a superficial acquirement. If education in a democratic society is a site of contestation over the kind of economic, social, and political formations we want schools to endorse, it is no wonder that English studies, with its concern for the literary and rhetorical texts students are to read and to write remains near the center of curricular decisions. So in English studies, writing instruction has remained at the heart of curricular decisions as to the kind of society we should advocate and the kinds of individuals we should encourage to make up that society. Decisions about writing pedagogy put into material practice our beliefs as to the purpose education should serve in society.

In the nineteenth century, when English studies was first taking shape, literature was primarily studied in classical texts, in Latin or Greek, leaving more curricular space for the development of written composition or public speech, the old rhetoric. Centering the English curriculum on literary texts—Aristotle's poetics—was a "modern" phenomenon that only occurred as language studies moved into the twentieth century. Yet instruction in writing always remained a part of English studies. Most histories of English studies until quite recently have failed to pay attention to the continuity of writing instruction. Both Arthur N. Applebee and Gerald Graff, for example, have written histories that intentionally exclude a consideration of composition instruction in school and college English programs.

In the last quarter of the twentieth century, with the professionalization of composition, our historians have been laboring to tell stories of this uninterrupted activity of instruction in writing. They are confirming that writing pedagogy has been a site of contestation and that no classroom pedagogy can long survive without in some way responding to its historical conditions, as this chapter considers.[1]

THE NEW SCHOOL AND COLLEGE

The modern high school and the modern comprehensive university took their shapes as part of an economic shift from a laissez-faire market economy of unbridled individual competition to a managed economy of corporate and government alliances and planning. Education in general, and the new formation of English, played a central role in this transition. For most of the nineteenth century, higher education served to prepare an elite for leadership in society. General education was common to all students—rhetoric, classical languages and literature, moral philosophy, and some mathematics and science. Specialized training in the professions—primarily law, the ministry, and medicine—was carried out primarily through apprenticeship programs, although a few professional schools were available.

The rise of the German research university model, with its specialized disciplines and rigorous research mission, joined with economic and social forces in the United States to produce the new comprehensive university. This momentous transformation was signaled early on by the passing of the Morrill Federal Land Grant Act of 1862, supporting states in establishing agricultural and technical institutions designed to apply the findings of science to the managing of economic and social affairs. In the new university, the curriculum was to be elective, not prescribed, specialized rather than general, and its purpose was to train certified experts in the new sciences to produce the knowledge that would move capitalist society forward.

When the act was renewed in 1890, a provision ensured that funds would go to both races, improving black institutions or establishing separate black colleges. Although no funds went to women, the commitment of

---

[1]Arthur N. Applebee, *Tradition and Reform in the Teaching of English: A History* (Urbana: NCTE, 1974); Gerald R. Graff, *Professing Literature: An Institutional History* (Chicago: U of Chicago P, 1987). This is consistent with Applebee's later work, *Curriculum as Conversation* (Chicago: U of Chicago P), which only mentions composition instruction in passing. In contrast, W. Ross Winterrowd's book *The English Department: A Personal and Institutional History* (Carbondale: Southern Illinois UP, 1998) attempts to synthesize composition and literary history.

public funds from both Morrill Acts put pressure on institutions to accept women. Colleges, especially state institutions, began to open their doors to more diverse people of talent—women as well as men, black as well as white—although genuine equality remained an unattained ideal of meritocracy rather than a reality. The change in higher education brought about changes in the high schools. While virtually all states by the time of the Civil War provided some form of common school for the lower grades, many secondary schools were private and were designed as places for college preparation.[2] The dividing line between high school and college was not clear. The same sort of political pressures that encouraged colleges to become places of scientific training for a more productive work force were effective in arguing that high schools should serve the same purposes.

In 1890, 202,963 students attended 2,562 public high schools; in 1900, the figure doubled to 519,251 students in 6,005 public high schools; and by 1912, enrollment reached one million. Attendance among fourteen-to-seventeen-year-olds continued to increase, with 28 percent of this age group in school by 1920 (2,200,389 students), 47 percent by 1930 (4,399,422 students), and two-thirds of this population by 1940 (6,545,991 students).[3] Increased attendance in colleges was almost as dramatic: 597,880 students in 1920; 1,100,737 by 1930; and 1,494,203 in 1940. As Lester Faigley has pointed out, an enormous expansion due to Baby Boomers came about just as composition studies was aspiring to disciplinary status: from 2.7 million in 1949–50, to 3.6 million in 1959–60, to more than 8 million in 1969–70, and over 11.5 million in 1979–80. By 1994, more than 14 million students were in college, with 16.4 million predicted by 2006. Thus, high schools became an institution serving the majority of American youth only in early twentieth century; it appears that colleges are crossing this line early in the twenty-first century.

The role of gender in these revised educational arrangements is crucial. More girls than boys graduated from high school at the start of the twentieth century, but few could go to college, although the number enrolled had grown from 11,000 in 1870 to 85,000 in 1900. But women persisted in gaining higher education informally or formally so that later in the century, much of the increase in college enrollment (in the 1970s and 1980s) would be made up of women, and many of the new college composition positions, both adjunct and tenure-line, were being filled by women, who

---

[2]Applebee 224, 243–45. The Morrill Act of 1862 led to the opening of public higher educational institutions to white women, but it took the second act in 1890 to begin the process of opening them to African American men and women by creating the historically black colleges and universities in a "separate-but-equal" extension. Frederick Rudolph, *The American College and University: A History* (New York: Vintage, 1962) 168.

[3]Joel Spring, *The American School, 1642–1985* (New York: Longman, 1986) 194.

earned doctorates at a sharply increasing rate beginning in the 1970s.[4] It should be noted, however, that throughout the twentieth century across the profession of teaching, women have dominated at the elementary and junior high levels, demonstrated a clear majority at the secondary level, and fallen in numbers to a small minority at the college level (with some exceptions in part-time teaching of composition). As Sue Ellen Holbrook has shown, the percentage of women in public school teaching remains high, while men dominate at the college levels. Moreover, women faculty teach in lower-paying areas such as education and the humanities. Overall, salaries for women in both college and in the schools were less than those for men doing the same work. This pattern of discrimination should be kept in mind in discussing the activity of a profession in which women played so prominent and successful a role.[5]

CONTEXT FOR A NEW CENTURY

Report of The Committee of Ten

By the turn of the twentieth century, the required classical course was generally abandoned, but not without a struggle.[6] This had much to do with the wider access to education, which also spurred the earliest debates over the composition course in the high school. Because high schools had seen their mission as preparing students for college, they had emphasized classical language and literature. In contrast, the new high school and college would organize around the study of English. By the nineteenth century, the rhetoric course had come to be taught in English.[7] As a result, the original courses in the emerging English department at the college level, most conspicuously at Harvard, were in composition. Harvard had indeed been the first to introduce the new entrance exam in writing, an exam destined to replace the classical language requirement, although it would be some time before this objective would be attained. In 1873–74, Harvard announced that each candidate for admission was required to write an essay on "such works of standard authors as shall be announced from time to

---

[4]Barbara Miller Solomon, *In the Company of Educated Women: A History of Women and Higher Education in America* (New Haven: Yale Univeresity Press, 1985), p. 63.

[5]Sue Ellen Holbrook, "Women's Work: The Feminizing of Composition," *Rhetoric Review* 9.2 (Spring 1991): 201–29.

[6]Rudolph 196, 214.

[7]Thomas P. Miller tells the story of rhetoric and the eighteenth-century vernacularization in *The Formation of College English: Rhetoric and Belles Lettres in the British Cultural Provinces* (Pittsburgh: U of Pittsburgh P, 1997).

time."[8] The essay, as Applebee has indicated, was designed to test writing ability, not knowledge of literature.

The prestige of Harvard, the fact that secondary schools had previously based the curriculum on college preparation, and the absence of any new curricular model for the new high school all conspired to make the new entrance policy decisive in shaping secondary English courses. Since Harvard's reading list—as well as the lists of those colleges emulating its example—changed from year to year, it was difficult for high school teachers to know what literary works to teach. As a result, regional organizations were established to provide uniform reading lists, and these groups were finally replaced in 1894 by the National Conference on Uniform Entrance Requirements. In addition, in 1892 the National Education Association appointed a group known as the Committee of Ten with Harvard president Charles W. Eliot as chair. Its purpose was to examine the entire curriculum on secondary schools.

The Conference on English, appointed by the Committee of Ten, was chaired by Samuel Thurber, master at Girls' High School Boston, and its secretary was George Lyman Kittredge of Harvard's new English department. Its mission was to formulate the purposes of English studies in the high school, its final report beginning with an important policy statement:

> The main direct objects of the teaching of English in schools seems to be two: (1) to enable the pupil to understand the expressed thoughts of others and to give expression to thoughts of his own; and (2) to cultivate a taste for reading, to give the pupil some acquaintance with good literature, and to furnish him with the means of extending that acquaintance.[9]

For our purposes, the elaboration of the first is crucial. The document encouraged the student in the elementary school "to furnish his own material, expressing his own thoughts in a natural way" and relying on his own "observation or personal experience."[10] This represented a concession to student interest and innovation that was, however, to be abandoned by the secondary school where the emphasis was to be on "training in expression of thought."[11] Here the orientation was provided by the tenets of mental

---

[8]Applebee 30. See also John C. Brereton, ed., *The Origins of Composition Studies in the American College, 1875–1925, A Documentary History* (Pittsburgh: U of Pittsburgh P, 1995).

[9]Alvina Treut Burrows, "Composition: Prospect and Retrospect," *Reading and Writing Instruction in the United States; Historical Trends*, ed. H. Alan Robinson (Urbana: International Reading Assoc., and ERIC, 1977) 24. The conference included the subjects of English language, grammar, composition, rhetoric, and literature, but excluded elocution from its purview.

[10]Burrows 25.

[11]Kenneth J. Kantor, "Creative Expression in the English Curriculum," *Research in the Teaching of English 9* (Spring 1975): 5–29.

discipline and faculty psychology, now offered in the service of the scientific values of precision, clarity, and conciseness—in short, of efficiency. Indeed, given that the members of the Conference on English were appointed by Eliot and that it included Kittredge, it is not unexpected to discover that the method of writing instruction for high schools recommended was the one later characterized as "current-traditional" rhetoric, the very method rigorously pursued in Harvard's English department.[12]

Current-Traditional Rhetoric

Harvard was one of the founding centers of current-traditional rhetoric during the last century, particularly through the textbooks of Adams, Sherman Hill, and Barrett Wendell (although those of John Genung of Amherst sold as well). Its epistemological base is positivistic and rational, offering writing as an extension of the scientific method. Since the basis of all reliable knowledge is sense impression, the writer is to use inductively derived data whenever possible. Language is a sign system that serves to stand in place of concrete experience. The mind is composed of a set of faculties that correspond so perfectly to the external world that these faculties inevitably give rise to the invariable forms of rhetorical discourse, "modes" such as exposition and argument, corresponding to the faculty of reason, or description and persuasion, arising from the emotions and will. The last is particularly suspect since it involves the ordinarily distortive feelings.

In this scheme, knowledge is always prior to the act of writing, to be discovered through the appropriate inductive method of one's scientific area of expertise. As a result, invention as the discovery of the available means of persuasion is excluded from rhetoric, and attention is shifted to arrangement—the modes of discourse—and style, now primarily conceived as correctness. This epistemology is complicit with a politics designed to preserve the interests of corporate capitalism and the university-trained experts who serve it. For this rhetoric, the inductive method of science is as effective in addressing questions of social, political, and ethical value as it is in responding to scientific problems. Indeed, all social problems are reduced to technical problems. Thus, the engineer who determines the

---

[12]For discussions of this term, see especially Berlin, *Rhetoric* 7–9, and Crowley, "Around 1971: Current-Traditional Rhetoric and Process Models of Composing," *Composition in the Twenty-First Century: Crisis and Change*, ed. Lynn Z. Bloom, Donald A. Daiker, and Edward M. White (Carbondale: Southern Illinois UP, 1996) 64–74. Robin Varnum's *Fencing with Words: A History of Writing Instruction at Amherst College during the Era of Theodore Baird, 1938–1966* (Urbana: NCTE, 1996), criticizes the concept of "current-traditional" for causing historians to neglect the mid-twentieth century through its homogeneously negative characterizations of writing instruction.

best location and the best method for building a bridge is regarded as possessing equal expertise in deciding whether or not the bridge ought to be built in the first place. Questions in the realm of public discourse—which in a democracy are commonly considered to be the responsibility of all citizens to decide—are now relegated to a emergent class of professional experts. These experts usually find through their scientific decision-making process the solutions to problems that best serve their own class interests. The new high school and college then were part of the creation of a meritocracy—a hierarchical class structure in which the certified professional is given an inordinate amount of power and reward for solving the problems considered worth solving by the demands of corporate capitalism. The objective, disinterested, and mechanical rhetoric they were learning in school reinforced their authority and concealed the economic and political sources of power on which their claims to privilege were based.

The Liberal Culture Ideal

Of course, current-traditional rhetorics did not go unchallenged in the new college and university. Their most important opponent was situated at Yale and other established prestigious Atlantic seaboard colleges. These schools came to stand for an ideal of English studies which has been labeled "liberal culture." It was Yale, after all, which in 1892 opposed Harvard's use of literature to teach composition, arguing that literature ought to be studied for its own sake. The proponents of liberal culture argued that the literary text was the expression of the highest potential of human nature, representing the perfect fusion of truth, goodness, and beauty. From this perspective, the claims of current-traditional rhetoric were altogether too democratic, arguing mistakenly that writing, like engineering or farming or pharmacy, could be taught.

A summary of the disagreement between Harvard and Yale was found in a 1912 essay by Glenn E. Palmer entitled "Culture and Efficiency through Composition." For Yale, if writing was to be taught at all in college, it ought to be taught to the few who were gifted, and then in order to encourage the creation of literature, not rhetoric. The Harvard method insisted all should be required to undergo writing instruction in order to cultivate "good language habits."[13] Yale was instead concerned with providing all its students "the inspiration of literature, recognizing that there can be no literary production without culture." This production, however, had as its chief objective the encouragement of a "few geniuses." The only way to learn to write for the liberal culturist was to read literature and to talk and write about literature under the direction of an expert in litera-

---

[13]Glenn Palmer, "Culture and Efficiency Through Composition," *English Journal 1* (1912): 488.

ture. Liberal culture represented the reaction of the old, elite colleges to the new meritocratic university. While it did not openly oppose democracy, it argued that the business of higher education was to train the leaders of society, unquestionably men, not women, with the innate gift for leadership, and that the only way to offer such training was to rely on a literary education. Liberal culture embraced the Arnoldian notion that literature represented the best thought of the best minds and was the appropriate basis for educating each new generation. Most proponents argued for the inevitability of class, gender, and race distinctions as a matter of genetic transmission and aspired to the status of an educated aristocracy of leadership and privilege, both to be granted on the basis of a spiritual superiority that was a result of birth and breeding.

Methods of Instruction in the Schools

The divisions in these two conceptions of writing instruction are fairly transparent in the debates taking place at the college level during this time. When we turn to the practices of high school teachers, however, the methods called upon in teaching writing are not nearly so clear-cut. Despite the fact that as high school enrollments increased the absolute numbers of students not going on to college increased, the curriculum remained tied to the needs of the college-bound. This meant that most of the writing a student attempted focused on literary texts. This writing, however, varied greatly depending on the nature of the literary study undertaken.

The philological method that emphasized responding to the text as an historical artifact to be studied scientifically lent itself to the composing processes of current-traditional rhetoric. Thus, the text could be used to demonstrate certain rhetorical principles, or the student could be asked to write about certain historical features of the text's production. A reading, on the other hand, that insisted on the unique ability of the literary text to provide a rare experience of truth and beauty would be more inclined to use the rhetoric of liberal culture.

This classroom encouraged students to offer an appreciative reading of the text, sometimes a unique response to the text in unique language or occasionally an original literary production. The point was to develop literary taste in students, which would equip them for a better life both morally and aesthetically, and to discover those with the talent for creative effort, if any were in fact in the classroom. This method, as will be seen later, often merged with the attempt to address the psychological needs and interests of the student, in this way moving against the elitist stance of the liberal culture ideal.[14] As is indicated by some of the high school textbooks

---

[14]For more on this aspect of creative writing in college, see D. G. Myers, *The Elephants Teach: Creative Writing Since 1880* (Englewood Cliffs: Prentice-Hall, 1996).

at the turn of the century, sometimes the two methods appeared in the same classroom.[15] In general, the high school English class at this early stage of its history was marked by uncertainty and experimentation, the only constant being the reading of literary texts and some sort of writing in response to them.

1900–1917—ENGLISH BECOMES A DISCIPLINE

During the first two decades of this century, the teaching of English in the high school and college attained professional standing. English teachers now were more confident about the special materials of their discipline and of the methods for teaching them. It is important to note, however, that there were still large disagreements. These, however, tended to take place among competing groups, each of whose members were themselves in agreement about their endeavors. A number of social and political developments at this time encouraged the new stability and status of English studies.

Social Efficiency and English Studies

During these decades, the vagaries of competitive capitalism became unacceptable to many so that the government and corporations attempted to manage a planned economy. A parallel concept of "social efficiency" was extended to the public schools. As Joel Spring explains, "social efficiency" meant that schools were to provide curricula that met "the future social needs of the student," taught "cooperation as preparation for future social activities," and provided for "the future social destination of the student."[16] Students were now to be prepared for work—primarily for life in the large-scale organizations where cooperation (as well as conformity) was valued over competition. This also included, however, some attention to the individual differences and needs of students. By this time, the developmental child-study efforts of such pioneers as G. K. Hall were flourishing. This movement argued for considering a student's stage of psychological development in planning instruction. Schools were also to become attentive to the needs of the workplace so that even high school students were expected to undertake some specialized study toward their future work. These programs were especially important to the parents of working class students intent on upward mobility, as well as to their employers.

---

[15]Nancy Van Tuyle McCoy, "A Relationship Between Rhetoric and Poetics: English Studies in Secondary Schools, a Composition-Literature Paradigm, 1874–1917," Purdue University Dissertation 1994 (UMI, AAC 9523405).

[16]Spring 198.

Finally, school and work were regarded as places of equal opportunity where the best, the brightest, and the hardest working were to be rewarded in accordance with strictest meritocratic principles, an ideal never quite realized.

High school teachers played an important role in working out the consequences of these new ideas for students. They were now freed of the obligation to groom all students for college. Young people were to be prepared for the economic and social roles they chose for themselves, not for the college education which at this time only four percent pursued by 1900.[17] Teachers of English were especially conspicuous in supporting this change. In fact, the National Council of Teachers of English was formed in 1911 in protest to the Uniform Reading Lists. A coalition made up primarily of teachers from the Midwest and New York City argued that teachers, not the colleges, should set reading and writing requirements for their students, taking into account their special needs. Their resolve was intensified by their concern for the learning problems of the many students not going on to college, particularly the increasing number of immigrant students.

Another effect of the move for social efficiency was the development of the comprehensive high school, offering a wide variety of curricula for students. One strong objection to these specialized curricula in the high school was that they brought about social fragmentation in the student community. Attempts to overcome the worst effects of this fragmentation included the formation of extracurricular activities for all—such as student government, social occasions, and athletic events—and the teaching of the "mother tongue."[18] English teachers were to provide through literature and composition the means for a common culture that would increase social cohesion. After World War I, this function was further encouraged through the "Americanization" programs provided for the new wave of immigrants. Finally, the efforts of secondary teachers to determine their own curricula led to support for separating the teaching of literature from the teaching of composition. If each was to be given its fair share of attention, each must be treated alone.

The effects on classroom practices in high school English of this movement to prepare students for economic and social life were in no way monolithic. The new emphasis on vocational education often led to English courses that ignored literature altogether, offering instruction in current-traditional rhetoric. As Applebee points out, these often included "units on salesmanship, advertising, and printing added for variety and breadth."[19] In other words, the emphasis on the high school as a place of

---

[17]Rudolph 152.
[18]Spring 203.
[19]Applebee 60.

training for work could restrict writing instruction to the strictly utilitarian and vocational, without regard for the personal or political life of the student. At its best, however, the drive for social efficiency promoted a democratic rhetoric that responded to the progressive agenda of John Dewey's full educational experience: self-development within a democratic environment, a concern for social reform and harmony, and the preparation for economic integration. This rhetoric is seen in the work of Fred Newton Scott of the University of Michigan, Joseph Villiers Denney of Ohio State, and Gertrude Buck of Vassar. Others who shared this perspective were George Pattee of Pennsylvania State, Katherine Stewart Worthington of Columbia, and Sterling Andrus Leonard of Wisconsin. Scott is particularly worth examining as an example of this social rhetoric because of his considerable influence in both public schools and colleges.

Alternative Social Rhetorics—Fred Newton Scott

Scott's rhetoric was consciously formulated as an alternative to current-traditional rhetoric with its emphasis on the scientific and practical, and to the rhetoric of liberal culture with its privatization of experience and elitism. Reality for Scott was neither exclusively sensory nor exclusively subjective, but was a product of the interaction of the private and public in a social setting. Scott's rhetoric was intent on providing for public discourse in a democratic and heterogeneous society. The writing course should not provide students exclusively with the means for presenting scientific truths or private visions or even persuasive appeals. It should enable students to undertake all of these tasks and others. The important consideration is that "any piece of discourse, or mode of communication, is to be measured by its effect upon the welfare of the community."[20] Scott thus proposes a rhetoric of public service, a commitment to using discourse for the public good.

Like Dewey, Scott argued that the first consideration of schools and colleges should be the preparation of citizens for a democracy who are trained to use their specialized knowledge for the welfare of the community as a whole. The subjects for writing Scott proposes in *Elementary English Composition*, a textbook for the schools written with Denney, accordingly emphasizes the relation of the writer or speaker to the entire rhetorical context—the audience and larger community, the subject from these perspectives, and the role of language in each and all. As Denney explains elsewhere, in leading students to topics it is necessary to choose "a typical situation in real life," express the topic so as to suggest to the stu-

---

[20]Fred Newton Scott, "Rhetoric Rediviva," *College Composition and Communication 31* (1980): 413–19.

dent "a personal relationship to the situation," and provide "a particular reader or set of readers who are to be brought into vital relationship with the situation."[21] Scott and Denney taught writing within a complete rhetorical situation, a situation that was thoroughly social without denying the importance of the individual.

Reorganization of English—1917

The larger effects of the social efficiency effort on English studies were presented in a report entitled *Reorganization of English in the Secondary Schools*, published by the United States Office of Education in 1917. It argued that English courses should emphasize personal and social needs rather than college requirements. They were to be "social in content and social in method of acquirement," to be attained by organizing them around "expressional and interpretative experiences of the greatest possible social value to the given class."[22] As for writing, there was to be, as in the Committee of Ten report, a progression from creative and individual activities at the lowest grades to social and more practical activities at the upper levels. Thus students in the seventh, eighth, and ninth grades were to engage in creative writing, such as stories about their experiences, sensory descriptions of memorable scenes, accounts of imaginary journeys, and fictional conversations. This creative effort was also to include oral expression, now returned to the English course. Imaginative work, however, was to appear less frequently in the upper grades except for those who display a special talent in this direction. Here the writing should be functional. It should grow out of the experiences of the students, but it should focus on social exigencies. Thus, the report recommended that writing should have a purpose, giving as an example the use of a school newspaper to publish student work. The student should write for a clearly designated audience, not "with the vision of a teacher, blue pencil in hand, looking over his shoulder." Therefore, the content and the form of the essay should be determined by "the purpose in view and the audience for whom the composition is prepared,"[23] and the same is true of the oral presentation. Finally, it should be mentioned that the report was, in general, a conservative document, emphasizing the utilitarian and social nature of mature discourse but saying little about the uses of writing in preparing students for citizenship in a democracy, or in enabling them to arrive at personal fulfillment. The strongest impulse for writing instruction is to

---

[21]Joseph Villiers Denney, *Two Problems in Composition Teaching*. Contributions to Rhetorical Theory, 3rd ed., Fred Newton Scott, editor (Ann Arbor: n.p., n.d.) 173.

[22]Applebee 66.

[23]Burrows 30.

prepare the student to be an efficient worker, as indicated by the opening
paragraph of the report on the senior high school:

> The purpose of teaching composition is to enable the pupil to speak and
> write correctly, convincingly, and interestingly. The first step toward effi-
> ciency in the use of language is the cultivation of earnestness and sincerity;
> the second is the development of accuracy and correctness; the third is the
> arousing of individuality and artistic consciousness.[24]

As already indicated, the third step receives little attention while the social
dimension of discourse is subsumed under efficiency.

THE PERIOD BETWEEN THE WARS

Self-Expression and Creative Writing

World War I served to establish beyond doubt the value of English studies
to the nation as a whole. While English teachers in the schools organized
courses around patriotic themes, their counterparts in the universities
turned their prewar training in German universities to the national interest, especially in the postwar occupation. The years immediately following
the war were a time of relative prosperity and optimism for the schools. In
English studies, the most notable turn was the concern for the unique individuality and creative potential of each student. The center of composition
activities for an increasing number of school and college teachers became
expressive writing about personal experience and occasionally creative
writing. As Berlin argued in *Rhetoric and Reality,* the insistence of liberal
culturists on genius as the essential element of writing at its best was now
given a democratic application. Each and every individual was seen to possess creative potential, a potential the proper classroom environment
could unlock and promote.[25] This was the result of a number of forces.
The child study movement represented by G. Stanley Hall had taken hold
at the new schools of education. In addition, as Lawrence Cremin explains, after the war there arose "a polyglot system of ideas that combined
the doctrine of self-expression, liberty, and psychological adjustment into
a confident, iconoclastic individuality that fought the constraints of
Babbitry and the discipline of social reform as well."[26] This description

---

[24]Burrows 30.

[25]See also Myers, *Elephants.*

[26]Lawrence Cremin, *The Transformation of the School: Progressivism in American Education,
1876–1957* (New York: Vintage, 1961).

well fits Theodore Baird, whose influential leadership of the writing program at Amherst spanned nearly 40 years, beginning in 1938.[27]

The resistance to social efficiency in the name of the individual was also aided by a bowdlerized version of Freud that depicted the innate impulses of children as innately good. The classroom was to unlock these virtuous and creative springs of feeling and conduct by providing a free and uninhibited environment. Finally, the example of aesthetic expressionism in dance, music, and poetry—particularly among the surrealists—was invoked as the paradigm for genuine writing. For expressionist rhetoric, writing—all writing—is accordingly art. This means that it can be learned, and learned by all, but not taught. The work of the teacher is to provide an environment in which students can learn what cannot be directly imparted in instruction. The expression of the writer is the product of a private and personal vision that cannot be expressed in normal, everyday parlance. This language, after all, refers to the public world of sense data and social experience. The writer must instead learn to use metaphor to express meaning that is separate and above this limited realm. Sensory experience, on the other hand, is also very important since it provides experiences that can be used as materials for metaphor. Writing from this perspective enables students to get in touch with the private and the personal, the source of all that is meaningful. It therefore empowers the student to shape a newly uncovered and better self—that is, half creating and half discovering the source of all truth and value. Furthermore, this product of the authentic writing experience—the truly personal—is organic, representing the perfect fusion of form and content. Finally, this method of teaching writing is concerned with power and politics, sometimes by implication and at other times openly in its critique of the dehumanizing effects of industrial capitalism. Its response is to enable each individual to realize his or her true self in order to bring about a better society. In other words, the private and personal is always prior to the public and social, the latter being an effect of the former.

In his historical perspective of creative expression in the school English curriculum, Kenneth Kantor offers an overview of the various features of the expressive movement between the two wars.[28] One form it took was to argue that English is an art subject-like painting or music—not preparation for the more efficient uses of language. Proponents such as Hugh Mearns and Harold Rugg argued that traditional English courses had encouraged conformity and imitation rather than self-expression, Mearns maintaining that "children speak naturally in a form that we adults are accustomed to call poetry, and without any searching for appropriate use of

---

[27]See Varnum.
[28]Kantor 12–21; see also Myers, 101–45.

the medium."[29] Rugg emphasized that the teacher must focus on the process of composing, not merely the product. John T. Frederick, originally at Iowa, argued that creative writing enables the student to recognize the dignity of his own experience. Writing, like art, becomes concerned with intrinsic rewards, rewards that are available to all, not just the creative few. Numerous claims for the benefits of expressive writing were also made. This writing can be therapeutic, "doing away with maladjustments of personality."[30] It can advance cultural values, although, as Kantor points out, these values were most commonly those of the comfortable middle class, ignoring, for example, the experiences of African Americans and other minorities. Expressive writing, others argued, can improve the mechanical elements of writing as students strive to communicate a message that really matters to them. It can also enhance students' enjoyment of literature since they can discover for themselves the values of literary discourse through their attempts to produce it. (Notice that this is the reverse of the earlier argument that reading literature will improve writing: here writing improves reading.) Finally, many argued that expressive and creative writing would enhance students' pleasure in writing of all kinds, encouraging an enjoyment of composing regardless of its purpose.

Challenges from Behaviorism

This enthusiasm for expressive, creative writing did not go unchallenged. One contrary consequence of the turn to the methods of psychology in studying the development of children was found in the quantitative method of Edward L. Thorndike. Thorndike argued that whatever exists, exists in some quantity and so could be measured. His research sponsored a behavioristic approach in which teaching objectives were stated in measurable terms and the learning then measured through the appropriate testing device. In English studies, this rage for quantification produced a variety of activities, some salutary, others unfortunate. The testing of student abilities led to tracking in English courses at both the high school and college levels, the latter in composition courses. This tracking on the basis of culturally biased tests tended to reinforce class, race, and gender relations at both levels.

In another area, the drive for efficiency in business and industry that came to be called Taylorism (after Frederick W. Taylor, one of the leaders in scientific management) combined with the influence of Thorndike to produce studies of the efficiency of high school and college writing courses. A joint survey conducted by the Modern Language Association

---

[29]Kantor 13.
[30]Kantor 18.

(MLA) and the National Council for Teachers of English (NCTE) found that high school students wrote on average 400 words per week while college freshmen averaged 650. The study revealed just how "efficient" English studies was, the course clearly overworking teachers to an appalling degree. The report argued convincingly for reform, although none was forthcoming.[31] A less useful application of this drive for quantitatively demonstrated efficiency came in the evaluation scales developed by Thorndike and Milo Burdette Hillegas, a device used to measure the quality of student essays in the secondary schools. The test itself had considerable merit, requiring the teacher to evaluate student work by comparing it to nationally normed models of varying degrees of excellence. Its pitfall was that it encouraged mechanistic approaches to writing instruction, teaching for the test and stressing matters of superficial form and correctness. The fact that results of the test were occasionally used to evaluate teacher effectiveness without regard for the ability level of students added to its destructive potential.

Challenges from Social Rhetorics

Another challenge to the dominance of expressive writing came in the form of socially-based rhetorics. These were found in courses inspired by Dewey and Scott, and were especially apparent during the Depression years. The insistence that writing is a social act performed through a complex interaction of writer, audience, subject, and language appeared at colleges in every geographical region.[32] These offerings tended to be specifically political in their orientation, addressing the economic crisis at home and the international crises abroad as failures of the total community, not of the individual. As we have seen, those supporting the value of expressive writing looked to private and personal resolutions to the economic and social catastrophes of the day. Those in the camp of social rhetoric, on the other hand, lay the blame for these disorders at the feet of the social and political arrangements generated by capitalism, a diagnosis in which they were led by strong factions in the American Historical Society and the Progressive Education Association.[33] While the expressionists looked to the individual to address the horrors of the 1930s and 1940s, the sponsors of social reform looked to collective solutions, beginning with a critique of the excesses of the free enterprise system.

---

[31]John Michael Wozniak, *English Composition in Eastern Colleges, 1850–1940* (Washington: UP of America, 1978) 169–70.

[32]Berlin 81–90.

[33]Applebee 115–16.

An Experience Curriculum

All of these conflicting positions on the most effective method for teaching writing are reflected in the NCTE-sponsored report *An Experience Curriculum in English* published in 1935. This is not unexpected considering that the shapers of the report, numbering more than 100, conceded the pluralistic nature of the document, explaining that any "attempt to create a single curriculum suited to pupils in environments so different as are to be found in the United States would be folly." Beginning with an assumption encouraged by the social efficiency movement as well as by certain strands of progressive education, the report asserted that "Experience is the best of all schools [. . .] *The ideal curriculum consists of well-selected experiences*" (italics in original). The experiences selected for students were those that were part of adults' daily lives as well as "desirable possible experiences they miss."[34] As far as writing is concerned, the report distinguished creative and expressive writing from social communication, providing experiences for each while favoring neither.

The report implied that both privatized expression and public discourse were to be encouraged in the classroom and were not in any way incompatible. Finally, the report came out against the mechanistic and formulaic methods of current-traditional approaches, most controversially in its recommendation that formal grammar training be abandoned in favor of teaching grammar as a part of composing. In this the report reflected the influences of such enlightened linguists as Sterling Andrus Leonard, Robert C. Pooley, Albert H. Marckwardt, Fred G. Walcott, and Charles Fries, all of whom argued for the social basis of language and the need for teachers to consider the importance of class relations and political contexts in teaching writing.[35]

1945–1960

During World War II, the Progressive Education Association sponsored a report entitled *Education for All American Youth* (1944), a document that became the major statement of what came to be called "life adjustment" in the schools. As Kantor explains, "Personal and social adjustment became the great concern of post war education," providing "a new security for those whose lives had been disrupted."[36] This effort was concerned with preparing students for the experiences they would encounter outside of

---

[34]Applebee 119.
[35]Berlin 88–89.
[36]Kantor 21.

school, including those associated with "civic competence." Unfortunately, the report contained excessive emphasis on "functional experiences in the areas of practical arts, home and family, health and physical fitness" as well.[37] Although such a holistic approach to education is commendable, what resulted in the composition course was a turn to the narrowly utilitarian. Applebee's judgment of the life-adjustment effort is probably accurate: "In spite of occasional disclaimers, the emphasis in both name and activities was on 'adjustment,' 'conformity,' and a stable system of values. The traditional concern of progressive education with the continuing improvement of both the individual and his society was submerged and ultimately lost in the formulation."[38]

Communication and Composition

While life adjustment became the dominant influence in secondary school writing instruction, the communications course offered an alternative that was especially influential in colleges and to a lesser extent in high schools. The communications course was a combination of writing, reading, speaking, and listening activities. It was strongly influenced by the General Education movement during the 1930s and by the General Semantics school of linguistics. It became a strong force in education, however, only after the army adopted it in its officer training programs during the war. As Berlin explains in *Rhetoric and Reality*, the communications course was varied in the form it assumed in colleges during the late 1940s and the 1950s, even including attempts to introduce life adjustment into the college. Most of these courses, however, were conservative, offering a current-traditional approach that presented communications in the service of the democratic ideals recently challenged from abroad. The assumption was that a rhetoric committed to a disinterested objectivity would inevitably discover the validity of United States economic, social, and political arrangements. In other words, these courses were unaware of or propagandistic about the ideological predispositions of the rhetoric they were forwarding. The communications course declined during the fifties. It did, however, for a brief time bring members of speech departments and English departments together, leading to an enrichment of rhetorical studies among English teachers. It also helped bring about the formation of the College Composition and Communication Conference (CCCC) in 1949. At century's end, George and Trimbur argued that the profession's sticking with the term "communication" in the face of arguments to abandon it has been "a good thing," pulling us "toward the worldly, the actual, the

---

[37]Applebee 144.
[38]Applebee 144.

material, " and making writing "[. . .] into an act of labor that quite literally fashions the world."[39]

Writing in the secondary schools during this time was pursuing the path of life adjustment or of communications, although both occasionally led, as noted, to the use of expressive and creative writing. The formation of the CCCC, however, signaled a renewed interest in composition at the college level, motivated in part by the large number of veterans attending college on the G. I. Bill. The pages of *College Composition and Communication* and *College English* during this time attest to this new activity. Three areas are especially worth noting: literature and composition, linguistics and composition, and the revival of rhetoric.

Literature and Composition

Using literature texts as materials for analysis in order to teach writing had of course been commonplace throughout the century. Despite the claims of college professors that students ought to come to college with mastery of the composing process, no generation of college students has ever in fact done so. Twentieth-century United States colleges, like their more elite counterparts in the nineteenth century, have continued to provide courses in writing, and there is obviously something perverse in labeling as remedial a course which is necessary for nearly all students.[40] Those colleges most opposed to this course have often concealed their admission of its necessity by offering a "Freshman English" course devoted to literature, a course which is in fact a class in rhetoric, albeit of a belletristic variety. The distinguishing feature of the 1950s in considering the relation of literature to composition is that, for the first time since the Uniform Lists, college professors were in large numbers insisting that the best way to teach composition is through reading literature and writing about it. This was, in large part, a result of a sense of professional identity achieved by teachers of literature following the war, a development described in Richard Ohmann's *English in America: A Radical View of the Profession.*[41]

As indicated earlier, the arguments offered in defense of this view came directly from the tradition of liberal culture, still alive in literary studies.[42]

---

[39]Diana George and John Trimbur, "The 'Communication Battle,' or Whatever Happened to the 4th C?" *CCC* 50.4 (1999): 682–98.

[40]Sharon Crowley, *Composition in the University: Historical and Polemical Essays* (Pittsburgh: U of Pittsburgh P, 1998). Crowley, a strong supporter of the Wyoming Conference Resolution Opposing Unfair Salaries and Working Conditions for Postsecondary Teachers of Writing, proposes eliminating the first-year composition requirement to end these problems.

[41]New York: Oxford UP, 1976.

[42]Berlin 107–11.

Students, it was charged, had nothing to say and literature provided them with rich subject matter. Writing about themselves required "a flair amounting to genius," and most were certainly "not geniuses."[43] Reading literary texts and writing about them provided the knowledge and stimulation that the student needed to become liberally educated and enabled the teacher (almost certainly at this time a male) to keep his career alive and vital. The communications course, this argument went on, failed to provide for the individual while literature preserved the integrity of the individual against the tyranny of the mob. In fact, the liberal culturist notion of the uses of literature in the writing class is offered in the name of democracy. College is to prepare the leaders of a democratic society, and literature is the best means for doing so. Writing about literature was also offered in the interests of the college teachers themselves: after all, it was literature that they knew best and, if they were to be forced to teach writing, they ought certainly to do so by focusing on their own area of expertise. That this might mean serving the professional interests of the teachers more than the instructional needs of the students was not considered. It should finally be noted that these arguments for placing literature at the center of English studies and marginalizing writing instruction were to prove extremely successful during the 1960s and 1970s when, as Applebee explains, "an academic revival [. . .] wrested the initiative in educational reform away from progressive education and returned it to college faculties of liberal arts."[44] This influence of college English teachers in curriculum formation will eventually have serious consequences for writing instruction in the schools.

Linguistics and Composition

Structural linguistics during the 1950s seemed for many to offer a panacea for the difficulties of learning to write. It was hoped that learning about the structure of language would enable students to learn about the structure of discourse, not to mention mastering grammar, making them better writers. The most frequently cited authors in *CCC* articles from 1950 to 1964 were linguists, Charles C. Fries (13 cites), Kenneth Pike (11), Paul Roberts (10), Donald Lloyd (8), and Noam Chomsky (7).[45] In the 1960s and 1970s, this would give rise to research in sentence combining in the work of Donald Batemen and Frank Zidonis, Kellogg Hunt and R. C.

[43]Randall Stewart, "The Freshman Course Needs a Current of Ideas," *College English 17* (1955): 16–19.
[44]Applebee 32.
[45]Phillips et al 452. Phillips, Donna Burns, Ruth Greenberg, and Sharon Gibson, "College Composition and Communication: Chronicling a Discipline's Genius," *CCC* 44.4 (1993): 443–65.

O'Donnell, John C. Mellon, Frank O'Hare, Lester Faigley and Stephen
Witte, and others, and to the classroom techniques based on their work,
particularly those of Francis Christensen and the team of Donald Daiker,
Andrew Kerek, and Max Morenberg. The interest in linguistics also led to
a strong interest in style on the part of many, including Edward P. J.
Corbett and Winston Weathers. In its wake followed discourse analyses of
various stripes including critical discourse analysis (Kress, Fairclough, Van
Dijk), social linguistics (Gee), and social semiotics (Hodge, Kress, and
Lemke) as well as semiotic cultural analysis including the late work of
Berlin.[46]

Perhaps most radically from the late-century viewpoint, the linguistics
emphasis encouraged the important 1972 CCCC position statement entitled "Students' Right to Their Own Language," in which James Sledd
played so important a part, a document that resisted dialectal imperialism
as class and race discrimination.[47] As Geneva Smitherman, another key
leader in the *Students' Right* resolution, has documented, the statement followed the 1968 annual meeting, which took place in Minneapolis during
the time in which Martin Luther King was murdered. A subsequent special
issue of *CCC* in December 1968 responded as well to the crisis precipitated
by events, containing articles by four black authors, most of whom also addressed linguistic issues in their historic discussion of race. Smitherman
describes the language crisis as "caused by the cultural and linguistic mis-
match between higher education and the nontraditional (by virtue of color
and class) students who were making their imprint upon the academic
landscape for the first time in history." Grounded in sociolinguistics, the
Students' Right resolution sought to enlighten on language attitudes, promote the value of linguistic diversity, and convey information on language
and language variation that would enable teachers to teach more effectively (359).

Historical Rhetorics

The attention to historical rhetorics, like that paid to linguistics, was part
of the rediscovery of the complexity of language in all its manifestations, a
complexity which many in English studies restricted to literary texts, seeing all other discourse as a simple signal system. The revival of rhetoric
studies was undertaken with special rigor by the Neo-Aristotelians at the
University of Chicago, most notably Henry Sams, Richard McKeon, and
Richard Weaver. A similar concern for rhetoric and literary studies was

[46]"Discourse Analysis and Literacy Education," Conference Paper, College Composition
and Communication, March 1997, Scottsdale, AZ.
[47]*College Composition and Communication* 25 (Special fall issue 1974).

also undertaken at this time in the work of Kenneth Burke, M. W. Croll, George Williamson, Sister Miriam Joseph, Rosemond Tuve, Wayne Booth, and others. A number of voices heard at this time have continued to be influential in rhetoric and composition studies, particularly James J. Murphy and the late Edward P. J. Corbett. This recovery of historical rhetorics reminded English teachers of the central place that text production had occupied in the educational institutions of the past, serving in many ages as the organizing element of the entire curriculum. In addition to uncovering valuable information about the history of language and of its place in larger cultural formations, these studies contributed to a sense of the importance of composition teaching at all levels of schooling. The New Rhetoric and its proponents—including such as Janice Lauer, Richard Young, Frank D'Angelo, Richard Larsen, James Kinneavy and George Yoos—would in the next decade work to establish rhetoric and composition as a discipline. Their vision of composition teaching would continue to impact theorists and practitioners through the end of the century, with the majority of graduate programs offering coursework in historical rhetoric.

1960–1975

Joel Spring argues that after World War II the "corporate liberal state"— that is, the combined resources of private corporations and various government agencies—had increased its effort to bring education in the United States in line with national economic and social policy. As he explains, "selective service, the NSF, the NDEA, and the War on Poverty are considered part of the general trend in the twentieth century to use the schools as a means of cultivating human resources for the benefit of industrial and corporate leaders."[48] One of the major concerns after the war was the continued provision of talented and trained workers to serve the economic growth of the nation as a means to prosperity and national security. Indeed, the introduction of selective service deferment for those who attended college and graduate school was motivated by this consideration as were the establishment of the National Science Foundation and later the National Defense Education Act (NDEA) of 1958.

As we have seen, life adjustment in the schools had originally begun as an attempt to provide for the socially efficient use of the nation's pool of talent. During the 1950s, however, the almost exclusively practical and excessively student-centered orientation of life adjustment came under attack from a variety of politically conservative critics of the schools. The major charge made was anti-intellectualism, the results of which were a

[48]Spring 282.

failure to provide the educated experts needed for a strong economy and a strong nation. The public schools, this argument went, should be subject-centered, not student-centered, emphasizing the scientific and scholarly disciplines around which the college is organized. This note was sounded in the popular critiques offered by Arthur Bestor, Hyman G. Rickover, Robert M. Hutchins, Mortimer Adler, James B. Conant, Mark Van Doren, and Paul Woodring. The Russian launch of Sputnik in 1957 gave instant credibility to these charges, providing concrete evidence to many that the United States's technological dominance was being eclipsed.

English Studies Responds

A number of measures by government agencies and by private foundations to address this crisis—the extent of which we now know was grossly exaggerated—were taken immediately. The important role of the schools in providing the expertise to address this perceived national threat was underscored by the passage of the National Defense Education Act in 1958. This measure was at first designed to improve school instruction in math and the sciences, but by 1964 it also included the study of literature, language, and composition—particularly the latter two.

Efforts to consider English studies itself at this time included the "Basic Issues" conference of 1958. A meeting of representatives from the MLA, NCTE, American Studies Association, and the College English Association, funded by the Ford Foundation, the conference was designed to address the English curriculum of the public schools. The recommendation was based on a cultural traditions ideal organized around language, literature, and composition.

The College Entrance Examination Board in 1959 appointed a Commission on English to "propose standards of achievement" and "to suggest ways of meeting them," resulting in the report titled *Freedom and Discipline in English* (1965).[49] The most important of the curricular efforts for composition, however, was, interestingly enough, the Woods Hole Conference sponsored by the National Academy of Sciences under the direction of Jerome Bruner. The result was reported in *The Process of Education* (1960), a document that served as an account of the new spiral curriculum. This plan organized the school curriculum around the structure of an established academic discipline which was then to be presented sequentially to students according to their level of cognitive development. Bruner's thought as found here and in several other of his essays from this period was highly influential. Its recommendation for the organization of a sequenced curriculum was influential in other curriculum studies, including

[49]Applebee 196.

Freedom and Discipline in English, and was central in the policies of Project English, a program for funding research founded in 1962 by the United States Office of Education. It was also important in the funding policies of the NDEA when it began granting money to English studies in 1964.

Cognitive Processes and Composing

Bruner encouraged the use of cognitive psychology in discussions of educational matters. His emphasis was on learning as "process," a concept that had been an important part of the progressive educationist's program. Bruner, however, conceived of the learning process in terms of the cognitive level of the student and its relation to the structure of the academic discipline being studied. He was not interested in relating knowledge to society. Instead, he argued that each academic discipline had a structure determined by the experts within its confines and that students should learn this structure at a level of complexity appropriate to their ages. Bruner relied on Piaget's thinking in determining levels of cognitive development. The crucial element, however, was the student's mode of behavior. Bruner emphasized the role of discovery in learning, arguing that students should use an inductive approach in order to discover on their own the structure of the discipline under consideration. This did not mean merely pursuing the scientific method in a slavish and mechanical fashion. Instead, Bruner placed a premium on intuitive methods, approaches that enabled the student to go from creative guesses to verification in the more orthodox manner. The student was to engage in the act of doing physics or math or literary criticism, and was not simply to rely on the reports of experts. Bruner believed that students learned the structure of a discipline through engaging in research as a practitioner of the discipline.

The implications of Bruner's thought for writing instruction are not difficult to deduce. Students should engage in the process of composing, not in the study of someone else's process of composing. Teachers may supply information about writing or direct students in its structural stages, but their main job is to create an environment in which students can learn for themselves the behavior appropriate to successful writing. The product of student writing, moreover, is not as important as engaging in the process of writing. Writing involves discovery, a practice requiring intuition and pursuing hunches—in short, acting in the way mature writers do. The emphasis in the classroom should be on individuals coming to terms with the nature of composing—its inherent structure—on their own, without regard for social processes. The individual must arrive at a unique, personal sense of the knowledge of the discipline concerned, and only through this private perception is learning to compose possible.

Teaching writing as a cognitive process was immediately encouraged by a number of researchers and teachers. Janet Emig's *The Composing Process*

of Twelfth Graders (1971) was especially important since it provided research evidence supporting the description of composing being forwarded by cognitivists. Emig also provided a great many of the terms
which were to mark discussions of cognitive rhetoric.[50] James Britton's *The
Development of Writing Abilities (11–18)* (1975), the results of research conducted in England, furthered the cognitivist agenda. Emig and Britton
were probably the two most respected empirical researchers in composing
among school and college teachers in the seventies, and both provided
suggestions for organizing a writing curriculum in the schools. The most
detailed curricular recommendation along cognitive lines, however, was
provided by James Moffett's *Teaching the Universe of Discourse* (1968).
Moffett presented a series of activities sequenced to correspond to the four
developmental stages of students as they passed from elementary school
to high school—the stages being interior dialogue, conversation, correspondence, and public narrative. The use of the cognitive model of composing was also found at the numerous summer workshops for high school
teachers sponsored by the College Entrance Examination Board's Commission on English in the 1960s. And at the college level, those concerned
with cognitive processes during this time were represented by Janice
Lauer, Richard Larson, and Frank D'Angelo, all of whom worked with
concepts of inventional arts from classical rhetoric.

Processes of Personal and Linguistic Growth

The cognitive version of the composing process was not the only alternative to be forwarded at this time. A related ideal of personal growth that is
finally much different was endorsed by the Dartmouth Conference of
1966. This meeting brought together approximately fifty English teachers
from Britain and the United States to consider their common problems.
The result was a revelation to the United States representatives. Contrary
to the emphasis on English as an academic discipline which emerged in
this country after the rejection of the child-centered approaches of the
progressives, the British offered, as Applebee explains, "a model for English instruction which focuses not on the 'demands' of the discipline but on
the personal and linguistic growth of the child."[51] For the British, the emphasis was not on subject matter, as had been the focus of recent discussions of the curriculum, but on providing "experiences through which the
child could experiment, testing and strengthening his linguistic and intellectual skills by using them in a variety of contexts." Once again, explains

---

[50]Emig has since protested being linked with cognitivism (plenary remark at the 1996
Watson Conference, University of Louisville).

[51]Applebee 229.

Applebee, process was the guiding concept: "it was process or activity rather than content which defined the English curriculum for the British teacher."[52] This process, however, was different from that of the cognitivists since its primary objective was, in the words of John Dixon, a major voice at the conference, "sets of choices from which we must choose one way or another of building our inner world."[53] Here the emphasis was not on mastering the composing process because of its value in solving writing problems, but experiencing it because of its value to the personal development of the student.

As Kantor has argued, the difference between the cognitivist process of Bruner and the expressionist process of the Dartmouth Conference can be stated in a number of clear-cut oppositions: cognitive learning and intellectual development against affective response; a process of knowing "a body of material in a 'spiralling' fashion" against a "process of personal development"; communication for practical purposes against symbolic expression for self fulfillment; discovery through induction against creation through intuition.[54]

The result of the Dartmouth Conference was to reassert for United States teachers the value of the expressive model of writing. Writing is to be pursued in a free and supportive environment in which the student is encouraged to engage in an art of self discovery. This method had never altogether faded from the public schools, and had even been recommended by Albert Kitzhaber in a report on a Commission on English summer workshop in writing.[55] It had, however, been de-emphasized in most curricular recommendations in the early sixties. The political activism of the late sixties and early seventies, on the other hand, gave it new life. A major feature of the counter-culture response to the Vietnam War, racial injustice, and environmental disasters had been based on the politics endorsed by expressionist rhetoric.

The highly personal, private, and individual process of composing once again became conspicuous at the high school level, most notably in the recommendations of Ken Macrorie. It was also at the center of the influential study among college students of Gordon Rohmann and Albert Wlecke, entitled *Pre-Writing: the Construction and Application of Models for Concept Formation in Writing*, published in 1964. (This report was the key document which launched the process movement in the schools.[56]) College

---

[52]Applebee 229.

[53]Applebee 230; see Dixon's *Growth Through English: A Report Based on the Dartmouth Seminar 1966* (Reading, Eng.: NATE, 1967), also Joseph Harris, *A Teaching Subject: Composition Since 1966* (Upper Saddle River: Prentice-Hall, 1997) 1–17.

[54]Kantor 24–26.

[55]Berlin 127.

[56]Winterrowd 4.

English teachers who employed the expressionist process methods were Donald Murray, Walker Gibson, William Coles, Jr., Elizabeth Cowan, and Peter Elbow.[57] It should finally be noted that the cognitivist process and the expressionist process were most often called upon to support divergent political perspectives. The expressionist process was frequently taught in classes organized around resistance to dominant political formations, particularly during the 1960s, in the interest of preserving the integrity of the individual. The cognitive process, on the other hand, most commonly adopted the stance of disinterested rationality, either avoiding political conflicts or addressing them as rational problems to be addressed in the terms of one academic discipline or another. The result was a tendency to reduce social, political, and personal problems to problems in technical management.

Both cognitivists and expressionists emphasized the private and psychological elements of composing, the first the rational and the second the emotional. Conceptions of composing that placed writing in a social context were most commonly found in college classrooms rather than in the public schools. These took two dominant forms: revivals of classical rhetoric and new formulations that came to be called "epistemic." The first, especially encouraged by those such as Edward P. J. Corbett and James Kinneavy, emphasized writing as a response to public discourse politically conceived. The text is a product of the interaction of the writer, the particular audience addressed, the community at large, and the subject considered. Decisions about language then arise out of this complex network in a process that involves invention, arrangement, and style. This rhetoric was criticized by the second group of social rhetoricians because it often privileges the rational over the pathetic and ethical appeals and because it regards language as an unproblematic part of the rhetorical act. (Kinneavy's position on this last matter later changed.)

Social Epistemic Theories

The central place of language in rhetoric was the distinguishing feature of those in the epistemic camp, a group including Richard Ohmann, Harold Martin, the team of Kenneth L. Pike, Alton Becker, and Richard Young, Ann E. Berthoff, Kenneth Bruffee, and W. Ross Winterowd. These diverse approaches agreed that language is constitutive rather than simply reflec-

---

[57]Varnum's book on Amherst shows the growth and development of an expressivist curriculum at Amherst which emphasizes the epistemological. She provides a genealogy of expressivists influenced by the Amherst program led by Theodore Baird including Walker Gibson, Roger Sale, and William Coles. George and Trimbur also link this group with the influence of F. R. Leavis (695).

tive of material and social realities. This means that the writer, the audience, the larger community, and the subject addressed are all at least partly constructed by their verbal formulations. From this perspective, we never know things in themselves, but only linguistic mediations which refract as much as they reflect. These rhetorics then are preeminently social in their orientation since they argue for the public and communal nature of language, a system of differences which is formed not by individuals or even by the system as a whole but by interaction among people. At its most extreme form, these rhetorics argue that we exist in a prison house of language, never reaching contact with any externally verifiable realities. More commonly, however, these rhetorics, as among those figures already mentioned, argue for a dialectical relationship among the elements of the rhetorical context. Their differences reside in how they conceive this dialectic and are especially apparent in their political positions—for example, in the liberalism of Bruffee versus the Marxism of Berlin.

1975–1985

The attempt to focus curricula on serving the needs of the liberal corporate state which began in the 1960s reached new extremes in the late 1970s and under the Reagan administration in the 1980s. Part of the success of this conservative turn was a national backlash engineered by the Nixon administration against what was portrayed as the political and personal excesses of the protest movements of the 1960s and 1970s.[58] During this period, corporate management models of profitability came to prevail in the organization of public institutions. A steady flow of reports beginning with *A Nation at Risk* (National Commission on Excellence in Education, 1983) made explicit connections between corporate interests and schools. Schools everywhere were charged with being "accountable" for the "products" they were producing. Students were now considered a commodity to be weighed and measured, and nationally normed achievement tests were introduced in virtually all of the states. As Daniel Koretz has demonstrated, the proliferation of these tests resulted in the decline of writing instruction in the public schools.[59] After all, machine-graded, multiple-choice tests do not require writing ability. Ordered to improve the scores of their pupils, teachers taught to the tests—indeed, so successfully that scores continued to improve in the 1980s. Unfortunately, since writ-

---

[58]Spring 312–27.

[59]Daniel Koretz, "Arriving in Lake Woebegon: Are Standardized Tests Exaggerating Achievement and Distorting Instruction?" *American Education* 12.2 (Summer 1988): 8–16, 44–52.

ing ability was commonly not measured in these tests, writing was often simply not taught at all. The "standards movement" as Myers has termed it, continued into the final decade of the century as society, with little understanding of the rising demands, insisted on a new, as-yet undefined, standard of literacy.[60]

There is still another important reason for the reduction of classroom time given to writing in the schools during this period. As was earlier indicated, in the 1960s college English teachers became responsible for guiding school curricula, a result of the spiral curriculum concept. College English studies, however, was then just beginning to develop rhetoric as a disciplinary formation. Indeed, the spiral curriculum can be partly credited with providing a hospitable environment for this development, arguing as it did that the college expert in an academic subject was to determine its structure. Thus when college teachers formulated the structure of English studies for the schools, their emphasis was understandably on their area of greatest expertise, the literary text. Writing instruction thus received short shrift in these curricular guides. The irony, of course, was that many college teachers of literature continued to insist that writing instruction was the sole business of the schools, yet were unable to advise these schools on the methods for carrying out their mission. In short, those who did not know how to teach writing were responsible for guiding those who did not know how to teach writing.

High School Writing

Indeed, the Squire and Applebee survey of successful high schools in 1966 discovered that while students were writing in the advanced tracks of schools, virtually no instruction in writing in these classrooms was taking place. Students in the tracks provided for those not going to college were writing little, if at all, and likewise receiving no instruction. The impoverished program provided these non-college-bound students was another unfortunate result of curricular thinking at this time, one for which neither the spiral curriculum nor English teachers can be held responsible. Since the emphasis in the 1950s and 1960s was on locating and training the best and the brightest for a time of national emergency, surprisingly little thought was given to appropriate instruction for average and below average students. Thus, the 1966 Squire and Applebee survey found that while advanced English classes were focusing on the study of literary tests, other tracks revealed "material of lower quality; the teaching technique less varied; the amount of time spent on worksheet and seat-work

---

[60]Miles Myers, *Changing Our Minds: Negotiating English and Literacy.* (Urbana: NCTE, 1996).

greater."[61] And as already mentioned, writing instruction in the composing process was virtually nonexistent at all levels, and writing itself found only at the highest tracks and in connection with the reading of literature. Finally, the decline of writing and writing instruction throughout the high schools during the seventies was further confirmed in Arthur Applebee's *Writing in the Schools in the Content Areas*, published in 1981.

In 1975, this failure of the schools to teach writing received national attention in a *Newsweek* cover story, "Why Johnny Can't Write." As Lester Faigley and Thomas P. Miller pointed out, at a time when the demand for workers who could write was increasing, the attention to writing in the public schools and even in the colleges, where many mistakenly argued that the best and the brightest did not need this instruction, was on the decline.[62] As Myers notes, while a few schools through the sixties and seventies adopted Dartmouth's personal growth model, most continued to use the older "decoding/analytical" model of literacy "in which 'low-track students' were given slot-filling exercises; the 'college-bound' were taught the forms of the triad—language, literature, and composition; and the 'general students' got a mixture of both."[63]

Literacy in Crisis

Viewed by the public as simply the latest public school failure, the public attention given to this literacy crisis coincided with a reassessment of the role of writing in English studies. Despite the baneful effects of accountability testing and the initial resistance of some college professors, attention to writing instruction in the schools and colleges has increased and improved. Teachers in the schools, sometimes allied with university education departments, have led the way in re-introducing lessons in the composing process to their students, often without the encouragement of the official curriculum with its emphasis on test scores.

Responding to social demands primarily geared to remaining competitive in global commerce and technology, writing programs in colleges were dramatically strengthened during the 1980s, and graduate programs began to train many specialists in writing instruction. These programs, including leading programs at Purdue, Ohio State, Rennselaer Polytechnic, Carnegie Mellon, and the University of Pittsburgh, would soon grow to number nearly 75, producing writing specialists to fill a growing number

---

[61]James R. Squire and Roger K. Applebee, *High School English Instruction Today: The National Study of High School English Programs* (New York: Appleton-Century-Crofts, 1968) 78.

[62]Lester Faigley and Thomas P. Miller, "What We Learn from Writing on the Job," *College English* 44 (1982): 557–69.

[63]Myers 5.

of jobs in composition-rhetoric. With plans for indexes and journals, composition, rhetoric, and for an increasing number, literacy specialists, were forming a new, interdisciplinary field of endeavor.

Unlike virtually every earlier period in the century, national leadership in the form of government and foundation support continued to be all but nonexistent. National education policy under Reagan was to blame the schools for the nation's economic failures while giving the administration credit for its successes. The numerous complaints leveled at the schools during the eighties, furthermore, shared the assumption that the sole business of education is to prepare a trained and disciplined work force. These discussions said little or nothing about readying students for citizenship or for providing them with means for personal fulfillment that go beyond mere commodity consumption. The making of money in order to be a bigger consumer continued and continues to be considered the chief end of education.

Teacher Initiatives

Teachers themselves took the initiative in filling this leadership vacuum. Three efforts are particularly worth noting: the National Writing Project, the teacher-as-researcher movement, and the whole language approach, the latter of which came under especially heavy attack with the nineties "back to the basics" movement.

The National Writing Project (NWP) was organized in 1973 as the Bay Area Writing Project. The NWP has established teacher-training centers to improve the teaching of writing in the schools in virtually every state. The unique feature of this effort is that its work is almost exclusively conducted by teachers in the schools. Although each site is usually situated at a university, the training programs are run by teachers and for teachers. Indeed, the major purpose of the university is to house and administer the program. Successful teachers of writing from all levels themselves design the instructional materials during a summer workshop, and then share them with other teachers in inservice workshops throughout the school year. Both activities, furthermore, provide financial compensation. The NWP sites reached more than 111,095 teachers and administrators in 1994–95, and the NWP has trained more than 1.5 million since 1973.[64] It should be noted that the NWP has no hard party line insofar as theory is concerned. It can, however, best be characterized as student-centered and expressive in its orientation.

---

[64]NWP 1996 Fact Sheet, U of California, Berkeley. See also Anne Ruggles Gere, *Writing Groups: History, Theory and Implications* (Carbondale: Southern Illinois UP, 1987).

The second initiative, the teacher-as-researcher phenomenon, was early on described in a collection of essays entitled *Reclaiming the Classroom: Teacher Research as an Agency of Change*, published in 1987.[65] Its proponents work to return control of the classroom to the teacher. Partly an attempt to resist narrow state and district-mandated curricula, this approach to pedagogy encourages teachers to study the unique features of their students in order to design the learning and teaching strategies best suited to their students' situations. The Bread Loaf School of English has been a leader in forwarding these methods, calling on the work of a broad range of established and new researchers, including Garth Boomer, James Britton, Anne E. Berthoff, Donald Graves, Shirley Brice Heath, Ken Macrorie, Janet Emig, Mina Shaughnessy, Nancy Atwell, Lucy Calkins, and others. The attention to ethnographic techniques in studying cultural contexts has made this approach to writing instruction sensitive to the social dimensions of learning and writing, particularly to issues of class, race, and gender. This social concern, furthermore, is present despite the fact that, as the previous list indicates, a number of the research studies invoked start from expressive or cognitive premises, especially the latter. One of the early exemplars of the pedagogical possibilities of the union of cognitive psychology and ethnographic study is seen in Nancy Atwell's *In the Middle: Writing, Reading and Learning with Adolescents*.

The third teacher initiative, the spread of the whole language approach to English studies in the schools, was closely related to the teacher-as-researcher movement in that a number of the same researchers and techniques were often invoked. Whole language teachers, however, were often less interested in cognitive and emotional processes and more interested in the social nature of learning. They also insisted on the integrated nature of reading, writing, speaking, and listening in all experience and argued for the need to create learning activities that brought them together in social environment.

In the 1980s, whole language theory became an international phenomenon, appearing in New Zealand, Great Britain, and Canada, as well as the United States. Among the leaders in this country were Yetta and Ken Goodman. By the end of the 1980s, a clear consensus in college writing instruction developed that paralleled the values of whole language approaches. However with the national turn to conservativism, whole language practices so abundant in the schools came under serious attack. Whole language teaching was opposed by "back to the basics" methods

---

[65]Dixie Goswami and Peter R. Stillman, eds., *Reclaiming The Classroom: Teacher Research as an Agency of Change* (Portsmouth: Boynton/Cook Heinemann, 1987); Donald A. Daiker and Max Morenberg, eds. *The Writing Teacher as Researcher: Essays in the Theory and Practice of Class-based Research* (Portsmouth: Boynton/Cook, 1990); Ruth E. Ray, *The Practice of Theory: Teacher Research in Composition.* (Urbana: NCTE, 1993).

such as phonics or traditional grammar instruction, although many teachers continued introducing such fundamentals in context while using a process approach to composing. One outcome of whole language theory in both school and college was the increasing shift to portfolio assessment of writing.[66] This was pioneered by expressionists such as Peter Elbow and Pat Belanoff and spread into both school and college writing assessment.[67]

College Writing Becomes a Discipline

Rhetoric and composition studies at the college level between 1975 and 1985 dramatically changed as the field attained disciplinary status, complete with graduate programs, undergraduate majors, major conferences, journals, and indexes. In the mid-1980s, the trajectory of its development was chronicled in Stephen North's *The Making of Knowledge in Composition*, Lester Faigley, et al.'s *Assessing Writer's Knowledge and Processes of Composing*, and Berlin's *Rhetoric and Reality*.[68] The encouragement of composition studies by college administrations was clearly a response to the demands of the workplace, where changing technologies and complex bureaucratic decision-making began to require writing ability to a greater extent than ever before. The discipline formulated a research program responsive to its own agenda rather than that of the economic needs of students and employers, although this has not precluded considering its relationship to the economic.

By the end of the 1980s, three major paradigms or problematics competed for attention in college rhetoric and composition programs. Some of those mentioned have already figured in the discussion of writing research in the schools, an indication of the rich interchange between school and college researchers that was beginning to take place. The most influential of the three paradigms may have been that of cognitive rhetoric. This paradigm argued for the primacy of cognitive structures in composing, arguing that any study of the process must begin with an analysis of these structures. Relying on the methods of qualitative research, especially protocol analysis, such researchers as Linda Flower and John Hayes, Sondra Perl, Nancy Sommers, Thomas Newkirk, and Carl Bereiter and

---

[66]Judith Newman, *Whole Language Theory in Use* (Portsmouth: Heinemann, 1985); Kathryn F. Whitmore and Yetta M. Goodman, *Whole Language Voices in Teacher Education* (Urbana: NCTE and Stenhouse, 1995). For discussions of portfolios, see Kathleen Blake Yancey and Irwin Weiser, eds. *Situating Portfolios: Four Perspectives* (Logan: Utah State UP, 1997), also Yancey, *Portfolios in the Writing Classroom: An Introduction* (Urbana: NCTE, 1992).

[67]See Yancey.

[68]North, *Making of Knowledge* (New Jersey: Boynton/Cook, 1987); Lester Faigley and Roger D. Cherry, David Joliffe, and Anna M. Skinner, *Assessing Writers' Knowledge and Processes of Composing* (New Jersey: Ablex, 1985), Berlin, *Rhetoric* (1987).

Marlene Scardemalia offered empirical data toward understanding composing behavior. Other workers in this area applied findings of research in cognitive psychology as well as cognitive rhetoric in discussing the composing process, among them being Joseph Williams, Lee Odell, and Charles Cooper. Cognitivist researchers were also using ethnographic studies, examining group behavior as well as cognitive processes, as seen, for example, in the later work of Flower and Hayes, Carol Berkenkotter, Anne Ruggles Gere, Lucy Calkins, Donald Graves, Thomas Newkirk, Barry Kroll, Kenneth Kantor, and others. The results of combining research in the privatized cognitive with research in group processes meant that the field was generally in agreement that social views of writing were the most productive. This perspective was most often called upon by those interested in the intersections of writing and the workplace—for example, in composing and the computer.[69]

Expressionists remained a force in rhetoric and composition studies. Such figures as Peter Elbow, Donald Murray, Ken Macrorie, William Coles, Jr., Walker Gibson, and others continued to emphasize the private and personal nature of writing. Despite a growing emphasis on the social nature of learning, it was this group that continued to insist on the importance of the individual against the demands of institutional conformity, staunchly holding out for the personal as the source of all value. Expressionists were most concerned with the individual studying her own composing process, regarding language as a probe for the discovery and formation of the self. Interestingly enough, while expressionists usually resisted cognitivist methods and pedagogy, cognitivists often cited expressionists as providing intuitive observations about composing that empirical research has verified. The ideological loyalties of expressionists, however, remained with the individual and against corporate activities, whether scientific, political, or economic.

With a growing concurrence about the primacy of the social and writing, the group of rhetorics variously labelled social constructionist or social epistemic constituted a third paradigm at the end of the 1980s. These rhetorics started with the social as the foundation of subject formation and so tended to call on neopragmatist, Marxist, or poststructuralist formulations in presenting their case. All emphasized, to a greater or lesser degree, the constitutive power of language in human activity. Sometimes the focus was on collaborative writing, as in Kenneth Bruffee, Elaine Maimon, and Andrea Lunsford and Lisa Ede. Others emphasized the social nature

---

[69]Berlin argued in a 1988 *College English* essay that one weakness of cognitive rhetoric was its reluctance to explore the ethical or political dimensions of writing in favor of the disinterested scientific stance ("Rhetoric and Ideology in the Writing Class." *CE* 50 (September 1988): 477–94.)

of composing, seeing the writer as always already socially situated—such as W. Ross Winterowd, George Dillon, Charles Bazerman, Theresa Enos, and Carolyn Miller. Still another group bore the marks of poststructuralist and Marxist elements, arguing for composing as political critique, moving in the direction of cultural studies—among whom were Ira Shor, Nan Elsasser, Greg Myers, Patricia Bizzell, Linda Brodkey, David Bartholomae, and John Trimbur.

By the end of the 1980s, feminists in college composition were strongly articulating the impact of feminist theories on their teaching practices. Early essays were found in two collections, one by Elizabeth Flynn and Patrocino Schweickart and the other by C. L. Caywood and G. R. Overing. This period opened the publishing floodgates to work on women in the history of rhetoric and writing and on effects of gender on composing.[70]

WRITING INSTRUCTION AT CENTURY'S END

The Turn to Literacy

Tensions over escalating demands for literacy accompanying global capitalism and developments in global communication and information technology continued to increase emphasis on literacy. Miles Myers writes of the new literacy demands arising in the 1970s and early 1980s linked with occupational changes as well as "international informational networks." He terms the new literacy standard "critical/translation literacy," a shift from the older model of "decoding/analytical comprehension."[71] Poorly understood by the public, these shifting demands occurred across society, showing up publicly in numerous assessments of literacy and writing in the

---

[70]*Gender and Reading: Essays on Readers, Texts and Contexts* (Baltimore: Johns Hopkins, 1986); *Teaching Writing: Pedagogy, Gender, and Equity* (Albany: SUNY, 1987). The earliest books on women in rhetoric and writing history were Andrea A. Lunsford, ed., *Reclaiming Rhetorica: Women in the Rhetorical Tradition* (Pittsburgh: U of Pittsburgh P, 1995); Shirley Wilson Logan, ed. *With Pen and Voice: A Critical Anthology of Nineteenth-Century African-American Women* (Carbondale: Southern Illinois UP, 1995); Louise Wetherbee Phelps and Janet Emig, eds. *Feminine Principles and Women's Experience in American Composition and Rhetoric.* (Pittsburgh: U of Pittsburgh P, 1995); Catherine Hobbs, ed., *Nineteenth-Century Women Learn to Write* (Charlottesville: U of Virginia P, 1995); and Cheryl Glenn, *Rhetoric Retold: Regendering the Tradition from Antiquity through the Renaissance* (Carbondale: Southern Illinois UP, 1998). Early discussions centered on Elizabeth Flynn, "Composing as a Woman," *CCC* 39.4 (1988): 423–35; "Composing 'Composing as a Woman': A Perspective on Research," *CCC* 41.1 (1990): 83–89; Susan Miller, *Textual Carnivals: The Politics of Composition* (Carbondale: SIU, 1991) and "The Feminization of Composition," *The Politics of Writing Instruction*, eds. Richard Bullock and John Trimbur (Portsmouth: Boynton/Cook Heinemann, 1991) 39–53.

[71]Myers 15–17.

schools that seemed to reveal an ongoing crisis. Writing in the schools was assessed in 1984 by the National Assessment of Educational Progress, which found that students in all levels needed to work on higher-level thinking. Students' enthusiasm for writing was shown to consistently deteriorate as they moved through school. The 1988 assessment found little overall change in a decade, reporting minimal levels of writing performance, although more writing was being done in schools. In the 1992 Writing Report Card, authors reported that students across grade levels "continue to have serious difficulty in producing effective informative, persuasive, or narrative writing" (3). Moreover, the best students' performance ranked far ahead of most of their classmates.' The 1993 NAEP Report found progress in what Myers calls decoding/analytical literacy, but announced that two-thirds of all twelfth graders failed their new standard of more complex literacy.

Other important reports that seemed to document a complex shift include the 1985 National Assessment of Educational Progress young adult literacy study and the similarly designed 1992 National Adult Literacy Survey.[72] Both found that although strict "illiteracy" is not the major problem, the nature and levels of literacy skills across the country need improvement for citizens to be able to function in a complex society. The turn to literacy served to draw together government, schools, colleges and communities in joint efforts to improve literacy through reading and writing instruction, often by volunteers, working with both younger and older adults. Inspired in part by pioneer Shirley Brice Health, important research in literacy was undertaken by scholars including David Bleich, Deborah Brandt, Kathryn Flannery, David Olson, Anthony Petrosky, Alan Purves, Mike Rose, Brian Street, J. Elspeth Stuckey, Myron Tuman, and Andrea Fishman.

Cultural Studies and Composition

In the colleges in the 1990s, literary cultural studies and critical pedagogy converged with ongoing, parallel social epistemic practices in composition studies. According to Leitch, in the 1980s, postmodern cultural criticism intensified traditional concerns with such issues as the social roles of the arts and intellectuals, education and literacy, postindustrial transformation, and the "relative status of popular, mass and canonical cultures, and

---

[72]Irwin S. Kirsch and Ann Jungeblut, *Literacy Profiles of America's Young Adults* (Report No. 16-PL-02, Princeton, NJ: National Assessment of Educational Progress, 1986); National Adult Literacy Survey, U.S. Department of Education, National Center for Education Statistics, various publications, 1992–94.

the possibilities for change" (ix, xx).[73] Since the open admission revolutions of the 1960s, compositionists had been confronted with cultural issues as the diverse, nontraditional students they were listening to and reading seriously reading demanded. Film, popular art, magazine and other journalistic forms and other noncanonical cultural materials such as advertising were staples of the composition classroom, early proponents including Joseph Comprone and Donald McQuade. Later multiculturalism and issues of diversity drew writing teachers into theories promising understanding, if not assistance, including Freire's relational, liberation theories of teaching and other leftist thought on handling difference and conflict.[74] While mass culture was a disease to be inoculated against and resisted in some pedagogies, in much composition, and subsequently in cultural studies, it became the portal to student learning and even to be celebrated in its own right.

Language Issues Continue to Arise

The "English Only" blow struck by California in its English Language Amendment of 1986 subsequently broadened to a national cause. In response, along with other organizations, CCCC took a stand, passing its National Language Policy in 1988. Smitherman describes this policy, as "a broad-based challenge to address linguistic diversity throughout the body politic" (368). The policy "stresses the need not just for marginalized Americans but for all Americans to be bi- or multi-lingual in order to be prepared for citizenship in a global, multicultural society" (369).

But by the mid-1990s, CCCC was swimming against the tide as a new language issue claimed the public's critical attention, this time over the teaching of "Ebonics" in the Oakland, California schools. Both blacks and whites nationally seemed to resist understanding the educational values of bi-dialecticalism, intensifying a nationwide commitment to the teaching of Standard Written English; public sentiment at century's end was far different from English teachers' of the 1970s, with their radical statement of "students' right to their own language." In part, such attitudes belied anxiety about future employment security despite a strengthening economy.[75]

---

[73]Vincent B. Leitch, *Cultural Criticism, Literary Theory, Poststructuralism* (New York: Columbia UP, 1992) ix–xx.

[74]For example, Mary Louise Pratt's metaphor of the "contact zone" became influential. See Pratt, "Arts of the Contact Zone," *Profession 91* (New York: MLA, 1991) 33–40.

[75]Arthur N. Applebee, Judith A. Langer, et al. *NAEP 1992 Writing Report Card* (Washington, DC: U.S. Government Printing Office for the National Center for Education Statistics, U.S. Department of Education, 1994).

Diversity

The civil rights movement of the 1960s had made diversity a familiar issue in the composition class, and this theme intensified as minorities entered colleges in larger numbers. But as Jacqueline Jones Royster pointed out, composition itself could function as an elite guild.[76] Nonetheless, despite some resistance, diverse groups and women in them made progress in the profession at century's end and served as exemplars for students in schools and colleges. The recovery of historical voices of scholars and rhetors remained pivotal, with researchers including Jacqueline Jones Royster, Christine Mason Sutherland, Rebecca Sutcliffe, Shirley Wilson Logan, JoAnn Campbell, Sheryl Fontaine and Susan Hunter, Anne Ruggles Gere, Keith Gilyard, Molly Meijer Wertheimer, and Glenn and Lunsford. At the decade's end, feminist theory became mainstream with an MLA volume by Jarratt and Worsham *Feminism and Composition Studies* (New York: MLA, 1998), reflecting thinkers and thought from across the decade. Most promising, the 1990s heard new and diverse voices in college composition including Shirley Wilson Logan, Victor Villanueva, Mike Rose, and Min-Zhan Lu, but our professional worlds, both in schools and colleges, remained far less diverse than our classrooms.

Computers and Technological Change

The introduction of computers into writing classrooms and, subsequently, networked forums and information sources challenged writing teachers across schools and colleges to further transform their already transforming classroom practices. By the mid-1990s, a "technology gap" had developed and widened between those with the latest technology and those without or struggling to stay abreast of changes.[77] In part because of the

---

[76]"In Search of Ways In: Reflection and Response," Phelps and Emig, *Feminine Principles*, 385–91; also Victor Villenueva, Jr., *Bootstraps: From an American Academic of Color* (Urbana: NCTE, 1993).

[77]Applebee, Langer, et al. *NAEP 1992 Writing Report Card* (Rep. No. 23-W01, June 1994). Gail Hawisher and Cynthia Selfe were pioneers in researching computers and composition with their *Critical Perspectives on Computers and Composition Instruction* (New York: Teachers Coll. P, 1989); see their "Reflections on Research in Computers and Composition Studies at Century's End," *Australian Journal and Language and Literacy* 19.4 (1996): 291–304. See also Gail E. Hawisher's edited book with Paul LeBlanc, *Reimagining Computers and Composition* (Portsmouth, NH: Boynton-Cook/Heinneman, 1992). Lester Faigley's *Fragments of Rationality: Postmodernity and the Subject of Composition* dealt with changes postmodernism and information technology are bringing to the writing classroom (Pittsburgh: U of Pittsburgh P, 1992.)

technological transformation of society, it is clear that writing instruction will continue to occupy a central place in the school and college classroom.

Much more complex literacy is required of skilled workers—the high-paying jobs President Clinton's Labor Secretary Robert Reich said will be held by "symbolic-analysts"[78]—than ever before. There is more sheer demand for writing, but writers also must be more flexible than ever before, possessing what has been called "multiliteracies," which now include understanding information technologies such as specialized computer programs, the Internet, and the World Wide Web. How these complexities will continue change the nature of both literacy and writing instruction is unclear. Looking ahead, we may wonder whether the ability to be a producer of text will be more widespread than ever before in history, or whether those in writing instruction will find ourselves a priestly caste preparing an elite of symbolic analysts, the scribes of twenty-first century consumer society.

In her 1997 Chair's Address to the CCCC in Chicago, Cynthia L. Selfe enjoined the conference to start "paying attention" to technology. Compositionists, trained as humanists, she noted, prefer their technologies and the material conditions associated with text production to remain invisible, a short-sighted attitude. She observed that technological literacy has been a primary goal of government reports, including the National Literacy Act of 1991 and the 1996 United States Department of Education report *Getting America's Students Ready for the 21st Century: Meeting the Technology Literacy Challenge*. Billions of dollars were being spent on educational technology at the turn of the millennium, yet with little input from literacy professionals or composition organizations. Regardless, this technology underlies present and future educational structures and priorities. Moreover, unequal distribution and use of computer technology exacerbates the problem of unequal literacies, Selfe warned, describing complex linkages among technology, literacy, poverty and race. Paying attention to technology and the human issues they raise can make us better humanists, she argued. Pioneers in researching technology and writing in addition to Selfe included Gail E. Hawisher, Patricia Sullivan, Lester Faigley, Myron Tuman, Johndan Johnson-Eilola, and Victor Vitanza.[79]

---

[78]Reich outlined three categories of workers in his book *The Work of Nations: Preparing Ourselves for 21st-Century Capitalism*: routine production services, inperson services, and symbolic-analytic services. As Spring notes, the majority of these occupations do not require a high level of education (93).

[79]"Technology and Literacy: A Story About the Perils of Not Paying Attention," *CCC* 50.3 (1999): 411–36. This was later incorporated into her book *Technology and Literacy in the 21st Century* (Carbondale: SIUP, 1999).

Cultural Formation and English Studies

Most governmental and business support of electronic literacy is geared to workplace writing to improve global competitiveness in the marketplace. At century's end, Clinton continued the strong emphasis on linking education to the needs of the business community. As this short history has indicated, however, other compelling reasons besides vocational training exist for teaching people to write.

The work of French poststructuralist language theory, of American neopragmatist philosophy, and of epistemic rhetorical theory argued that language is at the center of the formation of consciousness. From this perspective, culture is made up of an assortment of competing linguistic codes that "write" individual subjects. What this means is that each of us is a product of a combination of cultural codes or languages—class codes and gender codes, for example.[80] As analyzed in Berlin's *Cultural Studies and Composition*, the purpose of English studies was seen as an attempt to learn the way these codes operate, to learn to read and write them. It is important to note, however, that reading in this scheme becomes very close to writing since both are constructive acts requiring code formation as well as interpretation—both now being interchangeable. In the end then, writing and reading in the English class in the twenty-first century should aim at no less than to enable us to understand the central processes in forming culture, the self, and their relationship. Such a perspective brings rhetoric and poetic, composition and literature, back into more equitable and reciprocal relations, especially important in the schools, where literature and writing remain strongly linked in English classrooms and faculties.

COMPOSITION IN A NEW CENTURY

By century's end, composition studies, along with its allied studies of rhetoric, discourse analysis, and literacy (or composition-rhetoric as some were calling the field), had in one sense progressed from being overshadowed by literary studies to holding pride of place in addressing society's need for new literacies associated with competitive global capitalism and new information technologies. Throughout the 1990s, consensus emerged about some of the broader issues of writing instruction, while pedagogies emerged to flesh out and refine some significant theorizing from the

---

[80]Berlin's posthumously published book, first submitted to NCTE in 1992, uses a social semiotic framework to develop a pedagogical practice based on these ideas. See *Rhetorics, Poetics, and Cultures: Refiguring College English Studies* (Urbana: NCTE, 1996).

1980s. Expressive and cognitive rhetorics continued in both school and college programs, but a widespread emphasis on socially cognizant pedagogies blurred in practice some of the theoretical boundaries. Berlin's "epistemic rhetoric" moved into cultural studies and a renewed focus on civic discourse in the classroom.

This narrative of composition progress is commonplace in one sense, yet problematic in another. Despite professional growth and success in tackling problems seen as crucial by society and often allying ourselves with business and governmental institutions, composition remains in a hybrid position in many higher educational institutions, still serving as handmaiden to literary studies, producing serious economic consequences. Financial distress is usually blamed for the perennial problem of reliance on adjunct and graduate-student labor in teaching writing. In the late nineties, not CCCC, but the MLA stepped up to publicly protest professional issues related to college composition employment.[81] Meanwhile, despite the "feminization of composition" brought about by the subordinate status and the problems of being perceived as a service unit, many compositionists turned the tables to champion the service ideal, with service learning reaching out from universities to the local communities. This service learning ideal was helping bridge school and college relations.[82]

Looming on the horizon, however, were further challenges of responding to crises in funding, shifts in literacy demands, or transformations in educational institutions caused by new information technologies. If composition was born in response to open admissions and broadening access to higher education, the end of openness might likewise restrict its development. When New York City Mayor Rudolph W. Giuliani spearheaded efforts to ban "remedial" courses at the city's 11 senior colleges in 1998, open admissions policies established in 1970 disappeared and public understanding of knowledge gained by writing specialists was revealed to be thin or even non-existent. Such events are why composition is now said to be on a "professional faultline, a site where contradictions meet."[83] Poor public understanding of language diversity issues, the processes of writing and learning to write, and shifts in literacy needs and standards with global transformations exist. This suggests that school and college writing professionals may need to speak out more in this century as public intellectuals educating the public. But even if we do so, and if we succeed in

---

[81]"Final Report of the MLA Committee on Professional Employment," *PMLA* 13.5 (1998): 1154–77. The report outlined the crisis of the saturated market for PhD students in modern language and literature.

[82]For an historical look at service learning, see JoAnn Campbell, "Writing the Culture of Service," *College English* 59 (1997): 767–88.

[83]Cynthia Lewiecki-Wilson and Jeff Sommers, "Professing at the Fault Lines: Composition at Open Admissions Institutions," *CCC* 50 (1999): 438–62.

better educating the public in the knowledge we are producing, we may underestimate the magnitude of change happening in our institutions and our worlds. The pipeline of new posts in composition and rhetoric will no doubt one day produce a bulge, the extent the public is willing to fund existing institutions may continue to decline, and society may turn to new sites such as the workplace for literacy education. How—or if—these alternative sites will address key issues of cultural change, personal growth, or democratic access is not yet apparent. School and college writing programs themselves now struggle with the narrowness often imposed by economic priorities.

Nonetheless, as the twentieth century ended, secondary schools were paying serious attention to writing and attempting to cope with the technological revolution in literacy, often using collaborative process models and other pedagogies striving to address the need for new literacies. Secondary teachers challenged college writing teachers to toe the high mark they set. Colleges were generally training and educating their first-year composition instructors so well that in many cases, writing courses became a site for some of the finest undergraduate teaching taking place. The writing classroom in many large universities was often the only place where instructors knew their students' names. Whatever the challenges of the present millennium, the old one closed on a scene sometimes filled with contestation, but as often with a sense of challenge and of satisfaction on the part of many school and college writing specialists. In the face of contestation and change, it was a remarkable century for writing instruction, which transformed in multiple ways to respond to the pluralistic demands of the new century and its diverse constituencies.

Epilogue

James J. Murphy

OBSERVATIONS ON SOME POSSIBLE FUTURE HISTORIES

Given the widely varying approaches described in chapter 8, it seems clear that no single Malthusian projection can provide us with an accurate forecast of the future of writing instruction in America.

A century of diverse views on the goals and methods of writing instruction has left us without a national consensus. On one hand, this is reasonable enough, since democracy not only permits but encourages diversity, and different segments of the population may have different needs and capacities. On the other hand, to the extent that human beings all have some elements in common, it may well be possible to identify more commonalities than appear at present. The history of writing instruction in the twenty-first century, though, must necessarily be written by some scholars not yet born. It would be fruitless at this point for us to speculate about that history.

Instead, it may be more useful to look at practical steps we can take to understand better the history which this book only begins to outline. One reviewer of the first edition, John Flood of the University of London, wrote that "it is not short and it is not a history." In a sense he was right. No complete history of so complex a subject can be developed fully even in a volume of this length. We will be grateful if the book provides a general framework, a historical overview, which permits deeper investigation of a subject so important that people in our culture have devoted thousands of years to it.

Here, then, in no particular order of priority, are some possible realms of investigation that might further enhance our understanding.

Comparative Studies

We seem to know little about how other societies have handled writing instruction in the past, or how they have developed their modern forms. An educated citizen of The Netherlands, for example, can speak and write fluently in English, German, and French as well as Dutch. It should be of interest to know how this is accomplished. Is Urdu writing instruction in India the same as the process inherited from the English? Do Japanese students learn writing the same way Europeans do? Where can we look to find useful lessons in other societies and cultures?

Research Tools

Writers about writing instruction have of course produced thousands of articles and book chapters on the subject, but the field still lacks some of the basic research tools common in almost every other area of study. An encyclopedia of teaching methods would be a useful tool, especially if it included historical as well as contemporary items. An anthology of statements about writing instruction could be compiled fairly easily. Pedagogical biographies of leading theorists and teachers could provide more personal insights into particular times and places. Above all, though, the field needs systematic bibliographic access in electronic form; printed bibliographies, while useful, are necessarily selective and slow to produce. A good model would be the *ITER* project operated jointly by the University of Toronto and Arizona State University for medieval and Renaissance studies with the assistance of the National Endowment for the Humanities and other foundations; it includes not only articles but book reviews, is continually updated, and provides a wide range of search modes.

A Book-Length History of Twentieth-Century Writing Instruction

As the preceding chapter demonstrates, this is an extremely complex period. Yet regular reading of contemporary journals and books would seem to indicate that some people in the field are unaware of many developments which affect the subjects they are writing about. A coherent account would enable instructors to place themselves in relation to what has gone before. The late James A. Berlin, to whom this book is dedicated, was well on his way to producing such a study. Now other scholars should consider this challenge as well.

The Role of Women

Much as already been done in this area, especially by recent writers like Andrea Lunsford, Sheryl Glenn, Molly Wertheimer, and Christine Sutherland and Rebecca Sutcliffe. Yet much remains to be done. Historians of rhetoric and of writing instruction are often accused of overlooking the contributions of women in the periods they cover; their response often is that historians must recount what actually occurred in male-dominated societies like the Roman or the medieval. But Carol Dana Lanham points out an analogous problem in chapter three in relation to records of schools in late antiquity: is it a fact that schools disappeared under the barbarian invasions, or is it fact instead that the written records of exisiting schools were lost? In other words, we may have to look beyond the obvious to find new categories of evidence. For another example the bibliographer Robin Alston of the British Library in London once said that he had identified 2500 women writers of fiction of nineteenth-century England (though many used men's names to get their works published). His evidence was both direct and indirect, including title pages, diaries, correspondence, booksellers' sales records, publishing contracts, book reviews, and references in literary journals of the time. In other words the investigator of the role of women in writing instruction, regardless of the period studied, may need to be just as inventive in searching for sources.

The Role of Textbooks

Until the advent of printing there was very little likelihood that any teacher could offer a book to every student in the classroom. The "textbook" as we know it is a product of early modern times, the first one printed in England dating from 1480 when William Caxton published a Latin rhetorical text to be used by students in a class at Cambridge University. As we saw in the first four chapters in this book, ancient and medieval teachers relied heavily on oral reading, memorization, and repetition to bring written materials to the attention of their students. It might be profitable to examine more closely the question of whether the advent of textbooks changed teaching objectives and methods. And in modern America there is a particular question about textbooks which is seldom asked. Like the proverbial elephant in the living room that no one mentions, there is one subject too big to be noticed—the role of writing textbooks in respect to curricula and method. Some aspects of this subject are obvious: the regulatory influence of the committee which chooses a single textbook for twenty sections of college composition, or the committee which chooses a secondary textbook for an entire state. But it may be useful to probe a whole range of other factors. One is the urge for novelty which seeks obsolescence of the familiar for the sake of sales; perhaps the fact that a textbook is in its sixth edition is proof enough that the book was not very good to begin with? If you have ever heard a publisher say, "The used-book market is killing us," you have heard a common expression of the "need" for a "new" edition. Another factor is the desire of writers to push variations on the same theme by using new titles rather than new ideas. Of course textbook publication also allows teachers to promote their instructional ideas beyond their own classrooms. This too is a complex subject, but it would be illuminating to unravel its inner workings.

The Influence of Quintilian

While there is an immense range of Quintilian studies in print, including a recent three-volume collection published in Spain to commemorate the 1900th anniversary of his *Institutio oratoria* (AD 95), there is no definitive account of his influence over time. He is of course a major Renaissance force, but he is also cited by later figures like Alexander Pope in the eighteenth century and John Stuart Mill in the nineteenth. This historical account would indeed be a daunting task, but is hard to think of a single writer with more long-lasting effect on the teaching of speaking and writing in Western culture. (Apart from this historical account, it might also be interesting for a skilled educational psychologist, perhaps teaming with a classical rhetorician, to re-examine the pedagogical principles of the Roman school system as described by Quintilian.)

Non-departmental Writing Instruction

While this is partly a question of administrative history, the increase in the numbers of writing centers, projects, and institutes outside of English departments also has some philosophical/pedagogical implications. Coupled with calls for increased professionalism in the field and for an identity of writing-as-discipline, these distancing movements could possibly be shaping a new set of objectives for writing instruction. Recent events are always hard to study historically, since much of the needed data is not yet available, but it may well be that enough has been written already by and about these units that some analysis is now possible.

The History of English Departments

It is difficult for some American students to understand that English departments in their present form are barely more than a century old. Even the brief account of the events of the 1880s and 1890s provided here in chapter seven indicates the importance of far-reaching decisions made then at a small number of institutions to alter the national direction of instruction. There is such a dearth of informed research on this subject that virtually every recent study still cites an article published nearly 35 years ago: William Riley Parker, "Where Do English Departments Come From?" (*College English* 28 [1967]: 339–51). And Albert R. Kitzhaber's 1953 dissertation "Rhetoric in American Colleges: 1850–1900," now almost half a century old, has been printed as a book—presumably in the absence of a better account of the period. Yet this is such a critical period in this country's stance in respect to writing instruction that we ignore its details at our peril. One of the issues debated then was the question of who should teach writing—certainly a question of particular interest to today's part-time and adjunct faculty as well as tenured professors. Some of the other issues noted in chapter seven are still current today, which is still another reason for learning more about how those issues were resolved in that period.

Reading and Writing After the Advent of Printing

It is generally understood that the more rapid reading which followed the increase in the number of texts available had some visible effects on the page—punctuation and paragraphing are two examples. Walter Ong and others have studied the impact of the visual on the oral, but were there concomitant changes in the ways in which students were prepared to write for print? On the face of it, it would seem not, since fifteenth- and sixteenth-century schools seemed to follow conservative methods; but then the question has not yet been explored directly. Printing was not universally welcomed in its early years; Paris booksellers refused to buy any of the Gutenburg Bibles, for example, and the late fifteenth-century writer Trithemius, in a Latin work titled *In Defence of Scribes*, warned that printing would destroy careful writing, and ultimately grammar. Did writing instructors like or dislike the new medium, and what were their thoughts on the matter?

Vernacular Versus Latin

Chapters 5, 6, and 7 include reports on this issue. Their accounts are embedded in discussions of the schools and universities of their periods, but it might be useful to take the matter as a subject of its own. There are already a number of preliminary studies available, so that the project is not beyond possibility with what we already know. A related question for English-language users, too, is the history of the imposition of a traditional Latin grammar on a hybrid language with a Germanic base. This began to happen as early as the fifteenth century with English translations of the ancient Latin grammars of Donatus and Priscian. The historical basis of this development surely needs to be understood by anyone struggling with students who do not see any logic in the grammar we teach.

Old and New Technologies

This is a significant area to which little attention has been paid. The physical difficulty of writing was a factor in classroom teaching for most of the period covered in this book. Exploration of the means used over the centuries for coping with this problem may well provide us with clues to modern problems, especially at the lowest levels of instruction. We do not seem to know whether the fairly recent liberation from the inkpot, for example, or the ease of correction with a word processor have been matched by changes in pedagogy. We already see concerns about the putative erosion of grammatical standards in e-mail. The advent of voice-recognition technology may make computer writing once again the transcription of oral performance—an ironic return, perhaps, to the conditions in ancient Greece described in chapter one. If so, this would make it even more important that we understand the relationship of "dictation" to "text" in earlier periods, and to re-examine the age-old controversy over "oral" versus "written" styles. It is admittedly difficult to make historical assessments of current affairs, but a sure knowledge of the history of writing instruction can only enhance our ability to comprehend what is happening now.

These few suggestions, from among many possible ideas, may serve as illustrations of the many other things we do not yet know completely about the history of writing instruction. This is not simply a matter of filling in gaps in a chronological coverage. Rather, it is that chronological survey which makes it possible now to identify the key issues which have recurred over time. No doubt further research will continue to uncover more historical details of schools, their teachers, and their teaching methods, but it is also important to look at larger concerns.

Some of the approaches suggested above may require special skills, like a knowledge of Latin or a grasp of nineteenth-century educational history, but exploring these issues (and many others) can only enhance our understanding both of history and of our own situations.

Glossary of *Key Terms* in The History of Writing Instruction

Abbreviation. Compression of a given long text into a few lines of verse or prose. The reverse of Amplification.

Abcedaria. Letters of the alphabet that are written as an educational exercise for practice and memorization.

Adventure School. A private school which often specialized in teaching a particular skill, like dance. These schools were common in America during the seventeenth, eighteenth, and early nineteenth centuries.

After-lecture Summary. Proposal of George Jardine at Glasgow that students not take notes in class but instead write an abstract of the lecture's main points afterward.

Amplification. The dilation or verbal expansion of an idea or text. As an exercise in the "development" of concepts through additional detail, the main purpose is to give the student practice in handling multiple aspects of a given subject. See also copia, *progymnasmata*, and Topics.

Amplification of Outlines. Assignment of speech outlines prepared by the teacher for students to develop into complete orations for oral delivery in the classroom.

Analysis of a Text (praelectio). Detailed oral dissection of a text to evaluate the author's style and structure. The second stage in Imitation. This micro-analysis as used in English schools led to the term "parsing" (from the Latin question *pars orationis?* that is, 'what part of speech is this word?').

Analysis of Authorial Choices. Detailed discussion of an author's rhetorical choices in a given text, with reasons proposed for authorial decisions at each point. A part of the Imitation process.

Analysis of Structure. Discussion of a work as a whole, with particular attention to Arrangement (e.g., arrangement of parts, methods of beginning and ending, or proportion of the work devoted to a particular theme).

Anthologies of Standard Texts. Conscious retention of certain texts as best for exemplifying both stylistic form and moral content. The *Liber Catonianus,* Virgil's *Aeneid* and Lincoln's *Gettysburg Address* provide three examples.

Aodoi. Oral composers who appear in Homer's *Iliad* and *Odyssey* and are the forerunners to the rhapsodes.

Apprenticeship. The practice of sending a student to live with and emulate a practicing professional. The method was used into the nineteenth century, especially in law, and continues in a modified form in modern medical internships.

Artificial Order. Artistic alteration of normal chronological order in a narrative, to achieve a rhetorical effect. Medieval commentators, for example, saw a double order in Virgil's *Aeneid*—artificial because it begins *in media res,* natural because the first six books illustrate the six stages of a man's life.

Belletristic Writing. Writing with "taste" and aesthetic principles as the main features; greatly influenced by British and Scottish textbooks like Hugh Blair's *Lectures on Rhetoric and Belles Lettres (1783).*

Catechetical System. Lecture followed by a period in which the lecturer questions the students over the material covered in the lecture.

Chreia. Amplification of what a person said or did. One of the *progymnasmata.*

Cognitive Model of Writing. Writing instruction based on cognitive psychology, which analyzes learning as a process susceptible to empirical investigation.

Commonplace. Casting a favorable or unfavorable light (i.e., "coloring") on something admitted. One of the *progymnasmata.* Also, a language device to aid recall.

Commonplace Book. See Copy Book.

Communications Course. A course combining writing, speaking, reading, and listening activities. Popular during the 1940s and 1950s.

Comparison. Treating two subjects in one composition, praising or dispraising both or praising one and dispraising the other ("contrast"). One of the *progymnasmata.*

Composition Based on Classical Rhetoric. Composition in this sequence occurs in four chronological interior steps—Invention (discovery) of ideas, their Arrangement, their wording (Style), and their retention in Memory—followed by one exterior step: for oral language the step of Delivery (through Voice, facial Expression, and Gesture), and for written language through the step of physical inscription (Orthography) of words on some receptor like papyrus, wax tablet, or paper.

Conference on College Composition and Communication (CCCC). Association of writing teachers formed in 1949.

Continuity of Method. Re-use of proven teaching methods from one period to the next, even as conditions change.

Copia. Term used by Desiderius Erasmus to denote the ability to express oneself in different ways; analogous to Amplification. The term includes variation, abundance, and eloquence. The term is not original with Erasmus, being a major feature of Cicero's rhetorical theory.

Copy Book. Book of blank pages in which English grammar school students were expected to write commonplaces gleaned from the texts they read. Also called "Commonplace Book."

Correct Language as Social Status. The favorable effect, from Roman antiquity to present-day America, of the capacity to compose oral and written language according to accepted usage; the corollary has often been a heightened emphasis on grammatical "rules" and determined efforts to eliminate "dialects."

Correction. Public oral evaluation of student performance by the master and at times by the other students as well. The seventh stage in Imitation.

Courses in Composition. Separate courses in composition appear only in late nineteenth- and twentieth-century America, though (as Hobbs and Berlin point out in chapter 8), they are now the one element common to every level of education in America.

Craft Literacy. A system of writing that requires extensive time and energy for technical mastery, such as the training of an Egyptian scribe in hieroglyphics.

Cultural Studies. "Cultural studies deals with the production, distribution, and reception of signifying practices within the myriad historical formations that are shaping subjectivities" (Berlin and Vivion, *Cultural Studies in the English Classroom*, ix).

Current-Rational Rhetoric. Writing as an extension of scientific method, with emphasis on inductive method. Prominent at Harvard in the late nineteenth century.

Current-Traditional Rhetoric. Formalist rhetoric dominating writing instruction in North America for much of the twentieth century. Inspired by Alexander Bain's texts, it features topic sentences, modes of discourse, and an emphasis on correctness.

Curriculum. A systematic educational program designed to achieve a particular objective. (The word literally means "little course," from the Latin *curru* 'racecourse' to which the diminutive *-ulum* has been added.) As Professor Enos points out in chapter one, the itinerant Sophists of ancient Greece could have little opportunity for systematic development of their ideas before they moved on; Isocrates, on the other hand, developed a purposeful curriculum over many years in one place, greatly influencing the Romans in their systematizing of education.

Dame School. A private school owned and operated by a woman. These schools were common in American from the seventeenth to the early nineteenth centuries.

Declamation. Classroom speeches on assigned issues, either political *(suasoriae)* or judicial *(controversiae)*. Generally regarded as the most difficult of all the Roman exercises since it included all the others. During the Roman Empire, Declamation also became a popular form of public entertainment, with adult speakers performing.

Description. Dilation of detail in vivid description, "bringing before the eyes what is to be shown." One of the *progymnasmata.*

Dictation. Oral reading of a text for the purpose of student transcription. It was used in the Roman system for early training in sentence structure, but in early modern Scottish universities, in the absence of textbooks, some "lectures" were delivered slowly enough to allow verbatim copying.

Dissenting Academy. A high-level secondary school, equivalent to today's colleges, run by English Nonconformists, or "dissenting" Protestants, unhappy with the Anglican control of education in England from the late seventeenth through nineteenth centuries.

Dominance of Latin. The assumption, from Roman times into the late eighteenth century, that Latin was the language of literacy.

Dominance of the Oration. The assumption, common into the nineteenth century, that oral discourse—and, therefore, the rhetoric that underlay it—was the highest form of language use and should therefore serve as a model for all types of discourse.

Eight Parts of Speech. A taxonomy of Latin words popularized by Aelius Donatus (c. AD 350) in his Ars *Minor* and applied thereafter to large numbers of vernaculars as well.

Elliptical Exercise. Sentences with omitted words for students to supply.

Encomium. The praise of virtue or dispraise of vice in a person or a thing. One of the *progymnasmata.*

Epigraphy. The study of writing that appears on durable material such as marble, wood, or metal. Recent studies concentrating on marb inscriptions from Greece and Rome have yielded new primary evidence about writing practices.

Epistemic Rhetoric. Writing instruction based on language itself rather than social or audience-reaction elements.

Examinators. Selected students in George Jardine's classes at Glasgow who would read and correct other students' written work.

Exemplification of Figures. Two forms: (1) short composition giving an example of one figure; (2) composition consisting entirely of examples of a standard set of figures of thought and figures of speech, in the order given by a standard source. A famous one is in Geoffrey of Vinsauf's *New Poetics* (*Poetria nova*), using the 64 figures from the *Rhetorica ad Herennium.*

Exercise Book. Book of blank pages for student compositions; a draft is written on the left-hand pages, then a final copy is written on the right-hand pages after the instructor has commented on the draft.

Expressionist Rhetoric. Writing as art, which can be learned by the student but cannot be taught directly. Thus the work of the teacher is to provide an environment in which students can learn what cannot be directly imparted in instruction. "Creative" and "expressive" writing are forms of this method.

Fable. Re-telling of a fable from Aesop, either shorter or longer than the original. One of the *progymnasmata.*

Facility, (facilitas). The term used by Quintilian to describe the ultimate objective of the Roman educational system, that is, the ability to improvise appropriate and effective language in any situation. See Habit.

Faults in Language Use. Deliberate study of imperfect texts to illustrate defects to be avoided.

Forms. Student groupings or classes in English grammar schools, with specific curricula and timetables laid out for each form.

Grammar. In antiquity, "the art of speaking correctly and the interpretation of the poets" (i.e., literature). In modern times, standards of correctness based on well-known textbooks. In Renaissance English grammar schools, however, the term denotes an integrated curriculum of oral and written composition combined with literary criticism.

Habit. The deep-rooted capacity (*facilitas*) to produce appropriate and effective language under any circumstances; in Roman theory, habit is the result of long practice in a carefully planned set of incremental exercises like Imitation and the *progymnasmata*.

Hupogrammateus. A secretary used in ancient Athens for the purpose of recording the oral transactions of civil deliberations.

Imitation. A sequence of interpretive and reconstitutive activities using pre-existing texts to teach students how to create their own texts. One of the most pervasive and long-lasting methods of teaching writing and speaking, it appears in Greece in the fifth century before Christ; was systematized by the Romans; had continuing influence through the Middle Ages, the Renaissance, and early America; and continues in an altered form in many current textbooks. The complete Roman system has seven steps: reading aloud, analysis of text, memorization of model, paraphrase of model, transliteration of model, recitation of paraphrase or transliteration, and correction of the recited text.

Impersonation. Composition of an imaginary monologue that would fit an assigned person in certain circumstances. One of the *progymnasmata*.

Interactive Classroom. A Roman learning situation in which both students and teacher evaluated not only the model texts chosen for study but also each other's performance in recitation, in analysis, and in Declamation.

Language Acquisition. The natural process by which a child learns oral language on his own by listening to and imitating his elders; by contrast, writing requires external instruction and cannot be learned on one's own.

Laws. Composition of arguments either for or against a proposed law. The final and most difficult of the *progymnasmata*.

Lecture. The direct, uninterrupted, oral transmission of information by a teacher to a group of students. This method became popular only in early modern times, and was greatly spurred by the democratization of education that enlarged class sizes. See also Dictation.

Letteraturizzazione. Term used by George A. Kennedy to denote a movement from oral rhetoric ("primary rhetoric") toward written forms of discourse ("secondary rhetoric").

Letter writing. A basic mode of writing practice from the early Middle Ages into the nineteenth century.

Liberal Culture. Writing based on literary works, with emphasis on appreciation of literature as the best thoughts of the best minds. Prominent at Yale in the latter part of the nineteenth century.

Life Adjustment. A movement begun in the 1940s to use writing as a means to prepare students for specific real-life experiences they would encounter outside of school.

Lyceum. A nineteenth-century American institution found in cities across the country. Many had public buildings housing a lecture hall and library, with the aim of educating the public through access to libraries and lectures.

Melete (see *Declamation*). The Greek counterpart to the Roman *Declamatio*. Greek declamation stressed exercises in oral and wwritten composition, aas well as the study of *stasis* (qv.).

Metics. Free, non-citizens who resided in Athens. Sophists who came to Athens were frequently given this status.

Memorization. Verbatim memorization of a text for either (1) oral recitation in the classroom or (2) analysis of the text as a part of Imitation.

Modes of Discourse. Types of composition stressed by Alexander Bain at Aberdeen: narration, description, exposition, argument, and poetry. Bain also urged frequent and sequenced writing assignments. Some others attribute the "modes" to the influence of faculty psychology, through the Scottish rhetorician George Campbell.

Multi-purpose Exercises. A basic tenet of the Roman program, in which writing, speaking, listening, and reading are purposely combined wherever possible. Memorization for recitation was a common way to accomplish several ends in one exercise.

Narration as the Primary Step. Story-telling, and story re-telling (as in Imitation), as prior to any instruction in persuasion; exercises in Vivid Description *(ecphrasis)* accentuate the details of a narration.

National Council of Teachers of English (NCTE). Association of teachers founded in 1911 in protest to uniform reading lists. The NCTE argued that teachers, rather than the colleges, should set reading and writing requirements for their students.

National Writing Project. A teacher-organized program of teacher training centers in virtually every state, organized initially as the Bay Area Writing Project in 1974.

'Old Education.' The family-tutorship-apprenticeship mode of education common in ancient Greece and Republican Rome up to the time of Cicero before the prevalence of rhetorical schools.

Oratory. The art of public speaking.

Oxbridge. Term coined for Oxford and Cambridge universities, reflecting their similar conservative curricula.

Orthography. The physical act of writing words on a page. By late antiquity, Orthography was a standard part of treatises on Grammar. Quintilian and other authors as late as the nineteenth century comment on the effects that writing instruments and writing surfaces could have on the thinking aspects of writing. Until very recently, the sheer labor of transcription with stylus or quill pens encouraged writers to think their texts through very carefully before starting the difficult physical process of transcription.

Paideia. The virtue of intellectual excellence in Greece. Also, the educational program to achieve it.

Paraphrase of models. Re-telling of something in the student's own words. The fourth stage in Imitation.

Philology. The historical and comparative study of texts for their linguistic features and meanings. Philologists often studied texts as the key to cultural history.

Precept. The author of the *Rhetorica ad Herennium (86 BC)* defines Precept as "a set of rules that provide a definite method and system of speaking." In Roman education, Precept included both rhetoric and grammar, and was linked in the pedagogical triad with Imitation and Practice.

Progymnasmata. A set of graded incremental composition exercises; each exercise builds on the ones before it but adds a new element to create a higher level of difficulty for the student. The twelve common in antiquity are described by Hermogenes, whose revival in Renaissance Europe transmitted them to America as well. They are: Fable, Tales, *chreia*, Proverb, Refutation/Confirmation,

Commonplace, Encomium, Comparison, Impersonation, Description, Thesis, and Laws. See also Modes of Discourse.

Proverb. Amplification of an aphorism *(sententia).* One of the *progymnasmata.*

Reading Aloud (lectio). Oral reading of a model as the first step in Imitation. Also used with a student's own composition as prelude for evaluation by the master and his fellow students.

Recitation of Paraphrase or Transliteration. Oral presentation by student of his version of the text; sometimes recited from memory, sometimes read aloud from a written text. The sixth stage in Imitation.

Redbricks. British universities founded in the nineteenth and twentieth centuries, so named because they were built of common red brick in contrast to the medieval stone structures of Oxford and Cambridge.

Refutation and Confirmation. Disproving or proving a narrative. One of the *progymnasmata.*

Regent System. System in eighteenth-century Scottish universities in which one professor taught all the subjects and stayed with one group of students during their entire education. Writing instruction was connected with every course.

Rhapsodes. Greek minstrels who preserved, transmitted, and composed epic tales such as those associated with Homer. Rhapsodes traveled throughout Greece, and some formed guilds. Some are known to have used writing and are credited with helping to preserve the text of the *Iliad* and the *Odyssey.*

Rhetoric. Originally its precepts concerning the "art of speaking," though many of its doctrines have been and continue to be applied to writing as well. The subject was central in Western education from the first century BC until the late nineteenth century in America. Its traditional parts are Invention, Arrangement, Memory, Style, and Delivery. It is a term whose definitions have ranged broadly across the centuries, making it necessary to attach particular definitions to specific theorists and periods.

School. A system of group education under a dominant teaching master, who follows a plan of learning experiences designed to produce certain results in the knowledge-level and behavior of his students. The school in this sense is a Greek invention, though the Romans developed it further by establishing multiple sites with a common curriculum. Isocrates is the most influential Greek schoolmaster, being a major influence on Roman practice. His contemporaries Plato and Aristotle, on the other hand, operated "schools" devoted more to philosophical inquiry than to student development; they might rather be described in modern terms as "research institutes."

Self-correction. Quintilian urges that adults continue throughout their whole lives to use the methods learned in school to evaluate their own writing, to determine what to add, take away, or alter.

Sentence Diagramming. A process of visualizing syntactic relationships, begun by Alonzo Reed and Brainerd Kellogg in the 1870s.

Sequencing. The systematic ordering of classroom exercises to accomplish two goals: Movement from simple to complex, and Reinforcement by reiterating each element of preceding exercises as each new one appears.

Short Compositions. Student writings, as short as one sentence, or a pair of opposing sentences, to provide practice in the use of particular techniques (e.g. a rhetorical figure, a contrast, or a description).

Silent Reading. The dominant form of reading after the spread of printing, so that eventually writing became the medium for silent reading rather than the script for oral performance.

Social Efficiency. Writing instruction aimed at preparing students to be competent members of society.

Sophists. Literally, "wise" individuals who taught at the most advanced level of ancient education. Sophists emerged in the Fifth Century B.C. and continued well into the Roman empire.

Stasis. A Greek inventional system whioch provided heuristics to help in selecting the point at issue for an argument. *Stasis* is a central concept in Greek rhetorical education. Over the centuries, theoreticians constructed elaborate systems of *stasis*, but the most fundamental levels or focal points for argument are: fact, definition, quality, and appropriateness. The equivalent term in Roman rhetoric is *constitutio* or *status*.

Student Literary and Debate Societies. Self-organized student groups begun in eighteenth-century America and Great Britain; members sponsored oral and written forums and competitions and evaluated each others' work.

Structural Linguistics. Analysis of language structure, such as sentence combination, as an aid to learning how to write.

Sumposium (or symposium). A Greek term most commonly understood as a small gathering where (primarily) male aristocrats gathered to eat, drink, and discuss.The roots of the term, however, center on the practice of intimate family-oriented education where adult members of the household taught the youth.

Tales. Recounting of something that happened or may have happened. One of the *progymnasmata*.

Techne. A Greek term meaning "art" or "craft." Normally associated with a systematic method for facilitating oral or written expression. The Latin counterpart is the term *ratio*.

Theme. A prose composition as distinguished from a composition in verse.

Thesis. Composition of an answer to a General Question, that is, a question not involving individuals. One of the *progymnasmata*.

Topic. A method of discovering ideas (Invention) through designated "places" or "regions of argument" (to use Cicero's term). Aristotle names 28 in his *Rhetoric* II.23, though he discusses more than 200 in his book *Topics*. Cicero's *Topica* treats 14, divided into those inherent in the subject at hand and those extrinsic to it. Each Topic is a mental process which directs the mind toward a certain activity that will recall pre-existent knowledge so that it may be used in composition. Common examples still used in modern textbooks (usually without acknowledgement) are definition, comparison and contrast, cause and effect, division, circumstances, and testimony.

Translation. The exercise of reproducing a text in another language. It was prominent in Roman times with Greek and, beginning with the late Middle Ages, with vernaculars. It is a form of Transliteration in the process of Imitation.

Transliteration of Models. Student re-casting of a text in a different form: prose to verse, or verse to prose, or from one language to another. The fifth stage in Imitation.

Tutorial System. One-on-one teaching program in which the tutor assigns theme topics, then evaluates the written text orally with the student; especially prevalent at Oxford and Cambridge universities.

GLOSSARY

Universal Grammar. Assumption that there is a grammar common to all languages, permitting Latin grammar to be applied to the English language.

Whole Language Learning. Modern learning environment which stresses the integrated nature of reading, writing, speaking, and listening.

Word-play as First Exercise. Medieval practice of introducing students to tropes and figures, complemented by memorization and recitation, before taking up Arrangement and finally Invention.

Writing as Academic Sorting. An effect of middle-class expansion in nineteenth-century America, as increasing class sizes made oral recitation and oral disputation unworkable, making writing a useful means of assessing student ability.

Contributors

Don Paul Abbott is Professor in the Department of English at the University of California, Davis, CA 95616. E-mail: *dpabbot@ucdavis.edu*

James A. Berlin (1942–1994) was Professor in the Department of English at Purdue University, West Lafayette IN 47907.

Richard Leo Enos is Professor and Holder of the Lillian Radford Chair of Rhetoric and Composition in the Department of English, TCU Box 297270 at Texas Christian University, Fort Worth TX 76129. E-mail: *r.enos@tcu.edu*

Linda Ferreira-Buckley is Associate Professor of English and Rhetoric in the Department of English at the University of Texas at Austin, Austin TX 78712. E-mail: *linda-fb@uts.cc.utexas.edu*

S. Michael Halloran is Professor of Rhetoric in the Department of Language, Literature, and Composition at Rensselaer Polytechnic Institute, Troy NY 12180. E-mail: *hallos@rpi.edu*

Catherine L. Hobbs is Associate Professor in the Department of English at the University of Oklahoma, Norman OK 73019. E-mail: *chobbs@ou.edu*

Winifred Bryan Horner is Professor Emerita and former Holder of the Lillian Radford Chair of Rhetoric and Composition in the Department of English, TCU Box 297270 at Texas Christian University, Fort Worth TX 76129. E-mail: *hornerw@missouri.edu*

Carol Dana Lanham is Research Associate at the UCLA Center for Medieval and Renaissance Studies, 929 Bluegrass Lane, Los Angeles CA 90049.

James J. Murphy is Professor Emeritus in the Department of English and the Department of Communication at the University of California, Davis CA 95616. E-mail: *jermurphy@ucdavis.edu*

Marjorie Curry Woods is Associate Professor in the Department of English at the University of Texas at Austin, Austin TX, 78712-1164. E-mail: *jorie@mail.utexas.edu*

Elizabethada A. Wright is Assistant Professor in the Department of English at Rivier College, 420 Main Street, Nashua NH 03060. E-mail: *ewright@rivier.edu*

Bibliography for Further Study

Adams, John Quincy. *Lectures on Rhetoric and Oratory*. 1810. New York: Russell, 1962.

Applebee, Arthur N. *Tradition and Reform in the Teaching of English: A History*. Urbana: NCTE, 1974.

Archer, R. L. *Secondary Education in the Nineteenth Century*. Cambridge: Cambridge UP, 1921.

Ascham, Roger. *The Scholemaster*. 1863. Ed. John E. B. Mayor. New York: AMS, 1967.

Bain, Alexander. *English Composition and Rhetoric: A Manual*. London: Longmans, 1866.

Baldwin, T. W. *William Shakespere's Small Latine and Less Greek*. Urbana: U of Illinois P, 1944.

Barnard, H. C. *A History of English Education From 1760*. 2nd ed. London: London UP, 1961.

Beale, Dorothea. *History of the Ladies Colleges, 1853–1904*. London: n.p. 1905.

Beck, Frederick, A. B. *Album of Greek Education: The Greeks at School and Play*. Sydney: Cheiron, 1975.

---. *Greek Education, 450–350 B.C.* New York: Barnes, 1964.

Berlin, James A. *Rhetoric and Reality: Writing Instruction in American Colleges, 1900–1985*. Carbondale: Southern Illinois UP, 1987.

---. *Rhetoric, Poetics, and Cultures: Refiguring College English Studies*. Urbana: NCTE, 1996.

Blair, Hugh. *Lectures on Rhetoric and Belles Lettres*. London: Strahan, 1783. Philadelphia: Aitken, 1784.

Bledstein, Burton J. *The Culture of Professionalism: the Middle Class and the Development of Higher Education in America*. New York: Norton, 1976.

Bonner, S. F. *Education in Ancient Rome from the Elder Cato to the Younger Pliny*. Berkeley: U of California P, 1977.

Brinsley, John. *A Consolation for Our Grammar Schools*. 1622. New York: Scholar's Facsimiles, 1943.

---. *Ludus literarius*. English Linguistics 1500–1800 62. Menston, Eng.: Scolar, 1968.

Clark, Donald Lemen. *John Milton at St. Paul's School: A Study of Ancient Rhetoric in English Renaissance Education*. New York: Columbia UP, 1948.

---. *Rhetoric in Greco-Roman Education*. New York: Columbia UP, 1957.

Connors, Robert J. *Composition Rhetoric: Backgrounds, Theory, and Pedagogy*. Pittsburgh: U of Pittsburgh P, 1997.

Crowley, Sharon. *Composition in the University: Historical and Polemical Essays*. Pittsburgh: U of Pittsburgh P, 1998.

---. *Methodical Memory: Invention in Current-Traditional Rhetoric*. Carbondale: Southern Illinois UP, 1990.

Curtis, S. J. *History of Education in Great Britain*. 4th ed. London: U Tutorial P, 1957.

Davie, George Elder. *The Democratic Intellect: Scotland and Her Universities in the Nineteenth Century*. Edinburgh: Edinburgh UP, 1961.

Day, Angel. *English Secretorie*. English Linguistics 1500–1800 29. Menston, Eng.: Scolar, 1967.

Dionissotti, A. C. "From Ausonius' Schooldays? A Schoolbook and Its Relatives." *Journal of Roman Studies* 72 1982: 83–125.

Diringer, David. *Writing*. London: Thames, 1962.

Enos, Richard Leo. *The Literate Mode of Cicero's Legal Rhetoric*. Carbondale: Southern Illinois UP, 1988.

- - -. *Roman Rhetoric: Revolution and the Greek Influence*. Prospect Heights: Waveland, 1993.

Erasmus. *Adages*. Trans. Margaret Mann Phillips. Vol. 31 of *Collected Works of Erasmus*. Ed. Craig R. Thompson. Toronto: U of Toronto P, 1978.

---. *The Ciceronian: A Dialogue on the Ideal Latin Style*. Trans. Betty I. Knott. Vol. 28 of *Collected Works of Erasmus*. Ed. Craig R. Thompson. Toronto: U of Toronto P, 1978.

---. *Literary and Educational Writings: De copia/De ratione studii*. Trans. Betty I. Knott. Vol. 24 of *Collected Works of Erasmus*. Ed. Craig R. Thompson. Toronto: U of Toronto P, 1978.

Freeman, Kenneth J. *Schools of Hellas*. New York: Teachers Coll. P, 1969.

Frykman, Erik. *W. E. Aytoun, Pioneer Professor of English at Edinburgh*. Ed. Frank Behre. Gothenburg Studies in English 17. Gothenburg, 1963.

Gaff, Gerard. *Professing Literature: An Institutional History*. Chicago: U of Chicago P, 1987.

Gaillet, Lynee Lewis, ed. *Scottish Rhetoric and Its Influences*. Mahwah: Erlbaum, 1998.

Gaur, Christine. *A History of Writing*. London: British Library, 1984.

Gelb, I. J. *A Study of Writing*. Chicago: U of Chicago P, 1963.

Geoffrey of Vinsauf. *The "Poetria nova" of Geoffrey of Vinsauf*. Trans. Margaret F. Nims. Toronto: Pontifical Inst. of Medieval Studies, 1967.

Gere, Anne Ruggles. *Writing Groups: History, Theory and Implications*. Carbondale: Southern Illinois UP, 1987.

Glenn, Cheryl. *Rhetoric Retold: Regendering the Tradition from Antiquity through the Renaissance*. Carbondale: Southern Illinois UP, 1998.

Golden, James L., and Edward P. J. Corbett. *The Rhetoric of Blair, Cambell and Whatley*. New York: Holt, 1968.

Grafton, Anthony, and Lisa Jardine. *From Humanism to the Humanities*. Cambridge: Harvard UP, 1986.

Gwynn, Aubrey. *Roman Education from Cicero to Quintilian*. Oxford: Clarendon, 1926.

Hagaman, John. "Modern Use of the Progymnasmata in Teaching Rhetorical Invention." *Rhetoric Review* 5 1986: 22–29.

Hans, Nicholas. *New Trends in Education in the Eighteenth Century*. London: Routledge and Keegan Paul, 1955.

Harris, Roy. *The Origin of Writing*. London: Duckworth, 1986.

Harris, William. *Ancient Literacy*. Cambridge: Harvard UP, 1989.

Harvey, David. "Greeks and Romans Learn to Write." *Communication Arts in the Ancient World*. Eds. Eric A. Havelock and Jackson P. Hershbell. New York: Hastings, 1978. 63–80.

Havelock, Eric A. *The Literate Revolution in Greece and Its Cultural Consequences*. Princeton: Princeton UP, 1982.

Hobbs, Catherine L., ed. *Nineteenth-Century Women Learn to Write*. Charlottesville: UP of Virginia, 1995.

Hoole, Charles. *A New Discovery of an Old Art of Teaching Schoole*. English Linguistics 1500–1800 133. Ed. R. C. Alston. Menston, Eng.: Scolar, 1969.

Horner, Winifred Bryan. *Nineteenth-Century Scottish Rhetoric: The American Connection*. Carbondale: Southern Illinois UP, 1993.

Howell, Wilbur Samuel. *Eighteenth-Century British Logic and Rhetoric*. Princeton: Princeton UP, 1971.

- - -. *Logic and Rhetoric in England, 1500–1700*. Princeton: Princeton UP, 1956.

Humes, Walter M., and Hamish M. Paterson, eds. *Scottish Culture and Scottish Education: 1800–1980*. Edinburgh: Donald, 1983.

Isocrates. *Isocrates*. 3 vols. Trans. George Norlin. Cambridge: Harvard UP, 1954–56.

Jaeger, Werner. "The Rhetoric of Isocrates and Its Cultural Ideal." *Landmark Essays on Classical Greek Rhetoric*. Ed. Edward Schiappa. Davis: Hermagoras, 1994: 119–41.

Jamieson, Alexander. *A Grammar of Rhetoric and Polite Literature*. New York: Armstrong, 1818.

Jardine, George. *Outlines of Philosophical Education Illustrated By the Method of Teaching Logic, or First Class of Philosophy in the University of Glasgow*. Glasgow: Duncan, 1818.

John of Salisbury. *The Metalogicon of John of Salisbury: A Twelfth-Century Defense of the Verbal and Logical Arts of the Trivium*. Trans. Daniel D. McGarry. 1955. Gloucester, MA: Smith, 1971.

Johnson, Nan. *Nineteenth-Century Rhetoric in North America*. Carbondale: Southern Illinois UP, 1991.

Johnson, R. "Isocrates' Method of Teaching." *American Journal of Philology* 80 1959: 25–36.

Kaster, Robert A. *Guardians of Language: The Grammarian and Society in Late Antiquity*. Berkeley: U of California P, 1988.

Kellogg, Brainerd. *A Text-Book on Rhetoric*. New York: Maynard, 1896.

Kelly, Douglas. *The Arts of Poetry and Prose*. Typologie des sources du moyen âge occidental, Fasc. 59. Tournhout: Brepols, 1991.

Kelly, Louis G. *25 Centuries of Language Teaching: An Inquiry into the Science, Art, and Development of Language Teaching Methodology. 500 B.C.–1969*. Rowley: Newbury, 1969.

Kennedy, George A. *Classical Rhetoric and Its Christian and Secular Tradition from Ancient to Modern Times*. Chapel Hill: U of North Carolina P, 1980.

- - -. *A New History of Classical Rhetoric*. Princeton: Princeton UP, 1994.

Kimball, Bruce A. *Orators and Philosophers: A History of the Idea of Liberal Education*. New York: Teachers Coll. P, 1986.

Lanham, Carol Dana. "Freshman Composition in the Early Middle Ages: Epistolography and Rhetoric before the *ars dictaminis*." *Viator* 23 1992: 115–34.

- - -. *"Salutatio" Formulas in Latin Letters to 1200: Syntax, Style, and Theory*. Münchener Beiträge zur Mediävistik und Renaissance-Forschung 22. Munich: Arbeo-Gesselschaft, 1975. 60–63.

Lentz, Tony M. *Orality and Literacy in Hellenic Greece*. Carbondale: Southern Illinois UP, 1989.

Leonard, Sterling Andrus. *The Doctrine of Correctness in English Usage, 1700–1800*. 1929. New York: Russell, 1962.

Little, Charles E. *Quintilian the Schoolmaster*. 2 vols. Nashville: George Peabody Coll. for Teachers, 1951.

Lunsford, Andrea A., ed. *Reclaiming Rhetorica: Women in the Rhetorical Tradition*. Pittsburgh: U of Pittsburgh P, 1995.

Marrou, H. I. *A History of Education in Antiquity;* Trans. George Lamb. Madison: U of Wisconsin P, 1982.

McLachlan, Herbert. *English Education under the Test Acts: Being the History of Non-Conformist Academies 1662–1820*. Manchester, Eng.: Manchester UP, 1931.

McMurty, Jo. *English Language, English Literature: The Creation of an Academic Discipline*. Hamden: Archon, 1985.

Matthew of Vendôme. *The Art of Versification*. Trans. Aubrey E. Galyon. Ames: Iowa State UP, 1980.

Michael, Ian. *The Teaching of English from the Sixteenth Century to 1870*. London: Cambridge UP, 1987.

Miller, Thomas P. *The Formation of College English: Rhetoric and Belles Lettres in the American College, 1875–1925: A Documentary History*. Pittsburgh: U of Pittsburgh P, 1995.

Morgan, Alexander. *Scottish University Studies*. London: Oxford UP, 1933.

Morrison, Samuel Eliot. *Three Centuries of Harvard, 1636–1936*. Cambridge: Harvard UP, 1936.

Mulcaster, Richard. *Mulcaster's Elementarie*. Ed. E. T. Campagnac. Oxford: Clarendon, 1925.

Murphy, James J. "The Modern Value of Roman Methods of Teaching Writing, with Answers to Twelve Current Fallacies." *Writing on the Edge* 1 1989: 28–37.

---, ed. *Quintilian on the Teaching of Speaking and Writing: Translations from Books One, Two and Ten of the Institutio oratoria*. Carbondale: Southern Illinois UP, 1987.

---. *Rhetoric in the Middle Ages: A History of Rhetorical Theory from St. Augustine to the Renaissance*. Berkeley: U of California P, 1974.

---, ed. *The Rhetorical Tradition and Modern Writing*. New York: MLA, 1982.

---. "The Teaching of Latin as a Foreign Language in the Twelfth Century." *Historiographia Linguistica* 7 1980: 159–75.

Murphy, James, J., and Richard A. Katula, eds. *A Synoptic History of Classical Rhetoric*. 2nd ed. Davis: Hermagoras, 1995.

Newman, Samuel B. *A Practical System of Rhetoric*. 10th ed. New York: Dayton, 1842.

Ong, Walter J. *Orality and Literacy: The Technologizing of the Word*. London: Methuen, 1982.

---. *Ramus, Method, and the Decay of Dialogue*. Cambridge: Harvard UP, 1958.

Palmer, D. J. *The Rise of English Studies: An Account of the Study of English Language and Literature from its Origins to the Making of the Oxford English School*. London: Oxford UP, 1965.

Parks, E. Patrick. *The Roman Rhetorical Schools as a Preparation for the Courts Under the Early Empire*. Baltimore: The Johns Hopkins P, 1945.

Parkes, Malcolm B. *Pause and Effect: An Introduction to the History of Punctuation in the West*. Berkeley: U of California P, 1993.

Pattison, Robert. *On Literacy: The Politics of the Word from Homer to the Age of Rock*. Oxford: Oxford UP, 1982.

Parker, William Riley. "Where Do English Departments Come From?" *College English* 28 1967: 339–51.

Plato. *Plato on Rhetoric and Language: Four Key Dialogues*. Ed. Jean Nienkamp. Mahwah: Erlbaum, 1999.

Quintilian. *The Institutio oratoria*. Trans. H. E. Butler. 4 vols. Cambridge: Harvard UP, 1921–22.

Rainolde, Richard. *The Foundation of Rhetoric*. English Linguistics 1500–1800 347. Menston, Eng.: Scolar, 1972.

Ramus, Peter. *Arguments in Rhetoric Against Quintilian: Translation and Text of Peter Ramus's Rhetoricae Distinctiones in Quintilianum*. 1549. Ed. James J. Murphy. Trans. Carole Newlands. DeKalb: Northern Illinois UP, 1986.

Reed, Alonzo, and Brainerd Kellogg. *Higher Lessons in English*. New York: Clark, 1878.

Reynolds, Suzanne. *Medieval Reading: Grammar, Rhetoric, and the Classical Text*. Cambridge: Cambridge UP, 1996.

Riché, Pierre. *Education and Culture in the Barbarian West, Sixth Through Eighth Centuries*. Trans. John J. Contreni. Columbia: U of South Carolina P, 1976.

Robb, Kevin. *Literacy and Paideia in Ancient Greece*. London: Cambridge UP, 1983.

Rudolph, Frederick. *The American College and University: A History*. New York: Vintage, 1962.

Scholes, Robert. *Textual Power: Literary Theory and the Teaching of English*. New Haven: Yale UP, 1985.

Scott, Izora. *Controversies Over the Imitation of Cicero as a Model for Style and Some Phases of Their Influence on the Schools of the Renaissance*. 1910. Davis: Hermagoras, 1991.

Smith, Adam. *Adam Smith's Lectures on Rhetoric and Belles Lettres*. Ed. J. C. Bryce. Indianapolis: Liberty Classics, 1985.

Spring, Joel. *The American School 1642–1985*. New York: Longman, 1986.

Stowe, A. Monroe. *English Grammar Schools in the Reign of Elizabeth*. New York: Teachers Coll. P, 1908.

Vives, Juan Luis. *On Education [De tradendis disciplinis]*. Ed. and trans. Foster Watson. 1913. Totowa: Rowman, 1971.

Wagner, David L., *The Seven Liberal Arts in the Middle Ages*. Bloomington: Indiana UP, 1983.

Ward, John. *A System of Oratory*. 1759. Hildesheim: Georg Olms Verlag, 1969.

Watson, Foster. *The English Grammar Schools to 1660*. 1908. London: Cass, 1968.

Welch, Kathleen E. *The Contemporary Reception of Classical Rhetoric: Appropriations of Ancient Discourse*. Hillsdale: Erlbaum, 1990.

Wertheimer, Molly Meijer, ed. *Listening to their Voices: The Rhetorical Activities of Historical Women*. Columbia: U of South Carolina P, 1997.

Witherspoon, John. *Lectures on Eloquence and Moral Philosophy*. Philadelphia: Woodward, 1810.

Woods, Marjorie Curry, ed. *An Early Commentary on the "Poetria nova" of Geoffrey of Vinsauf*. Garland Medieval Texts 12. New York: Garland, 1985.

Wozniak, John Michael. *English Composition in Eastern Colleges, 1850–1940*. Washington: UP of America, 1978.

Index

University of Dublin, 203
University of Edinburgh, 197, 209n, 223
University of Glasgow, 200
University of London, 195, 209n
University of Manchester, 195
University of Pittsburgh, 277
University of Wales, 201
Upper classes, 24-25, 207
Upward mobility, 175, 229, 231, 256
Usage, 108
Usher, 149
Utility of ancient precepts, 166

V

Valerius Maximus, 89
Variation, 106-107, 116, 134, 163, 181
Variety, 163
Vernaculars, 4, 80, 152-153, 170, 175-177,
    180, 193-194, 196, 199, 209, 219
Vernacular poets, 156
Vernacular versus Latin, 295
Verse, 59, 118, 158, 212
Verse composition, 84, 98-103, 124, 151,
    156, 214
Vickers, Brian, 156n
Victor, Julius, *Ars rhetorica,* 83
Villanueva, Victor, 285
Virgil, 83, 88, 102, 112, 127, 151, 165, 214,
    215
    Aeneid, 57, 97, 137
    Aeneid, verse paraphrase of, 98n
Visual metaphors, 228
Visualized rhetoric, 228
Vives, Juan Luis, 154, 157-158, 169
    On Education (De tradendis disciplinis),
    152n
    The Instruction of a Christian Woman,
    168
Vivid description *(ecphrasis),* 68
Vocabulary, 90, 106, 215
Vocalized reading, 7
Vocational education, 257, 287
"Voice", 225
Voice-recognition technology, 296

W

Wales, 174, 200, 206, 208
"Wall lectures", 191
Ward, John, *A Sytem of Oratory,* 180, 219
Warnick, Barbara, 224

Watson, Robert, 175
Wax tablets, 5, 72n, 82, 92, 97
Weaver, Richard, 268
Welfare of the community, 258
Welsh, 176
Welsh education, 201
Welsh language, 201
Wendell, Barrett, 231, 253
Werthheimer, Molly, 293
Wesleyan College, 224
Whately, Richard, 185, 187
    Argumentative Composition, 183
    Elements of Logic, 183
    Elements of Rhetoric, 178, 183
White boys, 213, 233
White males, 216
White men, 240
Whole language approach, 278-279, 305
Wieland, Gernot R., 87n, 91
Will as distortive, 253
Williams College, 224
Wilson, N.G., 82n
Winterbottom, Michael, 42, 73n, 102n,
    106n, 109n, 134n
Winterowd, W. Ross, 249n, 273n, 274
Wisdom and eloquence, 158
Witherspoon, John, 231
    "Lectures on Eloquence," 219-220, 223,
    225
Witt, Ronald G., 124n
Women, 13, 41, 195-196, 205, 241, 249-
    251, 255, 293
    and degrees, 209
    and rhetoric, 167-170
    education, 168, 210, 235, 236n
    exclusion from public life, 168
    in debate, 237
    in history of rhetoric and writing, 282
    not taught rhetoric, 168
    notions of womanhood, 234
    oratorical skills, 237
    philanthropists, 207
    in public affairs, 208
    in public school teaching, 251
    sewing, needlework, and cleaning, 206
    writers of fiction, 293
Woods, Marjorie Curry, 48, 128n, 136n,
    137n, 138n, 142n
Word accent, 84
Word-play as first exercise, 305
Word processor, 296
Word separation, 97